"Appalachian dancer, dance scholar, and lover of dance Phil Jamison has crafted an artfully written, finely researched, groundbreaking, and comprehensive history of the multiple dance forms known as Appalachian dance."

—Patricia Beaver, professor emerita,
Appalachian State University

"No praise is too high for this book; I've been hoping for over half a century that someone would write it, and Jamison has done a superlative job."

—Tony Parkes, author of
Contra Dance Calling: A Basic Text

"Jamison's book presents clear proof of the true diversity of influences on this traditional art. The book is accessible, interesting, and enjoyable to read."

—Susan Eike Spalding, author of *Appalachian Dance: Creativity and Continuity in Six Communities*

Hoedowns, Reels, and Frolics

MUSIC IN AMERICAN LIFE

A list of books in the series appears at the end of this book.

Hoedowns, Reels, and Frolics

Roots and Branches of Southern Appalachian Dance

Phil Jamison

University of Illinois Press

URBANA, CHICAGO, AND SPRINGFIELD

Publication of this book was supported by
the L. J. and Mary C. Skaggs Folklore Fund
and Warren Wilson College

1 2 3 4 5 C P 5 4 3 2 1
∞ This book is printed on acid-free paper.

Library of Congress Control Number: 2015940887
ISBN 978-0-252-03927-0 (hardcover : alk. paper)
ISBN 978-0-252-08081-4 (paperback : alk. paper)
ISBN 978-0-252-09732-4 (e-book)

For Cathy, Sarah, and Alice

Contents

Illustrations

Figures

Tables

Preface

As a child growing up in the 1950s and early 1960s, long before I ever had the opportunity to attend a real square dance, I first became aware of this American dance tradition through images in the popular media. These were the dances of the pioneers and the cowboys, and I recall watching "hoedowns" and "barn dances" in Hollywood westerns and on television. These rural dances also appeared in old cartoons from the 1930s in which Mickey and Minnie Mouse, Clarabelle the Cow, and other cartoon characters would gather in someone's barn for a Saturday night dance.[1] The music always seemed to be "Arkansas Traveler" or "Turkey in the Straw," concluding with the customary tag: "Shave and a haircut, two bits." In addition to square dances, these barn dance cartoons also featured step dancing, with individual dancers kicking up their heels in time to the music. In contrast to the contemporary jazz music and popular swing dances of that time, these rural dances were portrayed simply as old-fashioned, down-home entertainment for ordinary country folk (or animals).

Portrayals of these rural social dances have not always been this favorable or nostalgic. "Hillbilly Hare," a Bugs Bunny cartoon from 1950, makes fun of square dancing and ridicules the dim-witted, barefooted hillbillies, who are eager to participate in it. The 1960s television show *The Beverly Hillbillies* likewise poked fun at these rural dances, but here the Southern folk culture was treated with a certain amount of respect, and in the end, the Clampetts always appeared more down-to-earth than the modern city slickers of Beverly Hills. Whether square dancing conjures up romantic images of preindustrial America or we dismiss it as unfashionable and "square," our perceptions of these rural dances have no doubt been influenced by the images we have seen in the media.

To some people, square dancing is a symbol of America's heritage and national identity, and as such, starting in the 1920s, these dances began to be taught in schools and community recreation programs. By the time I came along in the 1960s, square dancing had become a standard part of the physical education curriculum, and as a result, like many other children of my generation, I was exposed (subjected) to it. Taught by a physical education teacher with a record player, in the sterile setting of a gym class, this dance curriculum did little to instill a love of square dancing in the youth of America, but at least it made us familiar with these American folk dances.

I don't recall the first time I attended a real square dance in a community setting, but I do remember going to a few contra dances in New Hampshire as a teenager in the late 1960s. In the early 1970s, however, while attending college in central New York State, I discovered that old-time square dances could still be found in rural communities throughout the North Country. These dances took place on a regular basis at grange halls, schools, community centers, fire halls, VFWs, and even in bars and taverns. Unlike the square dancing I had done in middle-school gym class, this was a real, living folk tradition, in a community setting, with live music and dancers of all ages. I fell in love with it and attended dances wherever I could find them.

By the mid-1970s I had learned to play old-time banjo, and soon I began to sit in with the musicians at a local dance. One day, however, no one was there to call the dance, so I gave it a try; that is how I became a dance caller (around 1975). The first dances I learned to call were the four-couple squares I knew from attending local dances, but I soon discovered others in square dance books at libraries. These books had been written by physical education teachers and recreation leaders during the 1940s and 1950s, and they included a variety of squares, New England contras, dance mixers, and more. Given my interest in southern Appalachian music, though, the Southern dances were of most interest to me. Many of these were four-couple squares, similar to the ones I already knew, but I also read about dances involving any number of couples in a large ring.

Through my involvement with music and square dancing, I soon encountered another Appalachian dance tradition: percussive step dancing, more commonly known as buckdancing, flatfooting, or clogging. I had seen this kind of dancing in the old barn dance cartoons, and I remembered Jed Clampett occasionally kicking up his heels with a few steps on *The Beverly Hillbillies*.[2] But now I saw real people out on the floor "cutting a rug." When my band (the St. Regis Stringband) traveled south to play at the Carter Family Fold in southwest Virginia, I was amazed to see the dance floor fill with dancers of all ages—from old men in bib overalls down to young children. The rhythmic sound of the dancers' tap shoes on the concrete floor was deafening, but it was also exhilarating. It was part of the music that we were all making together. By this time, I had learned the basic steps myself, and in 1980 I was invited to join the Green Grass Cloggers, a professional clogging team based in western North Carolina. I spent the next seven years on the road, full-time, performing with this group throughout the country as well as overseas, and since that time I have remained active as a flatfoot dancer.

Since moving to western North Carolina thirty-five years ago, I have attended countless dance events in rural communities across the southern Appalachian region—in southwest Virginia, West Virginia, eastern Kentucky, East Tennessee, and western North Carolina. In addition to square dances, I have encountered flatfooting, clogging, two-steps, cakewalks, broom dances, mixers, and more, and at some point I became curious about the origins of these dance traditions. I discovered, however, that there was not much available in print. While I could find numerous books about the instrumental music of Appalachia (fiddles, banjos, dulcimers, and the like), vocal traditions (ballads, folksongs, and sacred singing), Appalachian crafts, Appalachian folklore, and other aspects of traditional Appalachian culture, there were no scholarly books devoted to Appalachian dance.[3] The old square dance books of the 1940s and 1950s and more recent publications provided descriptions of the dance figures, but the authors of these books had little to say about the history of these Southern dances. One author simply states, "The mountain square dance" was brought to America by "our ancestors from the British Isles," and it has been "handed down from generation to generation for many centuries."[4] The dances of today, however, differ significantly from the jigs and reels of the early settlers from the British Isles. There had to be more to the story.

Uncovering reliable evidence to explain the historical development of these American folk dances has been a challenge. Even so, over the years, I have discovered references to dancing in hundreds of primary documents dating from Colonial times up to the twentieth century. These include historical accounts, travel journals, slave narratives, newspapers, dance manuals, autobiographies, and oral histories, as well as works of fiction. The validity of fictional accounts, of course, depends on the author's familiarity with the social customs of the time and location where the story takes place. Dance manuals describing the popular ballroom dances of the eighteenth and nineteenth centuries have provided more concrete evidence, as have slave narratives, collected during the Federal Writers' Project of the 1930s, which include valuable first-hand recollections of the music and dances of the antebellum South through the eyes of former slaves.

The dance terminology that appears in these various written sources provides a wealth of information regarding the chronology of these dance traditions, although at times it can be misleading or ambiguous. When a specific type of dance is mentioned by name, there is no way to know for certain when it first became a part of the local dance repertoire, only that it was known there by that time. To complicate matters, terminology changes over time, and it is sometimes borrowed from one tradition and applied to another, even when the two are not related. For example, when Europeans first observed Africans dancing, they characterized these dances as "jigs." These, however, were not Irish jigs in 6/8 time;[5] at that time, this term was used more freely to describe any type of fast, energetic dancing. To add to the confusion, terminology is often retained when dance styles change. Throughout the nineteenth century, Americans continued to refer to square dances as "reels" and "cotillions" long after those earlier dances had become obsolete. (This phenomenon is not unique to dance. When I was growing up, we referred to our electric refrigerator as an "ice box," even though we no longer purchased blocks of ice to keep our food cold, and today ships still "set sail" even though they no longer have masts or sails.) The retention of old terminology, however, like ghosts of the earlier dances, provides clues to the ancestry and lineage of the dances found in rural Appalachia today.

As a supplement to these various written sources, dance calls that were recorded on nearly one hundred 78-rpm recordings of Southern string bands have proved to be a wealth of information about the Southern square dance tradition. These "Barn Dances with Calls," made during the 1920s and early 1930s, document the voices of forty-four Southern square dance callers from across the South. Contemporaries of the callers encountered by Cecil Sharp in Kentucky a few years earlier, they provide a broad view of the Southern square dance tradition, illustrating the commonalities, regional variants, and range of personal styles that existed in the early twentieth century.

Interviews and conversations with elderly musicians and dancers have also enriched my understanding of these dance traditions. These informants, however, grew up during the twentieth century, and their knowledge of the traditions does not extend beyond the "old-timers" of their parents' or grandparents' generations whom they remember from their childhood. This provides a shortsighted view, because customs are often considered "old" and "traditional" in as little as one generation. (Bluegrass music, which has roots in the traditional Southern old-time music but didn't develop until after World War II, is now promoted as a tradition that is "old as the hills" and "aged to perfection.") The dancers I would really like to interview are those who were alive in the mid-1800s.

In addition to these various sources, much of what I know about Appalachian dance comes from my personal experience, participating for more than thirty years as a musician, dancer, and dance caller at community dances within the region. At some of these dances, I kept detailed notes as a record of my observations. Other times, I was simply there to enjoy and participate in the music and dancing. In both cases, though, I have recollections of the events—the settings, the dance figures, the musicians, the callers, and the dancers. These personal experiences, as well as the many conversations I have had with callers and dancers over many years, have influenced my thinking and have broadened my knowledge of these Southern dance traditions.

A number of years ago, when I first considered writing about the history of these rural American folk dances, a friend and colleague cautioned me and suggested that I should refer to it as "a history," rather than "the history." No doubt there is more than one interpretation of the historical evidence. I have also been advised not to make assumptions or claim proof of a direct connection between dance figures and steps from different times and places, even when they appear similar. On the other hand, as I was recently reminded, spontaneous, completely original innovations are rare, and most of the Appalachian figures and steps do have precedents in earlier dance forms. Although further research may reveal more concrete evidence, my conclusions regarding the roots and branches of these dances are based on what I know at this time.

I hope this book will advance our knowledge of these dance traditions and that it will interest enthusiasts of traditional dance—dancers, musicians, and dance callers—but also scholars of American music and dance, and anyone with an interest in the Appalachian region. The history of these dance traditions is intertwined with the history and culture of the region, and an understanding of one sheds light on the other. I hope also, though, to inform a wider audience who may be aware of the stereotypes associated with these traditional American folk dances through their representations (and misrepresentations) in the media but who may know nothing of their history or of the southern mountains where they developed.

Some of the material in this book is drawn from articles I have written over the years for the *Old-Time Herald*, a magazine about traditional old-time music and dance. Other sections are adapted from "The Southern Appalachian Square Dance: African-American Influence on European-American Dance in Appalachia," which I completed for a master of arts degree in Appalachian Studies at Appalachian State University. As I have struggled with these ideas, I have had many fruitful conversations, in person and via email, with fellow dancers, musicians, and scholars. Many thanks to Glenn Bannerman, Ira Bernstein, Bob Dalsemer, Larry Edelman, Frank Hall, Alan Jabbour, Kate Van Winkle Keller, Dudley Laufman, Bill Litchman, Michael McKernan, Gerry Milnes, David Millstone, Jim Morrison, Michael Newton, Bill Nichols, Nikos Pappas, Tony Parkes, Brett Riggs, Susan Spalding, and many others. Thanks also to my family, friends, students, and colleagues for reading and providing useful feedback on parts of the manuscript; and to Fred Hay, Patricia Beaver, and Cecelia Conway of Appalachian State University, Ron Pen of the University of Kentucky, and LeeEllen Friedland, who provided me with guidance, encouragement, feedback, and useful suggestions. I am grateful to Warren Wilson College for faculty development funding and sabbatical leave in support of this project, and to the Appalachian College Association for its support through fellowship funding. Special thanks also to Mary Brown and Heather Harvey of the Warren Wilson College Library, for their assistance in filling my numerous requests for obscure old books through interlibrary loan, to David Abernathy and the GIS Crew at Warren Wilson for creating maps, to Sarah Kehrberg for her work on the index, and to Harry Rice of Berea College, Malcolm Taylor of the Cecil Sharp House, Helen Wykle of the University of North Carolina at Asheville, and Steve Weiss of the University of North Carolina for assistance at their respective archives. Thanks also to the folks at the University of Illinois Press: the late Judith McCulloh, who first suggested that I write this book; Laurie Matheson, who has remained patient and supportive throughout the project; and Julie Gay, for her careful and attentive copyediting. Most of all, I would like to thank my family, my wife Cathy Scott and daughters Sarah and Alice, for their unwavering support and endless tolerance as I shared my daily insights and obsession with Appalachian dance over these many years.

Introduction

Appalachia and Appalachian Dance

The place known as "Appalachia" refers to the southern portion of the Appalachian Mountain Range. This highland region, located in the southeastern United States, includes the Blue Ridge Mountains, the Great Valley, the Alleghenies, the Cumberland Plateau, and the Smoky Mountains. Appalachia does not have a clearly defined geographical border; it spans a number of states, and over the years its boundary has been drawn in several different ways. One of the first to delineate the region was John C. Campbell, who in a study for the Russell Sage Foundation in 1921 defined it largely based on elevation. Campbell's Appalachia included 254 counties in nine states: Kentucky, West Virginia, Maryland, Virginia, Tennessee, North Carolina, Alabama, Georgia, and South Carolina.[1] Clearly, though, the Appalachian region does not end abruptly at the Ohio River or the Mason-Dixon Line.

European settlement of the Appalachian region began during the eighteenth century, when the area was America's western frontier and the Eastern Continental Divide served as the boundary between the British colonies to the east and the French and Indian territories beyond the mountains to the west. As early as the 1730s, there were settlements in the Shenandoah Valley of northern Virginia; by the time of the American Revolution, settlers could be found throughout the southern mountains. Following the war, in 1783, the United States government opened the lands west of the Blue Ridge, allowing westward expansion into the Ohio Valley, and by the early nineteenth century, most of the region was settled.

Aside from being a geographical location, Appalachia is also often defined as a cultural region with its own unique customs and traditions. An early description of the people and ways of life in the southern backcountry comes from Charles Lanman, a New York journalist who traveled from Dahlonega, Georgia, to Abingdon, Virginia, in the spring of 1848. While in western North Carolina, invited to join a hunting and fishing party, Lanman traveled by

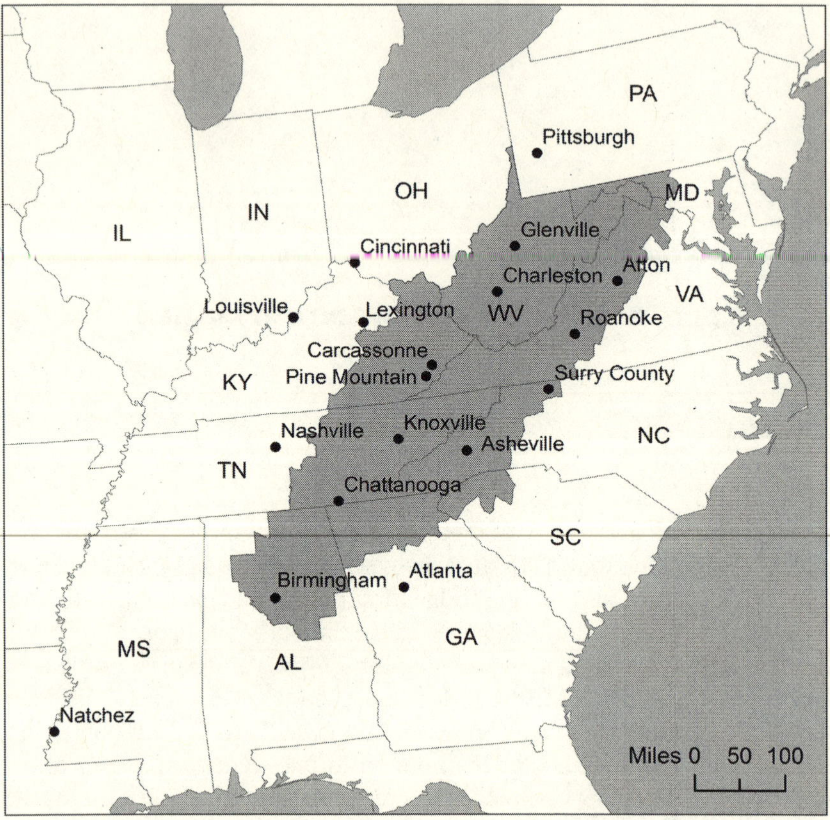

Figure 0.1. The Appalachian Region (John C. Campbell, 1921). Warren Wilson College GIS Crew.

wagon from Asheville up the Swannanoa Valley to a cabin at the foot of Black Mountain (Mount Mitchell). After supper that evening, a fiddler was summoned from a nearby cabin. Lanman wrote, "When the musical gentleman [fiddler] made his appearance, we were ready for the 'evening's entertainment.' We devoted hours to a series of fantastic dances."[2] We can only wonder what these "fantastic" dances were like. If Lanman had recognized them, he might have referred to them by name. Instead, he merely indicated that they were different, in some indescribable way, from the popular dances of the city ballroom.

Southern antebellum novelist and historian William Gilmore Simms, in a story set in the mountains of western North Carolina in 1847, likewise noted the distinctive dances of the southern backcountry. Simms characterized the dancing at a wedding as the "'Backwoods Breakdown,' and various other movements for which the fashionable nomenclature of the cities yield no name."[3]

Figure 0.2. "The Dance" (David Hunter Strother, Randolph County, West Virginia, 1872). *Harper's New Monthly Magazine* 45, no. 268 (September 1872)

The rural frolics of the southern mountaineers were indeed worlds apart from the refined public balls and dance assemblies of the city, and following the Civil War the gap between the two grew wider. Because of the rugged mountainous terrain, the early railroads bypassed large sections of Appalachia, and as the nation rapidly modernized, the rural culture of the southern mountains soon appeared old-fashioned and out of touch with mainstream America. This perception of the region is apparent in David Hunter Strother's account of a "frolic" following a "goose-plucking" party in Randolph County, West Virginia, in 1872. According to Strother, couple dances, such as the "polka, mazourka, waltz, or any other round dance," which at the time were fashionable at urban ballrooms, were unknown in this rural community. Instead, the dances consisted of old-fashioned "jigs, reels, and square figures."[4]

Strother was one of many "local-color" writers of the late nineteenth century who drew attention to (and often exaggerated) the regional customs, dialect, and folklore of the southern mountains in short stories and travelogues. These writers depicted the southern backcountry as a unique place that was somehow different from other parts of America, and their accounts of the quaint and "peculiar people" who inhabited this "strange land" stirred the imagination of their urban readers.[5] To many of these writers, the old-fashioned hoedowns, reels, and frolics of Appalachia epitomized the "otherness" of the region. In a story published in *Appletons' Journal* in 1874, Elizabeth

Whitfield Bellamy writes of a rural "ball" at "a country house . . . in one of those valleys between the straggling spurs of the great Appalachian chain." The "simple" people in this account are content to dance "interminable reels and antiquated Cotillons [sic] to one or two monotonous, melancholy jigs, played with damnable iteration."[6] Mary Noailles Murfree similarly writes of an "unending reel," accompanied by a "violin's monotonous iteration," in "The Dancin' Party at Harrison's Cove" (1878), a short story set in the Tennessee mountains.[7] English American author Frances Hodgson Burnett, who later wrote *The Secret Garden*, likewise characterized the "rough dances" held at a rustic cabin a few miles from Asheville in 1877 as "furious and erratic reel-dancing" accompanied by a "fiddler at work sawing industriously at one tune."[8]

In a romantic, fictional account of outsiders traveling in the Cumberland Mountains of East Tennessee, written in 1886, Mrs. Will Allen Dromgoole contrasts the formal waltzes and gallops of a mountain resort hotel ballroom with the raucous "whirligig figures" of the local "mountain dances" in nearby "Wild-Cat Cove."

> The house is a little, one-roomed hut, with the customary shed-room in the rear. We stand a moment in the porch looking in on the scene open before us: the low, square room is crowded with old men, old women, boys and girls; the bench set round the wall for lookers-on is full; the standing-room is taken to the last foot. The fiddler wedges his way in and out among the whirligig figures, dexterously avoiding protruding elbows and reckless heels, playing for dear life, the cracked fiddle fairly groaning with the terrors of the "Roaring River," or screaming the wonderful acts of "Cotton-eye Joe."[9]

These colorful accounts of frolics in the southern mountains (even if exaggerated), make it clear that these rural dances were different from the fashionable dances of the city ballroom, and this image of Appalachian "otherness" no doubt enhanced sales of the books and periodicals in which these stories appeared. Other people, however, used it to support other agendas. During the early twentieth century, benevolent workers and missionaries portrayed Appalachia as a backward place in need of outside help as they endeavored to justify and raise funds for church-sponsored mission schools. Around the same time, industrialists legitimized logging and mining operations in the mountains as a way to "lift up" the Appalachian people. Today, state agencies use the idea of Appalachia to promote tourism in the mountains and to market cultural heritage—craft shops sell "Appalachian" crafts; festivals feature "Appalachian" music. Historian Henry Shapiro, however, has questioned whether Appalachia even exists as a distinct place, or whether it is merely a romantic idea created in the late nineteenth century by the local-color writers, and one that persists today, making the southern mountains one of the most misunderstood and mythologized regions of the United States.[10] As John Campbell pointed out in 1921, Appalachia is "a land . . . about which, perhaps, more things are known that are not true than any other part of the country."[11]

Cultural traditions such as music and dance, which are passed on from one generation to the next, are clearly not contained by state lines, rivers, elevations, or other boundaries drawn on maps, and as people migrated through the Appalachian region and across the South during the nineteenth century, these customs became established in communities far beyond the southern mountains. Pointing out that the traditional music of Appalachia is not significantly different from that found elsewhere in the rural South, country music historian Bill Malone has suggested that "there is no such thing as 'Appalachian music.'"[12] Some might argue that this is also true of the "Appalachian" dances; these folk traditions likewise were not unique to the mountains but at one time could be found throughout the South. The relative isolation of the mountains, however, slowed the onslaught of the modern world, allowing these traditions to survive longer there, long enough to be discovered by outsiders in the early twentieth century and to be labeled "Appalachian."

The earliest detailed description of rural dances in southern Appalachia comes from English folk music and dance scholar Cecil Sharp, who with his colleague and young protégé Maud Karpeles encountered square dancing at several locations in eastern Kentucky in 1917. Like the earlier local-color writers, Sharp was struck by the otherness of these "most wonderful" dances, and the following year he and Karpeles published descriptions of the figures. Sharp believed that these Southern square dances, which he called the "Running Set," were survivals of an ancient type of English country dance that had remained pure and unchanged for many generations in the southern mountains.[13] Sharp was known as an authority on traditional dance, and his Anglocentric interpretation of the Kentucky dances, which his followers accepted without question, has subsequently been repeated (often verbatim) for close to a century.

Today, however, many scholars question Sharp's ideas and conclusions.[14] As an outsider he was unfamiliar with the Appalachian people and their culture, and he observed only a few dances in one area of the mountains during a single, brief visit to Kentucky. The dances he encountered were neither English nor ancient; they were instead uniquely American dances that developed in the southern backcountry during the nineteenth century. One has only to consider the musical traditions of the southern mountains to suspect this. These traditions developed concurrently, and they are inseparable. While the Appalachian fiddle repertoire does include a number of Scots-Irish reels that can be traced back to the British Isles, it also includes many breakdowns, blues, rags, and other musical pieces that are native to America. The traditional song repertoire is equally diverse, including British ballads and folksongs, as well as popular songs from the nineteenth-century minstrel stage, sentimental parlor songs, Tin Pan Alley songs, hymns, gospel songs, and African American blues. Given this musical diversity—not to mention the iconic presence of the banjo, an instrument with African roots—it would be naive to think that the dances could have remained pure, unchanged survivals of ancient English country dances. While some sections of the southern mountains are no doubt relatively isolated, the region has always maintained contact with the outside world through trade, travel, and immigration, and elements of popular culture, including social dances, have continually filtered into the rural Appalachian traditions.

The Appalachian dance tradition today comprises several different types of dance. These include step dances for individual dancers, couple dances ("round dances") for pairs of dancers, set dances for groups of couples, and other miscellaneous forms, such as cakewalks, play parties, and mixers. The step dances, once called "jigs" but now referred to as "buckdancing," "flatfooting," or "clogging," typically involve percussive footwork, which provides a rhythmic accompaniment to the music. Couple dances found in the Appalachian region include the two-step and the waltz, the former being more common among rural dancers. (In performing these dances, couples progress counterclockwise around the dance floor—hence the term "round dance.") The Appalachian set dance tradition consists of two forms of Southern square dance (square sets for four couples and circular sets for any number of couples) as well as the Virginia Reel and dance mixers.

These various forms of rural social dance, which are participatory by nature rather than performance oriented, could be considered folk dances; as such, traditional variants are passed on from one generation to the next by imitation, or, as dancers like to say, they are "caught, not taught."[15] As a living tradition these dances have never remained static; they have changed and evolved over the last two hundred years as popular dance forms and styles have been adopted into the tradition. Today, it is not unusual to encounter the Electric Slide and other modern line dances alongside traditional square dances, two-steps, and clogging.[16] Modern Western square dancing, contra dancing, swing dancing, salsa, and other types of dance can now also be found within the region.[17] These forms, however, are neither indigenous nor unique to the southern mountains, and they are not widespread in the vernacular culture of the region. Perhaps over time, though, like the popular social dances that preceded them, they will influence, if not become a part of, the rural dance tradition.

As I have sought a better understanding of the roots and historical development of these Southern dance traditions, I have been guided by the following questions: What are the defining characteristics of these dances, and to what extent are these same features found in earlier European, African American, and Native American dance forms? What facilitated the changes that occurred in the dance tradition during the nineteenth century? How should we interpret the dances observed by Cecil Sharp and Maud Karpeles in Kentucky? How did these Southern dance traditions change during the twentieth century, and how have they influenced dance traditions elsewhere in America? The answers to these questions help tell the story of these American folk dances.

The first part of this book (chapters 1 through 7) includes a discussion of the diversity (racial, ethnic, and social class) of the Appalachian population, the myth of Appalachian isolation, and the transmission of culture. I identify the defining characteristics of the Southern square dances, and I discuss the earlier European, African American, and Native American dance forms that contributed to their development during the nineteenth century. Following this, I examine Cecil Sharp's account of the "Running Set," his influence and enduring legacy, and his description of square dances at Afton, Virginia, in 1918. I conclude this section with my analysis of the Southern square dance calls that appear on close to one hundred 78-rpm recordings made between 1924 and 1933.

The second part (chapters 8 through 11) examines a variety of other social dances that have been part of the Appalachian tradition: the Virginia Reel; play parties and singing games; round dances, such as the waltz and the two-step; and other forms, including the "Grand March," German Cotillions, broom dances, cakewalks, and mixers. The longstanding conflict between religion and dancing is also discussed.

The third part (chapters 12 and 13) looks at the Appalachian step dance tradition, including buckdancing, flatfooting, and clogging. Like the square dances, these rural folk dances have roots in the earlier dance traditions of northern Europe, West Africa, and Native America. An understanding of the earlier traditions and styles, as well as a consideration of the terminology used to describe American step dancing over the years, provides clues that help explain the nature and development of these dances. Describing dance steps in print is difficult, and I have not attempted to notate the footwork using Labanotation (a dance notation system developed by Rudolf Laban in the early twentieth century) or any other notation system. The history and development of team clogging is also discussed. This modern performance-oriented dance form, which evolved from staged exhibitions of square dancing in western North Carolina in the late 1920s and early 1930s, combines the footwork of the step dances with the figures of the square dances, and in recent years it has spawned a contemporary style of clogging now popular across the country.

Finally, chapters 14 and 15 look at the Appalachian dance tradition in modern times with profiles of three rural community square dances in the early twenty-first century. I conclude with a discussion of folk dance as a symbol of national heritage and identity, the origins of the common stereotypes and images associated with square dancing, the proliferation of square dancing during the twentieth century, the "invisibility" of the African American contributions to the tradition, and the controversial issue of designating square dancing as our National Folk Dance.

Supplementary material appears in an appendix and a companion website. The appendix includes a discography of the "Barn Dances with Calls" (1924–1933) discussed in chapter 7, as well as tables showing the prevalence of the various features of the Southern square dances that appear on these 78-rpm recordings. Preceding the notes section is a glossary with descriptions of the square dance figures and other dance terms that are discussed in the text. I suggest that uninitiated readers consult the glossary to sort out the dance terminology. Audio files of the 78-rpm recordings, transcriptions of the dance calls, additional illustrations, links to dance videos, and other resources related to traditional Appalachian music and dance are available online at www.philjamison.com.

1 Diversity and Cultural Transmission in the Southern Mountains

"A Mixed Multitude of All Classes and Complexions"

Since the late nineteenth century, when local-color writers first popularized many of the common stereotypes now associated with the southern mountains, Appalachia has been perceived as an isolated and backward place that retained old-fashioned customs and lagged behind mainstream America. In 1899, however, Berea College president William Goodell Frost portrayed the southern mountains more favorably, as "one of God's grand divisions." In an appeal to Northern donors and philanthropists, he described the "highland stock" of eastern Kentucky as predominantly English and Scottish, but also "Scotch-Irish." Frost characterized these "mountain whites" as patriotic "Sons and Daughters of the Revolution" who had been isolated for generations in a "Rip Van Winkle sleep." Unlike the flood of immigrants who were arriving from Southern and Eastern Europe at that time, these supposedly racially pure, "native born" "mountain Americans" had preserved the Anglo-Saxon heritage of "our pioneer ancestors." In his mind, they were conservators of true "American" culture, and they clearly deserved an education at Berea College.[1]

Echoing Frost, American geographer Ellen Churchill Semple, in 1901, likewise portrayed the people who lived in "isolated communities" in the mountains of eastern Kentucky as "the purest Anglo-Saxon stock in all the United States." She described these "chiefly English and Scotch-Irish" people as "direct descendants of the early Virginia and North Carolina immigrants . . . kept free from the tide of foreign immigrants which has been pouring in recent years into the United States."[2]

This characterization of the southern mountaineers as a homogeneous population of racially pure Anglo-Saxons, however, is a myth. The population of the Southern backcountry, in fact, was a diverse mix of Europeans,

African Americans, and indigenous Native Americans. Charles Woodmason, an itinerant Anglican preacher based in the Piedmont of South Carolina between 1766 and 1772, characterized it as a "mixed Multitude of all Classes and Complexions."[3] Neither ethnically, racially, economically, nor culturally homogeneous, the region was home to wealthy landowners, poor tenant farmers and sharecroppers, well-to-do merchants, and isolated subsistence farmers, as well as enslaved African Americans.

In addition to the English and Scots-Irish, those of European descent included Germans and smaller numbers of Scots, Welsh, and French Huguenots. Some were recent arrivals; others were second- or third-generation European Americans. The Scots-Irish (and not the English), however, made up the single largest group among the early settlers. These people, also known as Scotch-Irish or Ulster-Scots, were primarily Presbyterians from northern Ireland whose ancestors had come from the lowlands of Scotland and northern England in the 1600s.[4] Charles Woodmason encountered many of these "Northern Scotch Irish" settlers in the foothills of the Blue Ridge Mountains. Venturing as far west as the Cherokee towns beyond the Saluda River, he noted their fondness for fiddling and "frolicking": "If You want to hire a fellow to Work, You'l not raise one for Money—But make a Dance, or a Frolic—and You'l see an hundred turn out." On one occasion, he wrote: "Married a Couple, who imprudently (or impudently) left the Service and staid not to Sermon, carrying with them 1/2 the Congregation to frolic and dance." Woodmason was appalled by the "Revelling Drinking Singing Dancing and Whoring" of these "poor wretches" and "licentious wenches," whom he dismissed as "ignorant, mean, worthless, beggarly Irish Presbyterians, the Scum of the Earth, and the Refuse of Mankind."[5]

Although Frost portrayed the Appalachian people as "mountain whites," and Semple claimed that the region "excluded the negroes," there have been people of African descent in the southern mountains since the time of the earliest explorers and settlers. African slaves accompanied Spanish explorer Hernando de Soto when he passed through western North Carolina in search of gold in 1540, and during the 1700s slaves and indentured servants arrived with the early white settlers. By the time of the first U.S. Census in 1790, there were many thousands of slaves as well as free blacks in the southern mountains.[6] In 1800, at the new settlement of Asheville in western North Carolina, one-third of the population was black—twenty-five free persons and thirteen slaves.[7]

The Appalachian backcountry was a fertile "cultural contact zone" that fostered interaction and cultural exchange between Native Americans, African Americans, and European Americans.[8] Thomas Ashe, an Englishman who traveled down the Ohio and Mississippi Rivers from Pittsburgh to New Orleans in 1806, experienced this blending of traditions one evening while staying at an inn in Wheeling, [West] Virginia: "I entered the ball-room, which was filled with persons at cards, drinking, smoaking, dancing, &c.

Figure 1.1. "(Voter) Registration at the South—Scene at Asheville, North Carolina." Black dancer and banjo player entertain a racially mixed crowd in this mountain town. (Alfred Wordsworth Thompson, 1867). *Harper's Weekly* 11 (September 28, 1867)

The 'music' consisted of two banjies, played by negroes nearly in a state of nudity, and a [flute], through which a Chickesaw breathed with much occasional exertion and violent gesticulations. The dancing accorded with the harmony of these instruments." Ashe was appalled by this crude "music" [Ashe's quotes] and dancing, which he characterized as "a violent vulgar uproar."[9] This raucous frolic, which was accompanied by African-derived banjos and a Native American flute, was no doubt quite different from the sophisticated, genteel music and dances of the European ballrooms with which he was familiar.

Though not as pervasive in the mountains as in the Deep South, slavery played a significant role in the development of the region, and it was important to the Appalachian antebellum economy. Prior to the Civil War, approximately 10 percent of white Appalachian households owned slaves (though typically fewer than five per household).[10] Slave labor was used to clear timber and for agricultural work; slaves were also crucial to the efficient transportation of goods (as livestock drovers and riverboat laborers), in gold mining and lumbering, in the ironworks, saltworks, brickyards, in carpentry as well as in travel and tourism, where slaves worked as stage drivers and hotel workers. Anne Royall, who traveled throughout the southern mountains in the early 1820s, observed blacks hard at work in all of these various occupations.[11] At that time, African Americans (mostly slaves) accounted for close to 12 percent of the total population of Appalachia.[12] They were, however, not uniformly distributed; black populations in some counties exceeded 30 percent, while elsewhere the proportion was less than 1 percent.[13] By 1860 more than 175,000 free and enslaved blacks lived in Appalachia, and slavery existed in every county, even on the Cherokee-owned plantations of East Tennessee, northeast Alabama, and north Georgia.[14]

Close to half of the households in the southern mountains were made up of poor white tenant farmers and sharecroppers who worked alongside slaves at corn huskings and other work parties. Daniel Hundley, who grew up in a slaveholding family in northern Alabama, wrote in 1860 of the music that was shared by these "industrious poor whites" and slaves who worked side by side: "And when the long winter evenings have come, you will see blacks and whites sing, and shout, and husk in company, to the music of Ole Virginny reels played on a greasy fiddle by some aged Uncle Edward, whose frosty pow proclaims that he is no longer fit for any more active duty, and whose long skinny fingers are only useful now to put life and mettle into the fingers of the younger huskers, by the help of de fiddle and de bow."[15] Such racially integrated labor forces no doubt provided opportunities for interaction between mountain blacks and the white majority.

Following the Civil War, the African American population of Appalachia became more concentrated in the urban centers and less apparent in rural communities, so that even though their numbers exceeded 274,000 by the end of the 1800s—many had come to the coalfields from the Deep South—the proportion of blacks in the overall population had declined.[16] By the start of the twentieth century, blacks made up less than 3 percent of the population of the mountain counties of eastern Kentucky—down from a high of 7 percent in 1850—and this may have led Semple to believe that "our Kentucky mountaineers" had had "no intimate knowledge of the negro."[17] From the time of the earliest settlers, however, the population of Appalachia was a "mixed Multitude of all Classes and Complexions," and the shared southern mountain culture that developed was a blend of the European, African, and Native American traditions.

The Myth of Appalachian Isolation

The local-color writers of the nineteenth century portrayed Appalachia as a remote and isolated place, and Frost and Semple, who suggested that the retention of eighteenth-century British culture in the mountains was due to the lack of contact with the modern world, perpetuated this idea. Semple claimed (in 1901) that the southern mountaineers' "speech and ideas" reveal their ancestry "as plainly as if they had disembarked from their eighteenth-century vessel but yesterday."[18] While some parts of Appalachia are certainly remote and relatively isolated, the region as a whole has never been completely cut off from the outside world. By the early 1700s, the southern backcountry was tied to the world economy through the fur trade with Europe. In the early 1800s, drovers routinely herded thousands of hogs, cattle, turkeys, and other livestock along the early roads that led from the mountains of western North Carolina to markets in Charleston and Savannah, and ginseng was shipped all the way to China by way of Philadelphia.[19] In her description of the "western country," Anne Royall listed some of the commodities that were exported from East Tennessee, including flour, corn, potatoes, whiskey, bacon, cider, apples, hemp, tobacco, beef, butter, cheese, beeswax, lard, feathers, onions, lumber, and timber. These goods were sent down the Ohio and Mississippi Rivers, where they were exchanged for cotton in New Orleans. Cotton was in turn exchanged for merchandise that was hauled down the Great Wagon Road from Philadelphia in heavily loaded wagons. Royall encountered a number of these wagons every day in her travels. The United States Mail also arrived three times each week. Lamenting the effects of consumerism in western Virginia in 1823, Royall wrote, "[The] taste they have for dress, foreign manufactures, coffee, tea, &c. will prove their ruin. I passed through this country about thirty years since, when the people hardly knew what coffee or tea was; in fact many of them did not; and now there is no family but what uses coffee and tea. . . . At that time nothing but domestic cloth was worn, and now every one in one hundred men . . . which I counted to-day at preaching, were clothed in foreign manufactures."[20]

Other commodities supplied to the nation by Appalachia included gold, salt, and iron, and with the coming of the railroad in the 1870s and 1880s, the region was opened up for the extraction of coal. Black laborers, who built the railroads, introduced new musical styles—the blues in particular—to the southern mountains, and the railroads brought in manufactured goods from the outside, including mail-order guitars and other musical instruments. In her autobiography, *Singing Family of the Cumberlands,* ballad singer Jean Ritchie (b. 1922) relates the story of her father and uncle making an eighty-mile round trip on foot from their home in eastern Kentucky to purchase a "talking machine" around 1905. As a result, Jean and her siblings in an "isolated" holler of eastern Kentucky grew up listening to cylinder recordings of minstrel songs, including "Whistlin' Rufus" and "Little Lizy Jane."[21] By the early twentieth century these and other popular nineteenth-century songs, as well as blues, had become part of the Appalachian musical tradition, taking their place alongside the older British and American ballads and folk songs.

The Back Door to Appalachia

The majority of the early settlers who came to the southern mountains (the "Western Country") followed the Great Wagon Road (what is now more or less Interstate 81) from Pennsylvania southwest through the Shenandoah Valley of Virginia. This was the main route for trade and transportation, providing a link between the southern mountains and the northeastern states. Other settlers arrived from the East—from Tidewater Virginia and Charleston, South Carolina.

Beyond the Eastern Continental Divide, however, the Ohio River provided a crucial conduit to the outside world. Flowing past West Virginia and Kentucky and eventually joining the Mississippi River, the Ohio River facilitated transportation and commerce all the way from Pittsburgh to New Orleans. As many as fifty Appalachian counties (in West Virginia, Kentucky, and Tennessee) were accessible by the navigable tributaries of the Ohio River,[22] and every year countless flatboats (some more than one hundred feet long), keelboats,[23] and barges loaded with goods descended these rivers.

The Ohio and other rivers that flowed into the Mississippi River were heavily traveled trade routes—the superhighways of their time. In 1787 *The Pittsburgh Gazette* reported more than 120 boats passing by Pittsburgh, bound for Kentucky, during a single week.[24] On board a thirty-six-foot-long flatboat that departed from Pittsburgh on the Ohio River in November 1796 were a young Englishman named Francis Baily and a French army general, who played the fiddle "exceedingly well." The first night out they stayed at a farmhouse: "The general . . . struck up a tune . . . and a dance was soon commenced, not much in the style either of Bath or Paris, but sufficiently pleasing to drive away the gloom inspired by the surrounding wilderness, and

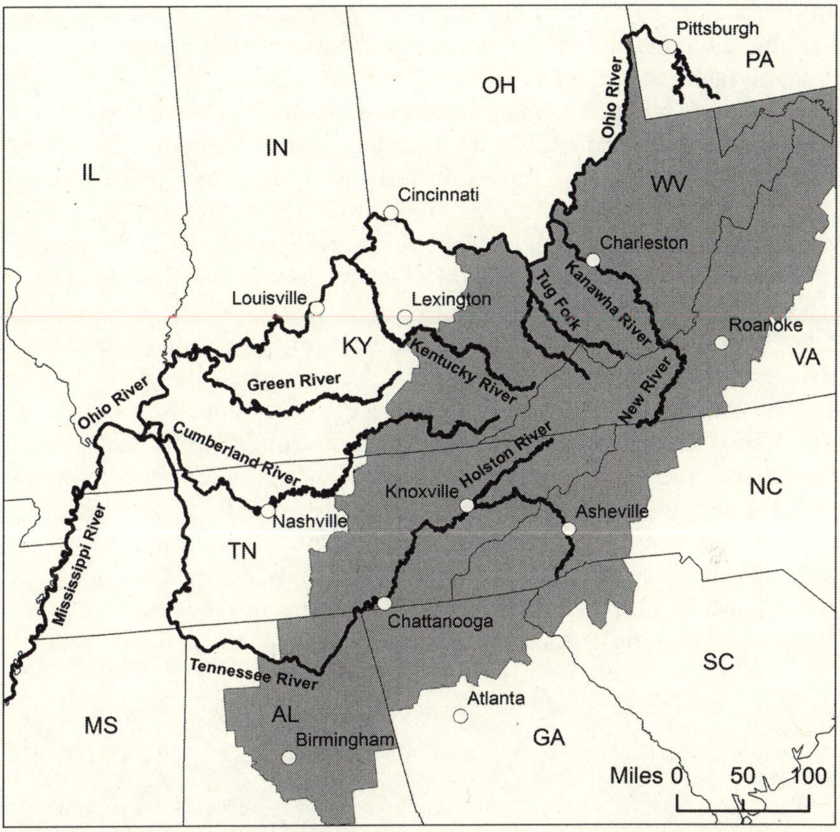

Figure 1.2. The Ohio River Watershed—The Back Door to Appalachia. Warren Wilson College GIS Crew.

to banish all idea of separation from civilized society."[25] Several months later, Baily and his companion eventually reached New Orleans. Baily had hoped to find passage to New York by boat, but none was available. So instead, like many others who descended these rivers, he returned to the mountains by foot, following the Natchez Trace, a 450-mile path through the wilderness from Natchez, Mississippi, to Nashville, Tennessee, and arriving in Knoxville in two months' time.

Francis Baily was just one of the many who arrived in New Orleans from the various tributaries of the Mississippi River. In 1806 a flatboatman noted as many as one hundred boats lining the banks of the Kentucky River at Frankfort, Kentucky, and the following year more than eighteen hundred boats landed in New Orleans.[26] The crews of these boats typically included a fiddler hired to provide entertainment over the many days it took to float down the river. A New Englander who traveled with his family down the Ohio and Mississippi Rivers on a keelboat in 1815 recalled the sound of "fiddles scraping continuously" on the flatboats and of the boatmen "dancing to the violin on the deck of their boat."[27]

One of these many flatboat musicians was Thomas C. Collins (1832–1907), a fiddler and dance caller of Scots-Irish and German descent who worked on the Ohio, Mississippi, and Missouri Rivers in the 1850s. Collins grew up along the Ohio River in Little Hocking, Ohio (across the river from West Virginia), and in his autobiography he wrote of playing the fiddle for dancers on the deck of the flatboat during the many weeks it took to float downriver to New Orleans.[28]

By night Collins and other flatboat fiddlers would provide the music for "dances got up at the hovels along shore."[29] One popular though notorious stop was the Natchez Under-the-Hill district in Mississippi, where the boatmen drank, danced, and caroused with "the refuse of the world." T. B. Thorpe described the scene in *Harper's New Monthly Magazine* in 1855: "With the professional flat-boatmen [the Negroes of the Mississippi] are always favorites . . . at night, when the 'old ark' is tied up. . . . On such occasions the master of the instrument will touch off the 'Arkansas Traveler,' and then gradually sliding into a 'Virginia hoe-down,' he will be accompanied by a genuine darkie keeping time, on the light fantastic heel-and-toe tap."[30] (See figure 12.7.)

Figure 1.3. "The Jolly Flatboatmen" (George Caleb Bingham, 1846). Library of Congress, Prints and Photographs Division (LC-DIG-pga-01064)

In addition to enabling the transportation of goods downriver to market, the Ohio River facilitated the transmission of popular culture throughout the Ohio Valley and up the many tributaries into the southern mountains. In 1793, while reporting on the occupational prospects for immigrants, Harry Toulmin, a Unitarian minister from England, had noted the great interest in dancing at settlements along the Ohio River in northeastern Kentucky: "A musical professor would not have much chance of succeeding at present, but a dancing master would meet with encouragement."[31] By that time a dancing school had already been established (in 1788) in the frontier settlement of Lexington, Kentucky.[32] With the Louisiana Purchase in 1803, more dancing masters arrived upriver from New Orleans. Shortly after arriving by barge in 1805, James Riddle opened a dancing school in Lexington, and the following year another dancing master, Mr. Terasse from the West Indies, arrived to teach "French language and dancing."[33] These and other dancing masters popularized the fashionable French quadrilles at settlements along the Ohio and Mississippi Rivers.

The advent of the steamboat accelerated the transmission of popular culture in the Ohio Valley. In 1811 the first steamboat traveled from Pittsburgh to New Orleans, and within a few years one managed to make the return trip upriver. By the late 1820s steamboats had reached Knoxville on the upper Tennessee River, and by 1830, others were venturing up the Licking and Big Sandy Rivers in Kentucky and the Kanahwa River in West Virginia.[34] In 1827 one observer wrote, "A steamboat, coming from New Orleans, brings to the remotest villages of our streams, and the very doors of the cabins, a little Paris, a section of Broadway, or a slice of Philadelphia, to ferment in the minds of our young people, the innate propensity for fashions and finery."[35] By the 1840s, steamboats were a common sight on all the navigable rivers that flowed from Appalachia.

Black and mulatto musicians, often slaves, typically provided entertainment for the passengers on the steamboats, and their music could be heard up and down the rivers. American actor Noah Miller Ludlow, who traveled with a theater company by steamboat down the Ohio River in 1817, wrote, "After dinner the tables were put out of the way, and an old 'darkey' with a fiddle was brought into the cabin, who could play an old Virginia reel 'to kill.' It was not long before the floor was occupied with dancers, and among the ladies were some of ours."[36]

A former steamboat pilot recalled the popularity and profitability of "colored" steamboat orchestras in the mid-nineteenth century:

> The cabin orchestra was the cheapest and most enduring, as well as the most popular drawing card. A band of six or eight colored men who could play the violin, banjo, and guitar, and in addition sing well, was always a good investment. These men were paid to do the work of waiters, barbers, and baggagemen, and in addition were given the privilege of passing the hat occasionally and

> keeping all they caught. . . . They also played for dances in the cabin, and at landings sat on the guards and played to attract [customers]. It soon became advertised abroad which boats carried the best orchestras, and such lost nothing in the way of patronage.[37]

One of these African American steamboat musicians was Milton Clarke, a slave from Lexington, Kentucky, who played bass drum and bugle. Clarke had worked as a steward on different steamboats on the Mississippi and Ohio Rivers; in 1838 he agreed to pay his owner, a Presbyterian minister, two hundred dollars a year for a pass to play for parties and dances with a group of fellow enslaved musicians. As Clarke related, "We made money fast and easy," and upon realizing their financial potential, he and his companions escaped to freedom in the North following engagement at a ball in Cincinnati.[38]

The many African American musicians who performed along the Ohio River provided source material for the early blackface minstrel performers. It was in Louisville in 1830 that Thomas Rice first performed as "Jim Crow," a character supposedly inspired by an elderly African American who lived along the Ohio River (either in Cincinnati or Louisville). Dan Emmett, who lived in Cincinnati prior to forming the Virginia Minstrels in New York in 1843, likewise drew from this rich musical environment.[39]

Flatboats remained a common sight on the rivers into the late 1800s, especially during the spring "tide" of each year, when timber was floated downriver to sawmills.[40] In the late 1870s hundreds of timber rafts descended the Kanawha River from West Virginia to the Ohio River, and in 1884 as many as one thousand timber rafts floated down the Clinch River.[41] William Frost noted that for many of the mountaineers of eastern Kentucky, "driving and rafting logs" was "the chief means of contact with the outside world."[42] Like the many others who traveled the rivers, these river workers would have been exposed to the popular music and dances of that time.

Although regular steamboat service still existed all the way to Pikeville in eastern Kentucky as late as the 1890s,[43] the railroads eventually made the steamboats, flatboats, and timber rafts obsolete. The legacy of these rivers, however, endures today in the names of numerous Southern fiddle tunes, especially in Kentucky and West Virginia. In addition to "Mississippi Sawyer,"[44] these include "Boatman," "Natchez-Under-the-Hill," "Ladies on the Steamboat," "Sail Away Ladies," "Big Sandy River," "Boatin' Up Sandy," "Sandy River Belle," "Sandy Boys," "Big Scioto," "Three Forks of Cheat," "West Fork Gals," "Forked Deer,"[45] and many more.

* * *

It is clear that the people of Appalachia were not a homogeneous Anglo-Saxon stock; they were, rather, a "mixed multitude of all classes and complexions" who, despite the relative isolation of the southern mountains, had contact with the outside world through trade and travel. The hoedowns, reels, and frolics of Appalachia likewise were not pure survivals of an ancient Anglo-Celtic heritage, locked away in isolation, but a constantly evolving folk tradition that incorporated elements of recently popular social dances with the older traditions. By the mid-nineteenth century a distinctive regional form of square dance had developed in the Southern backcountry that was distinctly different from the quadrilles and contra dances of the Northeast, and these Southern dances became part of the rural folk culture, not just in Appalachia but throughout the South. In the eyes of the local-color writers of the late nineteenth century, these rural dances no doubt appeared unfashionable and antiquated, especially when compared with the popular dances of the day, but in fact they were only a few generations old.

2 The Southern Square Dance

During the mid-nineteenth century, two separate but related square dance traditions became established in America—one in the Northeast and one in the South.[1] In both traditions, the dances are executed in closed formations, with all couples facing the center of the set—partners beside each other, the man on the left and the woman on the right.[2] Both have a verse-chorus structure in which a main figure, usually performed by two couples at a time, alternates with a chorus figure involving all of the dancers. A number of dance figures, such as the "Grand Right and Left," are likewise found in both traditions.

There are particular characteristics, however, that define the Southern dances (such as those found in Appalachia) and distinguish them from the "quadrilles" of the Northeast. To begin with, the Southern square dances have a circular visiting-couple structure, and although they are called "squares," in reality they are more like circle dances. This allows any number of couples to participate. The size of the set is flexible, depending on the available space, the number of dancers present, and the local tradition. While four-couple square sets—these can actually be thought of as circles with four couples—are common in some communities, big circle sets are the norm elsewhere. Regardless of the shape or size of the set, however, these dances are referred to as "square" dances.

In Southern squares each couple in turn leads the dance figure, working its way counterclockwise around the set, dancing ("visiting") with each of the other couples. If the set is large, more than one couple may lead the figure at the same time. Sometimes the couples are numbered, and every other couple—the "odd" (numbered) couples—progresses around the set from one "even" (numbered) couple to the next, as in a circular contra dance. More often, however, there is no designation of odds or evens, and the dancers

Figure 2.1. Square Dance at Soco Gap—Eight-couple square dance (Haywood County, North Carolina, 1930s). North Carolina Collection, University of North Carolina Library at Chapel Hill

spontaneously decide their roles on the fly. This is clearly different from the more rigidly structured Northern quadrilles, which are danced in four-couple sets. In those dances, the main figures are typically performed by pairs of couples across the set from each other—first the head couples and then the side couples. In circular sets, however, there are no "head" or "side" couples, and this may explain the absence of figures such as "Head Ladies Chain" from the Southern dance tradition.

In the Northern tradition, the figures of the quadrilles and contra dances are choreographed to fit the phrasing of the music, while in the South the choreography and timing of the dance figures are freeform and independent of the musical phrase.[3] Novelist George Tucker alluded to this characteristic of the Southern dances as early as 1824. In *The Valley of Shenandoah* he describes a dance in a Scots-Irish settlement in northern Virginia in the 1790s: "No regard was paid to suiting the figures to the tune, though, it must be admitted, they kept admirable time with their feet."[4] A century later, Cecil Sharp likewise observed, "The music controls the steps only and not the figures."[5]

Since the figures of the Southern dances do not follow the musical phrase, they require the use of a caller to coordinate the dancers, and it is the caller, not the music, that determines the timing of the figures. The caller, however, does not set the pace of the dance; the dancers do. While we might think of the dancers following the caller, in fact, the caller follows the dancers; the next call is not delivered until the dancers are ready for it, independent of the musical phrase or the tempo of the music. Although prompting (verbal cues preceding each dance figure) is now also common practice in the North, it is not necessary, nor was it originally done, in dances choreographed to fit the musical phrase. Once a contra dance has started and the dancers are familiar with the fixed sequence of figures, they can easily continue dancing without prompts, guided only by the phrasing of the music. This, however, is not possible with Southern squares.

Unlike the quadrilles and contra dances of the Northeast, which are written compositions with fixed sequences of figures,[6] the Southern square dances evolved as an unwritten oral folk tradition. There is no one definitive version of any particular dance; each caller has his or her own version. And even during the course of a dance, due to the freeform timing, the caller has the freedom to improvise and change the choreography at will.

The Southern square dance tradition includes a large repertoire of distinctive dance figures. Some, such as "Bird in the Cage" and "Chase the Rabbit," are visiting-couple figures for pairs of couples; others, such as "Wind Up the Ball of Yarn" and the "Shoo-Fly Swing," involve all of the dancers. Many of the visiting-couple figures are unique to one particular dance, and it is from these figures that the dances derive their names. In this oral tradition, however, neither the dance figures nor their names are standardized. Consequently, there are numerous variants and regional names for some of the figures, as well as unrelated figures known by the same name. By comparison, the quadrilles and contra dances of the Northeast are composed of a relatively limited menu of standardized figures, and the dances, rather than deriving their names from the dance figures, are typically named in honor of an important event or person (for example, "Hull's Victory," "Jefferson and Liberty," "Lady Walpole's Reel"), or the music that they are danced to ("Chorus Jig," "Money Musk").

Finally, it is important to consider the music that accompanies the Southern square dances. These two traditions developed side by side; they are inseparable, and an understanding of one sheds light on the other. Since the arrival of the early settlers in the eighteenth century, the European fiddle (or violin) has been the primary dance instrument in the southern mountains. Besides being small, portable, and loud, fiddles could be made by hand from materials readily available on the frontier—wood, hide glue, gut strings, and hair from a horse's tail for the bow—and up until the mid-nineteenth century, it was often the sole instrument at rural dances in Appalachia. Following the Civil War, however, the banjo, an instrument with African roots, became popular in the southern mountains as accompaniment to the fiddle. This may possibly explain why jig tunes in 6/8 time are not found in the Southern fiddle repertoire; unlike reels in 4/4 time, these tunes are not a natural fit with the rhythm of the banjo. By contrast, in the North, where fiddling has traditionally been accompanied by the piano, jigs have remained a part of the fiddle repertoire. Following the building of the railroad through the southern mountains in the late nineteenth century, other instruments became available through mail order, and the Southern old-time string band today typically includes a guitar and standup bass, and sometimes a mandolin or other instruments. The fiddle, however, remains the core of the traditional Southern dance music.

In the North, as in the South, it is the nature of the dances that determines the rhythm, tempo, and structure of the music—not the other way around.[7] The quadrilles and contra dances of the Northeast require thirty-two-bar dance tunes with AABB phrasing, which is why the Anglo- and Celtic-American dance tunes in that tradition have that structure. By contrast, the freeform timing of the Southern dances allows the use of "crooked" tunes with short parts, extra parts, dropped beats, extra beats, and other oddities, which may account for the presence of these kinds of tunes in the Southern fiddle repertoire, in particular in Kentucky and West Virginia. In the Southern dances, the rhythm and the tempo of the music are of much greater importance than musical phrasing, and because the Southern dance figures are not timed to the musical phrase, the music can be fast—sometimes as fast as 140 beats per minute.

* * *

These Southern square dances did not simply appear out of thin air in the Appalachian backcountry; they have roots in earlier dance traditions and were influenced by the fashionable social dances. A look at the traditions and popular dance forms that preceded them not only sheds light on their historical development but also helps to explain the presence of their distinguishing characteristics—their circular, visiting-couple structure, freeform timing, variable choreography, large repertoire of distinctive dance figures, and the fast tempo at which they are danced.

3 Square Roots

Scottish and Irish Reels

When European settlers first came to the southern mountains in the eighteenth century, the Southern square dance did not yet exist, and the dancing that took place at rural frolics consisted mainly of Scottish and Irish reels and jigs. The prevalence of these dances is not surprising, given the large number of Scots-Irish settlers who came to the region. Legendary frontiersman David Crockett (1786–1836), whose great-grandparents were among those who had immigrated to America from northern Ireland, wrote of dancing a "reel" at an all-night frolic in East Tennessee in 1805.[1]

In America, as in Scotland and Ireland, the term "reel" did not refer to one particular dance but to a variety of set dances with figures that involved a characteristic weaving movement.[2] The early Scottish reels included medieval "ring dances" ("rounds"), in which many couples might participate, but also a reel for three dancers, known as the "Reel for Three" (or "Threesome Reel"). This dance, which may have been imported from France during the sixteenth century, consisted of setting steps (rhythmic footwork) performed by the individual dancers, alternating with a traveling figure in the path of a figure eight.[3] Unlike the other, more formal European court dances that came to Scotland at around the same time, the simple repetitive pattern of this three-handed[4] reel was easily learned, making it popular with all classes of people. Furthermore, it did not require a large space, so it could be danced in private homes and taverns.

Joseph Doddridge (1769–1826) recalled the dances of his youth in southwestern Pennsylvania (just north of Berkeley Springs, West Virginia): "After dinner the dancing commenced, and generally lasted till the next morning. The figures of the dances were three and four handed reels, or square sets

Figure 3.1. "Dance in a Country Tavern"—Three-handed reel with setting steps accompanied by a black fiddler (John Lewis Krimmel, 1820). Library of Congress, Prints and Photographs Division (LC-USZ62-94848)

and jigs. The commencement was always a square four. . . . Contra dances, cotillions [square dances], and minuets were unknown."[5]

In addition to the three-handed reel, Doddridge refers to several types of four-handed reels (for four dancers). The "Scotch Reel" (or "Straight Four"), like the three-handed reel, involved a traveling figure in the shape of a figure eight, but with a third loop added (similar to a hey in English country dances and modern contras). This reel was widely known throughout America, and it is described in a social dance manual published in Philadelphia in 1856:

> The figure is danced by two Ladies and two Gentlemen forming a line of four, the Ladies in the center. . . . They begin with a chain in passing in and out of each other, (a straight right and left) until the two gentlemen return to places, the ladies finish facing the gentlemen; then they set (or balancé) before each other, the gentlemen exhibiting all their skill, the Ladies dancing as quietly as possible; after 8 bars of this set they begin again the chain and set, and this they do as long as they can—in fact they never seem tired, and seem to acquire fresh strength each time they come to the balancé.[6]

Doddridge also mentions another type of four-handed reel, called the "Square Four." Reels like this, with two couples facing each other, were known in Scotland and Ireland in the early nineteenth century and are likely the

Figure 3.2. Four-handed "Scotch Reel" (Thomas Hillgrove, *A Complete Practical Guide to the Art of Dancing*, 1863)

source of some of the common Southern visiting-couple dance figures.[7] One in particular, "Uilinn i n-uilinn (Link Arms)," a dance figure from Donegal that involved a series of alternating arm turns, resembles the Southern hand-turning "Do-si-do" (more about this figure later) and the "Georgia Rang-Tang."[8] Dancers in West Virginia today refer to this same figure as "running a reel."

Figure 3.3. "Merrymaking at a Wayside Inn"—Square Four reel with setting steps accompanied by a black fiddler (John Lewis Krimmel, c. 1811). Metropolitan Museum of Art, Rogers Fund

Four-handed reels were common throughout the South, and they are often mentioned in travel accounts and regional fiction. An Englishman who visited the South in 1817 wrote of dancing reels at a country tavern in Georgia as well as at a house in rural South Carolina: "In the evening, a black fiddler amused us for awhile, and I danced four reels in company with [two] girls and their brother."[9] Antebellum humorist and local-color writer George Washington Harris refers to what may have been similar "reels" at a Saturday night "frolick" at a house in East Tennessee in "The Knob Dance" (1845)—a lone fiddler plays "Forked Deer," "Natchez-under-the-Hill," "Rocky Mounting" [Mountain], and "Misses McCloud"—and in another of Harris's local-color "sketches" of life in East Tennessee, "Bart Davis's Dance" (c. 1850s), a black fiddler plays "tchunes" [tunes] for "reels" in a backwoods cabin.[10]

These four-handed Scots-Irish reels remained popular in Appalachia throughout the nineteenth century. In *The Heart of the Alleghanies* (1883), a book that resembles a tourist guide to western North Carolina, the authors describe how two pairs of couples, accompanied by a fiddle and a "homemade banjo," dance reels at an "old-fashioned hoe-down" in a mountain cabin in the Nantahala Valley:

> Four couples stepped into the center of the floor, forming two sets. Each one separated from and stood facing his partner. . . . The music was one of the liveliest jigs imaginable, and the musicians sang as they played. The dancers courtesied and then began a singular dance. There was no calling off; it was simply a jig on the part of each performer. The girls danced with arms akimbo, reeling sideways one way, and then sideways the other. Their partners . . . careened around in like manner.[11]

In the 1990s, Biss Honeycutt (1909–2000) of Yancey County told me of similar reels that he had danced in western North Carolina as a youth: "They called it the four-handed reel. It'd be two men and two women. And they could dance all kinds of different figures. . . . Just two couples. I've seen 'em dance all night long that way. One couple out after another. . . . They'd start out holding hands and circle."[12]

As mentioned earlier, reels in Scotland and Ireland were sometimes danced in circular sets involving more than four dancers. British military surveyor Charles Vallancey, who in 1786 wrote a history of ancient Ireland, noted these "circular dances" of the "vulgar Irish."[13] Author James Boswell encountered what may have been similar circular reels on the Isle of Skye when he accompanied Samuel Johnson on a tour of Scotland in 1773. These dances consisted of progressive visiting-couple figures in which one couple danced with another couple and then moved on to subsequent couples, with the others following up:

> We had again a great dinner, and in the evening a great dance. We made out five country squares without sitting down; and then we performed with much

activity a dance, which I suppose the emigration from Skye has occasioned. They call it "America." A brisk reel is played. The first couple begin, and each sets to one [a second couple], then each to another [a third couple], then as they set to the next couple [a fourth couple], the second and third couples are setting; and so it goes on till all are set a-going, setting and wheeling round each other, while each is making the tour of all in the dance. It shows how emigration catches till all are set afloat.[14]

Boswell refers to the great emigration across the Atlantic that was taking place at that time, and the Scots-Irish immigrants who came to America would have likely been familiar with these dances. Novelist George Tucker suggested this when he wrote of "reels, consisting of four, five, and even six couples" that were danced in Scots-Irish communities in northern Virginia in the late 1700s.[15] In the early decades of the nineteenth century, "reels, first six, then eight, then ten handed" (for three, four, or five couples) were also danced in the North Carolina Piedmont.[16] According to folklorist and dance researcher LeeEllen Friedland, circular dances such as these predate the four-couple square in the rural Appalachian dance tradition.[17] These Scots-Irish reels, therefore, likely served as a template for the Southern square dances, and this would account for the circular visiting-couple format of the later dances.[18] (Another type of reel, the Six-Handed Reel, performed in a longways set, will be discussed in chapter 8.)

Although the dance traditions of the southern mountains were changing and evolving during the nineteenth century, the dances continued to be called "reels." We read of "interminable reels" in the Blue Ridge in 1874 and "furious and erratic reel-dancing" in western North Carolina in 1877.[19] Even at the end of the twentieth century, some dancers continued to refer to square dances as "reels." Fiddler Tommy Jarrell (1901–1985) of Surry County, North Carolina, spoke of dancing the "old reels that's handed down from one generation to another (we called 'em reels back then)"; dance caller James Lawson (1928–2011), also of Surry County, recalled "six-couple reels" with one couple leading the figure at a time.[20] In addition to their importance as a precursor to the Southern square dance, the legacy of these various reels survives today in Scots-Irish fiddle tunes, such as "Billy in the Lowground," "Leather Britches" ("Lord Macdonald's Reel"), and "Miss McLeod's Reel," that remain a part of the Southern fiddle repertoire.

English Country Dances

When Cecil Sharp encountered square dances in eastern Kentucky, he mistook them to be survivals of English country dances, a type of dance that first became fashionable in the ballrooms of England in the late sixteenth century. Although the name suggests rural origins, most of these "country" dances were in fact composed by professional dancing masters for urban

Figure 3.4. "The Village Assembly"—English Country Dance (1776). Library of Congress, Prints and Photographs Division (LC-USZ62-59606)

dancers. By the mid-seventeenth century these dances began to appear in printed manuals, the earliest being John Playford's *The Dancing Master*. Playford's first edition (1651) includes 104 dances in a variety of formations: dances "for four" (dancers), "square dances for eight," and "rounds" and longways sets for six, eight, or "as many as will." The progressive rounds, in which each couple dances the figure with successive couples around the circle, are thought to be the oldest, with roots in earlier rural traditions,[21] and these are the dances that Sharp associated with the Kentucky square dances. In subsequent editions of Playford's manual, however, the progressive longways set "for as many as will" became the predominant form. In these dances partners stand across from each other in two facing lines, and each couple in turn leads the dance from the top of the set, dancing with successive couples down the line.[22]

By the end of the seventeenth century English country dances had spread to France, and the name changed to "contredanse," with the implication of opposing couples—the modern name "contra dance" is an Anglicization of the French name. By the early eighteenth century, longways country dances had also become popular in Ireland and the Lowlands of Scotland. The proliferation of these dances throughout Europe coincided with the colonization of the New World, so it is not surprising that they were also fashionable in colonial America.

Although "contra-dances" were reportedly known in some of the early settlements on the Cumberland Plateau of Tennessee in 1787,[23] they never became widespread in the southern backcountry. A few of the Southern visiting-couple figures ("Figure Eight," "Chase the Rabbit," and "Shoot the Owl"), however, likely have roots in these English dances.

Dancing Masters and Dancing Schools

English country dances were not prompted by a dance caller; instead, dancers were required to learn the figures at dancing school before attending a ball.[24] A dancing school was established in Boston as early as 1672, and by the early eighteenth century itinerant dancing masters were teaching the "latest and most fashionable" country dances in cities and towns throughout the American colonies.[25] While visiting eastern North Carolina in 1739, English evangelist George Whitefield wrote, "It grieves me to find that in every little town there is a settled dancing-master, but scarcely anywhere a settled minister to be met with."[26] These dancing teachers were not all men. Sarah Campbell advertised her services in Charleston as a "Dancing-mistress" in 1750, and ten years later another dancing mistress was teaching in Newport, Rhode Island.[27]

There were also black dancing masters. One was active in South Carolina in 1733, and others reportedly taught at dancing schools in Virginia in 1739 and 1775.[28] In the early 1800s, an African American dancing master held a dancing school at a tavern in Warrenton, North Carolina: "The dancing master was 'Uncle' Peter Feggins, a negro man, who was accompanied by his assistant, Hardy Artis, who played the violin."[29]

In America, as in Europe, attendance at dancing school distinguished the middle and upper classes from the unrefined common folk, and partly as a way to deflect criticism from the church, dancing masters also taught lessons in etiquette and proper manners. As a consequence, the dancers, who in Playford's time had been referred to as "women" and "men," became known as "ladies" and "gents."[30] These terms remain in use today, and dancers are still sometimes instructed to bow to their partners and corners at the beginning and end of a square dance.

The dancing schools of America were not confined to the cities of the eastern seaboard, and some itinerant dancing masters headed west into the backcountry, where even in small frontier towns dancing was considered to be a necessary part of one's education. By 1763 there were at least two dancing masters in the Shenandoah Valley of Virginia.[31] Robert Bailey, a young ploughboy, attended dancing school with students from the wealthier social class in Culpepper County around 1790. He recalled learning "country dances," which were "the fashion of the day."[32]

Not all gatherings, however, were as orderly as these dance assemblies of the Shenandoah Valley. Lacking the guidance of a dancing master, a house dance in Charlotte, North Carolina, in 1782 turned into a drunken frolic:

> The house was small and the floor was loose boarded, and they much warped with the heat of the fire. The company consisted of about three or four young married women, and about six or seven men, who were much worse than the girls, and most of them nearly drunk. The fiddle and fiddler was much alike for neither of them, nor both together could play; he, however, when he could not play a tune, would always sing it or attempt it. Their dancing was a continued scene of labor and confusion. We attempted a country dance or two, and except about three couples, the rest were intolerably awkward, as they hobbled through the figures without minding the tune.[33]

With the outbreak of the French Revolution in 1789, numerous expatriates from France and the West Indies fled to the United States, and taking advantage of the great popularity of dancing in America, many became dancing masters, opening dancing schools in Boston, New York, Philadelphia, Charleston, and New Orleans (which was not yet United States territory).[34] As mentioned earlier, French dancing masters traveled upriver from New Orleans to teach in remote settlements along the Ohio and Mississippi Rivers, and when Englishman Charles Janson visited Orange County in northern Virginia in 1803, he encountered a French dancing master teaching "minuets," "country dances," and "reels" at a dancing school in a local tavern.[35]

One of these French dancing masters was ornithologist and painter John James Audubon (1785–1851), who came to the United States from France in 1803 at age eighteen. In 1808 Audubon traveled down the Ohio River from Pittsburgh, and at the Falls of the Ohio (Louisville) he attended a "Barbicue on the Fourth of July," where he danced "reels and cotillons [sic]."[36] In addition to being an artist, Audubon played the fiddle and flute, and he later taught music, dancing, and fencing (as well as drawing) in various communities along the Ohio and Mississippi Rivers, including New Orleans. During the winter of 1825–26, as a way to finance travel to Europe, Audubon held a dancing school on Friday and Saturday nights at the village of Woodville, in southern Mississippi. Playing fiddle while he instructed sixty pupils in the popular dances of the day, Audubon earned about two thousand dollars that season, a considerable sum at the time—the equivalent of more than forty thousand dollars today.[37]

Audubon and the many other French dancing masters who taught dancing across the country left their mark on the dance traditions of America. Elements of the fashionable dances they taught filtered into the rural tradition, and the French dance terminology with which they prompted their students ("Allemande," "Balancé," "Chassé" [Sashay], "Dos â Dos" [Do-si-do], "Promenade") is still used by dance callers in America today.

French Cotillions

Around the time of the American Revolution, a French square dance called the cotillion (or cotillon) became popular in America. These "contredanses

Figure 3.5. "The Cotillion Dance" (James Caldwell, 1771). Lewis Walpole Library, Yale University

françaises" for four couples had a verse-chorus structure: a main figure danced by pairs of couples across the set from each other—first the head couples ("first four") and then the side couples ("second four")—alternated with a "change" figure involving all eight dancers. Some of the common change figures—"Circle" ("Le Grand Rond"), "Ladies (or Gents) Star," "Allemande Corners,"[38] "Grand Right and Left" ("La Grande Chaine"), and "Promenade"—would be familiar to square dancers today.

Cotillions were being taught in Philadelphia as early as 1772 and in Charleston, South Carolina, by 1774,[39] and following the revolution, these French square dances displaced the English country dances from the ballrooms of America. This was no doubt a reflection of the new nation's positive feelings toward France for its assistance in defeating the British. The exception was New England, which remained generally pro-British and retained the English country dances. Commenting on the dancing at victory celebrations in Williamsburg, Virginia, in 1781, French army officer Baron Ludwig von Closen wrote, "All of them like our French quadrilles [square dances], and in general, they find French manners to their taste."[40] As with the earlier English country dances, these dances were not prompted, so dancers were required to learn and memorize the various figures before attending a ball. Robert Hunter Jr. wrote of "practicing cotillions" in Baltimore before attending a wedding in eastern Virginia in 1785.[41]

The prevalence of French dancing masters throughout the country no doubt helped popularize these fashionable dances in America. Not everyone, however, had the privilege of attending dancing school; in the backcountry the old Scots-Irish reels remained popular in many rural communities. This was true in central Ohio, where in the first decade of the nineteenth century "cotillions were unknown," but "jigs, four-handed reels, the double shuffle and break down 'were all the rage.'"[42] While geographical isolation no doubt played a role, dance customs and preferences were also dictated by social class. This is illustrated in *Leather and Silk*, a novel set in western Virginia during the first decade of the nineteenth century. The daughter of a well-to-do German attends a dancing school taught by a French dancing master from Paris in the town of Martinsburg, and ten miles out of town, "an old fiddler" plays for jigs and reels at a "frolic" held at a hunter's cabin.[43] The stratification of dance styles by social class also appears in a recollection of dances that took place in a log courthouse in the Georgia Piedmont in the 1820s: "Them that's got on shoes and stockings [danced] the cotillion; them that's got on shoes and no stockings [danced] the Virginy reel; them that's got on nairy shoes nor stockings [danced] the scamper-down [step dance].'"[44]

When asked about the distinction between cotillions and reels, North Carolina fiddler Tommy Jarrell once differentiated them geographically, saying that reels were the ones danced "up in Virginia, up on top of the mountain," and cotillions were "the ones we danced at the foot of the mountain, on the south side."[45] This distinction may reflect the dichotomy that once existed between the older Scots-Irish reels of the rural mountain communities and the more refined four-couple French cotillions and quadrilles taught at dancing schools in the valley towns.

Over time, certain figures of the French square dances—those compatible with the circular structure of the Scots-Irish reels—became incorporated into the Appalachian dances. One of these is the Promenade. In the novel *Behind the Blue Ridge* Frances Courtenay Baylor describes a circular Scots-Irish reel followed by a promenade as a chorus figure at a wedding in the Shenandoah Valley in 1861: "The reels and reelers went thundering on, [then] all the couples bounded off in a 'grand cirkit' all around the room."[46] The "Promenade" and other change figures from the cotillions, such as the "Grand Right and Left," are still common as chorus figures in the Southern square dance tradition today.

The Quadrilles

Toward the end of the eighteenth century, advertisements for dancing schools—in New York (1792) and Philadelphia (1797)—began to mention a new kind of French square dance, "quadrilles."[47] These new dances combined figures from the earlier cotillions into longer dances that typically consisted of five separate parts, known as "changes."[48] The first four changes in a "set of

Figure 3.6. "The Quadrille Figure: Lady & Gent^{n} Advance & Retire" (Thomas Wilson, *The Quadrille and Cotillion Panorama*, 1822). Library of Congress, Music Division

quadrilles," like the main figures of the cotillions, were typically performed by pairs of couples across the set from each other (heads or sides). These would be followed by a fifth change (the "Finale") involving all eight dancers. Even though these dances were different from the older square dances, many dancers in America (much to the disdain of European visitors) retained the old terminology and continued to refer to them as "cotillions."

By the 1820s quadrilles had become the principal dance of fashionable society in America. English author Frances Wright, who visited New York in 1819, remarked that these new French dances, which were being promoted by the dancing masters, were "certainly prettier to look at than the interminable country-dance."[49] In the Northeast, these fashionable dances spread beyond the cities, becoming well established in the rural dance tradition by the end of the nineteenth century.[50]

The popularity of the quadrilles coincided with the steamboat era, and this no doubt helped disseminate these fashionable dances throughout the Midwest. Flatboatman Thomas C. Collins, who spent his life working on the rivers that flowed into the Mississippi, wrote of quadrilles involving twelve dancers at the hotel at Chouteau Springs, Missouri, in 1858: "Don't think I ever heard nicer music, or saw better dancing. They danced in sets of 12. Each of the 4 gents had 2 partners, and here was 3 sets of 12 each on the floor at once. The music was rendered by 2 German brothers, named Wettendorf. One played the violin and the other, the guitar. I thought I knew something about dancing, but I was nowhere."[51]

The quadrilles appear to have had the greatest influence on the dance tradition in the Ohio River watershed (especially in West Virginia and Kentucky), where by the end of the nineteenth century the earlier Scots-Irish reels adopted the four-couple form of these French dances. An account of a "ho-down" in eastern Kentucky from 1906 includes the calls, "First four [head couples], forward and back; forward again and cross over."[52] Cecil Sharp encountered a similar figure for head and side couples in this region in 1917, as well as other quadrille figures ("Basket Figure," "Cheat Figure," and "Divide the Ring").[53]

The influence of the quadrilles in this region is also evident from the dance calls that were recorded on 78-rpm discs in the late 1920s and early 1930s (see chapter 7). In the spoken introduction on a recording made in 1927, Uncle Dave Macon of Middle Tennessee shouts out, "Get your partners for your quadrille. Let 'er go, professor," and on a recording from 1932, Kentuckian Asa Martin announces that he is going to call "one more little quadrille."[54] The square dances on the recordings from this region are predominantly four-couple sets, and they include quadrille figures involving the head and side couples, such as "Ladies Chain," "Right and Left Through," and "Half Promenade."

Away from the rivers, quadrilles became popular in the ballrooms of resort hotels at the many mineral springs throughout the southern mountains.[55] Englishman G. W. Featherstonhaugh took part in these fashionable dances at the resort in Warm Springs, Virginia, in 1834: "After supper it is the custom at the Warm Springs to adjourn to a place called the Ball-room, which has a few wooden benches round it, and one fiddler . . . [to dance] quadrilles."[56] Not all mountain resorts, however, were as rustic as this. By the late 1830s, the hotel at Warm Springs in western North Carolina (now known as Hot Springs) boasted a 230-foot-long ballroom, the second largest in the state. When Charles Lanman stayed at Sulphur Springs Hotel in nearby Buncombe County in 1848, he observed that "the style in which people are entertained is well worthy of even such places as Saratoga."[57]

The quadrilles enjoyed by the summer guests at these mountain resorts likely did not go unnoticed by the hotel employees and local residents, and one figure adopted into the rural dance tradition across the South was the "Jig Figure." This fast-paced "Promiscuous Figure" (one in which dancers switch partners) was often danced as the "Finale" of a quadrille. The "Jig Figure" involved all of the women leaving their partners and swinging each of the other men in succession, counterclockwise around the set. Following this, the men would swing all of the women in a similar manner.[58] Unlike many of the other quadrille figures, this figure was compatible with the circular form of the Southern reels. David C. Barrow Jr. noted the spontaneity elicited by the "Jig Figure" at African American corn shucking frolics in northeast Georgia following the Civil War: "'Gemmen to de right!' . . . always calls forth a full display of the dancers' agility."[59] This spirited figure was also known in Middle Tennessee, where Dr. Humphrey Bate called it on a 78-rpm recording of "Take Your Foot out of the Mud and Put It in the Sand" in 1928: "Gents all to the right, all the way around boys, swing 'em all . . . now the little ladies, all to the right, swing all the boys." African American fiddler and dance caller Joe Thompson (1918–2012) called a similar figure at dances in the North Carolina Piedmont, and in recent years I have encountered it at community square dances in Surry and Madison Counties (North Carolina).

The Boulangère

Another European social dance that appears to have had an influence on the rural Southern dance tradition is the Boulangère. This French circle dance was popular in the ballrooms of England and America during the early nineteenth century. English author Jane Austen mentions "La Boulangère" in *Pride and Prejudice*, and in a letter to her sister Cassandra in 1796 she wrote, "We dined at Goodnestone, and in the evening danced two country-dances and the Boulangeries."[60] Described in nineteenth-century dance manuals as a dance "of great antiquity," the Boulangère was popular throughout North America, often danced at the end of the evening following the country dances, quadrilles, and waltzes.[61] According to William Gilmore Simms, the Boulangère was a regular feature of plantation balls near Charleston, South Carolina, in the 1830s: "Nothing can be imagined more simple or more fascinating than those Pineville balls. . . . The evening's entertainment was always concluded with the Boulanger."[62]

The Boulangère consisted of a series of hand turns with successive dancers in a circular set. A description of "La Balanjé or Concluding Dance" appears in a dance manual published in Philadelphia around 1810: "Circle eight (grand round)—One lady turn the next gentleman with the right hand—partner with the left & so on all round until all the ladies are done—grand round & the same by the gentlemen."[63] Here the women, one at a time, work their way around the circle, turning each of the men with their right hand, alternating with a left hand to their partners, who follow them around the inside of the set.[64] Like the "Jig Figure," this dance figure was performed first by the women and then the men. This movement is similar to, and may possibly be the source of, the reeling figures of both the Virginia Reel (see chapter 8) and the Scottish "Strip the Willow," though in the Boulangère it is done in a circular formation.

This lively figure was also danced at plantation frolics. Former slave Dave Lowry of Virginia referred to it as "Cashing the Ring" [Sashaying the Ring]: "That means de head lady would dance around the ring to everybody. Den de next one, and so on."[65] By the early twentieth century, this hand-turning figure was known as the "Shoo-Fly Swing," and it was used as an ending figure for square dances across the rural South. It is mentioned by name in a 1906 account of a "ho-down" in eastern Kentucky (mentioned above), and it also appears on several 78-rpm recordings made by dance callers from western North Carolina and Middle Tennessee in the 1920s.[66]

Native American Dance

The European dances were not the earliest in the Appalachian region. Dancing was an important part of the culture of the Native American societies of the Southeast, where it served a social purpose and was also a key ritualistic component of religious ceremonies. Dancing was a frequent occurrence in

Figure 3.7. "Dance Generale" of the Natchez Indians (Antoine-Simon Le Page du Pratz, *Histoire de la Louisiane*, 1758). Library of Congress, Prints and Photographs Division (LC-USZ6-679)

Native American communities, as attested by Henry Timberlake, an Anglo-American army officer who visited the Overhill Cherokee towns in East Tennessee during the French and Indian War in 1761: "I was almost every night at some dance, or diversion."[67] Englishman John Lawson had encountered similar Native American dances in the North Carolina Piedmont in 1701: "They made a circular Dance, like a Ring, representing the Shape of the Fire they danced about."[68] Accompanied by drums, rattles, flutes, and singing, these dances were typically performed by dancers moving single-file in a counterclockwise circle.

In 1775 a young Englishman named Nicholas Cresswell traveled by boat down the Ohio River from Pittsburgh to Kentucky, and at Coshocton, Ohio, he participated in one of these ring dances around a fire: "No regular figure, but violent distortion of features, writhing and twisting the body in the most uncouth and antic postures imaginable."[69] To Cresswell, these dances no doubt appeared spontaneous and freeform, especially when compared with the formal steps and figures of the European social dances. At that time, however, many of the native dances in the Southeast likewise followed a highly prescribed form, with particular steps and progressions. Sometimes, as noted at a Cherokee village in southeastern Tennessee in 1809, a circle of dancers was led in a spiral, coiling into the center and then reversing direction to uncoil: "They dance round a blazing fire, the Leader singing and his followers keeping chorus. . . . When the Circle is complete, another is formed within it, and so in continuation till it resembles the Coils of a Snake."[70]

While Cresswell and other Europeans observed and sometimes participated in these indigenous dances, Native Americans in turn were exposed to the European dances. According to John Oldmixton's 1708 edition of *The British Empire in America*, "A French dancing-master settling in Craven County, South Carolina [near Charleston] taught the Indians country-dances,"[71] and by 1711 Native American students (Tuscaroras and others) were learning these English dances at the College of William and Mary at Williamsburg, Virginia.[72]

In addition to the dances, Native Americans learned the European dance music, and by 1663 a Native American fiddler was routinely providing the music for white dancers in Maine: "The only Fidler that was in the Province of Meyn [Maine] . . . was an Indian called Scozway, whom the Fishermen and planters when they had a mind to be merry made use of."[73] In his travels down the Ohio River almost a hundred years later, Nicholas Cresswell likewise wrote of a Native American fiddler in the Indian territory of eastern Ohio: "Heard an Indian play upon a Tin Violin and make tolerable good music."[74]

Intermarriage between Europeans and Native Americans no doubt hastened the mixing of the two cultures, and by the early 1800s European social dances were being danced alongside the ceremonial dances in Native American communities. John Norton, whose father was Cherokee and mother was Scottish, wrote of the dances that took place in the Cherokee villages of East Tennessee in 1809. These included Native American dances as well as ones "in the English style" (most likely Scots-Irish reels) that were accompanied by Cherokee fiddlers.

> They began with one of their national dances on the green before the door, the leader singing and dancing in a circle, and the followers keeping chorus. Afterwards an English dance was struck up in the house. They now begin to be very fond of these dances, but for want of skilful teachers, none have yet acquired any proficiency in music; the fiddlers seem only to imitate their own simple notes, which however are sufficient to enable them to dance in cadence. The Entertainment continued with joy, sobriety and decorum, until near day, when all retired to rest.[75]

By the late nineteenth century, Native American communities had adopted many European American customs. Dancing was no longer a nightly ritual, but house dances took place on weekends, during the Christmas holiday, and on other occasions throughout the year. These social dances were common on the Cherokee reservation in western North Carolina well into the early twentieth century.[76] Cherokee elder Walker Calhoun (1919–2012) once told me about the house dances of his youth, which in addition to square dances and the Virginia Reel included the "Pot Dance." A big circle is formed around a lone dancer, and the circle moves first to the left and then back to the right. The lone dancer then turns each of the dancers in the circle, alternating with right and left arms before choosing the next one to be in the middle.[77] The arm turning movement of this circle dance is reminiscent of the French Boulangère ("Shoo-Fly Swing").

Folklorist and musician Bascom Lamar Lunsford believed that the Cherokee dances had an influence on the dances of the southern mountains and were the source of the "circle and the serpentine movements" in the square dances of western North Carolina.[78] An association between these two traditions is no doubt implied by the common square dance prompt for a single-file, counterclockwise circle: "Other way back, single file, ladies in the lead, Indian style." Snaking and spiral figures, however, are not unique to the Native American tradition. They also appear in European folk dances and in "The Grand March," a formal ballroom dance from the mid-nineteenth century (see chapter 10). The ring form likewise exists in both European and African traditions. It is impossible, therefore, to identify a single source for these features in the Southern square dances.

African American Dance

As in the Native American societies of the New World, music and dance were an integral part of the culture of West Africa. Englishman John Atkins described the dances of Sierra Leone in 1721: "Dancing is the Diversion of their Evenings: Men and Women make a Ring in an open part of the Town, and one at a time shews his Skill in antick Motions and Gesticulations, yet with a great deal of Agility, the Company making the Musick by clapping their hands together during the time, helped by the louder noise of two or three Drums made of a hollowed piece of Tree, and covered with Kid-Skin."[79] Atkins refers to several key characteristics of the West African dance tradition. These energetic dances were done in ring formations, with individual dancers taking turns dancing in the center, accompanied by rhythmic drumming, hand clapping, and singing.

African ring dances such as these came to the New World with enslaved Africans. Scottish doctor James Grainger wrote in verse of the slave dances at a sugar plantation on the island of St. Kitts in the West Indies in 1764:

> On festal days; or when their work is done;
> Permit thy slaves to lead the choral dance,
> To the wild banshaw's melancholy sound.
> Responsive to the sound, head, feet and frame,
> Move aukwardly harmonious; hand in hand,
> Now lock'd, the gay troop circularly wheels,

And frisks and capers with intemperate joy.
Halts the vast circle, all clap hands and sing;
While those distinguish'd for their heels and air,
Bound in the center, and fantastic twine.[80]

Like the dances observed by Atkins in West Africa, this dance takes the form of a "vast circle," with individual dancers ("distinguish'd for their heels and air") taking turns in the center. In addition to handclapping and singing, the dancers are accompanied by a banjo ("banshaw").

With the proliferation of the slave trade during the eighteenth century, African ring dances became known throughout North America. By the late 1700s "the original Congo dances," as danced in Africa, were part of Pinkster (Pentecost) Day celebrations in Albany, New York,[81] and in 1799 a passenger on a boat in New Orleans reported similar dances with "vast numbers of negro slaves, men, women, and children, assembled together on the levee, drumming, fifing, and dancing, in large rings."[82] According to former slave Tinie Force of Kentucky, "Ring dancing was largely practiced during the slavery period. Especially . . . throughout the [Louisiana] Purchase Region."[83]

When English-born architect Benjamin Latrobe (1764–1820) visited New Orleans in 1819, he "accidently stumbled upon an assembly of negroes" performing these dances. There, on Sunday afternoons, blacks would gather at "Congo Square" to dance, and as in the West Indies, the dancing was accompanied by a banjo: "They were formed into circular groups, in the midst of four of which that I examined (but there were more of them) was a ring, the largest not ten feet in diameter. In the first were two women dancing . . . hardly moving their feet or bodies. The music consisted of two drums and a stringed instrument [a banjo] . . . which no doubt was imported from Africa."[84]

While there was no distinction between sacred and secular dancing in Africa, by the early eighteenth century a separate secular dance tradition began to develop in the New World.[85] These black social dances were rooted in the ceremonial dances of Africa, but they also incorporated elements of the European set dances. In addition to dance figures, African American dancers adopted the one-on-one, male-female partnering of the European dances, which had not been part of the African tradition.[86] Even as the two traditions merged, former slave Robert Anderson (b. 1843) of Green County, Kentucky, was aware of the distinctions that still existed: "We danced the dances like the white folks danced them, and then danced our own kind of dances."[87]

This blending of the European and African dances can be seen in Christopher Columbus Franklin's recollection of antebellum dances. Franklin, born into slavery in Caddo Parrish in northwest Louisiana, spoke of outdoor frolics with forty or fifty dancers accompanied by "fiddle or banjo or windjammer" [accordion]: "De prompter call, 'All git ready.' Den he holler, 'All balance,' and den he sing out, 'Swing your pardner,' and dey does it. Den he say, 'First man [couple] head off to de right,' and dere dey goes. Or he say, 'All promenade,'

Figure 3.8. "Evening at the Quarters"—African American ring dance accompanied by a banjo (Wade Whipple, 1887). *New Harper's Monthly Magazine* 75, no. 449 (October 1887)

and dey goes in de circle. One thing dey calls, 'Bird in de Cage.' Three joins hands round de gal in de middle, and dance round her, and den she git out and her pardner git in de center and dey dance dat way awhile."[88]

The dance calls "sung out" by the "prompter" in Franklin's account reveal a circular visiting-couple dance (couples "head off to de right") with free-form timing that allows the dancers to "dance [that] way awhile." This dance includes European figures, such as "Balancé" and "Promenade," as well as "Bird in the Cage," a dance figure that involves an individual dancer within a ring of dancers. This Southern figure does not come from the European tradition, and it cannot be found in any of the nineteenth-century dance manuals. Instead, it appears to have come from the African tradition. In the ring dances of Sierra Leone, described by John Atkins, one dancer at a time "shews his Skill in antick Motions and Gesticulations." More explicitly suggestive of the "Bird in the Cage," however, are the ceremonial burial dances of southern Nigeria in which individual dancers imitated the motions of a bird within a ring.[89] These African ring dances may well be the source of this common Southern square dance figure.

Writer Lafcadio Hearn (1850–1904) wrote of African American ring dances in Cincinnati in 1876. Cincinnati, at that time, was the principal city along the Ohio River ("The Queen of the West") and an established stop for steamboats. According to Hearn, the African American "roustabouts" who worked on the river were "from all parts of the States, but chiefly from Kentucky and Eastern Virginia," and at night they would gather at the "dance-houses" and "'ball-rooms' of Bucktown" to enjoy the "old slave dances."[90] He describes these African American ring dances for eight couples as "double quadrilles."[91] The musicians started with the Scottish reel "Devil's Dream" on fiddle, banjo, and string bass, but then "the music changed to an old Virginia reel, and the

Figure 3.9. "Terpsichore in the Quarters"—African American frolic with a fiddler and dance caller (Alabama, c. 1860). *Scribner's Monthly 21* (January 1881)

dancing changing likewise, presented the most grotesque spectacle imaginable. The dancing became wild; men patted juba and shouted, the Negro women danced with the most fantastic grace, their bodies describing almost incredible curves forward and backward; limbs intertwined rapidly in a wrestle with each other and with the music; the room presented a tide of swaying bodies and tossing arms, and flying hair."[92]

David Barrow, who encountered equally energetic dancing at African American corn-shucking frolics in northwest Georgia in 1882, noted the adaptation of the European set dances: "The dance of late years is a modification of the cotillion [quadrille]. . . . There is a great deal of jig-dancing in these cotillions, and the man who cannot 'cut the pigeon wing' is considered a sorry dancer indeed; but still it purports to be a cotillion."[93]

Like the "double quadrilles" of Cincinnati, this "cotillion" was likely an African American ring dance for eight couples. These eight-couple sets were common throughout the Deep South, as well as in eastern Virginia and across North Carolina. Former slave Frank Menefee of Alabama referred to it as the "sixteen-hand reel," Liza Mention of Georgia called it the "16-hand cortillion,"[94] and by the early twentieth century, African American dance callers, such as Joe Thompson's father (b. 1880s), were calling the "sixteen hand cotillion" for white as well as black dancers in the North Carolina Piedmont.[95] Eight-couple square dances became common in western North Carolina, and consequently, when square dance groups began to perform on stage in the 1920s, they danced with eight couples. The most famous of these groups, the Soco Gap Square Dance Team, was led by Haywood County caller Sam Queen (1889–1969), who had learned from African American dance caller Bob Love. This ring dance formation for eight couples is still used by traditional clogging teams in western North Carolina today.

* * *

The Southern square dance is clearly an American hybrid that borrowed elements from all of these earlier dance forms. The circular Scots-Irish reels served as the foundation, providing the circular form, the visiting-couple structure, and the freeform timing of these dances. The French cotillions and quadrilles contributed the verse-chorus structure and chorus figures, such as the "Grand Right and Left" and "Promenade." The quadrilles, which were fashionable during the steamboat era, appear to have had the greatest influence on the western side of the Appalachians in the Ohio River watershed, where the four-couple square set became the predominant form. To the east of the mountains and in the Deep South, the eight-couple ring form of the African American dances was more common. All of these earlier forms and other popular social dances contributed to the large repertoire of distinctive Southern dance figures. Although these dances have roots in the earlier dance traditions of Europe, Africa, and Native America, by the mid-nineteenth century they had evolved into something new and different. In an account of a rural frolic (accompanied by a gourd fiddle and a dulcimer) following a quilting and log-rolling party in East Tennessee in 1843, George Washington Harris writes: "The music sounds high, and the wild woods ring; the feet of the company fly thick and fast; reels, cotillions, and waltzes, are all so mingled and blended together that it is a dance without a name."[96] Many dancers continued to use the old European terminology, referring to the Southern dances as "reels," "cotillions," "quadrilles," or "sets" (as in a set of quadrilles), but these new American dances needed a name of their own. As early as the 1860s, as a way to differentiate quadrilles from the increasingly popular "round dances" (the waltz and other couple dances), dance manuals began to use the term "square dance."[97] Adjacent dancers at the corners of a square set likewise became known as "corners," and by the end of the century these terms were also being used by dancers in rural Appalachia, regardless of the shape of the dance set or the number of dancers involved. Georgia novelist Will Harben refers to a "reg'lar square dance" (accompanied by an "old negro fiddler" who calls out the figures) in *Westerfelt* (1901), a novel set in rural north Georgia.[98]

All of the distinctive features of the Southern square dances—their circular visiting-couple structure, freeform timing, variable choreography, distinctive dance figures, and fast tempo—can be accounted for by the earlier traditions and popular social dances from which these dances developed. One important feature, however, has yet to be discussed, and that is the practice of dance calling. Introduced by African American musicians in the New World, it was the essential ingredient that enabled elements from the European, African American, and Native American dance traditions to merge together in the rural Southern backcountry to create these American dances.

4 Transforming Tradition

When Cecil Sharp visited Kentucky in 1917, he wrote, "It is customary for one of the company, not necessarily one of the dancers, to 'call' the dance as it proceeds."[1] Dance calling (the verbal prompting of the figures during the course of a dance) was not a part of the European dance tradition, and Sharp was not familiar with it. Instead, it was a New World innovation, a product of the confluence of the European and African American dance traditions that led to the development of the Southern square dances, which would not exist without it. Dance calling, though, did not originate in Appalachia. In fact, the earliest known reference to it comes far from the southern mountains, in New Orleans, where English-born architect Benjamin Latrobe attended a ball in 1819. Latrobe reported, "I have never been in a public assembly altogether better conducted. . . . Altogether the impression was highly favorable. The only nuisance was a tall, ill-dressed black in the music gallery, who played the tambourine standing up, and in a forced and vile voice called the figures as they changed."[2] Having the dance figures called out at a ball was not something that Latrobe was accustomed to, and he was clearly annoyed by this American custom.

African American Fiddlers

The black dance musicians Latrobe encountered at the ball in New Orleans were not an uncommon sight at that time. During the eighteenth and nineteenth centuries black fiddlers could be found throughout America, and these musicians routinely provided the music for dancing at social functions. White fiddlers certainly played for family and friends at private gatherings, and white musicians performed in formal concerts, but the musicians who played for dance assemblies and balls, especially formal ones, were nonwhite

Figure 4.1. "Tuning Up"—Dance musicians with fiddles and tambourine in East Tennessee (David Hunter Strother, 1858). *Harper's New Monthly Magazine* 17, no. 99 (August 1858)

more often than not. The role of a dance musician was that of a servant, and as was the case with hotel work, cooking and serving food, shining shoes, and cutting hair,[3] in America this work was typically done by blacks. This was true in the North as well as in the South.

The tradition of black fiddling, however, did not originate in the New World. West African fiddlers have accompanied singing and dancing with one-string gourd fiddles since the twelfth century, and many black musicians in America learned on similar homemade fiddles before switching over to the European violin.[4] As early as the mid-1600s, black fiddlers ("exquisite performers on three-stringed fiddles") were playing for both black and white dancers at street celebrations in the Dutch settlement of New Amsterdam

Figure 4.2. "Happy Little Bob and His Fiddle"—Homemade three-stringed fiddle (O. Pierre Havens, Chatham County, Georgia, c. 1870s). Robert N. Dennis Collection of Stereoscopic Views, Miriam and Ira D. Wallach Division of Art, Prints and Photographs, New York Public Library, Astor, Lenox and Tilden Foundations

(New York City), and by 1690 slave fiddlers were routinely providing the music at plantation balls in Virginia.[5]

Black and mixed-race fiddlers were common throughout North America during the eighteenth century. Colonial dance historian Kate Van Winkle Keller has cited nearly four hundred who were active between 1709 and 1789.[6] One of these fiddlers was Sampson, a slave who played for dances in Concord, New Hampshire, in the late 1700s. He was described as a "famous fiddler [who] for many years afforded fine fun for frolicsome fellows in Concord with his fiddle on election days."[7] Others include Beverly Hemings, Sally Hemings's son, who played fiddle for the Saturday evening dances at Thomas Jefferson's Monticello, and Cato Watts, who played jigs and reels for the early settlers at the Falls of the Ohio River (Louisville) in 1778.[8] Describing the rural frolics of colonial America in the late 1700s, French-American writer St. John de

Crèvecoeur wrote: "We have not the gorgeous balls, the harmonious concerts, the shrill horn of Europe, yet we dilate our hearts as well with the simple negro fiddle."[9] These fiddlers were not always male. A female slave fiddler named Clarinda played for dances in South Carolina, and Washington Irving wrote of a "negro wench" who served as the "principal musician" at a ball in Trenton, New Jersey, in 1807.[10] As elsewhere, dancing was the chief form of entertainment on the eastern edge of the North Carolina Piedmont, and in the early nineteenth century "every town and village had its ball-room, and its musician [was] almost always a negro fiddler."[11]

African Americans were noted for their musical skills, and slaves who demonstrated musical potential were highly valued—some were provided with instruments and given musical training. In a novel based on childhood recollections of life on her family's plantation near Charleston, South Carolina, in the early 1800s, Caroline Howard Gilman describes a slave who was "gifted with decided natural powers" and, though "unacquainted with the science of music," easily learned the fashionable tunes and dances of the urban ballroom. "We possessed the usual plantation luxury of a fiddler. I do not feel bound to say how many tunes Diggory played, nor how well a few visits to town had initiated his quick eye and ear into the tunes and figures of some newly-introduced cotillons. It is amusing to observe how soon a pretty air is appropriated, in Charleston by the negroes, by their quick musical organs."[12]

Being able to play music was a salvation to many who were condemned to slavery. In 1841 Solomon Northup, a free black musician from New York State, had the extreme misfortune of being kidnapped and sold into slavery. During his twelve years of bondage, he became the fiddler for a succession of slave owners. Northup, who could play the Southern "Virginia Reels," was frequently "called into the house to play before the family," and he was often hired to play for white dances. He later wrote, "I was indebted to my violin, my constant companion, the source of profit, and soother of my sorrows during years of servitude."[13]

In a nostalgic reminiscence of the antebellum South that appeared in the *Richmond Times-Dispatch* in 1921, Dr. C. A. Bryce recalled the plantation dances of his boyhood, where the music was "universally played by colored men." He writes, "For most of the dances . . . the musicians consisted of a violinist ('fiddler' they called him), who could call the figures, a banjo picker and tambourine player." According to Bryce, these musicians had a higher status and greater privileges than those working in the fields.

> The ability to play a "good fiddle" or "pick a banjo" was worth a good deal to its possessor if he was a slave, for he was given all manner of privileges and favors, the lightest work and good clothes, and the young men for whom he played always passed the hat around before he left and gladdened his heart with liberal returns. In addition, he got the best supper of all the guests and his measure of "peach and honey" or apple toddy was only regulated by his ability to contain and carry.[14]

Figure 4.3. "The Fiddler" (E. W. Kemble, 1887). Picture Collection, New York Public Library Digital Gallery, Astor, Lenox and Tilden Foundations

These black fiddlers were respected within their own culture as well, keeping alive the West African tradition of the "griot" musician well into the nineteenth century. Solomon Northup and other enslaved musicians routinely provided music for dances in the slave quarters, a service that some slave owners believed benefited morale and the efficient operation of the plantation. In an article titled "Management of Negroes upon Southern Estates," a "Mississippi Planter" wrote in 1851, "I must not omit to mention that I have a good fiddler, and keep him well supplied with catgut, and I make it his duty to play for the negroes every Saturday night until 12 o'clock. They are exceedingly punctual in their attendance at the ball, while Charley's fiddle is always accompanied with Ihurod on the triangle, and Sam to 'pat.'"[15]

As mentioned earlier, during the nineteenth century black musicians entertained the passengers on the steamboats of the Ohio and Mississippi Rivers, but they also provided the dance music at resort hotels across the country. Englishman J. S. Buckingham noted in 1840 that the dance bands at White Sulphur Springs and Salt Sulphur Springs in (West) Virginia were "almost always formed of coloured people."[16] Between 1830 and 1860 a string band of free blacks from Charleston and Columbia, South Carolina, played for dances at the Deaver Hotel near Asheville, North Carolina.[17] In the South, however, prior to Emancipation, many of the resort musicians, like the other hotel workers, were slaves, such as those who were leased during the summer months to play for dances at the Harrodsburg Springs Hotel in Kentucky.[18] After hours, these resort musicians shared their musical talents with their fellow workers at "kitchen balls."

Figure 4.4. "Kitchen Ball at White Sulphur Springs, Virginia"—African American dancers accompanied by fiddle, flute, and cello (Christian Friedrich Mayr 1838). North Carolina Museum of Art, Raleigh, purchased with funds from the State of North Carolina

These and many other accounts attest to the prevalence of black fiddlers throughout America during the eighteenth and early nineteenth centuries. At the same time, references to white dance musicians are rare. In 1788 a Scottish dancing master in Winchester, Virginia, advertised that his dancing school featured "the best white music that is to be had in these parts."[19] The fact that the musicians are specifically identified as "white," however, suggests that black fiddlers were common in the Shenandoah Valley at that time.

While African American musicians played the European violin (or fiddle) at white dances, the banjo, an instrument with African roots, was more often heard at plantation frolics, and some time during the eighteenth century, these two instruments—one European and one African—were played together. As early as 1756, a fiddle and banjo were played, along with a tambourine and drums, as accompaniment to singing and dancing at an African American celebration in Newport, Rhode Island.[20] In 1774 Nicholas Cresswell watched with envy as black musicians played a fiddle and banjo for white dancers at a "barbecue" on the banks of the Chesapeake Bay in Maryland. He wrote, "A great number of young people met together with a Fiddle and Banjo played by two Negroes, with Plenty of Toddy, which both Men and Women seem to be very fond of. I believe they have danced and drunk till there are few sober people amongst them. I am sorry I was not able to join them."[21]

Nicholas Cresswell may have been enthusiastic about the music he heard in Maryland, but not all European visitors appreciated the music played by black musicians in America. In 1788 a German traveler, commenting on the "public amusements" at "Bath-town," Virginia (Berkeley Springs, West Virginia), complained, "At balls one or at most two blacks supply the company with woful [sic] horn-pipes and jigs."[22] It may be that these black musicians were simply lacking talent, but it is also possible that their music contained African elements that did not conform to the aesthetics of this European visitor. This early critique of Southern fiddling foreshadows Cecil Sharp's dismissal of Kentucky fiddle tunes more than one hundred years later for what he called the "melodic poverty" of this "inferior" music.[23]

Today Southern fiddling is often thought of as a direct descendent of an old Anglo-Celtic musical tradition. Folklorist and musician Alan Jabbour has pointed out, however, that the regional fiddle styles of the British Isles and America are more like "cultural cousins" of the same generation.[24] These traditions developed concurrently during the second half of the eighteenth century, and while they have shared ancestry, they are distinctly different. Although the Southern fiddle repertoire includes American versions of tunes from the British Isles (for example, "Billy in the Lowground" and "McLeod's Reel"), a greater number of Southern dance tunes are native to America.[25] Some of these American tunes retain the melodic mode of the older Scots-Irish tunes and conform to the common AABB structure of the European dances. Others, however, have short repetitive phrases, rhythmic syncopation, and little melodic range (what Sharp referred to as "melodic poverty"). Many of the American tunes of this type are thought to have originated with, or at least to have been influenced by, the African American musical tradition.[26] Some became associated with blackface minstrelsy, and many are still common in the Southern fiddle repertoire today.

The interaction between white and black musicians in America no doubt led to imitation and exchange across racial lines. Thomas Jefferson's younger brother, Randolph, reportedly played fiddle and danced "half the night" with the slaves at Monticello, and in 1807, in "Salmagundi," a short story whose title indicates a mixture of different things, Washington Irving wrote of an integrated dance ensemble in New York, composed of "black, yellow, and white musicians."[27] The interracial sharing of music in the South continued well into the twentieth century. Banjo player Dock Boggs (1898–1971) of Norton, Virginia, said in an interview, "There was a colored string band playing for a dance in Norton. I stuck my head in at the door and I liked the way the banjo-player played, so I said to myself, I am going to learn to play that way."[28] Fiddler Hobart Smith (1897–1965) of Saltville, Virginia, recalled, "The first fiddle I ever heard in my life was when I was a kid. There was an old colored man who was raised up in slave times. His name was Jim Spenser. He played 'Jinny, Put the Kettle On' and all those old tunes like that. And he would come up to our house and he'd play."[29] Fiddlers Doc Roberts (1897–1978) of Kentucky and Tommy Jarrell of North Carolina likewise claimed to have learned from black fiddlers. The repertoires and syncopated bowing patterns of these and countless other Southern fiddlers were no doubt influenced by the African American musicians from whom they learned.

Dance Calling

In addition to playing for balls and dance assemblies, African American musicians also provided the music at dancing schools—some dancing masters owned slave fiddlers.[30] These musicians were no doubt familiar with the European dances, having heard the dancing masters prompting their students, and at some point they began to call out the figures of these dances at plantation frolics. This is suggested by an account of a gathering of about sixty slaves dancing "country-dances" on a Saturday night near Charleston that appeared in the *South Carolina Gazette* in 1772.[31] Obviously, slaves were not sent to dancing school, but dance calling provided an alternative, making these dances accessible to unschooled dancers. Calling out the figures during a dance was not part of the European tradition,[32] but it may have seemed a natural thing to do at plantation frolics, since dancing and singing are so closely linked in the African tradition. John Szwed and Morton Marks relate calling to the African "dance-instruction song tradition . . . which is at least partly rooted in the older African tradition of call-and-response in which master drummers signal and direct dancers."[33]

Figure 4.5. "Negro Ball"—African Americans dancing country dances and jigs; a white bystander (holding his nose) shows his disapproval (c. 1807). Library of Congress, Prints and Photographs Division (LC-USZ62-78129)

As early as the mid-1700s, African American fiddlers may have started calling out the figures for white dancers, too. James Ireland, a Scottish schoolmaster who emigrated from Edinburgh to New Market in the Shenandoah Valley of Virginia in the 1760s, noted the popular "recreations, pleasures and pastimes" of that frontier community, which included "balls," where "chanting to the sound of the violin, was the most prevailing practice."[34] Although Ireland does not specify the race of the musicians, this "chanting" is likely an early reference to African American dance calling.[35]

By the time Benjamin Latrobe encountered dance calling in New Orleans in 1819, this practice was widespread, and in subsequent years there are numerous references to black or mixed-race dance callers throughout the country. Most of these come from European visitors who, like Latrobe, were surprised, mystified, and amused by this unfamiliar American custom. In 1825, a visitor from Ghent (at that time a part of the Netherlands) attended a plantation ball near Columbia, South Carolina. Slave musicians provided the music: "The whole music consisted of two violins and a tamborine. This tamborine was struck with a terrible energy. The two others scraped the violin, in the truest significance of the word; one of them cried out the figures, imitating with his body all the motions of the dance."[36]

When English writer Frances Trollope encountered dance calling in Cincinnati around 1829, she remarked that it "has a ludicrous effect on European ears."[37] Carl Arfwedson of Sweden likewise was taken aback when he heard dance calling at a ball in a hotel near Boston in 1832. He wrote: "A practice which surprised me more than any other was, that one of the musicians attached to the band constantly called out to the dancers the different figures they were to go through. . . . The instrument on which he performed was a broken violin; and he often beat time so loud with one foot, that the music was drowned by the noise . . . He called out as loud as he could, in a hoarse and shrill voice: 'Advance!' 'Retreat!' 'Ladies chain!' 'Gentlemen's chain!' 'Sideways!' and so on."[38]

That same year, Englishman Thomas Coke visited the resort of Lebanon Springs, New York (near Albany), where "the evenings were usually passed in dancing." He, too, was puzzled by the African American musicians, who provided the music and called out the dance figures: "The band consisted of two negroes playing on violins, and a third upon a bass. The leader of the sable trio . . . acted as a kind of maitre du ballet, crying out "Balanciey!"—"Tan your patners!"—"La's shen!" and other jargon, utterly unintelligible even to those who were acquainted with the figure of every quadrille." Coke was no stranger to the ballroom, and he was familiar with the figures of the quadrille, but he did not know what to make of this musician (also the barber at the resort) who called out the dance figures.[39]

In *Georgia Scenes* (1835), a collection of sketches depicting life in Georgia, Southern writer Augustus Longstreet likewise describes a dance with African American musicians, including a fiddler who calls out the figures of the dance: "The musicians were all blacks, but neatly dressed. The band consisted of three performers on the violin, one on the clarinet, one on the tambourine, and one on the triangle. . . . 'Hands round!' said the fiddler."[40]

In 1832 English Shakespearean actress Frances "Fanny" Kemble complained that dancers in Philadelphia no longer bothered to learn the order of the dance figures but relied instead on the dance caller: "We stood up to dance a couple of quadrilles; but as they had not one distinct idea of what the figures were, the whole was a mess of running about, explaining, jostling, and awkward blundering. . . . At the close of almost every quadrille, a fancy figure is danced, which, depending entirely upon the directions of the leader of the band, is a very curious medley of all the rest."[41]

The bandleader to whom Kemble refers may have been Francis "Frank" Johnson (1792–1844), a free black fiddler and dance caller who at that time was popular in Philadelphia. Johnson and his band performed up and down the East Coast, from New York State (at Saratoga Springs) and Massachusetts to North Carolina, as well as in St. Louis, Pittsburgh, and even London.[42] Author James Battle Avirett recalled a ball (probably in the 1840s) in Raleigh, North Carolina, at which "Old Frank Johnson's (negro) band furnished the music," and Johnson called the figures for "double quadrilles."[43] Johnson was one of the many African American musicians who played for and called dances throughout America during the nineteenth century.[44]

The fact that *all* of these early dance callers were black or mixed race strongly suggests that dance calling originated in the black culture, and the fact that it shows up nearly simultaneously from New Orleans to New England suggests that it did not emanate from one particular region of the country, that it came from elsewhere—most likely the West Indies. Many of the enslaved Africans who ended up in North America were brought from plantations in the West Indies, where they had been taken for "seasoning" and acculturation before being sold at slave markets on the mainland. There, as in the British colonies of North America, slave musicians provided music for white dancers. Scottish reels, English country dances, and French cotillions were common at "negro balls," and the slaves who came to North America arrived with a Creole cultural mix of the African and European traditions.[45]

It is not surprising that Latrobe encountered dance calling in New Orleans: a French territory until the end of 1803, the city had strong connections with the West Indies, and its population had a known passion for dancing. Between 1719 and 1758 thousands of slaves had been brought there from the French colonies in the Caribbean, and in the first decade of the 1800s thousands more arrived, accompanying French planters who were refugees from Saint Domingue (now the Dominican Republic) following the slave uprising of 1791 and the ensuing Haitian Revolution.[46] In 1807 Washington Irving wrote of a Haitian musician in New York, who danced the "pirouet" and the "pigeon-wing" (French dance steps) and played a three-stringed fiddle.[47] It is quite possible that the black tambourine player whom Latrobe had heard calling dances in New Orleans had likewise come from the West Indies.

Nearly half of the slaves imported to Virginia during the 1700s as well as the majority of those brought to the northern English colonies came from the West Indies,[48] and this may explain why James Ireland encountered "chanting to the sound of the violin" in the Shenandoah Valley. Virginia subsequently played a large role in the interstate slave trade, and as people were dispersed through sale and escape, dance calling and "Virginia reels" (Southern dance tunes) became known throughout the country.

The appearance of dance calling in the ballrooms of America coincided with the introduction of the quadrilles. These French dances, which had multiple parts, were more complicated than the earlier reels, country dances, and cotillions, so a caller's prompts would have no doubt been welcomed by the less diligent dancers. The transition to called dances, however, was a challenge for some. In 1838 Caroline Howard Gilman wrote of the "confusion worse confounded" on the part of the older dancers when the figures of the new quadrilles were called out by a slave fiddler at a plantation ball near Charleston, South Carolina: "Poor mamma had never been much of a dancer; all her early associations were connected with the minuet and contra-dance. . . . Diggory called out, with the voice of a Stentor, 'Fore and back two, ole missis—ladies change—turn you partiner at de corner—shasha all round,' she was nearly beside herself."[49] The introduction of dance calling, however, did more than simply change the dances; no longer merely a servant providing music for the dance, the caller was now elevated to a position of authority as the master of ceremony.

By the mid-1830s European Americans were also starting to call dances. In a short story from that time set in southeastern Michigan, a white man, mimicking the motion of a fiddler sawing on a violin and "chaunting in a sort of iambic measure," directs the dancers at a dance in a "ball-room" at a country tavern, while three black musicians provide music on fiddle, banjo, and "jews-harp."[50] By the late 1830s Mark Beaubien, a white fiddler, originally from Detroit, was learning to call out the figures of the quadrilles while fiddling at his hotel in Chicago.[51]

Although by the 1850s published dance manuals began to include tips on elocution, pitch, rhythm, and timing for aspiring callers, this new custom was not universally accepted. In 1856 Charles Durang, a well-known Philadelphia dancing teacher and son of the stage dancer John Durang, dismissed it as "a vile custom, marring the melody of the airs."[52] With the advent of calling, would-be dancers no longer needed to attend dancing school, and Durang and other dancing masters no doubt saw it as a threat to their profession. A

Figure 4.6. *Prof. M. J. Koncen's Quadrille Call Book and Ball Room Guide* (1883). Library of Congress, Music Division

"Prompter's Guide," published in 1866, however, acknowledged the changing times and the growing popularity of calling: "The figures in this book can be danced without the dancers having any previous knowledge of them, if the caller or prompter will do his part. . . . So in this fast age this is the very thing the people want."[53]

One of the earliest known white callers in the Appalachian region was fiddler and flatboatman Thomas C. Collins, who, as mentioned earlier, grew up along the Ohio River, just across from West Virginia. Collins encountered numerous musicians in his travels on the rivers, including "Old Black Jim Walker," an elderly African American fiddler and dance caller from Virginia. By 1853, at age twenty-one, Collins had learned how to "play and call for cotillions [quadrilles]."[54]

Dance calling in the culturally rich environment of the Ohio River watershed was more musically refined than elsewhere in the southern mountains. There, instead of merely shouting out the calls, dance callers tended to use rhyming patter and pitched their voices to the music (see appendix, table 4). These characteristics were noted in 1864 by Scottish author and scholar of Gaelic folklore John Francis Campbell, who heard a black caller giving out dance calls "in a singing high key" at the hotel at Mammoth Cave, near the Green River in central Kentucky. Campbell wrote of this, his first encounter with dance calling: "The music was a fiddle, and the performer a darky dressed like a lord. Beside him sat an official [the caller] who was a new character." Recognizing many of the Scots-Irish tunes played by this black fiddler, Campbell also imagined a similarity between the dance calls sung out by the caller and the Gaelic tradition of lining out hymns:

> In Scotch churches where people cannot all read, the fashion is for the precentor [sic] to repeat a line before it is sung. Here was a man who called out the steps before they were danced, for people who did not all know how to do it. He called them out in a singing high key, like that of a London toast-master, and chimed in with the fiddle as well as he could. . . . FIRST *gent to the front*. Rum tidy idy—rum tidy idy—rum tidy idy. RIGHT *hand to your partner*. Tum tidy idy—tum tidy idy—tum tidy idy. TURN *the first lady*. Rum—, and so on till the country dance [quadrille] was ended. . . . I knew the Gaelic name of nearly every tune the [fiddler] played.[55]

The musicality of African American callers was also noted in an account of a "Negro dance" in Middle Tennessee from 1897: "The fiddler, inspired by the music of his fiddle and the muse of inspiration, has rhymed his calls to music, and, keeping time with his feet to the flying bow, sings out in his peculiar chant."[56]

This rhyming "chant" is what distinguishes patter calling from the sparser prompts delivered by dancing masters at dancing schools, which, as in the theater, are merely short spoken or shouted directives telling dancers what to do next. For example:

Circle left,
Allemande left,
Grand right and left,
Promenade.

By contrast, in addition to the prompts, patter calling includes improvisational rhymes that are chanted or sung with the music while the dancers are performing the dance figures. A colorful example of patter calling for these same dance figures comes from West Virginia dance caller Ernest Legg, who recorded with the Kessinger Brothers in 1928:

Circle up eight and you get straight,
And knock down Sal and pick up Kate,
And sixteen hands and circle eight,
And turn your corner like swingin' on a gate,
And meet your partner with a grand chain eight,
And hurry up boys and don't be late,
Chew your tobacco and rub your snuff,
And meet your honey and strut your stuff.[57]

By the end of the nineteenth century, dance calling was a well-established tradition in rural Appalachia, and, in the minds of the local-color writers, it no doubt highlighted the perceived "otherness" of the southern mountains.[58] While most of these writers depict dance callers as white, novelist Will Harben, as mentioned earlier, wrote of an old black fiddler, a fixture in the community, who provided the music and calls for an informal "reg'lar square dance" in a two-room cabin in the mountains of north Georgia.[59]

Following the Civil War, African American musicians, former slaves as well as free blacks, continued to play and call for white dancers throughout the country. Former slave "Uncle Jack Calhoun" played fiddle for dances in Habersham County (north Georgia) in the 1870s.[60] Isaac Stier of Mississippi recalled, "I use to call out de figgers. . . . Long after de war was over de white folks would 'gage me to come 'roun' wid de band an' call de figgers at all de big dances. Dey always paid me well."[61] In the North, Alvah Belcher (1819–1900) played the fiddle and called dances in the Catskills of New York State, and barber John Putnam (1825–1895) was active as a fiddler and dance prompter in Greenfield, Massachusetts.[62]

With the popularity of newer styles of music and dance in the early twentieth century, square dancing declined in African American communities, and black callers became a rarity. A few, however, can be heard on 78-rpm recordings made in the 1920s. These include Sam Jones of Cincinnati, Ohio (1924), Henry Thomas of Texas (1927), and Jim Baxter of north Georgia (1928) (see chapter 7). Joe Thompson (1918–2012), an African American fiddler from the North Carolina Piedmont who recently passed away, was perhaps the last of the continuous line of many generations of African American dance callers.

Figure 4.7. "The Music for the Dance" (Arthur Burdett Frost, 1891). *Harper's Weekly* 35, no. 12 (December 1891)

* * *

Initially, dance calling was simply a way to make the European dances accessible to unschooled dancers, regardless of race. By the mid-nineteenth century, however, this African American practice had transformed the dance traditions of America. William Hancock, an Englishman who visited America in the 1850s, noted that in addition to guiding the dancers through the figures, dance calling permitted the caller to change the choreography of the dance spontaneously, and he suggested that this was what separated the American dances from the European tradition: "The American cotillion, unlike the English quadrille, is not composed of a succession of well-known figures, but may be varied ad libitum, and extended or condensed at the pleasure of the leader of the band, who is consequently under the necessity of telling you throughout the dance what to do next."[63]

Although advice on calling could be found in dance manuals by the 1850s, as late as the 1890s some dancing masters continued to insist, "Dancing quadrilles without a 'prompter' is the only correct style of dancing."[64] One wrote, "It is to be hoped that the time will come when 'calling' will be obsolete in our ballrooms and parlors; and when the gentlemen who manage our social affairs will all be competent to conduct themselves and their partners through the mazes of the fashionable and popular dances without the assistance of a prompter."[65] But dance calling did not go away. Instead, it made the dancing schools obsolete and left the dancing masters unemployed. Taking their place was the dance caller, who became indispensible, as noted by David Barrow at African American corn-shucking frolics in northwest Georgia in 1882: "With the cotillion [square dance] a new and very important office, that of 'caller-out,' has become a necessity. The 'caller-out,' though of less importance than the fiddler, is second to no other. He not only calls out the figures, but explains them at length to the ignorant, sometimes accompanying them through the performance."[66]

Dance calling was crucial in the development of the Southern square dance. It allowed these dances to be flexible and free from the constraints of the structure of the European dance music, and it was the catalyst that enabled elements from English country dances, French cotillions and quadrilles, African American dances, and Native American dances to be incorporated with the Scots-Irish reels to create a distinct dance tradition in the rural South.

Most important, though, dance calling led to the democratization and proliferation of these dances. These were not composed dances, taught by dancing masters, with fixed choreography, fit to the musical phrase. They did not appear in social dance manuals, and they did not need dancing masters or dancing schools to flourish. Instead, they were folk dances that evolved organically in the Appalachian backcountry, passed on from one dancer to the next, from one community to the next, and from one generation to the next through the oral tradition. Dance calling facilitated the dissemination of these dances throughout rural America, so that by the end of the nineteenth century they were well established in the rural folk culture of the southern mountains, waiting to be discovered by Cecil Sharp and Maud Karpeles.

5 Cecil Sharp and the Kentucky Running Set

In the summer of 1917, English folksong collector Cecil Sharp, along with his assistant and colleague Maud Karpeles, traveled to the southern mountains in search of survivals of old English ballads and folksongs. In late August they arrived at the Pine Mountain Settlement School in eastern Kentucky, and while they were there, one of the teachers, knowing of Sharp's interest in old English dances, assembled a group of students to perform a square dance,

Figure 5.1. Cecil Sharp and Maude Karpeles collecting ballads in Kentucky (1917). English Folk Dance and Song Society

known locally as "set running." May Ritchie Deschamps (Jean Ritchie's eldest sister), who was among the students dancing that evening, later recalled that this demonstration included "our best set running people."[1] As no music was available, the dancing was accompanied by the clapping of hands. Evelyn Wells, one of the teachers at the school, recalled Sharp's reaction: "Out came his notebook, in which he jotted without taking his eyes from the dancers."[2] Sharp later wrote:

> It was danced, one evening after dark, on the porch of one of the largest houses of the Pine Mountain School, with only one dim lantern to light up the scene. But the moon streamed fitfully in lighting up the mountain peaks in the background and, casting its mysterious light over the proceedings, seemed to exaggerate the wildness and the break-neck speed of the dancers as they whirled through the mazes of the dance. There was no music, only the stampings and clappings of the onlookers, but when one of the emotional crises of the dance was reached—and this happened several times during the performance—the air seemed literally to pulsate with the rhythm of the "patters" and the tramp of the dancers' feet, while, over and above it all, penetrating through the din, floated the even, falsetto tones of the Caller, calmly and unexcitedly reciting his directions.[3]

Sharp, who had previously documented the rural folk dances of England, had studied social dance manuals dating back to the 1600s. He was also aware of the popular dances of his time, but these Appalachian dances were unlike anything he had ever encountered. In a letter to one of his Northern benefactors, he wrote of his "new discovery," which he referred to as "The Running Set":

> I came across a most wonderful dance the other day called "The Running Set." It is a form of circular country dance of a type about which I know nothing. There is certainly nothing of the kind in England at the present day and there is nothing that I know of in any of the old dance books. It is a very strenuous dance for six couples and extremely complicated. In many ways the general effect was not unlike that of the Sword-Dance.[4]

Sharp was fascinated by these Appalachian dances, and he inquired about others in the region. A few weeks later he and Karpeles were invited to a square dance at the town of Hindman. In his journal Sharp wrote, "In the evening [we] go to a dance, walking 2 miles along a very muddy road. All the men indulged in whiskey by way of a preliminary and danced badly—as badly as the half-dozen girls there. We didn't learn much about the Running Set, but we got something. It is a queer business because in these parts a party is always a public affair and we were crowded out with loafers who didn't dance but took up the space on the floor."[5]

Two weeks later a demonstration of the dances was arranged for Sharp and Karpeles at Hyden, with four couples who danced "sufficiently well for [them] to learn the figures."[6] The following day, however, when they attempted to recall and record the thirteen dance figures that they had witnessed the previous night, Sharp acknowledged, "There are a few points upon which we have some doubts."[7] Later that week Karpeles attended one more dance, at a bean-stringing party near Hyden—Sharp was too ill to attend.[8] To learn more about these Kentucky dances, they also spoke with a caller in Breathitt County.[9] In his diary Sharp wrote, "This dance is as valuable a piece of work as anything that I have done in the mountains. I may get some more figures to add but I do not think there is anything else to learn about it."[10] The following year, they published a detailed description of "The Running Set" in *The Country Dance Book, Part 5*.

Cecil Sharp (1859–1924) was a self-taught musician who first became interested in traditional dance in 1899, when at age forty he happened upon a group of morris dancers in the village of Headington, England (near Oxford). At that time the traditional folk dances of England were nearly extinct, having been replaced by popular ballroom dances—the polka, the waltz, and the quadrille—all imported from continental Europe. In these years preceding World War I, nationalism was on the rise, and folk culture came to be valued and promoted as the true expression of a nation's culture. Realizing that German music was being taught in English schools, Sharp made it his personal mission to revive his country's heritage of traditional folksongs and dances. In 1909 he wrote that he wanted to counter the "strange preference for foreign music" and overcome "prejudice against the native product."[11] That same year he succeeded in having morris dancing adopted into the physical education curriculum, and two years later he founded the English Folk Dance Society, an organization with the stated goal of "preserving and promoting the practice of English folk-dances in their true traditional form."[12]

Late in 1914, following the outbreak of war in Europe, Sharp traveled to America, arriving in New York City on January 1, 1915. By that time he was considered to be the leading authority on English folksong and folk dance, and he had been hired to arrange music and dances for a production of "A Midsummer Night's Dream." While in New York, Sharp helped establish the American branch of the English Folk Dance Society, and over the next few years, during several visits to America, he supplemented his income by lecturing on folksongs and teaching English country dances to folk dance enthusiasts across the country—in New York, Boston, Pittsburgh, Philadelphia, St. Louis, Chicago, Cincinnati, Kalamazoo, Asheville (North Carolina), and elsewhere.[13] In addition to his interpretations of Playford's English country dances, Sharp taught English morris and sword dances, thereby strengthening America's cultural identification with England on the eve of the United States entering the war in Europe.

Sharp made frequent trips to Lincoln, Massachusetts, to visit with his main benefactor, Helen O. Storrow, and while there in June 1915 he met with Olive Dame Campbell (wife of John C. Campbell), who shared with him the ballads and folksongs she had collected in the southern mountains.[14] Sharp was impressed by Campbell's collection, which included old British ballads that were no longer sung in England, and he decided to visit the southern mountains himself. The following summer, in July 1916, he and his young protégé Maud Karpeles (1885–1976) arrived by train in Asheville, and over the next several weeks they collected ballads from a number of singers in Madison and Buncombe Counties, as well as in nearby Flag Pond, Tennessee.

Like William Frost and Ellen Semple, Cecil Sharp perceived the "predominant culture" of the southern mountains to be "Anglo-Celtic."[15] In a letter to one of his benefactors, he wrote, "The people are very interesting, just English peasants in appearance, manner and speech. . . . They are said to have come largely from the lowlands of Scotland and the North of Ireland but I cannot detect many Irish or Scottish peculiarities."[16] Even though some of the singers from whom he collected ballads mentioned Scottish and Irish ancestors, in his eyes they were "English peasants" whose culture had remained "pure" and undiluted, even after many generations in the southern mountains. Therefore, he presumed the Kentucky dances to be survivals of old English country dances. These dances, however, were neither as old nor as English as Sharp imagined.

Sharp saw similarities between these Appalachian dances and the English dances, but he also noted differences. To account for the unfamiliar features, of which he admitted, "I know nothing," he hypothesized that the Kentucky dances predated those found in Playford's earliest printed collection of 1651, and they represented a "phase in the development of the Country-dance of which, hitherto, nothing has been known."[17] To explain how these dances could have remained untainted by the influences of contemporary fashions and popular culture for hundreds of years, Sharp suggests that not only had the Appalachian people been isolated in the southern mountains, but their ancestors had likewise been isolated in northern England and the Scottish Lowlands prior to coming to America. Sharp identifies three distinguishing features as proof of the antiquity of the Kentucky dances: "the construction of the dance"; the presence of "indubitably ancient figures"; and "the forceful, emotional character of the dance."[18] However, an examination of these features, which Sharp found so remarkable, undermines his own thesis. He did not entertain the idea that these rural American folk dances could have been influenced by non-English traditions as well as more recent popular dance styles in the New World.

"The Construction of the Dance"

Sharp and Karpeles encountered two different dance formations in Kentucky—six-couple circles at the Pine Mountain School and four-couple squares elsewhere. These dances, like others in the southern mountains, had a circular visiting-couple structure, and as in the French square dances, they involved a main figure for two couples followed by a chorus figure for all of the dancers.

Sharp noted, however, that unlike the French quadrilles, "no pause . . . is made between the Parts."[19] The progressive "circular" nature of these dances reminded him of the "rounds for as many as will" in the early editions of Playford's *Dancing Master*, and even though these traditions were separated by more than two and a half centuries, he imagined a direct connection between them.[20] This circular form, however, is not unique to the English dances, and given the preponderance of Scots-Irish settlers in the Appalachian backcountry, it is more likely derived from the circular Scots-Irish reels.

Sharp made particular note of the "Grand Promenade" that was used as a chorus figure to "bind the figures together and give continuity to the dance."[21] As mentioned earlier, a similar figure, in which "all the couples bounded off in a 'grand cirkit' all around the room," was known in the Shenandoah Valley of Virginia in the 1860s,[22] and by the twentieth century the Promenade was common as a chorus figure throughout the Appalachian region.[23] Sharp was aware that this figure, which does not appear in any of Playford's English dances, was one of the changes of the eighteenth-century French cotillions. He also noted the French dance terminology used by the dancers in Kentucky. He fails, however, to acknowledge any French influence on these Appalachian dances. Instead, he proposes that the ancestors of the Kentucky settlers, who lived in northern England in the sixteenth century, knew this figure two centuries before the advent of the French dances. He further suggests that these ancestral dancers somehow adopted the French term "promenade" before they had any knowledge of the French dances.[24] He writes, "The jargon of the dance travelled more quickly to the North of England than the dance movements themselves, a fact for which we have every reason to be thankful."[25] Dance terminology, however, as noted earlier, is often retained as dance styles change; it tends to lag behind, not precede, stylistic changes.

Although the "circular" visiting-couple structure of the southern Appalachian square dances may resemble some of the old English rounds, "the construction of the dance" suggests a closer kinship to the Scots-Irish reels and the more recent French cotillions and quadrilles.

"Indubitably Ancient Figures"

Sharp and Karpeles encountered a large repertoire of dance figures in Kentucky,[26] and Sharp recognized that some of the visiting-couple figures ("Hands-Across," "Hands-Four," "Hands-Three," and the "Figure Eight") had precedents in Playford's English country dances. "Shoot the Owl" resembles a figure in a round called "Mill-Field," as well as the later English country dance "Pop Goes the Weasel."[27] "Chase the Squirrel" is similar in both name and movement to "Hunt the Squirril" [sic] in Playford's later editions. Some of the chorus and ending figures of the Kentucky dances ("Circle Eight," "Ladies in the Centre," "Rights and Lefts," and the "Lock Chain Swing," also known as the "Double-Elbow Swing") can likewise be found in Playford's dances.[28] None of these figures, however, is unique to the English dance tradition. Many, like some of the other Kentucky figures ("Forward and Back," "Cross Over," "Going Down Town," and "Cutting off Three, Two, and One"), were also used in French cotillions and quadrilles.

Some of the Kentucky dance figures were new to Sharp, and since they did not appear in Playford's dances, he assumed that they must be older. He hypothesized that these unknown "indubitably ancient figures," some of which had been preserved in the British Isles in modern times as children's singing games, were "derived from ancient pagan ceremonials."[29] Sharp's thinking had clearly been influenced by his mentor and colleague Alice B. Gomme (1853–1938), whose extensive collection of children's games from the British Isles, *The Traditional Games of England, Scotland and Ireland*, appeared in two volumes, respectively, in 1894 and 1898.[30] Drawing directly from Gomme's work, Sharp attributes the serpentine movement of the "Wild Goose-Chase" to "dances of religious or magical significance," and he suggests that the figure "Wind up the Ball Yarn" originated as "an act of worship" that involved "encircling a tree or other sacred object."[31] Serpentine and spiraling figures, however, are not uniquely English, but they were common in folk dance traditions throughout Europe as well as in Native American dances. And more recently, during the second half of the nineteenth century, serpentine figures were also popular in the ballrooms of urban America (see chapter 10.)

According to Sharp, the "Basket" figure is an ancient ceremonial ritual associated with "well-worship"—an "imitation of the creeping of the devotee under the sacred bush, which was frequently found by the side of the holy well."[32] This figure, however, more likely comes from the "Basket Quadrille" (or "Basket Cotillion"), a figure that was popular in ballrooms on both sides of the Atlantic during the nineteenth century.[33]

Sharp suggests that "Bird in the Cage," in which a single dancer imitates a bird within a ring, is an ancient pagan figure "probably derived from some sacrificial ceremony." He writes, "The dancer within the ring may be the victim about to be seized and sacrificed as in several of the Sword dances and the Morris dance, Brighton Camp," and he associates this well-known Southern dance figure with the "Scottish Eightsome-Reel," although that popular dance was not composed until the 1870s.[34] He does not entertain the possibility that "Bird in the Cage" may have come from somewhere other than the British Isles, such as Africa.

Sharp associates the dance called "Tucker," which also involves a lone dancer within a ring, to an English children's singing game.[35] This dance, however, derives its name from the popular American minstrel song "Old Dan Tucker," and it was a variant of the "Ninepin Reel" or "Nine-Pin Quadrille," an "amusing dance for the parlor" that was known throughout Britain and America during the nineteenth century. According to a social dance manual from 1866, "a gentleman or lady place themselves in the centre of [the] Cotillion, then eight hands round . . . all balance . . . then all turn corners . . . now the person in the centre will take the place of [a partner in] any one of [the] couples, while the person discarded or cheated must go to the centre."[36] (More on this in chapter 9.)

Several of the other Kentucky dance figures likewise have precedents in nineteenth-century social dances. "Cheat 'em If You Can," which Sharp and Karpeles saw at Pine Mountain, was popular at dance assemblies in Washington in the 1820s.[37] Also known as the "Cheat," this "promiscuous" (partner swapping) quadrille figure appears in a dance manual published in 1841: "A lady may extend her hands to a gentleman and when he attempts to take them, may withdraw and turn by herself, or run to any lady or gentleman in the set, and turn them, without violating the rules of the figure—hence the title of Cheat."[38] The "Waltz-Swing" involves two circles of three turning clockwise while at the same time revolving around each other in a counterclockwise direction.[39] This figure, now known as the "Bouquet Waltz" (likely a corruption of the name "Polka Waltz" or "Pokey Waltz"), was no doubt inspired by the waltz and polka, popular nineteenth-century couple dances ("round dances") in which couples spin clockwise while at the same time progressing counterclockwise around the dance floor. "Treat 'em All Right," a figure in which each gent (one at a time) turns each of the ladies in succession with a series of hand turns, alternating with his partner, is similar to the "Shoo-Fly Swing" and may have roots in the nineteenth-century French dance, the Boulangère.[40]

The figure that Sharp calls "Box-the-Gnat" is an enigma, and his description of it ("partner half-way with the right hand and once round with the left hand"[41]) does not make choreographic sense in the context of a visiting-couple square dance. Perhaps this is one of the figures about which he admitted, "We have some doubts." The figure commonly known as "Box-the-Gnat" today involves two dancers trading places, with the right hands joined, the woman turning under their raised arms. This movement resembles a figure from the nineteenth-century quadrilles called "Pas d'Allemande."[42] Whether or not this is how it was done in Kentucky is unclear. The origin of the name "Box-the-Gnat" likewise remains a mystery.

Sharp offers no explanation for the Kentucky figure called "Do-si-do." He describes it as "one of the most characteristic movements of the Running Set" and one at that time that was "universally known in the mountains."[43] When playing the dance tune "Breaking Up Christmas," North Carolina fiddler Tommy Jarrell used to sing, "Way back yonder, a long time ago, the old folks danced the Do-si-do." It should be noted, however, that this Southern "Do-si-do" is not the common back-to-back movement familiar to most dancers today. The French dance prompt "dos-á-dos," from which its name derives, literally means "back-to-back," but this directive can be interpreted two different ways. In the Northern tradition it means for dancers to *pass* back-to-back, but in the Southern dances, it means for dancers to *stand* back-to-back. There are several different

Southern dance figures called "Do-si-do," but the Kentucky figure described by Sharp consists of a series of hand turns between two couples: a left-hand turn with one's partner, followed by a right-hand turn with the opposite partner, and then this is repeated. As mentioned earlier, this hand-turning figure for two couples is likely derived from ealier Scots-Irish hand-turning figures which likewise involved a series of alternating hand turns.[44] This figure starts easily if the two women stand back-to-back, as in the "Scotch Reel" ("Straight Four"). The calls "Ladies do-si," noted by Sharp and Karpeles, and the more common "Ladies Do-si-do" may have originated as prompts used by French dancing masters directing the two women to stand "dos-á-dos."

Like many of the other Southern dance figures, this "Do-si-do" figure was not unique to the southern mountains, and as settlers moved west during the nineteenth century, it became a part of the Midwestern and Western square dances. In *Little House in the Big Woods*, Laura Ingalls Wilder describes a house dance in Wisconsin in the 1870s: "Pa took his fiddle out" and "called the figures," including "'Doe see, ladies, doe see doe.'"[45] Western Kentuckian Bill Monroe likewise referred to it when he sang, "When the caller hollered 'Do-si-do,' you knew Uncle Pen was ready to go."[46] Various 78-rpm recordings from the 1920s reveal the prevalence of this hand-turning figure in Kentucky and West Virginia, used, as Sharp and Karpeles saw it, as a sub-chorus following a visiting-couple figure.[47]

Clearly, the distinctive Southern square dance figures that Sharp and Karpeles encountered in Kentucky were neither as English nor as "indubitably ancient" as Sharp thought. Instead, they were derived from a variety of sources, including recently popular social dances of the nineteenth century. Sharp, however, missed this important point. Although he had studied the "old dance books," he was blinded by romantic notions of cultural survivals that were popular at that time as well as by his own nationalistic ideology.

"The Forceful, Emotional Character of the Dance"

In addition to "the construction of the dance" and the supposed "indubitably ancient figures," Sharp cites "the forceful, emotional character of the dance" as further evidence of the old English heritage of the Running Set. In particular he notes "the absence from it of all the courtesy movements, . . . the speed with which the evolutions are executed, and the unconventional way in which the dancers comport themselves."[48] He claims that these characteristics were lost during the eighteenth century, when dancing masters "corrupted" the "freshness, spontaneity, and gay simplicity" of the rural English country dances and "stifle[d]" them "with the artificial graces and genteel posings of the drawing-room."[49]

Sharp reasoned the Appalachian dances must be older than the Playford dances because, in his eyes, they appeared unrefined, spontaneous, and primitive. He found it "interesting," however, that dancers in rural Kentucky used the terms "gentlemen" and "ladies." Perhaps he was unaware of the many dancing masters, who had taught dancing and etiquette throughout America during the eighteenth and nineteenth centuries. Sharp was impressed by the "break-neck speed" of the dancers as they "ran a set," and he suggested that the "charm" and "style" of the Running Set came from its "lack of style."[50] He did not consider the possibility that the "forceful," "emotional," and "unconventional" (new to him) nature of these dances might be attributed to non-English sources, such as the Scots-Irish, Native American, and African American dances.

The lively Southern dance music that Sharp heard in Kentucky contributed to his impression of the dances. He describes it as "jig-tunes," though by that he simply means that they were fast, not that they were in 6/8 time.[51] The only dance instruments he mentions are the fiddle and banjo, suggesting that the guitar had not yet become common in that region, as it was a decade later. Noting the "insistent beat" of the music, he writes, "The players in Kentucky generally managed, notwithstanding the melodic poverty of the tunes, to play them with such force and abandonment that they made excellent accompaniment to the dance."[52] Although he fails to identify any of the Kentucky tunes by name, in his later *English Folk Songs from the Southern Appalachians* (published posthumously in 1932) he includes transcriptions of fifteen of these Appalachian "jigs." Of these tunes, only two appear to have come from the British Isles, but they are Scots-Irish rather than English.[53] The rest are Southern breakdowns and popular blackface minstrel tunes native to America. Sharp dismisses these tunes as "not very good . . . far inferior, for instance, to those of the English peasant-fiddlers."[54] Karpeles likewise wrote that they were "of little value," and Sharp later suggested, "It will probably be advisable in the revival of the dance to substitute other and better tunes, such as, for example, the small-pipe airs of Northumberland."[55] In his mind, this improvement may have been more than simply an aesthetic enhancement; it may also have been an effort to reclaim and reframe these dances as English.

As mentioned earlier, the students at the Pine Mountain School had no musical accompaniment, so they danced to "patting" performed by the other dancers and bystanders. Sharp wrote, "the usual method is to stamp with the right foot on the strong accent and clap the hands on the weak one [the upbeat]."[56] Forty years earlier, in 1876, Lafcadio Hearn had noted similar handclapping and body percussion, known as "patting Juba," at African American dances in Cincinnati, not far from eastern Kentucky.[57] Sharp apparently did not know that this rhythmic accompaniment to dancing was derived from the African tradition and that it was once common at slave frolics throughout the South.

In addition to the patters, Sharp encountered "beaters" in Kentucky, who added to the "insistent beat" of the music by hitting the strings of the fiddle and banjo with flexible "wooden sticks."[58] Also known as "beating straws," this was likewise adopted from the black tradition. Blues composer W. C. Handy spoke of his grandfather's recollection of slave music in Alabama: "A boy would stand behind the fiddler with a pair of knitting needles in his hand. From this position the youngster would reach around the fiddler's left shoulder and beat on the strings in the manner of a snare drummer."[59] David Barrow described straw beaters at the African American corn-shucking frolics in northeast Georgia in 1882:

> The straw-beater is a musician. . . . The performer provides himself with a pair of straws about eighteen inches in length and stout enough to stand a good smart blow. . . . These straws are used after the manner of drum-sticks, that portion of the fiddle-strings between the fiddler's bow and his left hand serving as a drum. One of the first sounds you hear on approaching the dancing party is the tum tee tum of the straws, and after the dance begins, when the shuffling of feet destroys the other sounds of the fiddle, this noise can still be heard.[60]

Sharp took particular note of the dance callers in Kentucky: "It is customary for one of the company, not necessarily one of the dancers, to 'call' the dance as it proceeds," using "certain prescribed verbal phrases, a mixture of prose and doggerel rhyme that in the course of time has become stereotyped."[61] His use of quotes around the word "call" suggests that he (or his intended audience) was unfamiliar with the practice of dance calling, even though African American musicians had been calling out dance figures in America for more than a century. As Sharp noted, calling allowed the dances to be freeform and improvisational—"the division of the dance into Parts and Figures is quite arbitrary"—and this, along with the speed and "insistent beat" of the music, as well as the African American traditions of patting, beating straws, and banjo playing, contributed to the "forceful, emotional character" of these Southern dances.[62]

"The Inhabitants Have Been Partly Spoiled"

Cecil Sharp's personal background and cultural biases no doubt influenced his interpretation of the Kentucky square dances, but his views and experiences in Appalachia were also skewed by the opinions and prejudices of his contacts in the region on whom he relied to facilitate his work. Given his prior interest in traditional dance and the amount of time he spent in western North Carolina, it is surprising that he did not encounter any dancing while he was there. House dances still existed at that time, and public dances took place throughout the year at the many resort hotels in the region. Just over ten years later, in 1928, numerous square dance teams emerged from these same rural counties to compete at Bascom Lamar Lunsford's Mountain Dance and Folk Festival in Asheville. When Sharp visited Asheville, however, he stayed in the city at the home of Olive Dame and John C. Campbell and at the luxurious Grove Park Inn, unlikely places to experience rural hoedowns and frolics. Sharp was told of dances in the region, but as he later admitted, "Our informants had invariably led us to believe that [the southern Appalachian square dance] was a rough, uncouth dance, remarkable only as an exhibition of agility and physical endurance, [so] we had made no special effort to see it."[63] If he had ignored his informants and made the effort, he would have discovered, and perhaps documented, a thriving dance scene in western North Carolina, and perhaps today, then, we would speak of the "North Carolina Running Set."

In their search for folksongs in the southern Appalachians, Sharp and Karpeles took advantage of John Campbell's personal contacts, which included church-sponsored settlement schools ("Presbyterian Missionary Settlements"), and from these bases they visited singers within walking distance.[64] Presbyterian opposition to social dancing had declined somewhat by the twentieth century, but it was still considered by many to be a sin, so perhaps it is not surprising that their Presbyterian hosts, many of them outsiders themselves, did not send Sharp and Karpeles off to dancing parties and frolics. Sharp claimed to have found "the old Puritan dislike, fear, and distrust of dancing expressed in almost every log-cabin,"[65] and he reported, "I did not see any consumption of alcohol in the houses I visited."[66] Most likely, Sharp and Karpeles were only directed to homes approved of by their Presbyterian hosts.

While we can appreciate the ballads, folksongs, and dances collected by Sharp and Karpeles, we can only speculate about what they missed due to their cultural and ethnic biases and their narrowly focused search for English survivals. While in western North Carolina in 1917, Sharp visited Jackson County, home of Mary Jane Queen's ballad singing family, and Haywood County, home of legendary dance caller and dancer Sam Queen, but Sharp reported, "The inhabitants have been partially spoiled. . . . The log-cabins are primitive enough but their owners are clean, neat and tidy, looking rather like maid-servants in respectable suburban families. It is sad that cleanliness and good music, or good taste in music rarely go together. Dirt and good music are the usual bed-fellows."[67] From Sharp's perspective, these people had been tainted by the influences of modernity. They were too "clean" to have any music or dances worth documenting, so he moved on. Later, during a short visit to the Shenandoah Valley in 1918, finding the population to be "very largely of German extraction," he again looked elsewhere.[68] Sharp's personal biases clearly limited the extent of his fieldwork, but after all, he was interested *only* in English music and dances. He ignored the rest.

When Sharp and Karpeles visited Appalachia in 1917, the proportion of African Americans living in rural areas was low, so perhaps it is understandable that Karpeles claimed that there were "practically no Negroes in the mountains."[69] When they did encounter blacks, however, they intentionally avoided contact with them. While in western North Carolina, Karpeles wrote in her diary: "We arrived at a cove and got sight of log cabins that seemed just what we wanted. Called at one. A musical 'Good Morning,' turned round and behold he was a negro. We had struck a negro settlement. Nothing for it but to toil back again."[70] Referring to the same incident, Sharp wrote, "We tramped—a very hard and warm walk, mainly uphill. When we reached the cove we found it peopled entirely by niggers!! All our trouble and spent energy for naught."[71] It is understandable that Sharp and Karpeles believed African Americans to be unlikely sources for English ballads and folksongs.[72] Their comments, however, suggest more—that they were disturbed by the presence of blacks and sought to avoid them. The day after their chance discovery of the "negro settlement," Karpeles wrote, "Glad to leave Sylva. Do not like town. Too many negroes."[73] Sharp expressed a similar attitude in comments he made the following year after a visit to the North Carolina Piedmont. He wrote, "We *smelt* Winston-Salem about 8 miles away—tobacco and molasses! . . . The place is stuffed full with negroes—I presume they work in the factories whether they are attracted to this tobacco industry by their similarity in colour or not I do not know! . . . This is a noisy place and the air impregnated with tobacco, molasses and nigger!"[74]

A few years later, when commenting on the lack of purity of American music and dance, Sharp expressed contempt for the new jazz dances, which he claimed were "associated with music other than the first order." He characterized these dances as "inferior" and "objectionable" because they were "heavily charged with negroid characteristics, presumably contracted in the Southern States of North America."[75] Ironically, what Sharp failed to realize was that the Southern square dances, which he praised as "most wonderful" and having "great aesthetic value," were likewise influenced by the African American culture. His assumption of the racial purity of the mountaineers and their culture, combined with his nationalistic zeal to reclaim and revive the folk dances of his own country, led him to an uninformed and biased interpretation of the Kentucky dances. Although the black population of eastern Kentucky was small by the early twentieth century, the African American influence on the Appalachian music and dance traditions is undeniable, and in his attempt to trace these dances back to 'Merrie Olde England,' he missed this important fact. What made these Southern dances uniquely American and distinctly different from the European dances was not the imagined racial purity of the mountain culture but the *lack* of racial purity and the blending of various cultural traditions.

"Arrested Development" versus "Arrested Degeneration"

Ellen Semple and Cecil Sharp both saw the southern mountains as an isolated region, but they differed in their assessment of the effect that isolation had had on the mountain culture. Semple believed that the lack of contact with the modern world was a detriment. Commenting on "the pioneer character of the region," she wrote, "These mountain people are the exponents of a retarded civilization, and [they] show the degenerate symptoms of an arrested development."[76] Cecil Sharp, on the other hand, was thankful for whatever protection the southern mountains offered in slowing the "degeneration" of the traditional culture. Speaking of the mountain people at a literary club in

Asheville in 1917, he stated: "Their culture is hereditary, I found no such thing as 'arrested development'; rather I should say I found arrested degeneration. You can only improve people by preserving their racial inheritance, and the mountaineers of the south have preserved it in a large degree."[77]

While Semple may have lamented the fact that the Appalachian culture had lagged behind the modern world, Sharp was grateful that it had retained cultural elements from earlier times. To Sharp, the "amazingly rich" cultural heritage of the southern mountains was due to the "preservation" of the Appalachian people's supposed Anglo-Saxon "racial inheritance." Both concepts—"arrested development" and "arrested degeneration"—may help to explain the survival of certain old folkways, such as centuries-old British folksongs and ballads, but neither accounts for the richness of the traditional Appalachian culture, which was the result of racial and ethnic diversity and the transmission of culture that occurred both within the region and across the South during the nineteenth century.

The Running Set

For nearly a century Sharp's name for the Kentucky dances, the "Running Set," has been associated with these southern Appalachian square dances. Karpeles, however, admitted later that Sharp had "adopted [this term] for the sake of convenience."[78] The dancers in Kentucky did not use it; they referred to their dances as "frolics," "square dances," "dancing a set," or "set running."[79] When they spoke of "running a set," however, the word "running" was used as it would be if one were "running a business," "running a school," or "running a still"—they were simply doing dances. This use of the word "running" in connection with dance can be traced back to Scotland, where on both the Orkney and Shetland Islands the traveling part of a reel was called "running a reel."[80] North Carolina fiddler Tommy Jarrell likewise spoke of "running reels,"[81] and this phrase is still used by dancers in West Virginia today.

The dancers in Kentucky, however, did not speak of "running a reel" but of "running a *set*," a word that has several different meanings in relation to social dance. In the English country dances of the seventeenth century, dancers "set" to their partners (perform a few simple steps in place) before "turning" (swinging), and by the early nineteenth century, dancing masters were teaching elaborate "setting steps" for use in country dances, reels, and quadrilles. Over time, however, this flashy footwork fell out of fashion, and it was replaced by the simpler "balance" (from the French "balancé"). Sharp and Karpeles noted the figure "Balance Eight" in the Kentucky dances, and contra dancers still "balance" before swinging today.

In dance lexicon, however, there are two additional meanings for the word "set." It can refer to a set of *dancers* or to a set of *dances*, and the latter is what was meant by the expression "running a set." Maud Karpeles suspected as much: in 1930, she wrote, "It is very probable that the word 'set' implies a 'set

Figure 5.2. Running Sets at the Pine Mountain Settlement School (Pine Mountain, Kentucky, c. 1920s). Pine Mountain Settlement School Collections, PMSS Library, Bledsoe, Kentucky

of figures,' in the way that it is customary to speak of a 'set of Quadrilles.'"[82] These nineteenth-century French dances, which consisted of multiple parts (usually five), were often referred to as "sets," and this term became common in the southern mountains.[83] The expression "running a set" originally referred to dancing a set of quadrilles, not a set of running dancers. As Bascom Lunsford pointed out in 1942, the name "Kentucky Running Set" comes from "an erroneous foundation," and it was not meant to "qualify the tempo of the dance."[84]

In the early years of the Pine Mountain School, "set-running" was common as entertainment on Friday and Saturday nights. These dances were perceived as native folk dances, and minus the consumption of alcohol with which they were often associated, they were encouraged at the school as healthy and wholesome recreation.[85] In November 1914 one of the newly arrived teachers described her first experience with "set-running" at one of the school buildings that was under construction:

> Friday night I ran sets for the first time. The older boys and girls and some of the neighbors from eight miles away all went down to the "Foundation", as everyone calls the beginnings of Laurel House, and there, on the under-flooring, which is all there is as yet, we "ran" for about an hour. My partner was Bird Turner, one of the best set-runners in the county, and he pulled me through in great style. It was great fun, and not for anything would I have missed being whirled around as fast as I could go while the boys stamped and clapped their hands in time and called out the orders—"Ladies do C, Gents go gee", "Chase the squirrel", "Box the gnats" etc.[86]

Another teacher at the school wrote of dances at a molasses stir-off the following year (1915): "We all went down to the sawdust pile and watched the set-running. A set is really a quadrille, only danced as fast as you can do it, the boys snapping their fingers to speed things up and calling out the figures, 'Wild Goose Chase,' 'Home Swing,' etc."[87]

When Sharp visited the Pine Mountain School in 1917, he described the dancers' footwork as "a swift, short, and exceedingly smooth Country-dance running step. . . . [It was] so smooth that the dancers, as we saw them, seemed at times to be moving, or gliding, on wheels."[88] While these dances were no doubt faster and livelier than the slower, more reserved country dances and quadrilles, it is uncertain whether the "set runners" at Pine Mountain actually ran as they performed the figures. Sharp's reference to "the tramp of the dancers' feet" suggests a slightly slower pace. But even if the students at Pine Mountain did execute the figures "as fast as you can do it," as young people sometimes like to do, there is no evidence that Sharp encountered this elsewhere or that it was ever a common practice in Kentucky or anywhere else in Appalachia.

* * *

The dances that Cecil Sharp called the "Running Set" were not, as he believed, an ancient, unadulterated form of English country dance but represented a more recent American hybrid that developed from diverse roots in the American South during the nineteenth century. While some of the dance figures may have come from the English country dances, these American dances clearly show a greater debt to the Scots-Irish, French, Native American, and African American dances. Elements adopted from these other dance forms account for the "construction of the dance," the distinctive dance figures, and the "forceful, emotional character" of these dances, the very features that made these dances appear so unique and "wonderful" to Sharp.

In "prospecting" for survivals of British folksongs and ballads in the southern mountains, Sharp selectively mined the southern Appalachian vocal repertoire for songs of British origin. He was not interested in nineteenth-century minstrel songs, parlor songs, Tin Pan Alley songs, American hymns, gospel songs, or African American blues (though a few ended up in his collection anyway). The dances, however, were not as easy to identify, and either by intent or out of ignorance Sharp portrayed them all as English, overlooking the influences of other ethnic groups and popular culture. In spite of his flawed interpretation and biased notions, however, and the fact that he and Karpeles observed only a few dances during their brief visit to this one part of Appalachia, their description of the Kentucky dances is valuable, providing the earliest detailed historical documentation of square dancing in the southern Appalachian region.

6 Sharp's Legacy

Although Sharp and Karpeles spent only five days at Pine Mountain in 1917, their brief visit had a lasting effect at the school. While they were there, they taught English dances to the school's staff, and the following year the school instituted a "traditionally correct May Day" celebration, with English country dances, morris dances, and sword dances.[1] Beginning in 1923, these annual celebrations were directed by one of Sharp's young protégés, Dorothy Bolles of the American branch of the English Folk Dance Society, who would arrive from Boston each spring and spend the month of April at Pine Mountain teaching these English dances to the children. By 1926 the school's May Day celebration had become an established tradition that commenced with "a

Figure 6.1. Sword Dance at the Pine Mountain Settlement School (Pine Mountain, Kentucky, c. 1920s). Pine Mountain Settlement School Collections, PMSS Library, Bledsoe, Kentucky

group of Morris Dancers, going early in the morning from house to house and dancing to the accompaniment of a concertina or fiddle."[2] With the introduction of these English folk dances, however, what started out as simply a celebration of spring evolved into an acclamation of these Appalachian children's presumed British ancestry and heritage. One of the teachers at the school remarked that Sharp had "found there the right soil in which to plant again the native crop of songs and dances [and] made us realize our responsibility as never before and we have never since let the heritage of the children die out."[3] No one seemed to question the blatant Anglocentric bias of this supposedly "native" repertoire of songs and dances.

The Pine Mountain School took great "pride and pleasure" in having introduced Sharp to the "Running Set,"[4] and the May Day programs at the school concluded with a performance of "set-running." These performances became popular with a growing audience from the surrounding region, and in 1926 Evelyn Wells, who served as secretary at the school, took twelve students from Pine Mountain to perform at the State Convention of Women's Clubs in Middlesboro, Kentucky.[5] Wells was on the board of the American branch of the English Country Dance Society, with which the school maintained close ties, and within a few years students from Pine Mountain were performing the "Kentucky Mountain Running Set" at benefits across the country, raising much needed funds for the school. Performances by students from Pine Mountain in New York were noted in the *New York Times* in 1929, 1938, and 1939.[6]

John L. Turner (born c. 1890), who attended Berea College and called dances at Pine Mountain in the 1930s, recalled performing the Running Set for visitors at the school "from the North and New York."[7] One of these visitors was folklorist Alan Lomax, who filmed an outdoor demonstration of the dance in 1937. In this film, five couples can be seen running as they perform the dance figures.[8] Grazia Combs of Perry County (born c. 1890) was amused by, and skeptical of, these dance performances: "I'm going to tell you honestly that I always figured that somebody come in here from outside and concocted that thing up." It was not like any dancing that she knew. In her eyes, the Running Set was "not dancing," but "running."[9]

To Sharp, the Running Set was a valuable addition to the dance repertoire of the English Folk Dance Society, and in 1918 he included it in his series of instructional books for English country dances.[10] Following his visit to Kentucky, Sharp began to teach the Running Set, and even before appearing in print, it had already been performed publicly in New York and Boston. He wrote, "I shall be very surprised if within a few months of its publication, the members of the English Folk Dance Society here and in England are not dancing [the Running Set] merrily in every one of the society's Branches and Centres."[11]

Douglas Kennedy, who succeeded Sharp as director of the society, noted that Sharp had "adapted [the Running Set] to fit into the Society's dancing style."[12] Although he had seen six couples dancing at Pine Mountain, Sharp recommended that the Running Set was "most effective when the number of dancers is limited to four couples,"[13] and consequently the four-couple set became the "correct" form. By describing the footwork of the Running Set as a "country-dance running step" (a step he had previously invented for use in his revivals of Playford's dances[14]), Sharp not only made his "new discovery" consistent with the dancing style of the society, but he also reinforced the supposed connection between these two traditions, at least in his mind and in those of his disciples.

In 1930, six years after Cecil Sharp's death, Maud Karpeles published "Some Additional Figures for Set-Running" in the *Journal of the English Folk Dance Society*. She describes a number of four-couple square dance figures she and others had collected in Kentucky, northern Alabama, Ohio, Connecticut, Massachusetts, and Ontario, Canada; despite their wide-ranging geographical locations, she proposes that these figures be included in "the dance, which we call Running Set." Distinguishing between the "Square Dances" [quadrilles] of the Northeast and Canada and the "Running Set" of the southern Appalachians, Karpeles points out that while sharing many of the same figures, these dances differ mainly in "the style and character of the dance-execution." She contrasts the "quality of swiftness, . . . an essential characteristic of the Running Set," to the "more sophisticated" "shuffling or gliding walking-step" or "chassée step" of the Northeastern square dances. To account for this difference, she suggests that the quadrilles of the Northeast and Canada had been "influenced by modern 'civilization,'" while "the Set-runners of the Appalachian Mountains [had] been living for many generations in their mountain fastness with but little contact with the outside world." She describes the Northeastern square dance as a "hybrid, which contains elements both of an old form of Country Dance and of the later Quadrille and Cotillion," but she fails to say the same of the Southern dances. Instead, she repeats Sharp's claim that the Kentucky dances were survivals of old English country dances, and she denies the possibility that they "could have been developed from the Cotillion in so short a period as a century and a quarter, or thereabouts."[15]

Because of Sharp's reputation as an authority on English folk dance, his explanation of these southern Appalachian square dances was accepted as fact. No one questioned his Anglocentric bias and his self-admitted nationalistic agenda to promote English music and dance. As a result, Sharp's interpretation of the dances was cited in many of the subsequent dance instruction books that were written in the 1930s, 1940s, and 1950s.[16] In a self-published book, written in the mid-1930s, Neva Boyd, a recreational leader from Chicago, describes the figures of "Kentucky Set Running" ("Dance of the Mountain People") as well as English country dances, quadrilles, contra dances, and various European folk dances. Boyd apparently had seen the dance performed by "a group of Berea College students" sometime after

1933 (no mixed-gender dancing was allowed at Berea before that time).[17] She describes the footwork as "a swift but unhurried run," and she repeats Sharp's assertion that "Set Running" is "often performed without music, the dancers beating time with the feet and clapping their hands."[18] Although Sharp saw students at Pine Mountain dancing without music, this practice was not common; more likely there simply was no fiddler available at the school.

In *Cowboy Dances* (1939) Colorado educator Lloyd Shaw borrows heavily from Sharp ("the great authority") when he romantically describes the "Kentucky Running Set" as "one of the purest and oldest dance forms of England," with figures that can be traced back to "ancient pagan ceremonials" involving "well worship," "druidic tree worship," and "religious or magical significance." Shaw goes on to claim that the "Elizabethan" people of the Appalachians were an "isolated and changeless [people who] jealously preserved the ancient dance forms . . . unchanged and crystallized, fossils, if you will, for all time."[19] In *The American Square Dance* (1943) Margot Mayo, founder of the American Square Dance Group in New York City, praises the "Running Set" as "one of the most exciting and most beautiful of all American folk dances," one which "came directly from England to our highlands in the south."[20]

Frank Smith of Berea College likewise echoes Sharp's ideas about the English pagan origins of the Appalachian square dance. In *The Appalachian Square Dance* (1955) he claims that the "mountain square dance . . . was in full flower centuries ago on the village greens of England," and he states that "Birdie in the Cage" is a "ceremonial figure" which is "thought to be derived from the encircling of the sacred bush, this being an attempt to encourage fertility. In other words, it is a tribal act of prayer for protection against the terrors of starvation." Perpetuating the myth of an isolated Anglo-Saxon population, Smith writes, "The descendants of English villagers who found themselves in the Appalachian Mountains were isolated until a generation ago by lack of roads and navigable rivers."[21]

Smith, like Sharp, was an Englishman, and in 1937 he was recruited by the president of Berea College to initiate a "fitting recreational program" as an alternative to modern social dancing.[22] Students at Berea's Normal School division had been learning folk dances and singing games for the classroom since 1914, and Smith had been employed at the college from 1926 to 1933 as a teacher and recreational leader.[23] When he returned to Berea in 1938, after working as a recreation extension leader at the John C. Campbell Folk School in western North Carolina, Smith established a folk dance program that gave rise to the Berea College Country Dancers. This performing group drew from the repertoire of dances that were taught at Pine Mountain,[24] and throughout the years they have kept Sharp's Anglocentric image of Appalachia alive with performances of English country dances, morris dances, sword dances, and "Set Running," a highly stylized reenactment of the dances observed by Sharp and Karpeles at Pine Mountain in which the dancers literally run as they perform the figures, accompanied solely by hand clapping.[25]

One hundred years after his visit to the southern mountains, Cecil Sharp's legacy remains alive in the twenty-first century. The Berea College Country Dancers continue to perform the Southern square dances he first described in 1917, and the "Kentucky Running Set" is taught at Berea College's annual "Christmas Country Dance School."[26] Modern clogging competitions now include an officially sanctioned category, the "Running Set Hoedown," in which young dancers perform square dance figures with an exaggerated running step that resembles high-stepping jogging (see chapter 13). In London, the English Folk Dance and Song Society hosts concerts, lectures, workshops, and dances at the Cecil Sharp House, a dance center built in Sharp's honor in 1930, and in America, the Country Dance and Song Society (formerly the American branch of the English Folk Dance Society) continues to sponsor English and Anglo-American dance events throughout the country.

Although contemporary scholars and historians now reject Sharp's biased Anglocentric interpretation of these Appalachian dances, his ideas, having been repeated by generations of dancers and folk dance educators for a century, are deeply entrenched. And not unlike the Appalachian stereotypes popularized by the local-color writers of the nineteenth century, they continue to be recycled and perpetuated today, both in print and on the internet. According to an article by Dorothy Shaw (1891–1985) (Lloyd Shaw's widow) about the history of the "Appalachian Mountain Dance," which appears on a square dance Web site, "the great English folklorist, Cecil J. Sharp . . . was told that the people of this region had an interesting dance called a running set" that was a "living fossil" and "unquestionably an English country dance" brought to the region by the English ancestors of the Appalachian people. Elaborating on Sharp's romantic notion of the pagan roots of the dances, Shaw claims the dance "Old Dan Tucker is one of those human sacrifice dances . . . and 1,500 years ago, the one who was caught as 'Old Dan' in the centre, as the dance ended, really had his head cut off!"[27]

The Afton Square-Eight

Cecil Sharp likely imagined the "Running Set" of Kentucky to be just the beginning of his folk dance collecting in America. In December 1917 he wrote, "We happen to know . . . that many forms of the Country-dance—e.g., Square-eights and Longways dances—still survive in the Appalachians and other parts of America."[28] The following spring, he and Maud Karpeles returned to the southern mountains to resume their "prospecting" for ballads and folksongs, and while in Virginia they attended a house dance at Afton, a community in the foothills of the Blue Ridge, not far from Charlottesville. Sharp characterized these Virginia square dances, what he called the "Afton Square-eight," as "a somewhat tame and sophisticated version of the Kentucky Running Set." Although the music was "faster than usual" (138 beats per minute), he described the dancers' footwork as a "sluggish, C.D. [Country

Dance] running-step," and he was disappointed that the dancers "at times exhibited airs and graces savouring of the drawing room."[29] In Sharp's eyes, these dances were too "sophisticated." They did not seem as archaic as the ones he had encountered in Kentucky, and that may be why he never published his typewritten notes.

Sharp's account of the square dances at Afton, which appears in his *Autograph Notebook Collection*, provides a second detailed description of the Appalachian square dance tradition of the early twentieth century. Like the majority of the dances in Kentucky, these Virginia dances are four-couple, visiting-couple squares. The chorus figures of these dances (what Sharp calls "General Movements") all have precedents in the change figures of the eighteenth-century cotillions, and they include "Circle Right and Circle Left," "Balance Eight," "Swing Corners" (swing corners, then partners), "Rights and Lefts," "Promenade," and "Ladies in the Centre" (the four ladies form a star with right hands joined, and then left hands; the gents join the star beside partners, then "fall back" to the lady behind four times until they rejoin their original partners). Pointing out the spontaneity of these dances, Sharp notes that the chorus figures "were chosen and combined apparently on the spur of the moment by the Caller."[30]

Most of the visiting-couple figures ("Distinctive Figures") at Afton are similar to those Sharp and Karpeles saw in Kentucky. These include "Right Hands Across," "Figure Eight," "Chase the Squirrel" ["Lady round the lady and the gent also"], and variants of "Wild Goose Chase" and the "Waltz Swing." "Cheat 'em or Swing 'em" is a combination of two of the figures from Kentucky, "Treat 'em All Right" and "Cheat 'em If You Can," two of the "promiscuous figures" of the nineteenth-century quadrilles. Noticeably missing from these dances is the figure "Bird in the Cage," which at that time was more common west of the mountains, in the Ohio River watershed.

Sharp notes an unnamed hand-turning figure that resembles the "Do-si-do" he had seen in Kentucky. Here though, it starts with a right-hand turn with the opposite partner, rather than a left with one's own partner. Today, this figure is known in West Virginia as "running a reel" and in western North Carolina it is called the "Georgia Rang-Tang." At this dance in the Blue Ridge of Virginia, as well as in Kentucky and elsewhere in the Ohio River watershed, it served as a sub-chorus following the main visiting-couple figure, and that is also how it is used in West Virginia today.

Sharp describes two dance figures that he had not encountered in Kentucky. "Go to Cuba," likely a reference to the Spanish American War of 1898, involves the playful exchange of partners, reminiscent of the nineteenth-century German Cotillions (see chapter 10): four men circle around one woman, and she chooses one as her new partner. The figure Sharp calls "Do-si-do Ladies" is not the usual hand-turning "Do-si-do" (mentioned above) but a circular figure for two couples in which first the two women, and then the two men, orient themselves back-to-back, facing out. Unlike the hand-turning "Do-si-do," which was used as a sub-chorus, this figure was danced as a main figure, and it appears to have been widely known across the South in the early twentieth century. In Washington County, in the southwestern end of the state, it was known as "Ladies Do-si," and in the Tidewater region of Virginia, in Gloucester County, it was called "Ban Your Lady."[31] This circular "Do-si-do" figure appears on a number of the 78-rpm recordings of Southern dance callers that were made in the 1920s. Samantha Bumgarner of western North Carolina calls out, "Lady do-si-do, Gents you know," while callers in North Georgia tend to call, "Ladies do-si," "Do-si the lady," or simply, "Do-si." In *Kentucky Square Dances* (1928), Ida Levin refers to this same figure as "Do-si-do."[32] Grace Ryan, in her *Handbook for Dances of Our Pioneers* (1926), calls it "Dos-á-ballonette," a name that suggests the influence of the French dancing masters.[33] A similar figure, however, "Cúl le cúl" ("Back to Back"), was known in Ireland during the eighteenth century.[34]

The Afton square dances have a few other peculiarities that deserve mention. Sharp noted that the circles of eight in these Virginia dances turned first to the right (counterclockwise), before going to the left (clockwise). This is opposite the normal direction of English and most Appalachian dances, which turn clockwise first, but it is consistent with French dances of the late eighteenth century, which first turn counterclockwise.[35] Sharp also noted that the swings in the Afton dance were preceded by a "Balance" or "Balance Eight," and he likens this to the "Set" figure of Playford's English country dances. This setting movement, however, like the chorus figures and the French dance terminology, more likely comes from the French cotillions. As he did in Kentucky, Sharp ignores the obvious French influence on these dances. He remarks that the Afton set "consists of three parts only" (he was obviously aware of the usual five-part structure of the nineteenth-century quadrilles), but he avoids mentioning the French dances by name.[36] This three-part structure is consistent with the square dances of Tidewater Virginia and those of the Northeast, which by the twentieth century had likewise been shortened to only three parts, called "changes."[37]

The evening Sharp spent at Afton concluded his dance collecting in America. These square dances were not unlike others at that time in the Blue Ridge and Shenandoah Valley of Virginia, and despite a separation of more than three hundred miles across the Appalachian mountains, they were not significantly different from those he had seen in Kentucky. Like square dances elsewhere in the southern mountains, they had a circular visiting-couple structure, with a variety of distinctive visiting-couple figures that alternated with chorus figures. The timing of the figures was freeform, the calling was improvisational, and the music was fast.

7 "Barn Dances with Calls" (1924–1933)

Cecil Sharp's visits to the southern mountains preceded the birth of the commercial country music industry by only a few years, and soon Southern square dance music could be heard on the radio throughout the country. In 1922 Fiddlin' John Carson began performing on WSB in Atlanta, the first high-powered radio station in the South, and within a few years radio stations powerful enough to be heard across the nation were broadcasting "barn dance" programs that featured old-time fiddling. The first of these barn dance shows, on WBAP in Fort Worth, Texas, went on the air in 1923. The following year, WLS in Chicago began to broadcast the "National Barn Dance," and in 1925 a third "Barn Dance" program (later renamed the "Grand Ole Opry") was initiated by WSM in Nashville, Tennessee. These radio barn dance programs and others like them were basically variety shows, and even though they were billed as "barn dances," they more closely resembled vaudeville shows than square dances. However, they provided a commercial venue for the old-time dance music of rural America, and when Missourian Tom Owen called out square dance figures on the "National Barn Dance," it simulated the sound of a real barn dance, adding authenticity to the music and putting it in context.

When record companies began to make 78-rpm recordings of rural Southern music in the 1920s,[1] many of the early records likewise included square dance calls. Although these recordings were marketed as "Barn Dances with Calls," they were not intended for dancing. At about three minutes in length, they were too short for an actual dance, and in most cases little attention was given to the clarity and proper timing of the calls. Furthermore, at that time dance figures and terminology were not yet standardized, but they varied from region to region, so even in cases where the calls were audible and well timed, it is doubtful that dancers would have been able to follow the dances.

The calling was intended simply as a colorful addition to the music. Despite their shortcomings, however, these recordings inadvertently documented these rural traditions, providing a wealth of information about the music and dances of the southern mountains and across the South.

The first recordings to include Southern square dance calls were made by Samantha Bumgarner (1878–1960), a banjo player from Jackson County in western North Carolina. She recorded in New York on April 23, 1924, just four days after Tom Owen's dance calls were heard on the premier broadcast of the "National Barn Dance."[2] Perhaps this was a coincidence, or maybe Bumgarner or someone at Columbia Records had heard Owen's dance calls the previous Saturday night. Whatever the case, on these recordings (among the earliest of the five-string banjo) Bumgarner calls out square dance figures while playing "Shout Lou" and "Fly around My Pretty Little Miss." Her straightforward and sincere delivery suggests that, to her, these dance calls were simply a part of the music.

Not all of the dance callers who recorded on 78s were as genuine and sincere as Bumgarner. Later that same month Gene Austin (1900–1972) shouted out a few dance calls while George Reneau, a blind street musician from Knoxville, Tennessee, played "Turkey in the Straw" on harmonica and guitar. Austin, who a few years later would become famous for his hit "My Blue Heaven," was a studio musician and crooner, and his stiff delivery of the calls reveals that he was not a real dance caller but was merely reciting a few extraneous memorized lines to add rustic color to this otherwise instrumental recording. He delivers the calls in no particular order and interjects random remarks such as, "Hey Lem, why don't you swing that gal?" Unlike Bumgarner, Austin was not from Appalachia—he was from Texas—and his affected calling tells us nothing about the dance traditions of the southern mountains.[3]

That same year (1924), guitar player Henry Whitter, fiddler Henry Sutphin, and banjo player John Rector also traveled to New York to record. Billed as Whitter's Virginia Breakdowners, this trio from southwest Virginia recorded two dance tunes, "Mississippi Sawyer" and "Sourwood Mountain," while an unidentified person shouted out over-enunciated dance calls. Although the calls on these two recordings are identically worded and sound as if they were read from a script, they are valuable because they are true to the rural dance tradition of southwest Virginia.

As a way to differentiate this rural Southern dance music from the popular jazz music of the day, record companies marketed it as "old-time music," and the dance calls that could be heard along with the music clearly added to the rustic image. At the start of one recording made in 1927, north Georgia caller Bill Chitwood announces, "All right folks, we're going to give you an old-fashioned north Georgia square dance, just like our forefathers used to do."[4]

The heyday of these barn dance recordings (1927 and 1928) was just prior to the decline of record sales following the stock market crash of 1929 (see table 1). Subsequently, during the Depression of the 1930s western music became popular, and as the recording industry shifted its focus away from southern string bands to cowboy singers, dance calls were no longer included on commercial country music recordings.

It was not until the early 1940s, with the revival of square dancing in America, that record companies resumed making records with dance calls. These later recordings, however, were different from the earlier ones. They were specifically intended for dancers, with professional musicians and callers predominantly from the Midwest and West, and they no longer reflected the local music and dance traditions of the southern mountains. Advances in the recording technology, including the electric microphone, meant that the calls no longer needed to be shouted to be audible; clearly recorded, the dance calls and the caller became the main focus. These recordings of the 1940s reflect the increasing professionalism and standardization of dance figures and calling patter that led to the subsequent development of the modern Western square dance movement. Among the callers who recorded during this era are Roy Rogers (1940), Texan Shorty McCoy (1941), Missourian Luther Ossenbrink ("Arkie the Arkansas Woodchopper") (1941), and Iowan Lawrence V. Loy (1941).

78-rpm Recordings with Southern Dance Callers (1924–1933)

As a dance caller, I have long been intrigued by these voices from the past, especially those on the earliest recordings, who were contemporaries of the callers Sharp and Karpeles encountered in eastern Kentucky. Most of these callers were born in the late nineteenth century, and they learned by oral transmission, prior to the availability of radio and recordings. They grew up during a time when square dances were still common in rural America, and distinct regional dance styles and repertoires still existed. With the help of

Table 1. "Barn Dances with Calls" (1924–1933)

Year	Callers	Recordings
1924	4	8
1925	1	1
1926	1	1
1927	14	28
1928	14	30
1929	3	7
1930	2	4
1931	4	9
1932	3	4
1933	1	3
Total	44*	95

*Two callers made recordings in more than one year

two discographies, Guthrie Meade's *Country Music Sources* and Tony Russell's *Country Music Records*, I have identified and collected copies of close to two hundred commercial 78-rpm recordings with dance calls that were made between 1923 and 1941. Many feature callers from the Midwest, Texas, and the Northeast, but on ninety-five of these recordings, made from 1924 to 1933, we can hear the voices of forty-four Southern callers from the Appalachian region and its periphery.[5] (See appendix table 2, Discography of 78-rpm Recordings with Southern Dance Callers [1924–1933].)

Deciphering and interpreting the dance calls on these old 78s has been a challenge. On some of the records the calls are barely audible; some are in poor shape, and on others the calls were not clearly recorded in the first place. Even when the calls can be heard, changes in dance terminology since these recordings were made can lead to misinterpretation. For example, whereas today a "swing" refers to two dancers turning as a couple in a waltz hold, when these recordings were made, it meant to circle to the left with hands joined. This could be done with more than two dancers, as in "swing three," "swing four," or "swing all eight." Despite the challenges, however, these recordings are a valuable primary source. More reliable than the recollections of elderly informants, which are subject to lapses of memory, embellishment, and misinterpretation, they provide a first-hand glimpse at the square dances that were known across the Appalachian region in the early twentieth century.

The Callers

The forty-four callers who appear on these recordings are no doubt only a sample of the Southern callers who were active at that time, and they do not represent the entire southern Appalachian region. We can only speculate about the calling styles and repertoires of the many callers who were never recorded and the sections of Appalachia not represented on these recordings. The callers who were recorded, however, can be grouped into six geographic regions, based on where they grew up or lived. In cases where the caller's identity is unknown (fifteen instances), I have assumed that they were from the same county as the musicians, because most often the caller was one of the musicians or someone associated with them.

Among the callers who can be heard on these recordings are a number of well-known names in the world of old-time music. These include Fiddlin' John Carson, Uncle Dave Macon, Humphrey Bate, G. B. Grayson, Ernest Stoneman, and Clayton McMichen. Whether these musicians ever called dances or simply knew a few calls to shout out at a recording session is not known, but what is apparent is that they were familiar with the dance tradition. In this male-dominated field, Samantha Bumgarner is the only female caller represented on these recordings. There are also two African American callers. One is Sam Jones, who, billed as "Stovepipe No. 1," recorded in Cincinnati, Ohio, in 1924. Jones intersperses dance calls between the lyrics

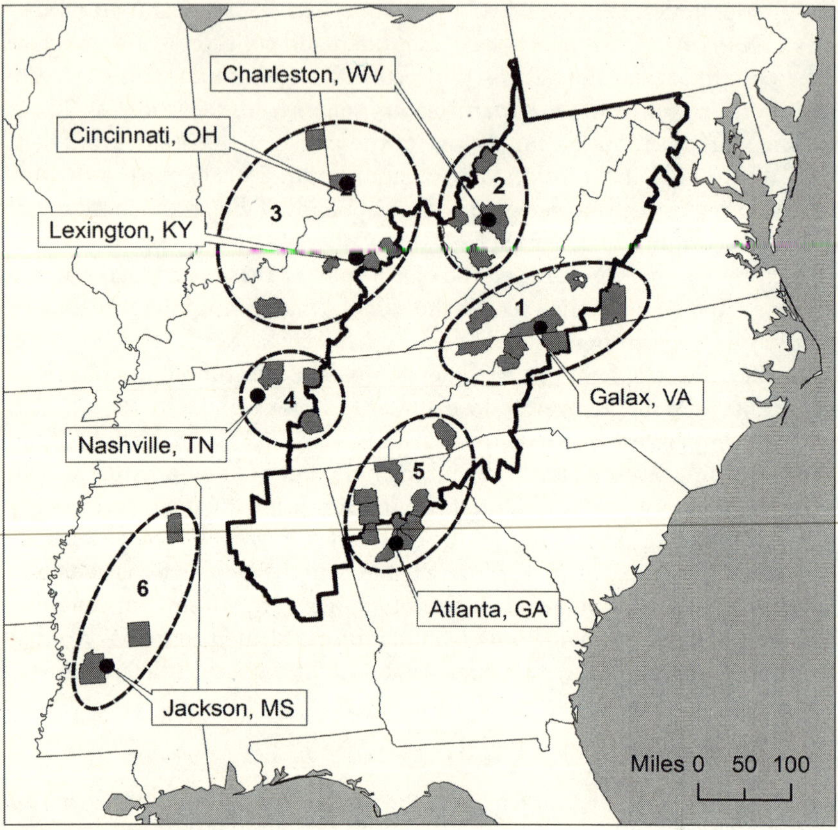

Figure 7.1. Six Regions: Counties of Dance Callers on 78s (1924–1933). Warren Wilson College GIS Crew.

of "Cripple Creek/Sourwood Mountain" and "Turkey in the Straw" while accompanying himself on guitar, harmonica, and kazoo. The other is Jim Baxter, an African American–Cherokee guitar player from north Georgia who was recorded in 1928. These recordings of Jones and Baxter are rare examples of the African American callers who once provided the music and calls for dances throughout America.[6]

The Calling Styles

Several different styles of Southern dance calling can be heard on these recordings. All of it, however, is freeform calling, and none of these callers fits the calls to the phrasing of the music. While some use rhyming phrases and pitch their voices to the tonic or fifth of the musical key, the majority simply shout out the dance prompts. A few sing out some of the dance calls, though none of these are fully developed singing calls. Many of the voices sound like those of experienced callers, with rhyming patter flowing easily from their tongues. The youngest of the callers, Ernest Legg (1904–1970) of Charleston, West Virginia, is also most verbose, and his modern style is markedly different from the older callers of the previous generation, such as John Carson (1868–1949) of North Georgia. Some of the voices on these recordings are clearly not actual dance callers but are instead perhaps one of the musicians merely shouting out a few random calls. Although we can learn the most from the real dance callers, even the imitators provide information about the Southern square dance tradition.

In addition to calling out the figures, many of the callers tease or reprimand the musicians and dancers. Sharp noted this practice in Kentucky: he wrote that the caller "will sometimes improvise remarks of his own . . . and crack jokes, chaff the dancers, and so forth."[7] Given that these callers are from across the Appalachian region and learned to call before the age of recordings, the uniformity of the content and wording of these phrases is remarkable. Five of the callers, from West Virginia, Tennessee, and Georgia, using almost identical wording, cajole male dancers to "Swing that girl with the red dress on." Ten callers in West Virginia, Ohio, Indiana, Kentucky, Tennessee, Virginia, and Georgia use the same opening call, "Partners to your places, like the horses to their traces," or a variant, "Partners to your places, and straighten your faces." These calls may have originated as a parody of the dancing masters and floor managers at balls who, during the nineteenth century, once directed dancers to take their places in squares for quadrilles.

The Music

On all but a few of the recordings the fiddle is the lead instrument, with the guitar providing accompaniment on the vast majority. Surprisingly, the five-string banjo appears on only about a third of the recordings and on none of those from West Virginia, Georgia, and Mississippi. With the exception of the Blue Ridge region, the four-string tenor banjo, an instrument that became popular in the 1920s, appears to have been more widespread at that time across the South, especially in Georgia and Mississippi. Other instruments on these recordings (listed in order of prevalence) include mandolin, ukulele, bass, harmonica, kazoo, bones, autoharp, piano, tiple, and washboard.

Most of the music on these recordings would be considered Southern breakdowns, with an average tempo of about 130 bpm (beats per minute). The fastest, at 150 bpm (assuming the speed of the recording is true), is from the Blue Ridge. Although some of these dance tunes are descended from British and Irish reels, the majority are native to America. This includes Southern breakdowns such as "Sally Ann" and "Cripple Creek," which were among the "jig" tunes noted by Sharp, as well as play party songs, nineteenth-century minstrel pieces, and African American blues.

The Dance Figures

The dance figures on these recordings should not be interpreted as the only ones known in these six regions, nor do they likely represent these callers' complete repertoires. Some of the regions are better represented, and some of the callers were more prolific than others. Also, while some of the recordings include fairly complete dances, on others we only hear a few random calls in no particular order—ones that might have come to mind during a three-minute recording session. Although the calls on these recordings reveal regional differences, taken as a whole they show a fairly homogeneous tradition that illustrates all of the defining characteristics of the Southern square dance. The prevalence of the dance forms and figures, as well as calling styles, dance terminology, instrumentation, and tempo of the music, are shown in tables 3 and 4 in the appendix.

All of the dances on these recordings are circular visiting-couple dances—four-couple squares and larger circular sets—with a verse-chorus structure. The four-couple set is the more common of the two forms, appearing in five out of the six regions. In these dances, as in the French cotillions, a chorus figure alternates with the main figure, while in the circular sets, it is used as an introduction or ending figure. The most common chorus figures are the "Promenade" and the "Grand Right and Left," which appear in five out of the six regions. Regardless of the form, these Southern dances are referred to as "square dances," and the terms "home" and "corner" (which are meaningless in a circular set) are widely used.

Several dozen different dance figures can be heard on these recordings. They come from a variety of sources: Scots-Irish reels, English country dances, French cotillions and quadrilles, African American dances, and Native American dances, as well as the popular social dances of the nineteenth century. Among the common figures are two different types of Southern "Do-si-do." (The Northern back-to-back "Do-si-do" is completely absent from these Southern dances.) As mentioned earlier, the hand-turning "Do-si-do," used as a sub-chorus following a visiting-couple figure, was common in regions adjacent to the Ohio River Valley, such as West Virginia and Kentucky. That is how Sharp and Karpeles saw it in eastern Kentucky, what is now called "running a reel" in West Virginia today. Ernest Legg, who recorded with the Kessinger Brothers in 1928, fills in the time required to execute this figure with a nonstop flow of rhyming patter:

It's ladies do and gents you know,
It's up by right by wrong you go,
And you can't go to heaven while you carry on so,
And it's home little gal and Do-si-do,
And it may be the last time, I don't know,
And oh by gosh and oh by Joe.[8]

The circular "Do-si-do," which Sharp and Karpeles encountered at Afton, Virginia, shows up on one of the recordings from southwest Virginia; it appears to have been more common in North Georgia and western North Carolina.

Regional Differences

The dance calls that can be heard on these ninety-five recordings illustrate a fairly homogeneous tradition across the South, one that is consistent with Sharp's observations in eastern Kentucky, but they also illustrate the regional differences that existed at that time. In the Blue Ridge of southwest Virginia, North Carolina, and East Tennessee (Region One), the four-couple square is the predominant form, though the ring form appears to have been known also in the Virginia Piedmont. The dance figures in this region are similar to those observed by Sharp in Afton, Virginia, a few years earlier. One common figure that appears to be common here but rare elsewhere (except for one instance in Kentucky and one in western North Carolina) involves the ladies standing back-to-back in the center of the set while the gents go to the right, single file, around the outside. The five-string banjo is most prevalent in this region, and the callers, with one exception, shout out the dance prompts, without using rhyming patter or pitching their voices to the music.

The calling styles appear to have been more developed in West Virginia, Kentucky, and southern Ohio and Indiana (Regions Two and Three). Here, most of the callers use rhyming patter and many pitch their voices to the music. Here, too, the dance repertoire includes a greater variety of figures. "Chase the Rabbit," "Bird in the Cage," and the hand-turning "Do-si-do," while common in this region, are relatively rare elsewhere. The Ohio River served as an important cultural conduit, and the influence of the nineteenth-century French quadrilles is apparent. The dances, which are all four-couple squares, include a number of figures derived from the French dances. These include "Balance," "Divide the Ring," "Right and Left Through," "Half Promenade," "Ladies Chain," "Basket," the "Jig Figure," "Pokey-Four," and "Allemande Left" (preceding the "Grand Right and Left").[9] Further evidence of the influence of the quadrilles in this region is the use of the term "first four" (meaning the head two couples in a quadrille) and references to "sets" and "quadrilles" (one of the Kentucky fiddlers plays a tune called "Washington Quadrille").

The dances in Middle Tennessee (Region Four) were likewise clearly influenced by the French quadrilles of the steamboat era. Not all of these dances, however, are four-couple squares. Two of the callers (Humphrey Bate and one other) call big-ring square dances with the "Shoo-Fly Swing." This figure is reminiscent of the French dance, the Boulangère, so its presence up the Mississippi River from New Orleans is perhaps not surprising. Some of the callers in Middle Tennessee pitch their voices, but none uses rhyming patter.

In North Georgia and western North Carolina (Region Five) the eight-couple circle is the predominant form, though there are also a few four-couple squares. The callers shout out the dance prompts without using rhyming patter or pitched voices. Most common among the relatively small repertoire of dance figures are "Right-Hands Across" and the circular "Do-si-do." Four callers, including African American–Cherokee caller Jim Baxter, call the figure "Single File to the Right," which likely has roots in the Native American and African American traditions.

The recordings of three callers from Mississippi (Region Six), though not from within the Appalachian region, shed light on the square dance traditions of the Deep South. Here, as in North Georgia, western North Carolina, and the Virginia Piedmont, the eight-couple circular set is the common form, and the calls are merely shouted out, with no rhyming patter or pitched voices. The prevalence of the circle form here, and its absence in West Virginia and Kentucky, illustrates the greater influence of African American ring dances in the Deep South.

* * *

Although these "Barn Dances with Calls" do not represent every section of the Appalachian region, this collection of recordings, made between 1924 and 1933, may be the closest thing we have to a primary source from which to learn about the southern Appalachian square dance tradition prior to the standardization of square dancing that occurred during the twentieth century. Like an audio snapshot of that time, these recordings support Sharp's and Karpeles's earlier observations of the dances in Kentucky, but they also provide a broader view of the Southern square dance tradition across the entire region, revealing the regional differences that existed at that time. More important, however, regardless of the quality of performance or the experience of these forty-four callers, these recordings can serve as a valuable resource for contemporary dance callers, providing role models from the last century. Audio files of these 78-rpm recordings, transcriptions of the dance calls, and additional information are available at the companion Web site, "Hoedowns, Reels, and Frolics" at http://www.philjamison.com.

8 The Virginia Reel

In a fictional account, set in 1850, an antebellum ball in Eastern Virginia concludes with the Virginia Reel:

> Then the chairs and tables were cleared away, and Pompey, the coachman, with his fiddle, was installed in one corner to do the orchestra for us. Waltzes, polkas, galops, and quadrilles, followed one another in quick succession, until Uncle Albert announced that the ball would end with a Virginia reel . . . the favorite dance of the "good old days."[1]

The Virginia Reel has often been portrayed as a beloved dance from colonial times—George Washington's favorite dance—but in fact, that is a myth. Washington was known to have enjoyed dancing, but the dance we know as the Virginia Reel did not become popular in the ballrooms of America until the early nineteenth century, several decades after his death in 1799. When the above account was written (in 1870), this "favorite dance of the 'good old days'" was no longer considered fashionable in urban ballrooms, and clearly, after the Civil War, it was no longer danced at plantation balls in the South. In the early twentieth century, however, this outdated nineteenth-century ballroom dance was resurrected. Erroneously promoted as a dance from colonial times, it was taught to the schoolchildren of America and was transformed into an iconic American folk dance that today, a century later, is known throughout the country.

Six-handed Reels

Part of the confusion regarding the supposed antiquity of the Virginia Reel (with a capital *R*) owes to the existence of older six-handed Virginia reels (with a lowercase *r*). These reels were danced with three couples in longways sets, the men on one side and the women on the other, and as in the

Figure 8.1. "Natchez Ballroom"—Six-handed reel accompanied by a black fiddler (Charles A. Lesueur, Natchez, Mississippi, c. 1830). Natchez Historical Society

four-handed reels (discussed in chapter 3), they involved footwork in place ("setting steps") that alternated with a traveling figure. Descriptions of the figures vary, but they typically included a sashay down the middle and back, heys within each of the lines, and a cast-off down the outside.[2] Like the four-handed reels, these six-handed reels did not require a large dance floor, so they could be danced in houses and other small spaces. This, and the fact that attendance at dancing school was not required to learn the simple repetitive figures, made these dances popular with all classes of people, rural as well as urban. During the late-eighteenth and early-nineteenth centuries, six-handed reels were popular throughout North America, from Canada to Mississippi.[3] They were especially prevalent in the South, however, where they (and the dance tunes that accompanied them) became known as "Virginia reels," the term "Virginia," used as a generic term for the American South, differentiating these American dances from the four-handed "Scotch reels" of the British Isles.

In 1785 Robert Hunter Jr., a young merchant from London, attended a wedding in eastern Virginia, and after dinner he and the other guests danced "cotillions, minuets, Virginia and Scotch reels, country dances, jigs, etc., till ten o'clock." Hunter wrote that he "admire[d]" the reels "amazingly," but "especially the six-handed ones."[4] John Enys, a British army officer who toured the United States in 1788, encountered similar reels at a private dance party in Baltimore: "These reels are not altogeather [sic] the Highland Reels [four-handed Scotch reels] tho I do not know how to describe the difference.

They are I find much used in the back parts of Virginia."[5] When Englishman Charles Janson visited the Blue Ridge Mountains of Virginia in 1803, he identified the "six-handed reel" as "the favorite dance in the southern states."[6] American writer James Kirke Paulding danced these reels when he visited White Sulphur Springs and Sweet Springs in [West] Virginia in 1816. He wrote: "It so happened that a servant of one of the gentlemen here was adept in playing Virginia reels, which are true native-born dances; and, in my mind, infinitely preferable to cotillions and waltzes."[7] Reminiscing in 1827 about his youth in western (now West) Virginia, Stephen T. Mitchell wrote: "How many Saturday nights have I beat time in the good old six-handed reel upon these split-log puncheon floors."[8]

These dances were not limited to Virginia, however; they were known throughout the South. When the early settlers of the South Carolina Piedmont (near Greenville) joined together for "cotton pickings" (to pick the seeds out of cotton) in the late 1700s, "after the evening's labors were finished, they would join in a regular old-fashioned Virginia reel, and keep time with flying feet to the delightful strains of music drawn from a gourd banjo."[9] As mentioned earlier, slaves worked alongside whites at such work parties, so it is not surprising that black dancers were also familiar with these six-handed reels. Former slave Matilda Henrietta Perry, who lived near Danville, Virginia, spoke of her mother, who "could dance and turn the Six-Handed Reel."[10] Antebellum Southern writer Augustus Longstreet (1790–1870) likewise recalled the "good ole republican six reel" with "setting steps," calling it the "native dance" of his youth in the Georgia backcountry, and Harden Taliaferro (1811–1875) wrote about "the old-fashioned 'seven-handed reel'" [sic] at rural frolics in Surry County, North Carolina, in the 1820s.[11]

Josephus Guild, who was born in 1802 to a family of Scots descent and grew up in Middle Tennessee, wrote of these dances ("old fashioned Virginia break-down reel[s]") at "log-rollings," "corn-shuckings," "house-raisings," and "reapings of the harvest." Guild wrote, "When the day's work was performed, the yard was swept, . . . [and] the word was given, 'Hand all round, set-to and face your partners' . . . I have seen several sets at the same time, both boys and girls, cutting the single and double pigeon wing" [setting steps].[12]

Guild mentions several dance tunes by name, including "a favorite reel called 'Miss McCloud.'" This Scottish tune ["Miss McLeod's Reel"] was widely known throughout the South during the nineteenth century, and it appears in George Knauff's 1839 collection of *Virginia Reels*.[13] Now also known as "Hop High Ladies" or "Hop Light Ladies," it is still played by Southern fiddlers today. The lyrics, "Hop high ladies, three in a row," may well be a reference to the setting steps ("cutting the single and double pigeon wing") performed by the women ("three in a row") as they danced these six-handed reels.

William Gilmore Simms fondly recalled six-handed reels, as late as the mid-1830s, at plantation balls in rural South Carolina (near Charleston): "And now, when a country dance, and one or two cotillions [quadrilles], had gently stirred up the spirits of the dancers, the signal would be given for the exhilarating reel. A six-handed reel! . . . The sets are formed, three couple in each, who generally agree to dance together. The music commences, and off they bound. In rapid succession, we have the chase, the hey, the figure of eight, right and left, cross hands, down the middle, grand round, cross again, and off the whole party darts again, to recommence the intoxicating reel."[14]

The Virginia Reel

At the beginning of the nineteenth century, a country dance called "Sir Roger de Coverley" became fashionable in the ballrooms of England. London dancing master Thomas Wilson, who published a description of the dance figures in 1808, refers to it as "The Finishing Dance," used at the end of an evening to conclude a ball.[15] In a later publication (1815), Wilson explains that this dance was intended to "promote the good humour of the company . . . causing them to separate in evincing a pleasing satisfaction with each other."[16]

"Sir Roger de Coverley" is danced in a longways set, with the men on one side and the women on the other. The dance figures begin with the top lady and bottom gent meeting on the diagonal in the center of the set and then returning to their places. The top gent and bottom lady then do the same. These same pairs of dancers (top lady and bottom gent followed by the top gent and bottom lady) meet four more times, turning with a right hand, and then a left hand, and then both hands, and, finally, passing back-to-back.[17]

Following these opening movements, the top lady and gent weave back and forth between the two lines, passing between the other dancers as they make their way to the bottom of the set.

SIR ROGER DE COVERLEY, OR THE FINISHING DANCE.

Fig. 1.

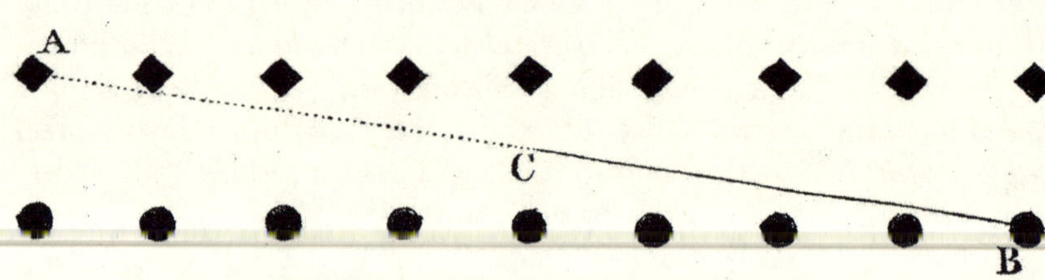

The top Lady at A, and the bottom Gentleman at B, advance to C, and retreat to their places.

Figure 8.2. "Sir Roger de Coverley"—opening figures on diagonals (Thomas Wilson, *An Analysis of Country Dancing*, 1808). Library of Congress, Music Division

SIR ROGER DE COVERLEY.

Fig. 3. 115

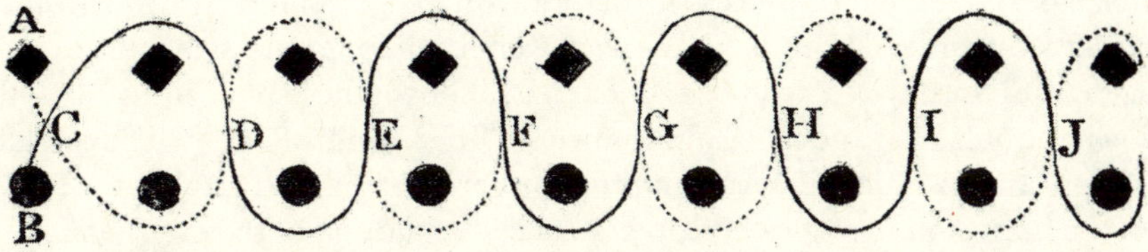

The top couple at A B, pass each other at C, and cross over every couple till they get to the bottom, they pass each other at D E F G H I J.

Figure 8.3. "Sir Roger de Coverley"—Top couple weaves between the other couples to the bottom of the set (Thomas Wilson, *An Analysis of Country Dancing,* 1808). Library of Congress, Music Division

The dance ends with a march figure. The top couple (now at the bottom) leads up the center of the set, with all of the other couples following in order (starting from the bottom). The couples split apart at the top and proceed down the outside in single-file lines to the bottom of the set. The dance then starts over and continues until all couples have had a turn as the top couple.

By the 1820s "Sir Roger de Coverley" had become popular in the ballrooms of America, and as in England, it was used as the last dance of the evening. Journalist and author Benjamin Perley Poore wrote of the Washington dance assemblies of that time: "The music was furnished by colored performers on the violin," and following the minuets, country dances, and quadrilles, the evening ended with "Sir Roger de Coverly" as a "concluding country dance." Poore reports that when John Quincy Adams's son was married at the White House in 1828, even the president participated in this dance.[18]

This English dance, however, changed in America. The American version starts out with the same opening figures as Wilson's "Sir Roger de Coverley" but then, instead of the top couple simply weaving back and forth between the other dancers, they reel down the lines with a series of alternating hand turns. This lively figure was described in 1857: "Then the top couple join right hands and turn once and a half round; the top lady then turns with the left hand every gentlemen down the line, while her partner turns every lady the same (between each of them turning their own partner with the right hand)."[19] This reeling figure may have been inspired by the French Boulangère, which was also popular at that time as a "Concluding Dance" on both sides of the Atlantic and involves a similar series of hand turns with successive dancers.[20]

When English Shakespearean actress Frances "Fanny" Kemble visited America in 1832, she encountered this dance (in addition to "waltzes" and "sundry quadrilles") at balls in New York. She describes it as "Sir Roger de Coverly turned Backwoodsman" (the dancers in New York referred to it as "a Kentucky reel").[21] This American dance was clearly different from the English country dance described by Thomas Wilson, but it shared certain features with the earlier six-handed Virginia reels—they were both longways sets with weaving figures (or heys), a promenade (or chassé) down the center, and a cast-off down the outside—and it became known as "The Virginia Reel" (with a capital *R*), appearing as such in a written program for a "Cotillion Party" at the Park House in Boston in 1835, where it was danced at the end of the evening.[22]

The earliest printed description of the figures for the Virginia Reel can be found in *Durang's Terpsichore; or, Ball Room Guide* of 1848. By that time the differences between the American dance and the English "Sir Roger de Coverley" had been clearly defined. Durang describes a variant of the ending figure: In addition to reeling down the line, the top couple, upon reaching the bottom of the set, dances ("chassés") back up the middle of the set to the top and then separates ("casts off"), leading the other dancers in single file lines down the outside. The dancers rejoin their partners at the bottom of the set and march back up to their original places. Finally, the top couple dances ("chassés") down the center, taking its place at the bottom of the set.[23] Another version of the ending figure, one that is commonly used today, appears in a dance manual published in 1868: the lead couple makes an arch at the bottom of the set and all of the other couples pass through the arch to the top of the set.[24]

Figure 8.4. "Soldier's Ball at Huntsville, Alabama—Dancing the 'Virginia Reel.'" *Harper's Weekly* 8 (April 9, 1864)

By the mid-nineteenth century, the Virginia Reel had become popular in ballrooms throughout the country, including in the South, where it took the place of the older six-handed reels at plantation balls. William Gilmore Simms of South Carolina lamented this change in 1854: "Many persons, thinking [the six-handed reel] too fatiguing, have fancied that the Virginia reel [Reel] might be a happy substitute for it. But this is long and languid. It is like diluted spirits, substituted for pure champagne."[25]

As with the other fashionable European American set dances that were featured at antebellum balls in the South, the Virginia Reel also became popular at slave frolics. Charles Lanman wrote of slaves dancing the Virginia Reel at a corn shucking in Georgia in 1850, and ten years later, two English visitors encountered it on a plantation near Montgomery, Alabama: "The men seemed to shuffle on their heels in a wonderful manner and a negro was standing on a chair, calling out what figures were to be performed in the Virginia Reel, which they were dancing."[26] Former slave Tom Mills recalled dancing the Virginia Reel at a wedding party in Texas, and Harriet Jones of North Carolina told of slave frolics at Christmastime that would "break up with de Virginny Reel."[27] Here, as at the white dances, it was danced at the end of the evening.

Despite its popularity on Southern plantations, there is no evidence that the Virginia Reel was ever widely known in the southern Appalachian backcountry during the nineteenth century. Nonetheless, the local-color writers who wrote of the southern mountains in the 1870s and 1880s refer to this dance. By that time it was no longer considered fashionable in urban ballrooms,[28] so its inclusion in their narratives may have been simply a way to illustrate the backwardness of the region. Another explanation is that these writers had heard locals refer to Southern square dances generically as "Virginia reels." Whatever the case, by intent or out of ignorance of the vernacular traditions, these writers created the misconception that the Virginia Reel was popular in rural Appalachia. In a story set in the Allegheny Mountains of West Virginia that appeared in *Harper's New Monthly Magazine* in 1872, David Hunter Strother alludes to this dance at a rural frolic: "The old house shook to the chimney tops with the cadenced tramp of many feet. . . . So fast and furious was the reel that our entrance was unheeded. Dilly, the fiddler, occupied a chair elevated upon a table, . . . [the dancers] whirling right and left, casting off, promenading, and hey down the middle with a reckless jollity."[29] In "The Dancin' Party at Harrison's Cove" (1878), a short story set in the Tennessee mountains, Mary Noailles Murfree likewise writes of two dancers "flying down the middle together" in an "unending reel."[30] The Virginia Reel also appears in Katherine Sherwood Bonner McDowell's "The Bran Dance at the Apple Settlement" (1881), a short story set during the antebellum period in the Cumberland Mountains of East Tennessee: "Men on one side, women on the other. It was a reel they were to dance. . . . Down the middle danced the leading pair, and separating with an air of being braced for duty, began their advances at opposite ends of the line."[31]

Figure 8.5. "The Bran Dance"—The Virginia Reel (Katherine Sherwood Bonner McDowell, "The Bran Dance at the Apple Settlement," *Dialect Tales*, 1883)

It is uncertain how much firsthand knowledge these writers had of the dance traditions of rural Appalachia. Strother, who grew up in Martinsburg, Virginia (now West Virginia), but left the region to study art, likely knew the most. Although Murfree spent summers at a resort in the Cumberland Mountains, she was an outsider from an upper-class family in Murfreesboro, Tennessee, and McDowell, who was born in Mississippi, lived in Boston. A more knowledgeable source (though biased in her own way) would be folk music and dance collector Annabel Morris Buchanan, who in the 1930s helped organize the White Top Folk Festival in Virginia. She wrote, "I have never found the Virginia Reel ('Sir Roger de Coverly') danced as such in the mountains."[32] This dance does not appear on any of the 78-rpm recordings of Southern callers made in the 1920s and 1930s, and it is also missing from the dances documented by Cecil Sharp and Maude Karpeles in Kentucky in 1917 and the following year in Virginia. If they had encountered it, Sharp surely would have recognized it and perhaps touted its English heritage as further evidence of an Anglo-Saxon presence in Appalachia.

At the turn of the twentieth century the Virginia Reel developed a new identity. No longer simply an obsolete social dance from the mid-nineteenth century, it began to be mistakenly promoted as a colonial-era dance. This misrepresentation of the dance appears to have been invented and popularized by the Daughters of the American Revolution (DAR), a hereditary patriotic society founded in 1890. At that time, millions of immigrants were coming to the United States from Southern and Eastern Europe, and the DAR sought to reaffirm America's Anglo-Saxon colonial heritage and identity (more on this in chapter 15). As reported in the *Daughters of the American Revolution Magazine*, by the late 1890s various chapters of the DAR were dancing the Virginia Reel at Colonial-themed costume parties. In 1898 in Eire, Pennsylvania, following the singing of the "Star-Spangled Banner," DAR members, wearing colonial costumes and powdered wigs, celebrated George and Martha Washington's wedding anniversary by dancing "the old-fashioned dance, the 'Virginia Reel.'"[33] At another event, held on George Washington's birthday in Gouverneur, New York, in 1900, the dances ("mostly the old type employed in the colonial days") likewise included the Virginia Reel.[34] Before long, this dance was also being featured in school pageants. Instructions for a Colonial ball that include the "old-fashioned dance, the 'Virginia Reel,'" can be found in *Masquerades, Tableaux and Drills* (1906). Performed by boys and girls ("colonial dames and squires") in Colonial costumes, this dance was to be accompanied by "any appropriate selection of patriotic airs for the 'Virginia Reel,'" played by a pianist.[35]

The Virginia Reel is likewise portrayed as a colonial-era dance in an illustration that accompanies a poem that appeared in the *Richmond* [Virginia] *Planet* in 1908. In "The Old Virginia Reel: A Christmas Reverie in Verse," the poet Robertus Love accurately refers to the "old Virginia reel" as being popular ("some half a hundred years ago") before the war. The illustrator, however, seems to have picked the wrong war (the Revolutionary War instead of the Civil War) and depicts dancers in powdered wigs and colonial dress.[36]

Folk dance educator Elizabeth Burchenal (1877–1959) unwittingly perpetuated this myth in 1918, when she included the Virginia Reel in her collection of American "Folk-Dances," *American Country Dances, vol. 1*. Burchenal had founded the American Folk-Dance Society in 1916, and though she admits that the Virginia Reel was known "more as a society dance than a country-dance," she justifies its inclusion in this publication because it was "considered by many as the most representative American folk-dance." In accord with the authors of numerous nineteenth-century dance manuals, Burchenal writes that the Virginia Reel is "nothing more or less than the well-known popular English country-dance known as 'Sir Roger de Coverly,'" but she mistakenly claims that it was "brought by the English to Virginia" during colonial times.[37] There is no evidence, however, that "Sir Roger de Coverly" was ever known in colonial Virginia; in fact, the early references to this "society dance" are not from Virginia but instead are from Washington and the Northeast.

As early as 1915 Burchenal was supervising the production of recordings made by the Victor Record Company that were intended to accompany her folk dance curriculum in schools and recreation programs, and the advertisements for these records reveal the changing perception of the Virginia Reel.[38] One of these recordings, "Country Dance (Virginia Reel)" (Victor 17160), was advertised in 1915 as an appropriate way "to celebrate Lincoln's Birthday."[39] Four years later, however, following the publication of the Virginia Reel in Burchenal's folk dance book, this same recording was being promoted for school celebrations of patriotism (with children dressed in "colonial costumes") in honor of Washington's birthday.[40] Later that same year Victor's competitor, Columbia Records, recommended its recording, "Sir Roger De Coverly, a Colonial or Virginia Reel" (Columbia A3079), for use at May Day festivals.[41]

Thanks to the folk dance and recreation movement, the Virginia Reel did eventually become known in Appalachia during the twentieth century. In 1926, as chair of the American Folk-Dance Society, Burchenal initiated a "campaign" to make the Virginia Reel and several other dances (Sicilian circle, quadrille, waltz, and polka) "universally known" throughout America, and she began to teach them to educators across the country at "Folk Dance Institutes."[42] That same year, Grace Ryan, a physical education professor from Michigan, included the Virginia Reel in her *Handbook for Dances of Our Pioneers*.[43] Thanks to Burchenal, Ryan, and other dance educators, the Virginia Reel became part of the standard physical education curriculum taught in schools throughout the United States. Cherokee dancer Walker Calhoun (1919–2012) and Surry County dance caller James Lawson (1928–2011), both from rural North Carolina, and Charlie Whitaker (1929–2009) of eastern Kentucky, were among the many people who, as children in Appalachia, learned this dance at school.[44]

* * *

Today, having been taught to several generations of children through physical education, recreation, and folk dance programs, the Virginia Reel has become a folk dance known in communities across the country. Variants of it have been exported as part of the standard ceilidh dance repertoire of the British Isles. (In Scotland it is known as "Strip the Willow"; in Ireland, "The Haymakers Jig"; in England, "Drops of Brandy.") This dance, however, has changed from its original form in the mid-1800s. By the 1930s the long, drawn-out opening movements of the nineteenth-century ballroom dance were being performed by all of the couples simultaneously, each person with his or her partner across the set. Beth Tolman and Ralph Page wrote in 1937 that this updated version of the dance in New Hampshire "seems to fit the temper of modern times a great deal better" when compared with the "old dance which never failed, when announced, to call forth groans and bored expressions."[45] Likewise, in Colorado, Lloyd Shaw wrote in 1939 that this "new form of the dance" was "gradually growing in favor." Shaw mentions another twentieth-century innovation, the top-couple sashaying down the center and back before reeling down the line[46]—how Rhett Butler and Scarlett O'Hara dance it in the film *Gone with the Wind*, made that same year. These changes livened up this formerly "long and languid" nineteenth-century ballroom dance and transformed it into the spirited American folk dance known by dancers across the country today.

9 Religion and Dancing

As a teenager growing up in rural western North Carolina in the 1940s, Loyal Jones found himself caught between two worlds: his church, and the temptations of music and dancing at the nearby John C. Campbell Folk School. Jones, who later became the founder and director of the Appalachian Center at Berea College, was born in 1928. His parents were tenant farmers, and as fundamentalist Southern Baptists, they "looked with some suspicion on dancing." He recalled, "I think people were uneasy with the whole business of sexual maturation, with young people being too close together. With their arms around each other and so forth; it might give them ideas." On nights when his church's revivals coincided with dances at the Folk School, he said, "You certainly wouldn't make the choice of going to a dance rather than to the revival in your own church." He admitted, however, "I would sometimes sort of slip out and go down and dance a while and maybe come back and be seen at both places."[1]

The conflict between religion and dancing has a long history. In the sixteenth century John Calvin condemned social dancing as the work of the devil and an "incitement to whoredom."[2] In 1632 English Puritan William Prynne declared that "all mixt effeminate, lascivious, amorous dancing [is] utterly unlawful unto Christians," and he preached that by participating, dancers were apt to "incite themselves or others to lust."[3]

Following the arrival of a French dancing master in Boston, Puritan minister Increase Mather wrote an antidance treatise in 1685, titled "An Arrow against Profane and Promiscuous Dancing Drawn out of the Quiver of the Scriptures." Borrowing many of his arguments from earlier European writers, Mather cites Scripture to condemn "Mixt or Promiscuous Dancing," which he defined as "Men and Women (be they elder or younger persons) [dancing] together." According to Mather, "Scripture condemns Promiscuous dancing" because dancing violates, or may lead to a violation of, the Seventh Commandment—Thou shalt not commit adultery. He warned parents not to entrust their children to dancing masters, whom he claimed encouraged lascivious behavior. He likewise denounced disorderly reveling, which he saw as heathen and pleasing to the devil.[4] Despite Mather's disapproval, social dancing continued to grow in popularity in New England, in homes and taverns as well as at weddings and other festive occasions. Dancing was prohibited by law only if it disturbed the civic order or if it was perceived to be a pagan ritual, such as maypole dancing.

Since Mather's time, religious leaders of various denominations across America have selectively used passages from the Bible to condemn various forms of dancing (usually whatever form is currently popular with young people) from a religious and moral point of view. Objections to dancing have varied over time, but they tend to fall into four general categories: dancing is an expression of vanity and a sinful worldly pleasure that contradicts the ideal of quiet introspection and piety; formal dances are flagrant displays of luxury and self-indulgence and an irrational waste of money and time that could be better spent on charity and serving God; dancing is associated with alcohol and drunkenness; and dancing encourages sexual promiscuity and the violation of the Seventh Commandment.[5]

As the popularity of dancing increased in America during the eighteenth century, so did opposition from church leaders. This was true in the South as well as in New England. While visiting the Southern colonies in 1739, English evangelist George Whitefield encountered numerous dancing masters throughout eastern North Carolina, and he preached against balls and dancing assemblies, claiming that dancing diverted the mind and soul from God. On New Year's Day in 1740 he attempted to stop a dance at an inn near the South Carolina border: "It being New Year's Day, several of the neighbours were met together to divert themselves by dancing country dances. By the advice of my companions, I went in amongst them whilst a woman was dancing a jig. At my first entrance I endeavoured to shew the folly of such entertainments, and to convince her how well pleased the devil was at every step she took. For some time she endeavoured to outbrave me; neither the fiddler nor she desisted; but at last she gave over, and the musician laid aside his instrument."[6] Apparently, Whitefield's influence on this fiddler and dancer was short-lived, for later that night, after having gone to bed, he heard the music and dancing resume.

Itinerant Anglican preacher Charles Woodmason was likewise appalled by the rural frolics he encountered in the Carolina backcountry on the eve of the Revolutionary War, but he also condemned the provincial magistrates, whom he found "rioting in Luxury and Extravagance—Balls—Concerts—Assemblies—Private Dances—Cards—Dice."[7] At that time, however, even in small towns, dancing was considered to be a necessary part of one's education, so despite the efforts of Whitefield, Woodmason, and others, dancing schools, balls, and rural frolics continued to proliferate throughout the country. In an effort to counter religious opposition, dancing masters placed greater emphasis on etiquette and proper behavior for "ladies" and "gentlemen" at their dancing schools.

In some cases religious leaders were successful in the suppression of dancing. One account tells of Clarinda (1730–1832), a female slave fiddler in South Carolina, who "learned to play on the violin, and usually, on the first day of the week, sallied forth with her instrument, in order to draw persons of both sexes together, who, not having the fear of God before their eyes, delighted, like herself, in sinful and pernicious amusements." One day, "whilst participating in a dance, she was seized with fits, and convulsively fell to the ground. From that moment she lost her love of dancing, and no more engaged in this vain amusement."[8] Clarinda later became a preacher.

The religious attacks on dancing intensified following the Great Revival of 1801, when as many as twenty thousand Methodists, Baptists, and Presbyterians joined together for a camp-meeting revival at Cane Ridge, Kentucky (near Lexington). That same year, sixteen-year-old Peter Cartwright attended a wedding in southwestern Kentucky: "There was a great deal of drinking and dancing," he wrote, "[which] was very common at marriages those days." Later that night, at home, Cartwright, like Clarinda, had a religious conversion. He decided to quit dancing as well as playing cards and subsequently became an itinerant Methodist preacher and circuit rider. In his autobiography Cartwright tells of traveling through the Cumberland Mountains of Tennessee in 1820 and staying overnight at an inn. A dance party took place that night, and he was invited to join in. Pretending to participate, he took his place on the dance floor, but as the fiddler was about to play, Cartwright dropped to his knees and began to pray. Some of the dancers joined him in prayer, but others, including the black fiddler, fled, thus breaking up the dance party.[9]

A similar antidance tactic was employed the following year in Randolph County, North Carolina, where a rural dance was turned into a prayer meeting: "When the young men began to select their partners for the first dance, one of the most popular girls there refused to join the rest; and when the music started, she dropped to her knees and prayed aloud. The fiddler fled for home and most of the dancers likewise sought protection in escape, believing that the Devil was in hot pursuit. The less superstitious who stood their ground were soon won by the praying girl. From that time, prayer meetings took the place of dance frolics in that neighborhood."[10]

In other communities, however, dancing won out. Robert Nelson Mount, the brother of American painter William Sidney Mount, was an itinerant dancing master who taught in small towns in central and western Georgia and in South Carolina between 1836 and 1840. From Monticello, Georgia, he wrote to his brother in New York: "I spent five of six weeks quite pleasantly at Hillsboro, and met with good success in my business. My class was principally made up of back sliding Methodists, and on that account it was called the Methodist Dancing School."[11] Through letters from his brother, Mount kept up to date with the latest and most fashionable dances of New York, which he taught to dancers in the rural South.

Due to its association with dancing, church leaders also condemned the fiddle, which they portrayed as the Devil's instrument—the "Devil's Box." The challenge of mastering this difficult instrument has no doubt added to its mystique, and stories of fiddlers making Faustian contracts with the Devil have proliferated in European and American folklore as well as popular culture throughout the centuries. Often, as in Washington Irving's short story "The Devil and Tom Walker" (1824), Satan is perched on a stump. In this vein, the African American folklore of the South sets out that one learns to play the Devil's instrument by going to a fork in a road or a crossroads at midnight.[12] An account from the late 1700s, predating the legend of bluesman Robert Johnson selling his soul to the devil at the crossroads, tells the story of a free black who lived in Lincoln County in the Piedmont of North Carolina. This young man purchased a fiddle and asked the advice of an elderly friend on how he should learn to play it.

> He was told to go out into the middle of a field, get into a hollow stump and devote three evenings to practice, when the devil would appear and learn him. He went into the stump the third evening with fear and trepidation, and looking around, "not a leaf was movin in de trees, not a speck of cloud in de sky, it was a perfect calm and de sun shinin in spendor. I got into de stump and commenced drawin de bow cross de violin when all at once there was a noise as if a great tree had fallen, de limbs and leaves strikin right on de stump sir." This was the arrival of his satanic majesty. He received instructions, and from that time on was an expert violinist.[13]

This fiddler is reported to have died around 1880, at well over one hundred years old.

The association between the fiddle and the Devil survives today in the titles of many Southern dance tunes—"Devil's Dream" (also known as "Devil among the Tailors"), "Hell Broke Loose in Georgia," "Hell among the Yearlings," "Devil in the Woodpile," "Devil on a Stump," "Whip the Devil Round the Stump," and others—and in 1979, Charlie Daniels revived this image with his country-rock song, "The Devil Went Down to Georgia." Daniels's song tells the story of a fiddle contest with the Devil, and as in the earlier legends, the Devil plays the fiddle on a hickory stump.

The Ring Shout

When slaves converted to Christianity in America, the Protestant Church discouraged their participation in secular dancing. The ceremonial ring dances, which had been used in Africa to honor the ancestors, however, survived as a religious ritual. Charles Lyell, an English geologist who visited a plantation near Savannah, Georgia, in 1845, wrote: "Of dancing and music the negroes are passionately fond. On the Hopeton plantation above twenty violins have been silenced by the Methodist missionaries. . . . At the Methodist prayer-meetings, they are permitted to move round rapidly in a ring, joining hands in a token of brotherly love, presenting first the right hand and then the left, in which manoeuvre, I am told, they sometimes contrive to take enough exercise to serve as a substitute for the dance." Comparing it to the French circle dance, the Boulangère, Lyell refers to it as "a kind of spiritual boulanger."[14]

This ritual, which became known as the Ring Shout, was described by an observer in Port Royal, South Carolina in 1865: "The 'shout' is a peculiar service in which a dozen or twenty participants jog slowly around a circle behind each other with a peculiar shuffle of the feet and shake of the arms, keeping time to a droning chant and hand-clapping maintained by the bystanders. As the exercise continues, the excitement increases and occasionally becomes hysterical."[15]

The Ring Shout incorporated several aspects of the African dance tradition. The footwork involved shuffling steps with the feet close to the ground—"The foot is hardly taken from the floor, and the progression is mainly due to a jerking, pitching motion"[16]—and the participants moved counterclockwise in a single-file circle accompanied by vocalizations and handclapping. To avoid the condemnation of the church and to differentiate the Ring Shout from secular dancing, the participants were careful not to cross their legs or let their feet leave the floor. That would have been considered "dancing" and therefore "worldly" and sinful.[17] This belief is conveyed in an African American folktale from North Carolina in which Brer Rabbit leads dancers astray with his fiddling. "Brer Rabbit worked the fiddle in his own devilish way at all the dances and picnics in the country, and made people lose their religion. And a whole lot of them had been turned out of their churches because they had crossed their feet to his dancing tunes, because when Brer Rabbit played, there aren't any feet around that can take any notice whether they are crossing or not!"[18]

Play Parties and Singing Games

In rural communities throughout America where religious opposition to social dancing was strong, play parties and singing games sometimes took the place of dances. These dance-like activities for young people, which were accompanied by singing and the clapping of hands, rather than the "Devil's Box" (the fiddle), were not considered to be "dancing" and were therefore tolerated by the church.

Singing games for young children typically involved skipping, marching, and play-acting, and the participants would act out the story told in the lyrics

Figure 9.1. Singing Game at the Pine Mountain Settlement School with lone dancer in the middle of the ring (Pine Mountain, Kentucky, c. 1920s). Pine Mountain Settlement School Collections, PMSS Library, Bledsoe, Kentucky

of the song (for example, "The farmer takes a wife . . ."). Many of the American singing games evolved from earlier examples from the British Isles, and as with the traditional ballads, the lyrics sometimes retained references to the old country ("London Bridge is falling down . . ."). In the South this folk tradition was shared across racial lines as black and white children played together. Henry Bedford, who was born a slave on a plantation in Tennessee in 1859, recalled the singing games of his childhood, which included "Goose and Gander," "Hide and Seek," "Drop the Handkerchief," and "Ring 'round Rosie."[19] African American children, however, also played African-derived ring and line games, such as the "ring-play songs" of the Georgia Sea Islands.[20] Children's singing games that are still known today, having been taught to many generations of American school children, include "The Farmer in the Dell," "Ring around the Rosie," and "London Bridge."

Singing games for teenagers or young adults were called "play parties," or simply "plays." These involved more complex figures adopted from the country dances, reels, and square dances of the adults, and they often entailed choosing partners and sometimes kissing (as in the game "Spin the Bottle"). Like the singing games for younger children, the dance prompts were embedded within the lyrics that were sung by the participants.

Play parties are often attributed to the church's condemnation of dancing, and in some communities they were the only type of dancing permitted. Elsewhere, however, play parties existed side by side with square dances, so it was not always a case of one or the other. Their prevalence in rural communities, rather than in towns or cities during the nineteenth century, may have had more to do with cultural and social isolation. Play parties tended to be more common in newer frontier settlements, where dance musicians may not have been available.[21] Historian Henry Howe wrote of the "dancing and other innocent amusements" of the settlers along the Ohio River in the early 1800s: "If they had no fiddler (which was not very uncommon), some one of the company would supply the deficiency by singing."[22]

An early reference to play parties in the southern backcountry appears in David Crockett's autobiography. He recalls going to an all-night dance in Tennessee as a young man in 1805: "We continued our frolic till near day, when we joined in some plays, calculated to amuse the youngsters."[23] An anonymous, unauthorized "autobiography" of Crockett published in 1833 likewise testifies to Crockett's love of dancing and the "old fashioned plays . . . which served to help him along amazingly" at courting. It tells of a rural frolic following a neighborhood "reaping and flax-pulling" around 1806:

> Plays which had been fashionable when their grandmothers were girls, were called up, and wearied out. Nothing seemed to give more enjoyment than a play termed, "We are on our way to Baltimore" . . . [which] derived its chief charm from the circumstance, that every couple who composed it, had to kiss each other at stated pauses. It consisted of a wild and irregular dance, during which, with measured steps, the following lines were sweetly chanted:
>
> We are on our way to Baltimore,
> With two behind, and two before;
> Around, around, around we go,
> Where oats, peas, beans and barley grow,
> In waiting for somebody. (A kiss.)
>
> Tis thus the farmer sows his seed,
> Folds his arms, and takes his ease,
> Stamps his feet, and claps his hands,
> Wheels around, and thus he stands,
> In waiting for somebody. (Another kiss.)
>
> David's partner was a bewitching creature, and ere they had finished dancing "We are on our way to Baltimore," she had led him far on the road to Love. . . . For we will here find him, though introduced as a stranger, engaged to be married before the evening is over.[24]

With such quick results, it is no wonder that play parties and kissing games were popular with young people.

During the nineteenth century new play parties were invented to accompany the popular songs of the minstrel stage. One of these was "Old Dan Tucker," which within a few years of its publication in 1843 was being sung throughout America. By the early 1860s this song had inspired an "amusing dance for the parlor" called "Old Dan Tucker" (also known as the "Ninepin Reel" or "Nine-Pin Quadrille"), which Sharp and Karpeles encountered in Kentucky as "Tucker."[25] The absence of "Old Dan Tucker" from William Newell's 1883 collection, *Games and Songs of American Children*, suggests that it had not yet become common as a play party. By the early twentieth century, however, it was known not only in the southern mountains but in the Ozarks, the Midwest, Oklahoma, and Texas.[26]

As in the "Ninepin Reel," "Old Dan Tucker" (the play party) includes an extra dancer in the middle of a four-couple square set. The verse is sung:

> Old Dan Tucker's back in town,
> Swingin' the pretty girls all around,
> First to the east and then to the west,
> Then to the one he loves the best.

While these words are sung, the dancers circle to the left around "Tucker." Then, while the dancers turn their partners with a right hand ("east") and their corners with a left ("west"), "Tucker" attempts to secure a partner. The couples then promenade around the ring, and the dancer left without a partner becomes the next "Tucker." During the Promenade, the chorus is sung:

> Get out of the way old Dan Tucker,
> You're too late to get your supper,
> Supper's over and breakfast's cookin',
> Old Dan Tucker just stands there lookin',

Like many other American play parties, "Old Dan Tucker" is a composite of elements drawn from a variety of sources. Only a few of the lyrics come from the original minstrel song; others are from an earlier English singing game, "Little Sally Waters" (also known as "Little Sally Walker"), and the figures are borrowed from the nineteenth-century quadrilles.

In *Sunny Side of the Cumberland* (1886), a romantic fictional account of outsiders traveling through the Cumberlands of East Tennessee, local-color writer Will Allen Dromgoole mentions the play party, called "Weavily Wheat," which was based on the figures of the Virginia Reel.[27] This play party was popular at church socials in north Georgia and Florida in the 1880s and 1890s, where it was known as "Twistification,"[28] and as recently as the 1940s it was danced at Cumberland Gap, Tennessee (see figure 9.2).

In general, play parties and square dances can be thought of as parallel and complementary forms of recreation that fulfilled the social needs of different age groups in Appalachia. As a child growing up in eastern Kentucky in the first half of the twentieth century, Jean Ritchie experienced both. In her autobiography, *Singing Family of the Cumberlands*, she tells of young people at a molasses making who wanted to have a square dance, but there was no music

Figure 9.2. "Singing Games"—The Virginia Reel as a singing game (Cumberland Gap, Tennessee, c. 1940s). Photo: Joe Clark. Clark Photography Collection, University of North Texas, Denton, Texas

available—"Can't run a set 'thout music. Not a solitary fiddle amongst us." So instead, they play a singing game until a fiddler shows up.[29] Ritchie once told me that whenever a new preacher came to her community, the "dancing" would cease, and they would resort to play parties for a while, but before long, the restriction would be relaxed and the square dances would resume.[30]

By the 1940s play parties were mostly extinct, and they are no longer a part of the rural Appalachian culture today, but their influence can still be seen in the dance music of the region. A number of fiddle tunes in the Southern repertoire originated as play party songs. At one time, "Old Joe Clark" was a play party in Virginia, North Carolina, Tennessee, Kentucky, and West Virginia, as well as further west in Mississippi, Texas, Oklahoma, and Indiana, and "Fly around My Pretty Little Miss" (also known as "Pretty Little Pink" or "Coffee Grows on White Oak Trees") was a play party in North Carolina, Kentucky, the Ozarks, and the Midwest. Other Southern fiddle tunes that were once play parties include "Cindy," "Fire on the Mountain," "Polly Put the Kettle On," "Black-Eyed Susie," and "Sally Goodin" as well as the song "Jennie Jenkins." The lyrics from long-forgotten play parties survive today as nonsensical floating verses that are often sung to these and other old-time fiddle tunes.[31]

* * *

Although religious opposition to dancing had declined by the time Sharp and Karpeles visited Appalachia in the twentieth century, it was still considered by many to be a sin and was prohibited at many of the church-sponsored schools in the southern mountains. Dancing was, however, allowed at the Pine Mountain School, because at the time the school was founded, in 1913, that community had no established church.[32] In Ashe County, North Carolina, even though dancing had become part of the physical education curriculum by the mid-1920s, the school board, under the influence of the local Baptist church, forbade schoolteachers from attending dances.[33] In the 1930s, "dancing of any sort was prohibited" by the Presbyterian Board of the Asheville Farm School (now Warren Wilson College), also in western North Carolina. Instead, on Saturday nights the school's staff and their spouses were required to participate in singing games, taught by the school's farm manager.[34] At the John C. Campbell Folk School, as a way to avoid condemnation from the church and the local community, dancing was referred to as "folk recreation."[35] Although by the 1940s many denominations no longer opposed dancing—it may have seemed insignificant compared to bigger issues, such as the Great Depression and World War II—some conservative Baptists in the southern mountains still disapprove of it today, and at regional music venues dancers invariably refrain from dancing during gospel songs.

10 Couple Dances

Rebecca Latimer Felton (1835–1930)[1] grew up in the frontier settlement of Marthasville (renamed Atlanta in 1845) in northwest Georgia. Recalling her childhood in the early 1840s, she wrote:

> It was a cold day in the late fall and my father and mother, with my small self, reached Thompson's Hotel in Decatur, where the excursionists assembled and where a fine dinner was provided. . . . Maria Gertrude Kyle took a seat in our barouche on my mother's invitation, and she was well known as authoress and poetess, in our few Georgia papers. She had lately married and her new clothes interested me, and I was even more interested to see her dance that night in some of the new sort of dances, different from the Virginia Reel and cotillions that I had been accustomed to.[2]

Figure 10.1. Couple dancing accompanied by fiddle, banjo, and harmonica (c. 1870s). Courtesy: Lydia Hamessley

These "new sort of dances" that so fascinated this young girl in rural Georgia were not set dances, like the reels and square dances, but couple dances. They had recently become fashionable in the urban ballrooms of Europe and America, and during Felton's lifetime they became a part of the rural dance tradition of the southern mountains.

Round Dances

Couple dances have been part of the social dance repertoire of America since colonial times, when formal balls typically opened with stately French minuets. These ostentatious dances of the aristocracy, which were performed by one couple at a time, were, however, more of a performance than a social dance, and they were becoming obsolete by the early 1800s. Taking their place, during the first half of the nineteenth century, was a succession of popular European couple dances, in particular the waltz, the polka, and the two-step. These dances became known as "round dances" because the couples progress in a circular path around the perimeter of the floor as they dance. The convention is to travel counterclockwise around the room, the same direction that couples promenade in a square dance (as is the case for roller skaters, ice skaters, track runners, racehorses, and even NASCAR drivers).

The first round dance to become popular in America was the waltz, a triple-meter social dance that became fashionable in Germany in the late eighteenth century. An advertisement for a ball in Philadelphia in 1797 claimed that in addition to "new Quadrille[s], Cotillions, and Reels," the "German Waltz" would be "introduced for the first time in this country." The dancing public was assured that these "new dances will not infringe upon the usual routine of the evening."[3]

The waltz introduced the closed ballroom position, which involved dancers standing face-to-face with arms around each other. This was a radical departure from the earlier set dances in which dancers merely held hands, and to many people these new dances appeared immodest and immoral. In 1832 a visitor from Sweden noted the disapproval of some of the older dancers at a ballroom near Boston: "Waltzing had but lately been introduced in society, in spite of strenuous opposition on the part of elderly ladies. At intervals it was resorted to in the course of the evening, but subject to many restrictions and exceptions."[4]

The term "waltz" means to revolve or turn, and originally this dance entailed a continuous spinning motion—couples turning clockwise while moving counterclockwise around the room. Critics of this new dance claimed that the constant twirling motion posed a danger to the health of women of "delicate constitution," causing "violent emotions" as well as "vertigo and nervous symptoms."[5] In the 1840s, however, the original waltz, the "Waltz á Trios Temps," was replaced by a newer, simpler version, without the constant spinning, and this new form, called the "Waltz á Deux Temps" (or Two-Step Waltz), was adopted by dancers throughout America.

The second of the many types of round dance to become popular in America was the polka, a duple-meter couple dance that originated in Bohemia in the 1830s. With its characteristic turning motion similar to that of the waltz, it was originally known as the "Polka Waltz." In 1856, Philadelphia dancing teacher Charles Durang wrote: "Like the earth in its orbit, the Polka Valse consists of two circles, a great and small one. It turns on its axis while it revolves round its great centre of a circle."[6] In other words, as in the waltz, the couples traveled counterclockwise around the dance floor, while at the same time spinning clockwise, resulting in a "giddy effect."

These and other fashionable round dances, while popular in the cities, were slow to catch on in the rural southern backcountry, where the older set dances were preferred. While visiting Knoxville, Tennessee, in 1858, David Hunter Strother wrote: "I have already attended two balls, and find the ladies eminently handsome and intelligent, and pretty good dancers in the reel. They entirely ignore hoops and the polka, to the great delight of Uncle Broadacre; and even our ladies, yielding to the prevailing sentiment, have lessened the circumference of their skirts by a foot or so, and figure only in reels and cotillions."[7] As late as 1872, Strother claimed that the "polka, mazourka, waltz, or any other round dance" were still unknown in the Allegheny Mountains of West Virginia.[8]

While dancing masters promoted these new round dances as representing a "new era in the art of dancing," church leaders of all denominations saw them as an even greater evil than the earlier reels and square dances, and this no doubt suppressed their popularity in the southern mountains. In an antidance tract originally presented as a sermon in Kentucky in 1849, Baptist preacher William W. Gardner portrayed the "German Waltz and the French Round-dances" as "impure and vain amusement(s)," taught to the "elite" by "carnal professors" and "prostituted by the ungodly." Recycling some of the old arguments against dancing, Gardner condemned waltzing as a "worldly pleasure" that went against the teachings of the Bible. In particular, he objected to the physical contact and close proximity of the closed dance position. He wrote, "There is no disguising the fact, that promiscuous dancing, including the Waltz and Round-dances, to which the 'square dances' naturally lead, are essentially licentious, and legitimately tend to the violation of the Seventh Commandment."[9]

The old-fashioned reels and square dances by comparison appeared more innocent, but they likewise were to be shunned, because like gateway drugs, they were seen to lead to the more promiscuous and addictive round dances. In 1881 an "ecclesiastical court" in Charlottesville, Virginia, considered a proposal to allow square dances as the lesser of two evils, while prohibiting the round dances altogether. During the discussion one of the assembled spoke out, "Ah brethren, I mightily fear that if we authoritatively permit the square dance that some people may soon pinch off the corners and make it a round dance." The proposal to allow square dances did not pass.[10] As with drinking, total abstinence was seen as the only way to avoid downfall and damnation.

As a way to capitalize on the growing popularity of the waltz and the polka, dancing masters began to invent new hybrid set dances that incorporated footwork from the fashionable round dances, and by the 1850s there were "Waltz Cotillons," "Waltz Quadrilles," "Polka Cotillons," "Polka Quadrilles," a "Mazurka Quadrille," and even "Waltz Contra Dances" and "Polka Contra Dances."[11] Urban dancers, however, were more interested in couple dancing, and the older set dances soon became unfashionable relics of the past. Some of the figures of these new quadrilles, though, filtered into the rural Southern dance tradition. In the 1920s, West Virginia caller Ernest Legg called the "Pokey Four," a figure in which two couples polka around each other.[12] (The word "pokey" is slang for Polka, as in the "Hokey-Pokey.") As noted earlier, Cecil Sharp and Maude Karpeles observed a related figure in eastern Kentucky, called the "Waltz-Swing," in which two circles of dancers turn clockwise while at the same time revolving counterclockwise around each other, not unlike the amusement park ride "Tilt-a-Whirl." Today, this figure is still danced by pairs of couples (in circles of four) at square dances in West Virginia, and it is called "Four-by-Four around the Floor."

The waltz and the polka never became as popular in the southern mountains as in the Midwest, and this may account for the relative scarcity of waltzes and polkas in the Appalachian fiddle repertoire. A form of the two-step, however, likely derived from the early "Waltz á Deux Temps," did eventually become widely known during the twentieth century. The common footwork of this couple dance (from the man's point of view) consists of two steps forward, leading with the left foot (step-close-step-close), followed by one step backward, leading with the right foot (step-close). The woman's footwork is opposite. This type of two-step, danced in the closed ballroom position to slow music regardless of the meter, either songs in 2/4 time—"Faded Love" is a favorite—or waltzes in 3/4 time, is popular with dancers today across the rural South from the Blue Ridge to the Ozarks.

The German Cotillion

Building on the popularity of the waltz and the other newly fashionable round dances, a new type of dance called "German Cotillions," or simply "Germans," became popular in American ballrooms in the mid-nineteenth century. Germans were dance parties that combined couple dancing with the playful choosing and exchange (or rejection) of dance partners. With couples seated around the sides of the room, leaving the center open for dancing, a dance leader ("conductor") would initiate game-like situations that involved the trading of dance partners, props, and role playing. The conductor would choose a few couples to begin a designated dance figure, and then, using a whistle, he would signal these dancers to choose new partners. At the end of each dance, amusing party favors would be awarded to the participants: pencils, button-hooks (for shoes), or fans, but more often simply festive decorations made of "colored silk, or muslin, and tinsel" to "pin on the coat or dress, or in the hair, as ornaments for the evening."[13]

Instructions for these new "cotillions" can be found in many nineteenth-century social dance manuals. French dancing master Henri Cellarius, who in 1847 stated that this fashionable dance should be the "essential finale of every ball," provides instructions for more than eighty different figures.[14] Hinting at their playful, sometimes risqué nature, Germans are described by one author as "one of those foreign importations that may be justly suspected of being 'naughty' as well as 'nice.'"[15] As these dances became increasingly popular, new Germans were invented; by 1900, dance manuals included as many as 250 different figures.[16]

One of the most common figures, "The Cushion," is described as follows: "The first couple perform a tour de valse, the gentleman holding a cushion in his left hand; he then presents to the lady the cushion, which she offers to several gentlemen, inviting them to kneel upon it. She withdraws it from those she desires to cheat, and places it before the gentleman with whom she desires to dance."[17] This dance figure may have its origins in an earlier "Cushion Dance" (also known as "John Sanderson"), which appears in John Playford's *The Dancing Master* of 1698.

Another common nineteenth-century German was "Blind Man's Buff":

> Three chairs are placed in the centre of the room. First couple lead off. The conductor takes another gentleman, whom he blindfolds and seats on the centre chair. The lady selects another gentleman, whom she leads (walking on tiptoe) to one of the chairs next to the blind man, whilst she seats herself on the other. The first gentleman then invites the blind man to select from the right or left. If he hits upon the lady, he waltzes with her to her place; if he indicates the gentleman, he must waltz with him, whilst the conductor dances with the lady.[18]

These are just two of the hundreds of figures for the German Cotillion that were once popular in the ballrooms of America. The legacy of this nineteenth-century ballroom fad continues today with party games such as "Musical Chairs" and "Blind Man's Buff" as well as the practice of handing out party favors.

During the nineteenth century, Germans also became popular at the many summer resort hotels that were scattered throughout the southern mountains. In 1837, shortly after the construction of the resort hotel at White Sulphur Springs, (West) Virginia, a visitor wrote: "To-night, for the first time, we had the German cotillion."[19] By 1869 this same resort, which catered to planters from the Deep South, had gained a "national reputation," and the "fashionable" guests, who arrived by railroad from Philadelphia and New York, "danced morning, noon and night, literally. Six nightly balls had proved insufficient to satisfy their hunger, so they had 'morning germans.'"[20] Germans were equally popular at the resort hotels in western North Carolina, where in Asheville during the summer in the 1880s dances were held every weekday night at both the Swannanoa and Eagle Hotels, and at the Swannanoa Hotel even during the day.[21] One visitor in 1884, reporting that "the German was still 'on' at the hotel when we ascended to our chamber [at eleven o'clock]," was "satisfied that Asheville was a lively town."[22]

Dance Mixers

Although the German Cotillions never became widespread at rural frolics in Appalachia, these fashionable dances inspired a number of dance mixers that became popular in the early twentieth century throughout the southern mountains and elsewhere in rural America. Mixers are playful, game-like dances that, like the Germans, involve the exchange of partners. The most common one was the "Paul Jones," supposedly named for John Paul Jones, the Scottish naval officer who fought in the American Revolution.[23] As with the Germans, a designated leader, or master of ceremonies, conducts the dance. The "Paul Jones" begins with any number of couples in a large ring circling to the left, and at a signal from the master of ceremonies (often a whistle), the dancers begin a Grand Right and Left around the room. At another sounding of the whistle, or the call "Paul Jones," the dancers take new partners and waltz or two-step around the room. This is then repeated. A dance manual from 1922 recommends the "Paul Jones" as "an excellent diversion" that "breaks the monotony" of couple dancing, "stimulating enthusiasm by a complete change in dancing partners" and "offering to the self-conscious a sufficient way to overcome their timidity."[24] West Virginia dance caller Bill Ohse (b. 1938) recalls seeing, as a child in the late 1940s, the "Paul Jones" danced on Saturday nights at "beer joints" in Jackson County, West Virginia.[25] In more recent years, this mixer has been popular at community dances in southwest Virginia and the North Carolina Piedmont.[26]

The "Broom Dance" is another common mixer that is sometimes seen at rural community dances in Appalachia. Like the "Paul Jones," it involves couple dancing and changing partners. While couples two-step or waltz around the dance floor, an extra dancer (usually a man) without a partner dances with a broom. At some point the lone dancer drops the broom (loudly) to the floor, and at this signal, everyone takes a new partner, including the lone dancer. As in the game "Musical Chairs," there is a frantic scramble, and someone is left over, without a partner, to dance with the broom. While resembling the Germans in spirit, the widespread popularity of the "Broom Dance" across America may be attributed to Elizabeth Burchenal's folk dance curriculum. In *Dances of the People* (1913) she describes a German dance game, called "Besentanz," in which an extra person dances with a broom, and all of the dancers seek new partners when the broom is dropped to the floor.[27]

The Grand March

During the nineteenth century, formal balls in Europe and America often opened with a promenade figure called the "Grand March" (or "Grand Promenade"). Derived from a seventeenth-century Polish dance called the "Polonaise," this ceremonious processional for couples provided dancers an opportunity to show off their finery and to be seen by others. The "Grande Polonaise" is mentioned in an English social dance manual in 1815, and in 1826 a "promenade . . . resembling a Polonaise with pretty figures" took place between the two halves of a concert in New Harmony, Indiana.[28]

The Grand March consisted of a variety of figures directed by a conductor or master of ceremonies. It begins with a Grand Promenade in which all of the couples promenade counterclockwise around the perimeter of the dance hall and then up the center of the floor toward the musicians. Upon reaching the top of the hall the couples turn alternately to the left and to the right and

Figure 10.2. Grand March at the Farmer's Ball (Swannanoa, North Carolina, c. 1940s). Author's collection

promenade down the sides of the hall. They proceed back up the center in lines of four and then again in lines of eight dancers side by side.[29]

The Grand Promenade and other figures of the Grand March were common in the ballrooms of the resort hotels in western North Carolina during the second half of the nineteenth century, and being compatible with the big-ring format of the region's square dances, they were adopted into the local dance tradition. One of these figures is described in a social dance manual from 1841: "All march forward till they arrive at the end of the room; the ladies turn to the right and gentlemen to the left . . . the ladies march down on one side and the gentlemen on the other, till they arrive at the opposite end of the room—here the ladies meet their partners, and taking arms, again turn up the room to their place."[30] Dancers in western North Carolina today would recognize this single-file figure as the "King's Highway" (when the ladies go to the left and the gents go to the right, it is called the "Queen's Highway"). In the "Arbor March" couples raise joined arms to make an arch, creating a tunnel through which all of the other couples pass. This figure became known in western North Carolina as "London Bridge."

Another of the figures of the Grand March, the "March Jig," is described in a dance manual from 1863: "The column separates, forming in two lines facing each other, the gentlemen standing directly opposite to their partners. The march music then stops, and is followed by a jig [a fast tune]." The top couple balances and swings and then

> . . . polka[s] or promenade[s] down the middle, taking their positions below the last couple. As soon as the first couple commences to promenade down the middle, the next couple begins to balance and turn; and when the second couple has gone down the middle, the next couple commences, and so on for all the rest. As fast as they leave from the top, the entire lines move up, so that every couple starts from the same place, and takes position below the previous couple, until the first couple have arrived at the head again.[31]

This nineteenth-century dance figure, in which each couple dances down the middle showing off their individual steps and style, is known by cloggers today as "Rise and Shine."

By the time square dance teams began to perform on stage in western North Carolina in the late 1920s, these nineteenth-century ballroom figures were well established in the local tradition; today, nearly a hundred years later, they remain a part of the standard choreography of southern Appalachian clogging and smooth dance teams (see chapter 13).

In recent years, at community dances in western North Carolina, I have encountered a dance mixer called "The Shuffle," which may be related to the "March Jig." Any number of dancers can participate, and no partners are required. As in the "March Jig," the dancers form two lines that keep moving up the hall toward the band while the music plays—the men in one line and the women in the other. The two dancers at the heads of the lines swing each other and then promenade (or dance) down the center, rejoining their respective lines, at the bottom. As long as the number of participants in the two lines are unequal, the dancers find themselves paired up with a new partner each time they reach the top, hence the name "Shuffle" (as in a deck of cards).

When the Grand March takes place at a square dance in Appalachia today, it often concludes with the dancers being led in a serpentine path or a spiraling coil. As mentioned earlier, snaking and spiral figures were common in Native American dances as well as in the folk dance traditions of Europe. Dances with human chains, however, were also popular in ballrooms on both sides of the Atlantic during the nineteenth century. One of these spiraling figures, described by French dancing master Henri Cellarius in 1847, is called "The Labyrinth." Starting with a circle moving clockwise, one dancer leads the others, with hands joined, in an ever-narrowing spiral. Upon reaching the middle, the first couple waltzes out of the spiral ("labyrinth"), followed by the other couples.[32] In another version, from 1865, as the coil becomes tight, the leader passes under the arms of the other dancers to reach the outside; the others follow without dropping hands.[33] And in a third variant, known in the 1880s as the "Serpentine March," after the dancers are led single file into the spiral, but before the coil becomes tight, the leader turns and leads the dancers back (counterclockwise) between the coils to the outside.[34] Sharp and Karpeles encountered this figure in Kentucky.[35] Now known as "Wind up the Ball of Yarn," it is still common today as a closing figure for big-ring square dances in Appalachia.

* * *

The great popularity of the waltz, the polka, the two-step, and the other "round dances" of the nineteenth century transformed the social dance traditions of America. Unlike the earlier set dances, these "new sort of dances" that so fascinated Rebecca Felton in rural Georgia in the early 1840s were danced in the closed ballroom position, and they involved male-female partnering that was independent of the other dancers on the floor. Despite the strong objections of religious leaders, these "promiscuous" couple dances (the "waltz and her more licentious sisters") became increasingly popular, and by the late nineteenth century they had replaced the older country dances, reels, and quadrilles in ballrooms of urban America. Although set dances survived in Appalachia, elements of these urban ballroom dances filtered into the rural dance tradition. The waltz swing (closed ballroom position) replaced the older two-handed swing, dance mixers modeled after the Germans (such as the "Paul Jones" and the "Broom Dance") became popular, and the two-step, no longer considered "promiscuous," became common throughout the rural South. Figures from the Grand March, popular in the ballrooms of mountain resort hotels, likewise became incorporated into the square dances of western North Carolina, and these subsequently became the standard choreography of clogging teams. The Grand March also served as the inspiration and model for the Cakewalk, an African American dance that ridiculed the pompous formality of plantation balls (discussed in chapter 11), and the legacy of this Promenade figure continues today at cotillion balls for young debutantes in the South, not to mention the yearly ritual of the formal high-school prom (short for Promenade).[36]

11 The Cakewalk

At community dances in Appalachia today, it is not unusual for a cakewalk to take place during an evening of square dances, flatfooting, and two-steps. A cakewalk is a fundraising activity, and, for a small fee, participants have a chance to win a donated cake. How the winner is determined varies from community to community. Sometimes numbered paper plates are arranged in a large circle on the dance floor, and as the music plays, the participants walk (or dance) single file, moving counterclockwise around the circle. When the music stops, as in the game "Musical Chairs," each dancer steps onto a

Figure 11.1. Cakewalk (Glenville, West Virginia, 2011). Photo: Phil Jamison

plate. A number is then drawn, and the dancer with the winning number "takes the cake." This is just one of many ways to decide the contest. At one community, near Buckhannon, West Virginia, in 1915, a fishing pole was lowered at a given signal to designate the winner.[1] Elsewhere in West Virginia (in the 1990s) the winner was chosen by spinning a bowling pin, as in the game "Spin the Bottle."[2] Sometimes cakewalks are conducted more like raffles, with the dancers purchasing numbered tickets before the music begins. However the winner is decided, the cakewalk is repeated until all of the donated cakes have been "walked off."

Cakewalks have a long history that precedes their popularity as a dance game in rural Appalachia, and it is a story that illustrates the repeated exchange of music and dance across racial lines and social classes in America. While these dances were inspired by African American dances that took place on Southern plantations in the nineteenth century, the practice of awarding cakes to dancers is in fact older than that. An account from 1682 describes a dance contest in County Westmeath, Ireland, in which a cake is given to the couple that can dance the longest:

> On the patron-day in most parishes, as also on the feasts of Easter and Whitsuntide, the more ordinary sort of people meet near the ale-house in the afternoon, on some convenient spot of ground, and dance for the cake; here to be sure the piper fails not of diligent attendance; the cake to be danced for is provided at the charge of the ale wife, and is advanced on a board on the top of a pike about ten foot high; . . . the whole number of dancers begin all at once in a large ring, a man and a woman, and dance around the bush, so is this garland called, and the piper, as long as they are able to hold out; they that hold out longest at the exercise, win the cake and apples, and then the ale-wife's trade goes on.[3]

These cake dances, which continued in western Ireland throughout the eighteenth century and into the nineteenth, are thought by some to be the origin of the expression, "That takes the cake."[4]

In the New World, a different cake dance tradition developed on plantations in the American South. African Americans who worked as servants and musicians in the big house were familiar with the formal European ballroom dances that were danced there, and they entertained themselves after hours with parodies of the white dancers. In 1772 the *South Carolina Gazette* reported a "Cabel" of about sixty slaves, who gathered together near Charleston to dance on a Saturday night: "The entertainment was opened, by the men copying (or taking off) the manners of their masters, and the women those of their mistresses . . . to the inexpressible diversion of the company."[5]

The Grand March was an easy target for such satire. Antebellum balls typically opened with this formal processional, and slaves watched as the white dancers, dressed in their finest clothes, promenaded ceremoniously as couples around the ballroom. Later, at their own plantation frolics, dressed in their best clothes, they mocked the high manners and pompous, self-important airs of the white dancers, promenading arm-in-arm in the yard of the slave quarters with ridiculous strutting steps. Recalling the plantation frolics of the 1840s, a former slave from Beaufort, South Carolina, explained: "Us slaves watched white folks' parties where the guests danced a minuet and then paraded in a grand march, with the ladies and gentlemen going different ways and then meeting again, arm in arm, and marching down the center together. Then we'd do it, too, but we used to mock em, every step. Sometimes the white folks noticed it, but they seemed to like it; I guess they thought we couldn't dance any better."[6]

Slave owners and other white onlookers were entertained and amused by these comical performances, and perhaps failing to realize that they were the ones being ridiculed, they saw these dances as an amusing and entertaining performance of a supposedly inferior race. Over time, these dance performances became contests, with the slave owner serving as judge, and as in the old Irish custom, a cake was awarded to the "best" dancer. If the cake came from the slave quarters, it was made of cornmeal, but sometimes a cake was donated by the white mistress of the big house. Estella Jones, an ex-slave from Augusta, Georgia, recalled the plantation cakewalks of her youth: "Cake walkin' wuz a lot of fun durin' slavery time. Dey swept de yards real clean and set benches 'round for de party. Banjoes wuz used for music making. . . . De couple dat danced best got a prize. Sometimes de slave owners come to dese parties 'cause dey enjoyed watchin' de dance, and dey 'cided who danced de best."[7] Unlike the Irish cake dances, which were tests of endurance, these plantation cakewalks had evolved into competitive dance performances.

With the advent of the blackface minstrel show in the 1840s, white performers began to present reenactments of African American slave dances on stage. Initially, these self-described "Ethiopian delineators"[8] performed the "Walk-Around" (or "Chalk Line Walk"), a dance finale in which individuals took turns showing off their steps and style while the others shuffled around in a circle, as in the African American ring dances. With comical embellishments to entertain the audience, these performances, like other aspects of minstrelsy, evolved into an offensive and degrading caricature of African Americans.[9] It is not known when cakewalks were first performed on the minstrel show stage. As early as 1877, however, Ed Harrigan and Tony Hart were entertaining audiences in New York with their song "Walking for Dat Cake," and one of their later productions, *Cordelia's Aspirations* (1883), featured African American dancers in a comedy sketch called "Sam Johnson's Cakewalk."[10]

Offstage, following Emancipation, cakewalks continued to be popular as social entertainment in African American communities throughout the country. No longer a parody of formal white dancers, however, these dance contests had become exhibitions of grace and dancing ability. At a Christmas cakewalk in Richmond in 1870, a white observer characterized the winner of the contest as the dancer who "excels in the fine art of walking" with "head and shoulders erect," "toes out," and a graceful movement of the arms and hands.[11] In 1883, the *New York Times* reported a "Walkin' Fo' De Cake" at an African American dance hall in New York City. Shortly after midnight, "colored men and women" gave "an exhibition of their marvelous grace in walking" in an "old-fashioned cake walk." In addition to a "fruit cake," prizes included a "gold-headed ebony cane" and a "silver watch and chain."[12] Such prizes no doubt provided a greater incentive than a mere cake.

An account of an African American cakewalk in rural Virginia in 1892 describes a competition with a number of different categories:

> A suitable hall or barn being obtained, the spectators gathered along the sides of the room while the contestants let themselves out the best they knew how in the central portion of the floor. There were prizes for the "best gentleman walker," for the "most graceful lady walker," for the "most graceful couple," for the "best matched couple," for the "best high stepper," for the "lady with the smallest foot," and so forth, and so forth. In a genuine cake walk it is a sight to see the airs and graces some of the more ambitious contestants do lay on in their desire to get the best foot forward in the race for the cake.[13]

In *The Autobiography of an Ex-Colored Man* (1912), African American novelist James Weldon Johnson tells of a cakewalk that took place following "quadrille-dancing" at a dance hall in Jacksonville, Florida, in the 1890s. Johnson, who points out that the original plantation cakewalk was based on the square structure of the Grand March, portrays it as a formal exhibition of precision stepping, in which a dozen or so couples compete for a cake:

> The floor was cleared for the cake-walk . . . and twelve or fourteen couples began to walk for a sure enough, highly decorated cake, which was in plain evidence. . . . The couples did not walk round in a circle, but in a square, with the men on the inside. The fine points to be considered were the bearing of the men, the precision with which they turned corners, the grace of the women, and the ease with which they swung around the pivots. . . . This was the cake-walk in its original form.[14]

In Asheville, North Carolina, Mrs. George Vanderbilt surprised her husband on Christmas Eve in 1898 with a demonstration of a cakewalk at their home, the Biltmore House. She arranged for eight African American couples from the local community to perform "a regular old-time cake walk, figure dancing, quartet singing, and a lively old Virginia breakdown." Following this demonstration, these black performers provided music, and the Vanderbilts and their guests danced through the night until Christmas morning.[15]

By this time, African Americans were also performing cakewalks on stage. African American performers had been involved in minstrel shows as early as the 1850s, and by the 1860s black minstrel companies were touring the country.[16] Adopting the existing minstrel-show format, these black performers, like their white counterparts, applied burnt cork to their faces and played the established stereotyped caricatures of African Americans. Black minstrel troupes were perceived by many to be more authentic than the white performers in blackface, and it was through one of these all-black minstrel shows that the cakewalk eventually gained national prominence and became a popular dance sensation.

"The Creole Show," an all-black production that opened in Boston and New York in 1890, followed the standard minstrel-show format, but it was the first to include women: prior to that time, only men performed in minstrel shows, playing the roles of both men and women. This, for the first time, made it possible to stage a cakewalk with mixed-gender couples, taking the place of the old minstrel show Walk Around. Within a few years, "The Creole Show" was touring the country on the vaudeville circuit, and the show's highly stylized "Cakewalk" finale, performed by dancers Charles Johnson and Dora Dean, sparked a national dance craze both on stage and off.[17]

The great popularity of Johnson's and Dean's "Cakewalk" performance inspired cakewalk competitions throughout the country in which African American dancers competed in front of an audience for more than just a cake. When fifty African American couples, winners of local competitions, competed in a "Grand Cake Walk" championship at Madison Square Garden,

Figure 11.2. "Primrose and West's Big Minstrels" (1896). Library of Congress, Prints and Photographs Division, LC-USZ62-24432

in New York City in 1892, the first prize was a grand piano.[18] The dancers who participated in these cakewalks clearly prided themselves on their finesse, and it is thought that these dance contests popularized the common expressions, "It was a Cakewalk" and "It was a piece of cake," to indicate an easily accomplished task.[19]

By the late-1890s, white dancers were also competing in cakewalk contests. At one competition in New York in 1897, a white couple, with chests thrown out, heads held back, and exaggerated high stepping, competed against ten black couples in front of an audience of more than one thousand.[20] By that time, weekly cakewalk competitions for cash prizes were also being held on Coney Island.[21] The high stepping and strutting associated with these contests inspired the "Cakewalk," a new social dance that soon became the rage of white society—the first of many African American vernacular dances to be adopted by white dancers in the early twentieth century.[22] Soon dancing masters were teaching the "Cakewalk" at dancing schools; Mr. and Mrs. William K. Vanderbilt hired African American dancer Tom Fletcher to give them cakewalking lessons in New York City (around 1900).[23] In response to the growing social dance fad, in 1899, A. C. Wirth, president of the American National Association of Masters of Dancing, incorporated steps from the "Cakewalk" into a new quadrille, the "Cake Walk Quadrille," which he promoted as "The Popular Fad of Popular Society."[24]

The "Cakewalk" had crossed racial lines once more, raising the question of who was imitating whom. Here were upper-class whites imitating black

Figure 11.3. "Le Cake-Walk dans un Salon Parisian" (*L'Illustration*, No. 3124 [January 10, 1903]). Bibliothèque Nationale de France

performers, who had patterned themselves after white minstrel performers in blackface, portraying African American slaves, who in turn were satirizing the white Southern aristocracy!

It is not known how or when cakewalks became adopted into the rural Appalachian dance tradition. While it is possible that the custom of awarding cakes to dancers came to the southern mountains with the early Scots-Irish settlers, more likely this tradition was adopted from African Americans, or it was inspired by the minstrel shows of the late nineteenth century. When American novelist Charles Dudley Warner traveled through the region on horseback in 1884, he encountered an innkeeper's daughter in East Tennessee, who informed him: "Well, there's gay times here in the winter—dancing. Like to dance! Well, I should say. Last winter I went over to Blountsville [Blountville, Tenn.] to a dance in the court-house; there was a trial between Union and Blountsville for the best dancing. You bet I brought back the cake and the blue ribbon."[25]

Today, more than a century after the "Cakewalk" craze of the 1890s, cakewalks continue to be popular at community dances throughout the country. No longer dance contests, however, they are now simply an entertaining way to raise money. This was done in African American communities in the South as early as the 1870s, when cakewalks were held "to aid some poor person or some deserving charity."[26] In 1894 ten or twelve white couples in Louisville, Kentucky, likewise participated in a cakewalk to raise twenty dollars for a "Christian Widow's and Orphan's Home."[27]

The story of the cakewalk illustrates the repeated appropriation of culture across racial lines. Today's cakewalks, however, bear little resemblance to the earlier cake dances—the Irish cake dances (contests of endurance), the African American plantation dances (mocking white people), the minstrel show cakewalks (mocking black people), the African American cakewalks (contests of grace and ability), or the social dance fad that swept the country at the turn of the twentieth century. Gone are the satire, theatrical spectacle, exaggerated high stepping, and finesse of the earlier dances. Instead, at community dances in Appalachia today, the dancers merely walk around the circle while the music plays, hoping that they will be the one chosen to "take the cake."

12 Appalachian Step Dance

Following his visit to eastern Kentucky in 1917, Cecil Sharp wrote, "The only kind of dancing other than the Running Set [square dances] that we have as yet seen in the mountains is a species of step- or clog-dance, locally known as the hoe-down . . . i.e. a heel-and-toe, shuffle, or clog-dance step."[1] This type of step dancing, now known as "buckdancing," "flatfooting," or "clogging," is still common in rural Appalachia today, and every Saturday night, dancers of all ages fill the dance floor at the Carter Family Fold in Hiltons, Virginia.[2] Traditionally performed to old-time and bluegrass music, this is for the most part a solo dance form, but it is also a social dance, and when a lively breakdown is played, dancers of all ages mingle out on the dance floor, trading steps and learning from each other by imitation. It is not a performance or a contest, and no partners are required. It is simply a way to enjoy

Figure 12.1. "Old Fashioned Hoedown"—Appalachian step dancing accompanied by patting (Cumberland Gap, Tennessee, c. 1940s). Photo: Joe Clark. Clark Photography Collection, University of North Texas, Denton, Texas

and participate in the music and to interact with other dancers, regardless of age, gender, or acquaintance.

While Appalachian step dancers may share certain steps, there is no prescribed footwork; some perform memorized sequences of steps; others, "doing their own thing," are more improvisational and freeform in their movements. Depending on one's personality, age, and stamina, the steps may be energetic, loud, and percussive, or smooth, subtle, and relaxed.[3] Generally, though, the feet stay close to the floor, and the footwork consists of a variety of rhythmic movements involving the toe, the heel, or the entire foot. As Robert Anderson, a former slave from Kentucky once explained, individual dancers often like to "play a tune with their feet."[4] Often, however, as at the Carter Fold, where many of the dancers wear taps on their shoes, the sound of the feet simply creates a loud rhythmic cadence in time to the music.

The step dancing that takes place at the Carter Fold and other music venues throughout Appalachia is improvisational and idiosyncratic by nature, but it is not completely freeform, and many of the common steps and movements clearly have roots in earlier traditions. This form of step dancing did not develop in isolation, nor does it come from a single source; but like the Southern square dances, it is a hybrid mix of the northern European, West African, and Native American dance traditions that developed in the New World. As early as the mid-1600s, blacks and whites danced together at Christmas and Pinkster (Pentecost) celebrations in the Dutch settlement of New Amsterdam (New York City),[5] and since that time, generations of dancers have shared dance steps and styles across racial and ethnic lines to create this uniquely American form of step dancing. Traces of the earlier dance traditions from which these step dances evolved, however, can still be seen in the characteristic movements, common footwork, and general style of dancers in Appalachia today.

These dances have roots in the step dances of the British Isles, but they also incorporate elements adopted from the sub-Saharan African dance tradition. As a way to recognize the influences of these two traditions, jazz historian Marshall Stearns, in the 1960s, identified several characteristics of the African dances that differentiate them from those of the Northern European tradition. Stearns describes African dancing as a flatfooted style that involves "gliding, dragging, or shuffling steps."[6] This style, with the heels down, is compatible with dancing barefoot on the ground, and it is distinctly different from the percussive dances of Europe, which are typically performed in hard-soled shoes, on a wooden floor, with the dancer's weight on the balls of the feet. European observers noted that while African dancers "scarcely moved their feet," they were particularly "distinguish'd for [the use of] their heels."[7] "Master" Pierce, an early blackface minstrel performer ("Ethiopian Delineator") who imitated this style in the 1840s, was billed as "the great heelologist."[8]

According to Stearns, African dancers generally perform in a crouched position, with bent knees and the body bent at the waist. This body posture, which fits with the flatfooted dance style (with the heels down), is radically different from the upright, erect posture of European dancers. In Africa a straight body was associated with death and rigor mortis, while a relaxed crouching posture with flexed joints evoked life and energy.[9]

Stearns points out that unlike the highly choreographed sequences of steps and formal styles taught by European and American dancing masters, African dance involves improvisation and individual expression. Englishman John Atkins noted dancers in Sierra Leone in 1721 who "one at a time shews his Skill in antick Motions and Gesticulations, yet with a great deal of Agility."[10]

Finally, as opposed to the phrased, melodic music of the European dance tradition, African dances are performed with rhythmic accompaniment. Black dancers in North America commonly danced to tambourines, bones, jawbones, handclapping, and foot stomping, as well as body percussion known as "patting Juba." (Drums were outlawed in South Carolina and elsewhere in the South following the Stono Slave Rebellion of 1739.) When slaves from Long Island and New Jersey gathered to dance "jigs" and "breakdowns" at public markets in New York in the 1790s, "their music or time was usually given by one of their party, which was done by beating their hands on the sides of their legs and the noise of the heel."[11] A dance instruction manual from 1873 recommends this "old fashioned patting on the thighs" as the appropriate accompaniment for "plantation breakdowns."[12]

Figure 12.2. John Dee Holeman (Orange County, North Carolina) and Fris Holloway (Durham County, North Carolina)—African American buckdancing accompanied by patting. Photo: Kathy James. National Council for the Traditional Arts Archives

These characteristics of African dance can all be seen in the Appalachian step dances of today, and they are part of what distinguishes these American dances from those of the British Isles. The Appalachian step dances are improvisational by nature, and the posture of the dancers is relaxed. The footwork includes close-to-the-floor flatfooted steps involving a forward-and-back sliding motion, and some dancers in the South still use body percussion to keep time.[13]

The Appalachian step dance tradition was also no doubt influenced by Native American dances, which, as in Africa, were performed on the bare ground with rhythmic accompaniment. Henry Spelman, an Englishman who lived with the Powhatan people of Virginia in the early 1600s, compared their dances to the jigs and hornpipes of Derbyshire: "When they meet at feasts or otherwise they use sports much like to ours heare in England as ther daunsinge, which is like our darbysher Hornepipe. A man first and then a woman, and so through them all, hanging all in a round, ther is one which stand in the midest with a pipe and a rattell with which when he beginns to make a noyes all the rest Gigetts [jigs] about wriinge ther neckes and stampinge on ye ground."[14] Englishman John Lawson, who traveled through the piedmont of the Carolinas in 1701, likewise noted the heavy footwork of these dances: "Their way of Dancing, is nothing but a sort of stamping Motion, much like the treading upon Founders [foundry] Bellows."[15] Other than being lively, these Native American step dances (sometimes described as "stomp dances") likely had little in common with the step dances (jigs and hornpipes) of Derbyshire, but their legacy may be reflected in some of today's clogging steps.

Over the years, step dancing in Appalachia has been known by a number of different names. Cecil Sharp (like Henry Spelman) used familiar European dance terminology when he referred to the step dances of eastern Kentucky as "clog-dances"; the locals called them "hoe-downs." In rural communities where dancing is traditionally learned by imitation, however, there is little need for labels or standardized names—to many, it is simply "dancing." It is only for the purposes of documentation, teaching, performance, or competition that dance steps require standardized names and definitions. Nevertheless, the terminology that has been used to describe these rural Southern step dances over the last two hundred years, even when applied somewhat indiscriminately, provides clues to their lineage, nature, and historical development.

Jigs

Prior to the European settlement of the New World, there was a tradition of step dancing in the British Isles. Scottish poets of the mid-sixteenth century mention certain steps and styles by name: the "Light-fute" (lightfoot), "Backfute" (backstep), "Ow'rfute" (overfoot), "Futebefore" (foot before), "Splae-fut"

Figure 12.3. "Dance of the Haymakers (Music is Contagious)" (William Sidney Mount, 1845). Two white dancers face off for a jig in a barn. An African American boy watches the fiddler, and another contributes rhythmic accompaniment with sticks on the side of the barn. Two girls, one white and one black, watch the dancers from the hayloft. Long Island Museum of American Art, History and Carriages. Gift of Mr. and Mrs. Ward Melville, 1950

(splayfoot), and "Platfute" (flatfoot).[16] These step dances are thought to have been influenced by the refined dances of the French court, and by the end of the sixteenth century they were generally referred to as "jigs," possibly derived from the Old French "giguer," meaning to leap or gambol.[17] (The use of this term does not necessarily mean that these dances were in 6/8 time, only that they were fast and lively.) Although descriptions of these early step dances do not exist, the footwork would not have been highly percussive; at that time, houses and barns in rural Scotland typically had dirt floors and shoes had soft soles. Once wooden floors and hard-soled shoes became common, however (in the Scottish Highlands that was not until the late eighteenth century[18]), the steps became percussive, and setting steps taught by itinerant dancing masters began to filter into the rural tradition.[19]

These percussive step dances of the British Isles were also popular in colonial America. Future president John Adams, a descendant of the early

Puritans, wrote of dancing a "gigg" as a young man at a Boston tavern in 1760: "Every Room, kitchen, Chamber was crowded with People. Negroes with a fiddle. Young fellows and Girls dancing in the Chamber as if they would kick the floor thro . . . caught a Girl and danced a Gigg with her."[20]

By that time the European and African dance traditions had already begun to merge in the New World. Following a visit to America in 1759, English clergyman Andrew Burnaby recounted a formal ball in Virginia: "Towards the close of an evening, when the company are pretty well tired with country dances, it is usual to dance jiggs; a practice originally borrowed, I am informed, from the Negroes. These dances are without any method or regularity: a gentleman and lady stand up, and dance about the room, one of them retiring, the other pursuing, then perhaps meeting, in an irregular fantastical manner."[21]

These lively jigs, in which two dancers faced off against each other within a ring (sometimes referred to as "Congo dances"), clearly have roots in the ring dances that were common on plantations in the West Indies and the American South.[22] John Stewart described such a slave dance in Jamaica in 1823 in which "an assemblage of both sexes . . . form a ring around a male and female dancer. . . . When [these] two dancers have fatigued themselves, another couple enter[s] the ring, and thus the amusement continues."[23] Informal, improvisational dancing such as this would not have been seen at balls in England, but these African Caribbean–inspired "jiggs" became common throughout America, no doubt providing a welcome relief during an evening of formal country dances.

Nicholas Cresswell, who encountered these jigs at formal balls in Alexandria, Virginia, in 1775, noted the uninhibited spontaneity that was elicited by the "Negro tunes" that were played by African American fiddlers:

> Here was about 37 ladies dressed and powdered to the life, some of them very handsome and as much vanity as is necessary. All of them fond of dancing, but I do not think they perform it with the greatest elegance. Betwixt the Country dances they have what I call everlasting jigs. A couple gets up and begins to dance a jig (to some Negro tune) others comes and cuts them out, and these dances always last as long as the Fiddler can play. This is sociable, but I think it looks more like a Bacchanalian dance than one in a polite assembly.[24]

These competitive "cut-out jigs" were also popular in the Appalachian backcountry. Joseph Doddridge wrote of all-night frolics that followed weddings in southwestern Pennsylvania (just north of Berkeley Springs, West Virginia):

> The commencement was always a square four [a four-handed reel], which was followed by what was called jigging it off; that is, two of the four would single out for a jig, and were followed by the remaining couple. The jigs were often

> accompanied with what was called cutting out; that is, when either of the parties became tired of the dance, on intimation, the place was supplied by some one of the company, without any interruption of the dance. In this way a dance was often continued till the musician was heartily tired of his situation.[25]

A similar "cut-out jig" took place at a wedding party in Providence, Rhode Island, in 1788: "Somebody props'd a cutout jigg—I forget who began it but a ring was instantly form'd around the actors—and every creature that never cut a caper before now tried the suppleness of their feet . . . as true a husking frolic as ever you saw."[26] As early as 1797, a French dancing master was teaching these African American jigs ("Congoes") to white dancers at a dancing school in Chapel Hill, North Carolina.[27] When English actor and comedian John Bernard, encountered these American "jigs" at a wedding party in North Carolina in 1801, he characterized them as "violent exercise under the title of a ball." He wrote, "The diversion commenced by a gentleman leading a lady to the middle of the room, and, after a formal salutation, bursting into an eccentric movement, which to me had a new and peculiar significance. No regular steps, but a latitude of shuffle was adopted, in a system of alternate pursuit and retreat, now the lady, now her partner gaining the advantage, testing at every turn the respective strength of their sinews."[28] It is not surprising that these impromptu dance contests are also mentioned in slave narratives. James Smith of Texas recalled: "There am dancin' and singin' mostest every Saturday night. He [Master] had a little platform built for de jiggin' contests. Cullud folks comes from all round, to see who could jig de best."[29]

Informal jigging contests continued to be popular in the South and the Midwest throughout the nineteenth century. In *Behind the Blue Ridge*, a novel set in the 1860s, Frances Courtenay Baylor writes of such a contest taking place at a wedding party in the Shenandoah Valley of Virginia, and in *Little House in the Big Woods*, Laura Ingalls Wilder describes a "jig" contest at a house dance in Wisconsin in the 1870s.[30]

As an added challenge, dancers would sometimes place cups of water on their heads—a practice that likewise comes from the African tradition—to "see who could jig de hardest without spillin' any."[31] In 1876, Lafcadio Hearn noted an African American "jig-dancer" in Cincinnati who "could dance with a glass of water on his head and not spill a drop."[32] Some white dancers, including Sam Queen's mother in western North Carolina, also mastered this skill, and today, octogenarian Fred Skeens of Church Hill, Tennessee, can sometimes be seen out in the floor at the Carter Fold, dancing with a plastic water bottle balanced on his head.

Step dancing in the Ozarks of Missouri and Arkansas as well as western Kentucky is still known as "jig dancing" or "jigging" today, and although these terms are no longer common in Appalachia, it is clear that these informal social dances left their mark on the step dances of the southern mountains.

Hornpipes and Setting Steps

In the late eighteenth century, dancers in America began to incorporate footwork adopted from stage step dances, called "hornpipes," with the earlier British and African American jigs. These percussive step dances were derived from the earlier hornpipe dances of rural northern England (mentioned by Henry Spelman in the early 1600s), and like the Scottish and Irish jigs, they were influenced by French dance steps. Danced in wooden-soled shoes, hornpipes involved choreographed sequences of steps that were designed for both audio and visual effect, and by the mid-eighteenth century, they were being performed on stage as entertainment ("entr'actes") between the acts of plays on both sides of the Atlantic.[33]

Sometime around 1783 American dancer John Durang (1768–1822) began to perform these percussive dances in America. Durang wrote that he learned "the correct stile of dancing a hornpipe in the French stile" by watching a French dancer named Roussell, who was performing with a theatrical dance company in Durang's hometown of Philadelphia. Durang, who went on to become America's first professional stage dancer, later wrote, "I saw him dance a hornpipe which charmed my mind. . . . I practiced at home and I soon could do all his steps besides many more better hornpipe steps."[34] The following year, Durang traveled to Boston to study with dancing master William Turner; in 1785, dressed in a sailor's costume, Durang began performing hornpipes at theaters in Philadelphia. These step dances, like the earlier jigs, were shared across racial lines, and in 1808 a circus in New York City advertised a "Young African" who could "exhibit many steps of Hornpipe, on Horseback, in full speed, without losing the measure of the music."[35]

The duple-meter dance tunes that accompanied these stage dances likewise became known as "hornpipes." Durang wrote in his memoir that "Durang's Hornpipe," a tune composed in his honor in 1785 by "Mr. Hoffmaster, a German dwarf," had within his lifetime already become "well known in America": "I have since heard it play'd the other side of the Blue Mountains as well as in the cities."[36] "Durang's Hornpipe" (though now played as a reel) is one of the many once-popular hornpipe tunes that remain common in the southern Appalachian fiddle repertoire today.

In the late eighteenth century, it became fashionable to perform hornpipe steps as setting steps while dancing country dances and cotillions. As one author later wrote, "Dancers at that time often boasted that they 'put in so much work' as to wear out a pair of dancing slippers in one evening."[37] One of these common setting steps was the "Double Shuffle," a step that John Durang had used in his hornpipes.[38] A "Shuffle" step typically involves the foot moving forward and back with the toe striking the floor twice, and a "Double Shuffle" simply repeats this motion. This percussive step was taught at dancing schools, and it soon became part of the vernacular step dance tradition on both sides of the Atlantic. Harden Taliaferro wrote of the "Double Shuffle" at rural frolics in Surry County, North Carolina, in the 1820s.[39] This step is also mentioned in the lyrics of a minstrel song (c. 1848), acknowledging the superior abilities of black dancers:

> Oh! De long Island nigger,
> He good at de dance,
> In de double shubble [shuffle] figger,
> He beat the man from France.[40]

Another popular setting step was the "Backstep." This step, which may be related to the Scottish "backfute" of the sixteenth century, was described by Scottish dancing master Francis Peacock in the early 1800s: "This is an easy familiar step, much used by the English in their Country Dances. You have only to place the right foot behind the left, sink and hop upon it, then do the same with the left foot behind the right."[41]

Confederate soldier, doctor, and writer John Allen Wyeth wrote of slaves dancing the "back-step" on his family's plantation near Huntsville, Alabama. Rather than an "easy familiar step," he characterizes it as an energetic step that "required not only a keen sense of keeping time with the music, but agility and muscular power of a high order."[42] A fictional account of a rural "mountain dance" in East Tennessee from 1886 likewise depicts the "back step" as a difficult step and "quite an accomplishment."[43] Joe Hood, a dancer from Middle Tennessee who grew up in northern Alabama in the early twentieth century, learned the "Old-Time Back Step" from his father.[44] Hood's step resembles the "easy familiar" setting step described by Francis Peacock, but with a shuffle added. In West Virginia this step is now known by some as the "Double Shuffle Backstep,"[45] and its proper execution is considered to be the sign of a skilled dancer.

Another step that is frequently mentioned by name in accounts from the nineteenth century is the "Heel-and-Toe," which was, however, not one particular step but a variety of steps involving different combinations of the heels and the toes alternately striking the floor.[46] While dancers from the British Isles typically performed this step with the weight on the balls of the feet, African American dancers did it differently, with their heels down. New Orleans mayor Edward Henry Durell described this close-to-the-floor, flat-footed dance style in 1853: "The feet scarce tread wider than their own length; but rise and fall, turn in and out, touch first the heel and then the toe, rapidly and more rapidly."[47] An Englishwoman who observed slaves dancing at a Christmas ball in Montgomery, Alabama, in 1860, likewise noted that the dancers "seemed to shuffle on their heels in a wonderful manner."[48] Charles Dickens wrote of similar flat-footed black dancing at a "public-house" in England in 1860: "The male dancers were all blacks. . . . The sound of their flat feet on the floor was as unlike the sound of white feet as their faces were unlike white faces. They toed and heeled, shuffled, double-shuffled, double-double-shuffled, covered the buckle, and beat the time out."[49] Although these accounts are lacking in detail, it is clear that the African-derived flat-footed heel-and-toe step was distinctly different from the heel-and-toe steps of the British Isles.

By the mid-nineteenth century, flashy setting steps were no longer fashionable at urban balls, and dancing manuals prescribed "walking or sliding through the different changes" of the quadrilles, with the feet "raised but very little from the ground."[50] By that time, however, these percussive steps were well-established in the vernacular dances of the rural South. In fact, they had become so common that dancers began to refer to step dancing generically as the "Double Shuffle" and the "Heel-and-Toe." Frederick Law Olmsted encountered white dancers in rural northern Mississippi in 1854 who spoke of dancing the "Heel and Toe" on wooden planks at dance parties, and in a fictional account of a "break-down" contest in the Shenandoah Valley around the time of the Civil War, two dancers face off with "shuffling and double-shuffling."[51] Cecil Sharp used both of these terms—"shuffle" and "heel-and-toe"—in his description of the "hoe-down" steps of eastern Kentucky, as did Biss Honeycutt of Yancey County, North Carolina, who still referred to these two steps by name in the late twentieth century.[52]

The Shuffle step remains a common step in the rural Appalachian dance tradition today; however, it is executed in two different ways. "On-the-toe" buckdancers as well as contemporary cloggers typically perform "double toe" shuffle steps, with their weight on the balls of the feet and the toe striking the floor twice. This is how, in the European tradition, it was taught at dancing schools, and this is also how it is done in Irish and Cape Breton step dance as well as tap dancing. The other way of executing a shuffle step, though, is to let first the heel and then the toe strike the floor as the foot moves forward and back. Many traditional dancers in the South use this flat-footed "Heel-and-Toe" shuffle step, which is danced with the heels down and likely reflects the influence of the African American dance tradition.

The Pigeon Wing

"An when I cut de pigeon wing, I fan de ceilin wid my fling."[53] These song lyrics from the 1840s refer to the "Pigeon Wing," an energetic dance step that was performed on stage in the blackface minstrel shows of the nineteenth century. Although this step is often cited as an "authentic" African American plantation dance, it has, in fact, an earlier history. The "Pigeon Wing" was originally a French dance step ("Ailes de Pigeon") that was taught to dancers on both sides of the Atlantic during the late eighteenth century. This step, which was likely derived from a classical ballet step called the "Entrechat," consists of an acrobatic leap into the air, the dancer crossing and re-crossing

Figure 12.4. The Pigeon Wing performed by Burton Edwards (Haywood County, North Carolina, 1990s). Photo: Mike Seeger

the legs as many times as possible while airborne.[54] This movement mimics a pigeon's wings, as it flutters up off the ground, not really flying away, but flapping its wings several times before landing again.

John Durang, who performed the "Pigeon Wing" onstage, wrote in his memoir that he had learned this step from the French dancer Roussell around 1783:

> The pigeon wing I never saw done by any other person. . . . I learned the correct stile of dancing a hornpipe, an allemande, and steps for a country dance. Except the pigeon was the only difficulty I had to encounter. . . . The mystery of the figure occurred to me in bed, for my thoughts were constant on that subject. I dream'd that I was at a ball and did the pigeon wing to admiration to the whole company; in the morning, I rose in the confidence of doing the step. By this strange circumstance on trial I was the master of the step.[55]

Durang taught the "Pigeon Wing" to his students, and by the early 1800s dancers across the South were performing "pigeon wings," in addition to "double shuffles," as setting steps.[56] Josephus Guild spoke of "both boys and girls, cutting the single and double pigeon wing" while dancing six-handed reels in Middle Tennessee.[57] Augustus Longstreet, who recalled dancing it in his youth at rural frolics in Georgia, referred to it as the "double cross-hop": "It was performed by rising and crossing the legs twice or thrice before lighting, and I used to carry it to the third cross with considerable ease."[58]

Although urban dancers had discarded these setting steps by the mid-nineteenth century, a simplified version of the "Pigeon Wing" (with the crossing of the legs replaced by the clicking of the heels) remained popular with rural dancers. In his account of a rural frolic in East Tennessee published in 1843, George Washington Harris wrote: "The mirth becomes uproarious, the men jump high, 'cut the pigeon wing,' and crack their heels together."[59] Former slave Liza Jones remembered dancing this step at plantation frolics: "I could cut de pigeon wing, jes' pull my heels up and clack dem together."[60] William M. Adams, who likewise spoke of slave frolics recalled, "Some of dem would jump up and see how many times he could kick his feets 'fore dey hit de groun.'"[61] The "Pigeon Wing" subsequently became popular on the minstrel show stage as an "authentic" plantation dance, and over time it evolved into the "Wing," an early stage tap-dance step in which toe taps are combined with a leap into the air.[62]

By the late nineteenth century the "Pigeon Wing" had become another generic name for flashy step dancing. In *Little House in the Big Woods* Laura Ingalls Wilder writes of her uncle dancing "a pigeon wing" in the Midwest in the 1870s, and Sam Queen spoke of his grandmother in western North Carolina who likewise could "cut the pigeon wing."[63] This common expression likely comes from the French word "coupé" (meaning to cut). In the eighteenth century a "cut step" occurred when one leg or foot struck against the other,[64] and in nineteenth-century dance manuals the "Pigeon Wing" appears as "Coup d'Ailes de Pigeon" (Blow of the Pigeon Wings). Today, a "cut" in tap dance involves a crossing of the legs, and dancers in the rural South still refer to step dancing as "cutting a step" or "cutting a rug."

A number of years ago I met a traditional folk dance group, the Bleuniadur Ensemble, from Brittany, France, when they were performing at an international folk dance festival in western North Carolina. I asked the group's director about the step called "Ailes de Pigeon," and he leaped into the air with a sideways click of his heels. He informed me that it was a traditional step from Brittany. Perhaps the "Pigeon Wing" originated in Brittany, but more likely—there, as in the American South—this step reflects the legacy of the French dancing masters.

Breakdowns, Hoedowns, Buckdancing, and Flatfooting

It is clear that by the early nineteenth century, the step dances of America, having been influenced by the African American dance tradition, were different from the jigs and hornpipes of the British Isles. Consequently, they acquired new American names and began to be referred to as "breakdowns" and "hoedowns." The term "breakdown" is derived from the expression "breaking down corn," which meant to break an ear of corn from the stalk,[65] and the

AN OLD-FASHIONED BREAK-DOWN.

Figure 12.5. "An Old-Fashioned Break-Down" accompanied by fiddle and patting (Mark Twain, *Life on the Mississippi*, 1883)

energetic step dances that took place at African American corn shucking frolics were known as "breakdowns."[66] John A. Quitman, who later became the governor of Mississippi, wrote of a "Virginia 'break-down'" dance along the Ohio River at Point Pleasant, [West] Virginia in 1819.[67] Quitman's use of quotes suggests that the term was new at that time.

By the mid-nineteenth century the term "breakdown" had become yet another generic term for rural Southern step dancing, regardless of race. In *Life on the Mississippi* (1883) Mark Twain writes of the "break-down" dancing of the boatmen of the Mississippi River in the 1840s. As in the earlier "cut-out jigs," these step dances are accompanied by a fiddle and someone patting juba: "Next they got out an old fiddle, and one played, and another patted juba, and the rest turned themselves loose on a regular old-fashioned keel-boat break-down."[68]

In *Behind the Blue Ridge* (1887), a novel set in a mountain community in the Shenandoah Valley of northern Virginia at the start of the Civil War, two young men challenge each other in a "break-down" contest at the conclusion of a wedding dance, and as in Twain's story, they are accompanied by a fiddler and a bystander "patting Juber."[69]

Figure 12.6. *Jig, Clog, and Breakdown Dancing Made Easy* (1873). Library of Congress, Music Division

Noting the African American roots of these dances, American historian and writer John Russell Bartlett, in his *Dictionary of Americanisms* (1859), defined a "breakdown" as "a riotous dance . . . in the peculiar style of the negroes . . . with which balls are often terminated in the country."[70] Alice Hutcheson, a former slave from Georgia, recalled the dancing at corn shucking frolics: "After supper dey started playin' dem fiddles and banjoes, and de dancin' begun. White folkses danced de twistification [set dances] up at de big house, but us had reg'lar old breakdowns in a house what Marster let us have to dance in."[71] Minstrel show performers who wished to perform these Southern slave dances could find instructions for a choreographed "Plantation Breakdown" in the dance manual *Jig, Clog, and Breakdown Dancing Made Easy* (1873).[72]

In the mid-1800s the term "hoedown," also derived from the agricultural work of African Americans, was used synonymously with "breakdown."[73] As early as 1835, a dancer is described in a periodical as "hoeing it off like a regular Juba," and in 1854 David Hunter Strother wrote of blacks dancing a "kitchen hoe-down" in northern Virginia.[74] This term, however, also referred more generally to the informal rural dance parties where these step dances took place. During William Henry Harrison's presidential campaign of 1840 his supporters celebrated his (invented) identity as a common frontiers-

Figure 12.7. "Virginia Hoe-Down"—Black dancer accompanied by white fiddler (Jacob A. Dallas, 1855). *Harper's New Monthly Magazine* 12, no. 67 (December 1855)

man by dancing the "Tippecanoe Quick Step" at "Harrison Hoe-downs," and years later, in 1883, a dance that took place at a cabin in the Nantahala Valley of western North Carolina was likewise described as an "old-fashioned 'hoe-down.'"[75] Cecil Sharp referred to the step dances of eastern Kentucky as "hoe-downs," and this term is still in use today. As Clifton Caudill, an elderly dancer in eastern Kentucky, once explained to me, a hoedown is what you do when the day's work is done—you put your hoe down and dance.[76]

As with the earlier European dance terms (jig and hornpipe), the terms *breakdown* and *hoedown* became associated with the music that accompanied these dances. In "Remembrances of the Mississippi," a story that appeared in *Harper's New Monthly Magazine* in 1855, a flatboat fiddler plays a "Virginia hoe-down" for an African American dancer, who keeps time with a "heel-and-toe tap."[77]

During the second half of the nineteenth century, rural Southern step dancing also became known as "buckdancing," an American term which, like "breakdown" and "hoedown," originated with the dancing of African Americans. As early as the 1830s, African American males were demeaningly referred to as "bucks"—that is how they are listed in advertisements for

Figure 12.8. Buckdancer Thomas Maupin of Murfreesboro, Tennessee, accompanied on banjo by grandson, Daniel Rothwell (2009). Photo: R. L. Geyer

slave auctions—and their dancing was referred to as "buckdancing."[78] Agatha Babino, a former slave from Louisiana, recalled the antebellum plantation dances: "We have dance outdoors sometime. Somebody play fiddle and banjo. We dance de reel and quadrille and buck dance. De men dance dat."[79]

By the 1870s, "Buck Dancing" was being featured on stage in blackface minstrel shows, and by the end of the century, instructions for "Buck Tap Dance" could be found in dance manuals.[80] Over time, "Buck Dancing" combined with "Wing Dancing" (derived from the "Pigeon Wing") and became known as the "Buck-and-Wing," the precursor to modern stage tap dance. As with the other popular step dance styles that preceded it, buckdancing and the "Buck-and-Wing" became two more names for rural step dancing, regardless of the race or gender of the dancers, and by 1925 there was a "buck dancing" contest at the Alabama Fiddlers' Convention in Birmingham.[81]

Today, in the Blue Ridge of southwest Virginia and western North Carolina and in West Virginia, traditional step dancing by individual dancers is often referred to as flatfooting (or flatfoot dancing)—basically a style of buckdancing in which, as the name suggests, the dancer's feet stay close to the floor. Rather than being up on the balls of the feet, the dancer keeps his or her heels down, and the footwork often involves a forward-and-back sliding motion, sometimes referred to as a "chug."[82] Although Scottish poets back in the sixteenth century referred to a dance called the "platfute," Appalachian flatfooting is more likely derived from the flat-footed "gliding, dragging, or shuffling" footwork of the African tradition.

Pantomime Dances and the Charleston

While some of the dance steps in the Appalachian tradition are highly percussive, others are more visual by nature. This includes pantomime steps, which, like the Pigeon Wing, mimic animals or common activities. Some of these steps are the personal creations of individual dancers; other steps, however, with roots in the European, African, and Native American traditions, at one time were widely known across the South, crossing racial and ethnic lines.

In the European tradition, pantomime steps often imitated work activities. An Irish dance from Connacht, the "Maide na Planndaí," mimicked the tilling, planting, and digging of the potato.[83] Washington Irving may have been referring to this dance step (as well as the "Double Shuffle") when he wrote admiringly of a young African American dancer in 1807: "No Long-Island negro could shuffle you 'double trouble,' or 'hoe corn and dig potatoes' more scientifically."[84] This same step appears in an anonymously written "autobiography" of David Crockett published in 1833. At a rural "frolic" in East Tennessee, the dance steps include "kiver [cover] taters" and "weed corn," as well as the "double shuffle," "heel an' toe," and "back step."[85] Shell Coffee, an African American dancer from the Cumberland Plateau of Kentucky, described what may be a similar step called "Diggin' Potatoes" in 1992: "You take this foot, it's like the shovel, gets dirt here, puts it over there."[86]

In the Cherokee tradition of western North Carolina, pantomime dances often mimic animals. Dances from the Qualla Reservation in western North Carolina include the "Beaver Dance," "Bear Dance," "Ground-Hog Dance," and others.[87] Anglo-American dancer and storyteller Stanley Hicks (1911–1989) of Watauga County performed several animal dances—the "Frog Dance," "Eagle Dance," and "Bear Dance"—that were likely adopted from or inspired by the Cherokee tradition.[88] Hicks's "Bear Dance," which is performed by leaning back on all fours with palms on the ground, at one time was known by different names throughout the South. In the North Carolina Piedmont, African American dancer Lily Roberts called it the "Rabbit Dance," Arthur Pryor, from the Cumberland Plateau of Tennessee, referred to it as the "Rabbit Hop," and to Hoy Haden in southwest Virginia, it was the "Possum Dance."[89]

Pantomime dances from the African tradition often involved the motion of birds, and dances known as the "Turkey Trot," the "Buzzard Lope," and the "Chicken Wing" were common at plantation frolics.[90] As mentioned earlier, dances such as these, in which an individual dancer imitates a bird within a ring of dancers, are likely the source of the American square dance figure "Bird in the Cage." They also, however, served as inspiration for the blackface performers of the minstrel stage, and it is probably no coincidence that Thomas Rice used a bird's name for his "Jim Crow" dance.

With the subsequent advent of the blackface minstrel show, these and other African American dances became popular with white dancers, too. A newspaper in Kansas in 1894 described "Break de chicken's neck" as "a twist of ankle and knee as a man twists a chicken's neck."[91] John Reeves, a dancer from Haywood County, North Carolina, knew some of these steps. Growing up in the early twentieth century, Reeves learned the "Broken Wing," "Dust the Pigeon Toe," and "Wring the Chicken's Neck" from his uncle Sam Queen, who in turn had learned from African American dancer Bob Love.[92]

One of these African American bird pantomime dances, a dance from rural South Carolina called the "Jay-Bird" that involved a sideways twisting of the feet, is thought to be the source of the Charleston.[93] After becoming fashionable in Charleston, South Carolina, and Savannah, Georgia, in the early 1900s, the Charleston became a national dance craze when, in 1923, it was featured in the all-black Broadway musical comedy *Runnin' Wild*. Within a few years, film shorts, featuring the latest Charleston steps from Hollywood, were being shown in movie theaters across the country, and young women in rural western North Carolina (both black and white) began to incorporate these steps into their dancing. One of these steps, now known as the "Windmill" or "Wagonwheel," has since become a standard clogging step.

When the railroads were built through the southern mountains in the late 1800s, a new kind of pantomime dance entered the Appalachian dance tradition. The African American workers who built the railroads devised new percussive steps, imitating the rhythm of the steam engine, which was a part of their daily work environment. African American blues guitarist and dancer John Dee Holeman (b. 1929) from the North Carolina Piedmont used alternating heel and toe sounds in his "imitation of a steam train," as did white dancer Arthur Pryor from Tennessee in a step called "Train a-Puffin."[94]

Willard Watson (1905–1994), a flatfoot dancer from Watauga County, North Carolina, likewise danced African American pantomime steps. He once told me that he had learned these steps from an uncle who had spent time in the penitentiary working alongside African American convicts. There was a huge steam-powered rock crusher, and the inmates kept time with it using a variety of percussive steps. These steps included "Walking the Heel," "Shoe Shine," "Barnyard Slide," "Wring the Chicken's Neck," and "Snake in the Grass."[95]

Clog Dancing and Clogging

During the twentieth century, Appalachian step dancing also became known as clogging, and this is the most common term used today. This name was adopted from stage clog dances based on the English Lancashire Clog, which became popular in America in the 1840s.[96] Like the earlier English hornpipes, these step dances involved percussive sounds made by striking the toes and heels on the floor, and they were performed in stiff, wooden-soled shoes called "clogs" (hence the name). In the European tradition, clog dances were performed with the dancer's weight on the balls of the feet, as indicated in *Clog Dancing Made Easy*, an instruction manual from 1874: "In clog dancing never stand with the heels touching the floor, unless required by the step in use at the moment."[97]

By the 1850s and 1860s clog dancing had become common in the blackface minstrel shows that toured America. Ohio River flatboatman Thomas Collins recalled "the best clog dancing [he] ever saw" at a theater in Pittsburgh in 1865.[98] These percussive step dances were later featured on the vaudeville stage, remaining popular well into the twentieth century. English silent film actor Charlie Chaplin performed these dances in English music halls as a member of a clog-dancing troupe when he was a child.[99]

In the early twentieth century, Helen Frost, an instructor of physical education at the Teachers College of Columbia University, promoted clog dancing as part of the physical education curriculum of America. In *The Clog Dance Book* (1921) Frost provides instructions for choreographed clog dance routines. In addition to the dance steps, she suggests costumes for a number of "character dances" for children, including two blackface dance routines that would be considered racially offensive today: "Rastus" ("a merry old Negro who still loves to dance") and "Liza Jane" ("a roly-poly pickaninny").[100] It is not known how widely this stage clog dance curriculum was taught or what, if any, influence it might have had on the dance traditions of rural Appalachia.

Although dancers in Appalachia did not wear wooden-soled shoes or perform dance routines on stage, in the early twentieth century rural Southern step dancing became known as "clog dancing." One of the first to use this term was local-color writer Mary Noailles Murfree. In her short story "The Dancin' Party at Harrison's Cove" (1878), Murfree writes of "awkward young mountaineers [who] clogged heavily about in their uncouth clothes and rough shoes . . . to the violin's monotonous iteration of The Chicken in the Bread-Trough, or The Rabbit in the Pea-Patch."[101] Murfree's use of the word "clog" may have been due to her lack of knowledge of the vernacular—she also refers to the "fiddle" as a "violin." She was an outsider who grew up in an upper-class family in Middle Tennessee and vacationed with her family each summer at the Beersheba Springs resort in the Cumberland Mountains.

When Cecil Sharp, another outsider, visited eastern Kentucky in 1917, he used the term "clog-dance" for what was locally known as a "hoe-down," and by the 1920s dancers in the southern mountains had likewise adopted this term. At an "old-time fiddlers' convention" in Winston-Salem, North Carolina, in 1924, a prize was awarded to the "best clog dancer," and in 1935 the Old Fiddlers Convention at Galax, Virginia, included a contest for "Clog or Flatfoot Dancing."[102]

By the early 1930s the step dances of western North Carolina were also called "clogging." There is an often-repeated (but fictitious) story that when Sam Queen and the Soco Gap Square Dance Team performed at the Roosevelt White House for the king and queen of England in 1939, the queen likened their dancing to English "clogging," and the press picked up the term and popularized it. This term, however, was already in use in Asheville six years earlier.[103]

The adoption of the term clogging coincided with a change in the regional dance style, and dancers in Haywood County, who had been buckdancing on the balls of their feet, began to use heavier steps with their weight on the heels. Some have attributed this stylistic change to the Native American dancers of nearby Cherokee, who danced on the early clogging teams, but the shift may also have resulted from the introduction of amplified music.[104] Dancers needed to dance with heavier, louder steps in order to hear their own feet. By the 1950s a characteristic style of clogging had developed in western North Carolina that incorporated elements of the various earlier step dance traditions: the percussive double-toe shuffle of the British step dances, the heavy heel of the Native American "stomp dance," and the flat-footed forward-and-back "gliding, dragging," and "shuffling" motion of the African American dances.

* * *

The various names that have been used to describe step dancing in Appalachia over the past two hundred years—"jig," "double shuffle," "heel-and-toe," "Pigeon Wing," "breakdown," "hoedown," "buckdance," "flat-foot," "buck-and-wing," "Charleston," "clog dance," and "clogging"—are an indication of the diverse roots of these dances. Like the square dances, the step dances are a composite of the northern European, West African, and Native American dance traditions, and they have also continuously borrowed from the popular dances of Europe and America. They have evolved over time as dancers have observed, imitated, and shared their steps and styles, and in some cases they have fed back into popular culture, creating a cycle. The "Pigeon Wing," like the Cakewalk (discussed earlier), moved back and forth between urban and rural settings as well as across racial lines more than once: from French dancing masters to white dancers at dancing schools, then to black dancers (enslaved as well as free), to white minstrel performers in blackface (who were imitating the black dancers), and finally to urban tap dancers (both black and white), rural Southern buckdancers (both black and white), and contemporary cloggers (predominantly white).

Traditional freestyle step dancing, by whatever name we choose to call it, remains common in rural Appalachia today, and individual dancers still take to the floor wherever old-time music and bluegrass is played. In rural communities, where dancing is still often learned by imitation, steps continue to be shared informally between dancers on the dance floor, and while there are common movements and steps, dancers are free to "do their own thing" within the boundaries of the tradition. As one elderly dancer in western North Carolina once told me, "I get up and do my thing. . . . I don't know what I do."[105] The true essence of Appalachian step dancing, however, was perhaps best expressed by Pauline Zimmerman, a dancer from Madison County, North Carolina, who described her dancing to me simply as "a jubilant spirit within me."[106]

13 Clogging

Appalachian Step Dance on Stage

On Saturday evenings during the summer, "long about sundown," musicians and dancers from throughout western North Carolina gather in front of the Buncombe County courthouse in downtown Asheville for Shindig-on-the-Green. This free outdoor celebration of traditional music and dance has been in existence for almost fifty years (since 1967), and each week thousands of spectators, locals and tourists alike, turn out to enjoy the old-time and bluegrass music, known locally as "mountain music." While some of the

Figure 13.1. The Southern Appalachian Cloggers at the Mountain Dance and Folk Festival (Asheville, North Carolina, 1974). Mountain Dance and Folk Festival, D. H. Ramsey Library, Special Collections, University of North Carolina at Asheville

musicians sign up to perform on the stage, others are simply there to socialize and participate in the many informal jam sessions that take place around the periphery. Several times during the evening, however, the microphones are moved aside to make room for dancers. The Stony Creek Boys launch into a fast breakdown, and a clogging team dressed in colorful matching costumes and tap shoes takes to the stage, entertaining the audience with choreographed square dance figures and loud percussive footwork. This performance-oriented dance form, which combines the earlier traditions of southern Appalachian square dancing and step dancing, is a relatively new tradition, one that originated in western North Carolina in the late 1920s as a byproduct of the region's tourism industry.

Western North Carolina has been a popular tourist destination since the early nineteenth century, when summer visitors, seeking cooler temperatures and beautiful mountain vistas, first started coming to the "Land of the Sky." Arriving by stagecoach, these summer guests stayed at resort hotels, such as the one at Warm Springs (now Hot Springs) in Madison County. Built in 1831, this grand hotel in the Appalachian backcountry boasted 350 rooms, dining facilities for six hundred, and a large ballroom.[1] Other hotels in the region catering to summer visitors included Asheville's Eagle Hotel (1814) and the nearby Sulphur Springs Hotel (1830). Once the railroad to Asheville was completed in 1880, summer guests began to arrive by passenger train, and in the 1890s and early 1900s, many more hotels were built to accommodate the increasing number of visitors. Like the earlier mountain resorts, these hotels featured large ballrooms and dance pavilions where, each evening, the guests enjoyed the popular dances of the day: quadrilles, waltzes, Germans, and the Grand March.

By the early twentieth century, these old ballroom dances were no longer considered fashionable, and in Haywood County some of the hotels began to hold mountain square dances for the summer visitors. Local dance caller Sam Queen was hired to teach the dances, and he put together a team of dancers to demonstrate the figures. During the summer tourist season, Queen and his group were kept busy as many as six nights a week. Albert Burnette (1912–2005), who grew up in Haywood County, recalled watching these dances as a child with his older brother and sister at the Wildwood Inn near his home in Dutch Cove. Peeping through the windows from the porch, Burnette learned the figures and eventually became a square dance caller himself.[2]

The Mountain Dance and Folk Festival

By the 1920s Asheville was a rapidly growing metropolis, and in 1928, in an attempt to boost tourism and attract additional development to western North Carolina, the Asheville Chamber of Commerce established the annual Rhododendron Festival. For the most part, the Rhododendron Festival was an extravagant display of parades, beauty pageants, and costume balls, but the

Figure 13.2. The Pigeon River Square Dance Team at the Mountain Dance and Folk Festival (Asheville, North Carolina, late 1930s). Library of Congress, Prints and Photographs Division, Lomax Collection (LC-DIG-ppmsc-00462)

organizing committee also decided to include a "folk song and dance festival" on one of the evenings. Bascom Lamar Lunsford (1882–1973), a banjo player and folksong collector from nearby Madison County, was enlisted to organize the event. This was the jazz age, and Lunsford, who was concerned that the region's traditional music and dances were in danger of dying out, welcomed the opportunity to promote these mountain traditions onstage. Expressing the prevailing Anglocentric view of these local traditions, the *Asheville Citizen* stated that Lunsford's program would feature the "songs and dances of the mountain folk," which "had their origin in England before Colonial days" and "have been preserved in their pure form by the mountaineers."[3]

Lunsford's show took place at Pack Square, just uphill from the present site of Shindig-on-the-Green. An area was roped off, and a wooden platform was built as a stage. Lunsford invited five "dancing clubs" from western North Carolina to compete in an exhibition of "old corn-shucking square dances,"[4] several thousand spectators crowded around the dance floor for what the *Asheville Citizen* described as a "throwback from the modern jazz-mad world."[5] Among the dance teams was Sam Queen's demonstration group, whom Lunsford named the Soco Gap Square Dancers. That first year, however, the "Leicester dancing club" won the first prize of one hundred dollars as the best "square dance team."[6] Lunsford's square dance competition became an annual event, and within a few years (in 1930) it separated from the Rhododendron Festival, becoming known as the Mountain Dance and

Folk Festival, the first and oldest continuously running folk festival in the United States.

Freestyle Clogging and Smooth Dance

The square dance teams that competed at Lunsford's Mountain Dance and Folk Festival danced in circular sets of eight couples, breaking into smaller two-couple circles for traditional visiting-couple figures such as "Right-Hands Across," "Bird in the Cage," and "Georgia Rang-Tang." These dance performances would conclude with all of the dancers joining together again in one big ring for closing figures, such as "Shoo-Fly Swing," "London Bridge," "King's (or Queen's) Highway," and "Rise and Shine," all likely adopted from the nineteenth-century Grand March, which had been popular in the hotel ballrooms. For the most part, the dancers used a smooth, sliding step, as they would at a community square dance. While dancing the "King's Highway" and "Rise and Shine," however, the individual dancers had the opportunity to show off with a few buckdance steps.

Figure 13.3. Bascom Lamar Lunsford watches square dance team at the Mountain Dance and Folk Festival (Asheville, North Carolina, 1960s). Photo: Bob Lindsey. Mountain Dance and Folk Festival, D. H. Ramsey Library, Special Collections, University of North Carolina at Asheville

Although Lunsford's original intent had been to promote and preserve the mountain square dances, by putting teams of dancers on stage in competition, he inadvertently changed the tradition and created a new one. Competition invariably leads to innovation, and whatever caught the attention of the audience and judges one year was imitated by rival groups the next, soon becoming common practice. At first, the dancers at the Mountain Dance and Folk Festival dressed as they would at a community square dance, but within a few years (by the early 1930s), despite Lunsford's objections, some of the dance teams started wearing matching outfits. Some also began to include percussive footwork throughout their performances. This no doubt had a powerful effect. One of the first to do this was the Limestone Team, from nearby Henderson County, described by the *Asheville Times* in 1933 as an "all-clogging team." That same year, local radio station WWNC began to provide an "amplification system" for the music.[7] Once PA systems became the norm, it was difficult to hear the dancers' footwork, and by the early 1950s, to Lunsford's dismay, some of the dancers began to wear metal taps on their shoes to make a louder sound.[8] Tap shoes had not been worn at the earlier community dances, but they soon became standard attire for the square dancers at Lunsford's festival.[9]

The dance style that developed as a result of the annual dance competition at Lunsford's Mountain Dance and Folk Festival is now known as "traditional freestyle clogging." In this style of clogging, the footwork is not synchronized, but the dancers maintain a percussive rhythmic cadence with their feet as they perform big-ring square dance figures with eight couples. The individual dancers are free to use whatever steps they choose, as long as they keep with the overall rhythm and timing of the music.

By the 1960s, clogging teams had adopted a uniform, stylized costume, not unlike those worn by modern Western square dancers of that era. The men typically dressed in Western-style shirts, often with white pants or white belts; the women wore short, brightly colored square dance dresses, adorned with pinafores or aprons and puffed out by multiple layers of crinolines. The tap shoes worn by these cloggers were (and still are) most often white, but red, lime green, or even gold shoes were not uncommon.[10]

Some of the dance groups at Lunsford's festival preferred to dance in a more traditional style, using a smooth step rather than incorporating percussive footwork into their performances. As a result, in 1958 the square dance competition was divided into two categories: Clog Dance and Smooth Dance. Over the years, smooth dancing, like freestyle clogging, has evolved into a performance-oriented dance form with a uniform style and costuming for the stage. The choreography used by smooth dancers, like that of the clogging teams, is based on the traditional big-ring square dance figures, but instead of percussive footwork, smooth dancers use a highly stylized sliding step, with hands on their hips. Rather than the short skirts, crinolines, and tap shoes worn by cloggers, the women typically wear old-timey floor-length dresses, suggestive of the pioneer days.

Figure 13.4. The Pisgah View Ranch Smooth Dancers at the Mountain Dance and Folk Festival (Asheville, North Carolina, 1980s). Mountain Dance and Folk Festival, D. H. Ramsey Library, Special Collections, University of North Carolina at Asheville

Lunsford had insisted that the music and dances presented at his festival be traditional, and he stated that he would "book no performance which is not 'in the tradition.'"[11] He watched, however, as these new dance forms, the unintended byproducts of his festival, developed during his lifetime. By putting square dancers on stage in competition, he had created new traditions, ones that came at the expense of the older mountain dance traditions he had hoped to preserve. This was not unlike what was happening to the Appalachian musical tradition at that time. The commercialization of rural Southern music through radio, recordings, and stage shows had likewise spawned new, performance-oriented styles, in particular country and bluegrass music.

Although it was not his intent, Lunsford's efforts to promote traditional square dancing at the Mountain Dance and Folk Festival may have in fact hastened the decline of community dancing in western North Carolina. Square dancing in this region ceased being a community-based social activity where everyone, regardless of age or ability, was welcome to participate; instead, it became a rehearsed exhibition of choreographed dance routines and percussive footwork performed onstage by energetic young dancers in front of a passive audience. This was noted in the *Asheville Citizen* in 1952: "In the first Festivals, most of the square dance teams were adults, many of the members were middle-aged, and most of them had known how to square dance all their lives. . . . Today, the square dance teams are mostly young people, many of them teenagers."[12]

By the 1960s, many high schools, junior high schools, and even elementary schools in western North Carolina sponsored clogging and smooth dance teams. These groups competed each year at Lunsford's festival as well as at the Mountain Youth Jamboree in Asheville, and square dance trophies from that time can still be seen on display in the trophy cases of many local schools. In western North Carolina, "square dancers" were no longer simply members of the community but skilled members of a "team" who dressed in matching costumes, wore tap shoes, and performed choreographed dances.

From its inception in 1928 the Mountain Dance and Folk Festival has had a mutually beneficial relationship with the tourism industry of western North Carolina. Originally conceived and promoted by the Chamber of Commerce as a way to boost tourism, it became so successful at attracting out-of-towners that in 1977 a local observer noted the large number of "Florida folks" attending the festival and the "conspicuous lack of 'mountain people,' excepting performers and their families."[13] This influx of outside attendees no doubt helped spread clogging to other parts of the country, and as early as the 1950s, dance groups were coming from outside the mountains to perform at the festival. In 1959, the Florida Town Square Dance Team from Milton, Florida won first place as the "best mountain cloggers."[14] Lunsford's festival, however, also provided opportunities for performers of traditional music and dance in western North Carolina. Visitors to the region came to expect to see cloggers and hear mountain music, and while the context of the music and dances had changed—from private community affairs to public performance venues—this cultural tourism helped sustain these traditions in the region. Although the dance competition at the Mountain Dance and Folk Festival was discontinued in 1987, traditional freestyle clogging teams and smooth dancers are still featured at the festival each summer, as well as on Saturday nights on the newly constructed Bascom Lamar Lunsford Stage at Shindig-on-the-Green.[15]

Precision Clogging

Over the years, as dance teams competed against each other at Lunsford's festival, the performances became increasingly refined and polished. When the Plantation Team won first place in 1942, the *Asheville Times* attributed their success to "the precision with which the group danced, not as individuals, but as a team." "So well drilled was this group that every step was synchronized with other members of the team, the position of the bodies was similar, the position of the hands the same, and even the position of the head, all made to conform to the general rhythm of the team."[16] This new, synchronized style of clogging, which was a departure from earlier freestyle clogging, became known as "precision clogging."

Figure 13.5. The Blue Ridge Mountain Dancers at the Mountain Dance and Folk Festival (Asheville, North Carolina, 1968). Photo: Bob Lindsey. Author's collection

The person most often credited with popularizing precision clogging is James Kesterson (b. 1937). Kesterson grew up in a family of traditional dancers in Henderson County and learned his first dance steps from his brother and some friends at age eleven. Within a few years he had joined the Connemara Farms square dance team, a local dance group associated with Mrs. Carl Sandberg's Connemara Farm in nearby Flat Rock. By the 1950s he was performing with Ben Smathers's Stony Mountain Cloggers as well as the North Carolina Cloggers. Kesterson traveled with these two groups to perform at county fairs and other venues beyond western North Carolina, including the Grand Ole Opry. Although the North Carolina Cloggers danced traditional mountain square dance figures using freestyle footwork, they would sometimes end their performances by opening up into a line facing the audience. According to Kesterson, they were the first clogging group to do this.[17]

By 1959 Kesterson had his own clogging team, the Hendersonville Cloggers, and this group took precision clogging to a new level. Practicing as many as three nights a week, Kesterson's dancers set themselves apart from the other clogging teams of that time, and in 1962, with their synchronized figures and footwork, they won first place at the Mountain Dance and Folk Festival. While much of the group's choreography was based on the traditional mountain square dance figures, they, like the North Carolina Cloggers, ended their performances in a chorus line facing the audience. In 1964, however, when they danced in a production of the musical *Annie Get Your Gun* in nearby Maggie Valley, the show's New York choreographer suggested that they move the chorus line to the middle of their routine for a more dramatic effect, and that became a permanent part of the group's choreography from then on. That same year, Kesterson and his group of young dancers were featured in a film that was made about Lunsford, *Music Makers of the Blue Ridge*.[18] Lunsford decided that Kesterson's group needed a more traditional-sounding name, so he renamed them the Blue Ridge Mountain Dancers.

During the 1960s the Blue Ridge Mountain Dancers and other dance teams led by Kesterson dominated the dance competition at the Mountain Dance and Folk Festival with this new precision style, winning seven out of eight years from 1962 to 1969. Their success, year after year, discouraged other groups from entering the contest, so one year, Kesterson was asked to organize and bring three different teams just to fill out the competition. In 1972, as a way to discourage precision clogging and encourage the more traditional freestyle teams, the festival committee adopted stricter contest rules and judging criteria with a "strong emphasis on traditional figures."[19] This effectively eliminated precision clogging from the festival.

In addition to being a perennial crowd pleaser at Lunsford's festival, Kesterson took the Blue Ridge Mountain Dancers on the road. In 1964 and 1965, at the height of the folk music revival, they performed with four couples at the Newport Folk Festival, where they shared the stage with fiddler Clayton McMichen and musicians Pete Seeger and Mike Seeger.[20] Other notable performances included the Festival of American Folklife in Washington, D.C. (1964), the New York World's Fair (1964), Expo 67 in Montreal (1967), and the Olympic Games in Mexico City (1968).

The stylistic innovations initiated by the Blue Ridge Mountain Dancers were an important step in the evolution from traditional freestyle clogging to the contemporary clogging of today. Their use of synchronized precision footwork was certainly important, but equally significant was their choreography. Breaking out of the closed circular form of the mountain square dance figures into a chorus line, their performances were no longer simply a demonstration of the old mountain square dances but were instead a well-rehearsed, choreographed dance show. Similar to the changes that were occurring in traditional music at that time—away from community-based old-time music to more performance-oriented bluegrass music—this development influenced the style and choreography of subsequent dance groups.[21]

The Green Grass Cloggers

In the early 1970s a group of young dancers from North Carolina, the Green Grass Cloggers, developed a new style of clogging that was a departure from both the freestyle and precision clogging of that era. I first saw this group on stage at the Great Hudson River Revival in 1977, and like many others in

Figure 13.6. The Green Grass Cloggers at the Mountain Dance and Folk Festival (Asheville, North Carolina, 1974). Mountain Dance and Folk Festival, D. H. Ramsey Library, Special Collections, University of North Carolina at Asheville

the audience at this folk music festival, I was captivated by the free-spirited, dynamic choreography and rhythmic footwork of these young performers. It looked like a lot of fun, and I wanted to learn how to do it too. The following week, I met some members of the group at a music party, and late that night, on a dancing board, I learned my first clogging steps. What I did not know when I first encountered the Green Grass Cloggers was that they did not dance in a traditional style. They were not from the mountains—they lived in Greenville, in the coastal plain of eastern North Carolina—and only a few of the members of the group came from families or communities with strong dance traditions. So rather than perpetuating a regional style, they developed one of their own. Three years later, I was invited to join the Green Grass Cloggers, and in subsequent years I became aware of the significance of this influential group. They not only popularized their unique repertoire of steps, but they also established a noncompetitive style of dancing that now, more than forty years later, can be found across the United States as well as in the British Isles.

The Green Grass Cloggers were founded by Dudley Culp (b. 1948), who in the spring of 1971, shortly after graduating from East Carolina University, attended the annual Fiddlers Convention at Union Grove, North Carolina. Inspired by a performance by the Smoky Mountain Cloggers, a precision clogging team from the western part of the state, Culp asked Evelyn Farmer, a dancer from southwestern Virginia, to show him a few basic clogging steps, and he shared these with friends back in Greenville. That fall, Culp, along with a few of these novice cloggers, returned to Union Grove for the annual Autumn Square-Up at Fiddlers Grove. They watched as traditional freestyle, smooth, and precision dance teams competed on stage, and upon returning to Greenville, they decided to start a clogging team of their own; thus, the Green Grass Cloggers were born.

Although the Green Grass Cloggers drew inspiration from and had great respect for the traditional dance teams of western North Carolina, partly out of ignorance they developed a unique, eclectic style of their own. Their choreography, which borrowed from the earlier traditions, included traditional square dance figures and precision lines, but also figures from Western square dancing that they had learned in a square dance class at East Carolina University. As a result, unlike the traditional freestyle teams who performed Appalachian square dance figures with eight couples in large circular sets, the Green Grass Cloggers performed in square sets with four couples. Betty Casey, a veteran square dance caller from Texas who was living in Greenville at that time, helped them understand how to fit the dance figures to the musical phrase, and with an awareness of performance dynamics, the group created short, energetic dance routines that incorporated synchronized footwork—a mix of traditional clogging steps and innovative steps of their own creation, including head-high kicks—with fast-moving figures.

In addition to learning from dancers on other clogging teams, the Green Grass Cloggers befriended, visited, and learned steps from traditional flatfoot dancers, whom they met at fiddlers' conventions. These include North Carolina dancers Willard Watson of Deep Gap, Hansel Aldridge of Avery County, and Robert Dotson (1923–2015) of Sugar Grove. These older dancers had watched as dancing had become increasingly standardized during their lifetime, and they emphasized that it should be an expression of individuality, rather than conformity. Following the advice of these mentors, the Green Grass Cloggers were willing to break any rule in the book. Their attitude was to have fun and to "do their own thing" rather than conform to the standards of the day—after all, this was the rebellious 1970s. While their innovative style was an affront to many in the traditional clogging world, their uninhibited, high-spirited dancing was popular with audiences.

In their first year, the Green Grass Cloggers performed mostly at benefits near their home in Pitt County, but the following spring (1972) the group traveled to the Union Grove Fiddlers Convention, where they performed in exhibition for an audience of thousands. In contrast to the clean-cut appearance and carefully matched polyester outfits of the other clogging teams, the Green Grass Cloggers presented a more relaxed (some would say scruffy) look. These young dancers were a product of their time, and they embraced the back-to-the-land ideals of the 1970s. The men dressed in blue jeans and work shirts with western-style calico yokes; the women wore black tights and calico square dance dresses of assorted colors, minus the enormous crinolines that were standard at that time. Instead of white tap shoes, they wore black or brown shoes, often acquired at second-hand stores. That fall, the Green Grass Cloggers returned to Fiddlers Grove to compete in the clogging competition at the annual Autumn Square-Up Festival, and despite their radical style, high kicks, and long-haired "hippie" appearance, they won first place in "Traditional Mountain Clogging."

The following year (1973) the Green Grass Cloggers traveled to Asheville to compete at Lunsford's Mountain Dance and Folk Festival, and once again they received an enthusiastic response from the audience. Who knows what ninety-one-year-old Lunsford thought of these longhaired dancers as he watched from offstage? The following spring, at a planning meeting for the Mountain Dance and Folk Festival, however, one of the committee members expressed concern about the authenticity of the dancing at the festival. He felt that "choreographed" routines, such as those done by the Green Grass Cloggers, were not "true mountain dancing" but "merely a modern offshoot of the real thing (like bluegrass is to traditional mountain music)."[22] Consequently, when the Green Grass Cloggers returned to the festival that year, they were disqualified during the competition and instead received a "special award."[23]

After winning for a second time at Fiddlers Grove in 1974, the Green Grass Cloggers were eliminated from the competition, as the contest rules there likewise became more explicit. By this time, however, the group had an established reputation, and they began to receive invitations to perform at major folk festivals throughout North America.[24] In 1977 half of the group, hitting the road in an old converted bus, decided to become a full-time professional dance company. This "Road Team" relocated to Asheville in 1980 (that is when I joined them) and continued to travel and perform full-time both nationally and internationally until 1987. During this decade of full-time touring, the Green Grass Cloggers performed at numerous festivals, concerts, and schools across the country. Overseas tours included performances in Sweden, Spain, and Singapore, as well as a USIA-sponsored tour of South and Central America. Both branches of the Green Grass Cloggers, what was formerly the Asheville Road Team and the Greenville Home Team, are still active today, having recently celebrated the group's fortieth anniversary.

Through their travels, the Green Grass Cloggers taught their style of clogging to countless dancers across the country, and by the end of the 1970s, dance teams patterned after them could be found coast to coast. In 1979 several former Green Grass Cloggers formed a four-person dance group in Maryland, the Fiddle Puppet Dancers (now known as the Footworks Percussive Dance Ensemble). Combining Green Grass–style footwork with innovative choreography for two couples, this group helped popularize Green Grass–style clogging, not only across the United States, but also, starting in

Figure 13.7. The Feet First Appalachian Clog Dancers (Durham, England, 2004). Photo: Ken Routledge

the mid-1980s, in the British Isles.[25] Green Grass–style clogging continues to be popular in England, Wales, and Scotland (where it is known as "Appalachian clogging"), with as many as sixty active groups.[26] Some of these groups perform with four mixed-gender couples, like the Green Grass Cloggers; more common, though, are all-female ensembles, some with as few as three or four dancers.

There are certain characteristics that clearly identify Green Grass–style clogging. As in precision clogging, the footwork of dancers on teams is synchronized, but dancers in the Green Grass lineage generally lead steps with the right foot at the start of the musical phrase. This is different from contemporary cloggers, who typically lead with the left foot, and self-taught dancers, who may lead with either foot. Certain named steps that are now widely known, as well as the use of high kicks in dance routines, can also be traced back to the Green Grass Cloggers. Among the more common named steps are the "Indian" and the "Earl" (a step created by, and named for, Earl White, one of the original members of the group) and flatfooting steps such as Willard Watson's "Walking the Heel" and the "Walking Step" learned from Robert Dotson.

In addition to dance style, Green Grass–style clogging groups (though not the Green Grass Cloggers themselves) often perform in retro "old-timey" costumes suggestive of pioneer days. Suspenders are not uncommon for the men, and the women often wear calico dresses. Brown or black shoes, with or without taps, are typical footwear, rather than the standard white tap shoes worn by most cloggers today.

Since their inception many of the Green Grass Cloggers (myself included) have also been musicians, and the group has always had a close connection with and appreciation for traditional old-time and bluegrass music. Whether performing as a group onstage or dancing informally as individuals on dancing boards ("step-a-tunes"), the Green Grass Cloggers have always danced to live rather than recorded music, and this appreciation for live traditional music has been conveyed to subsequent generations of dancers. Consequently, Green Grass–style dancers and clogging groups tend to perform to live traditional, rather than recorded, music.

Having been passed on from one dancer to the next through the informal sharing of steps (the "folk process") for more than four decades, the dance style established by the Green Grass Cloggers in the 1970s has now become a well-established form of American clogging that is known throughout the country.[27]

Contemporary Clogging

Independent of the Green Grass Cloggers but building on the innovations pioneered by the Blue Ridge Mountain Dancers and the other early precision groups, team clogging continued to develop as a performance art during the 1970s and 1980s, evolving into what is now known as "contemporary clogging." Bill Nichols (b. 1937) is sometimes credited with being the "grandfather" of this modern style. Nichols grew up in East Tennessee, where he attended community square dances as a child. As a young man, in 1955 he

Figure 13.8. The Bailey Mountain Cloggers of the then Mars Hill College (Mars Hill, North Carolina, 2006). Photo: Cindy Whitt

found employment at the Fontana Village Resort in nearby western North Carolina. At that time square dances were held at this mountain resort three nights a week during the summer, and Nichols, along with some of the other young employees, formed a four-couple freestyle team, the Fontana Cloggers, to entertain the guests with exhibitions of clogging between the dances. By the early 1960s Nichols had developed a method and vocabulary to teach the basic clogging steps, and he began to hold clogging classes at nearby Western Carolina University, where he refined and standardized his methods. When teaching steps, Nichols led with his left foot, as in couple dances, where the man likewise leads with the left foot. For the purpose of teaching, he also named the steps. These innovations were a departure from the tradition in which dancing is learned by imitation rather than in classes, and in which there are no standardized steps or style. According to Nichols, "The basic thing that grew out of Fontana was being able to teach a group of people. . . . A lot of people saw the potential and started dance studios."[28]

In the 1970s clogging began to be taught throughout the South, undergoing a major transformation that distanced it from its roots in the community-based social dances of Appalachia. Taught in dance studios, with dancers facing a mirror, line formations facing an audience replaced the closed circular choreography of the earlier traditional Appalachian square dances. These line dances were no longer based on the male-female partnering of the traditional social dances, so they had the advantage of being able to be performed by any number of dancers, regardless of gender. Consequently, today's contemporary clogging teams are not gender-balanced and are overwhelmingly composed of girls or women. At many dance studios, clogging is taught alongside other styles of dance, and over time, steps and movements borrowed from tap, jazz, Canadian and Irish step dancing, hip-hop, and even gymnastics and cheerleading have been incorporated into the dances. With little or no physical contact between the performers in these line formations, many dancers now perform with their hands on their hips, and since the early 1990s contemporary cloggers have also incorporated upper-body and arm movements adopted from hip-hop.

The use of recorded music at dance studios and performances, by choice as well as necessity, has further separated contemporary clogging from the Appalachian tradition. Dancers now perform routines consisting of sequences of steps that are choreographed to specific recordings. The music ranges from the latest commercial pop and modern country, to rock, techno, and rap. Dance instructors justify the use of popular music by saying that it's what young people want to listen to: the music gets them involved in clogging, and thus nontraditional music has now become standard.

With the rising popularity of clogging during the 1970s, several clogging organizations were established to promote and regulate this developing dance form. These include the National Clogging Organization, C.L.O.G. (originally Clog Leaders of Georgia, 1973), America's Clogging Hall of Fame (western

North Carolina, 1981), and the National Clogging and Hoedown Council (western North Carolina, 1974), which in 1978 adopted a standardized step terminology defining "Eight Basic Movements" of clogging.[29] While the standardization of steps and styles has no doubt facilitated teaching, it has taken contemporary clogging further away from its traditional roots.[30]

In addition to training "national certified" clogging instructors, these organizations sanction competitions. At those sponsored by the National Clogging and Hoedown Council, there are now as many as seventeen "Contemporary" categories for solos, duos, or any number of dancers ("any combination of males and/or females"). While "country, bluegrass, western or hoedown music" and "traditional style steps" are used in a few of these categories, others permit "any type of music" and "any type of steps." "Showmanship" and creativity are emphasized in the "Show" category, and dancers, often dressed in sequins and spandex, are encouraged to use "stage props."[31] The seven age divisions, which range from "Tiny Tot" (six and under) up to "Adult" (thirty and over), are an indication of the age range of the participants; these contests are not intended for old folks.

In recent years, however, America's Clogging Hall of Fame and the National Clogging and Hoedown Council have sought to promote and preserve the traditional aspects of clogging by including "Traditional (Appalachian)" categories at clogging competitions. These categories stipulate the use of "traditional mountain figures," "traditional style music" (bluegrass), and traditional "southern Appalachian" clogging, either "hoedown" (freestyle) or precision. One of the Traditional categories, called the "Running Set," involves four couples performing traditional visiting-couple figures in an "English quadrille formation" (Sharp's Anglocentric myth lives on!). The footwork may be either freestyle clogging or a "Running Step," which is defined as "a soaring, graceful run with the ball of the foot bearing the dancer's weight."[32] This highly stylized step, which the dancers maintain as they perform the figures today, however, more closely resembles high-stepping jogging than the "exceedingly smooth" running step originally described by Sharp.[33]

Since the 1980s contemporary clogging has become increasingly popular outside the southeastern United States, and clogging groups have sprung up across the country and as far away as Australia and New Zealand. Many of these dancers simply enjoy clogging as a recreational activity. For others, however, it is primarily a competitive sport. Some young dancers, distancing themselves from the rural images associated with Appalachia, now prefer to call this modern form of competitive step dancing by a new name, "Power Tap," which they describe as "a blend of clogging and hip hop."[34] In fact, today's contemporary clogging has evolved so far from its roots in the traditional dances of the southern mountains that perhaps it should no longer be characterized as either "clogging" or "Appalachian."

According to Bill Nichols, the contemporary clogging of today is less family-oriented than the Friday and Saturday night square dances he knew as a child growing up in the mountains of western North Carolina and East Tennessee. Like modern western square dancing, it has become a club-based activity and a commodity that is promoted and regulated by national organizations. Today's clogging teachers, though, are the dancing masters of our time. Like the French dancing masters of two hundred years ago, they teach "the latest and most fashionable" dances, and now, as in the eighteenth and nineteenth centuries, dancers attend dancing school to learn sequences of standardized steps and figures that are choreographed to the popular music of the day. This may be an inevitable consequence of dancing schools, but it is contrary to the spirit of traditional step dancing, which is idiosyncratic and improvisational by nature and is learned through observation and imitation. Today's contemporary clogging is light years away from the traditional square dances that were first celebrated at Lunsford's Mountain Dance and Folk Festival more than eighty years ago. Perhaps over time, however, elements of these dances will filter back into the rural Appalachian folk tradition, as "the latest and most fashionable" dances have continually done over the past two hundred years.

* * *

When Bascom Lunsford invited square dance teams to compete on stage at what was to become the Mountain Dance and Folk Festival, he unintentionally initiated a new performance-oriented dance tradition. Now, more than three generations later, team clogging not only remains an established tradition in western North Carolina, but it has spread far from the southern mountains. Clogging teams can now be found across the South as well as throughout the country. This is a living tradition, and as such, it continues to change and evolve as each generation adds its own innovations, starting in the 1930s, when square dance teams began to wear matching outfits. By the 1940s, dancers were adding precision footwork, and by the end of the 1950s, taps were the norm. James Kesterson's Blue Ridge Mountain Dancers popularized synchronized footwork and line formations. The Green Grass Cloggers created an eclectic style that incorporated traditional Southern clogging and flatfoot steps with choreography from Western square dancing. Today's contemporary cloggers have now added footwork and body movements from other dance forms, to create a modern form of percussive step dance performed to nontraditional music. While each of these performance-oriented innovations has taken Appalachian step dancing further from its original context (as a community-based, social dance), they have also made it more dynamic as a performance art, attracting successive generations of young dancers and perhaps ensuring the viability of this form of American step dancing into the future, both within and beyond southern mountains.

14 Community Dance in Appalachia

Throughout the nineteenth century, dancing served an important social function in rural communities in Appalachia and throughout the South. Harden Taliaferro recalled the dances that took place following "grubbings, log-rollings, reapings, and corn-shuckings" in Surry County, North Carolina, in the 1820s: "As soon as night came, or the work was done, the fiddle sounded, and they danced and courted all night."[1] These "workings" (work parties) and the dances that followed were not public events but gatherings of family, friends, and neighbors, and they fulfilled the needs, both work and social, of the local community. Dancing at these events and at other times of the year most often took place in private homes. All of the furniture, even the woodstove, would be taken from the largest room to create a space large enough to dance. Sometimes the musicians were situated in a doorway, and dancers were accommodated in two adjacent rooms. These house dances were private affairs, and while alcohol was consumed by the guests, it generally did not present a problem. William Norman, who likewise recalled "frolics" in Surry County prior to the Civil War, wrote, "Most of such visitors were dram drinkers, but it was a very rare thing indeed to see anyone intoxicated. Anyone was treated with a great deal of contempt that would indulge to too great an extent in dram drinking. Everything flowed freely and all were made welcome. Everything was peaceable and moved off in perfect harmony."[2]

By the early twentieth century, community workings were mostly a thing of the past, and although house dances continued to be held in some communities into the 1930s, with the availability of the automobile and better roads, public dances began to take their place. These dances were held in newly built community centers such as schoolhouses, firehouses, VFW halls, and National Guard armories. With larger dance floors and PA systems to amplify the music and dance calls, more dancers could participate. In some communities, large circle sets replaced four-couple squares. In these larger sets, the couples were designated as "odd" or "even" (numbered), an innovation that allowed every other couple in a big ring to lead the figure, with no waiting.[3] Unlike the earlier house dances, these public dances were no longer limited to the local community, but they attracted dancers from a wider geographic region. There was often an admission charge to pay the musicians, and the consumption of alcohol sometimes led to fights.

One of these public dances, known as the Farmer's Ball, took place in the Swannanoa Valley, ten miles east of Asheville. Around 1935 several families joined together to build a small dance hall for neighborhood dances. Before long, dozens of dancers from across the region were showing up every Saturday night, and the structure had to be enlarged to accommodate the growing crowd. The dancing, which would start around seven o'clock, included big-ring square dances, flatfooting and clogging, round dances (waltzes, two-steps, and even the jitterbug), and an occasional Virginia Reel. Raymond Peak called out the figures from the floor as he danced, without using a microphone. On some nights, if the crowd was large, two rings would be formed, one inside the other or side by side. Common dance figures included "Right-Hands Across," "Georgia Rang-Tang," "Bird in the Cage," and "Clover Leaf," and at the end of each dance, Peak would lead the dancers through

Figure 14.1. The Farmer's Ball, Raymond Peak, caller, with dancers in a conga line (Swannanoa, North Carolina, 1940s). Author's collection

closing figures such as the "Shoo-Fly Swing," "In and Out the Windows," "London Bridge," and the "Grand March" (see figure 10.2). Sandwiches, peanuts, cakes, hot chocolate, and coffee were sold to keep the dancers going until eleven o'clock or later, and while alcohol was tolerated in the parking lot, it was not allowed inside the building. This was an intergenerational gathering that served the social needs of the entire community each Saturday night. Nondancers filled the benches lining the sides of the hall, and children, as well as beginners, were welcome on the dance floor, assisted by those with more experience.[4]

By the late 1940s, square dances, within driving distance, could be found in western North Carolina as many as six nights a week throughout the year. As at the Farmer's Ball, a typical evening would include flatfooting and round dances, as well as big-ring square dances. At that time, Sam Queen was still actively calling dances at the various hotels in Haywood County, and his Soco Gap Square Dance Team would perform between the dances. The amplified music at these public dances was no longer simply a fiddle and banjo but larger ensembles that often included mandolins, guitars, and basses, and sometimes pedal steel and electric guitars. Popular dance tunes of this era ("Down Yonder," "Under the Double Eagle," "Alabama Jubilee," "Steel Guitar Rag," "Black Mountain Rag") were played alongside the older fiddle tunes ("Lost Indian," "John Henry," "Paddy on the Turnpike," and "Grey Eagle").[5] Although these public dances were commercial enterprises whose floors filled each summer with tourists from Florida, like the Farmer's Ball, they still functioned primarily as community dances—events that served the local community and were organized and attended, for the most part, throughout the year by the local residents.[6]

During the 1950s the number of dances in western North Carolina began to decline. The Saturday night dances at the Farmer's Ball ended in the mid-1950s, and by the end of the 1970s almost all of these public dances, like the earlier house dances, ceased to exist. What happened to this rich tradition of mountain square dancing, and why did it die out after so many generations? Many dancers who were active at that time blame the coming of rock-and-roll and the stratification of communities by age. Better transportation, which allowed these public dances to exist in the first place, likewise may have had an effect, providing more choices for entertainment beyond the immediate community. In western North Carolina the square dance competitions at the Mountain Dance and Folk Festival may have also had an unintended negative impact. "Square dancing" was no longer seen as an intergenerational community activity but had been redefined as the staged performances of young people on clogging teams. Newer popular dance forms, such as the Texas two-step, line dances, and modern Western square dancing also competed for potential dancers, and some people, no doubt drawn to the addictive allure of television, simply stayed at home. As in rural communities across

America, all of these factors likely contributed to the decline of community square dances in Appalachia.

Community Dances in the Twenty-First Century

Surry County, North Carolina

Although old-time community square dances are now rare, they can still be found. One place is in Surry County, North Carolina, where the tradition of dancing over Christmas holidays goes back two hundred years. Harden Taliaferro recalled the dances that took place there in the 1820s: "Christmas was a great festival. . . . For a whole week they would dance from house to house day and night, 'sparking' going on at a 'big lick' all the time."[7] William Norman likewise wrote of the dances that took place in this rural Southern community in the mid-1800s: "During holidays all the youngsters and the neighbors, generally, were invited to meet at a neighbor's house to take dinner. On that day another house was selected, at which all were to meet. Thus it continued for one week. Then all frolicking would cease and all would return to their respective avocations of life."[8] Tommy Jarrell's son, Wayne Jarrell (1927–2011), told me of similar house dances that took place in Surry County as recently as the 1940s: "Well, I was fifteen years old, I went to a dance up in Round Peak. They moved the furniture out of the house, put it out on the porch, and we danced, we danced all night without stopping. It was New Year's Eve and we danced from New Year's Eve into the next year."[9]

Figure 14.2. Square Dance at Beulah Ruritan Club (Surry County, North Carolina, 2009). Photo: Phil Jamison

Dances continue to be held in Surry County today, and until recently an annual "Breaking Up Christmas" dance still took place on New Year's Eve at the Beulah Ruritan Club, near Mt. Airy.[10] People of all ages attended this free community event. Some came to dance, others were there simply to listen to the old-time music, watch the dancers, and visit with family and friends. This annual dance, as well as the weekly square dances that took place at Beulah throughout the year, unfortunately came to an end following the death of James Lawson (1928–2011), who grew up in this rural community and called out the figures of the square dances from the floor as he danced. On a typical night, though, he only called a few square dances. The rest of the evening was taken up with two-steps, flatfooting, the Broom Dance, cakewalks, the Virginia Reel, and a popular mixer known in this region as "The Shuffle" (see chapter 10). The music at Beulah, played on fiddle, banjo, guitar, and bass, included dance tunes from the local Round Peak repertoire, such as "Sally Ann," a favorite with the flatfoot dancers.

In Surry County, square dances are danced in large circle sets, often with twenty or more couples. There is no walk-through or teaching of the dance figures, but when the music starts, the dancers join hands in one large ring. These dances typically begin with an introductory figure: "Circle left, back to the right," and then "Promenade." At a given call, the men place their partners on their left-hand side and then turn back, walking single file around the outside of the set, passing all of the women, until finally meeting and swinging their partners. This simple introductory figure, with all of the dancers joining together in the one large circular set, contributes to the sense of community at these dances.

After this opening figure, the dancers break into circles of four to perform the main figure of the dance, a visiting-couple figure for two couples. The most common figure in this region is "Georgia Alabam" (known elsewhere as "Georgia Rang-Tang"). Other common figures include "Right-Hands Across," "Figure Eight," "Garden Gate," "Lady Round the Lady and the Gent Also," "Take a Peek," "Bird in the Cage," "Chase the Rabbit," "Ocean Wave," and a local variant of the Southern "Do-si-do" in which the woman is simply passed to the man's left side and around behind his back. Following each figure, the dancers swing the "opposite partner" (the other person's partner) and then their own. Some couples swing by merely dancing forward and back in the ballroom position, without any turning motion. After swinging, each couple moves on to repeat the dance figure with a new couple.

At these Surry County square dances, once the caller has initiated the main figure, the calling ceases and the dancers continue at their own pace, working their way around the room from one couple to the next, completely at random. This freeform visiting-couple dancing without active calling is reminiscent of the Scottish reels described by James Boswell on the Isle of Skye in the late eighteenth century. After about five minutes, the caller signals the dancers to once again join in one large circle for an ending figure such as the "Grand Right and Left," "Grand March," "King's and Queen's Highways," "London Bridge," or "Ball of Yarn."

Carcassonne, Kentucky

In eastern Kentucky, about thirty miles from Pine Mountain, where Sharp and Karpeles encountered the "Running Set," an old-time community square dance takes place once a month at the old Carcassonne School in Letcher County. The school is located on top of a mountain, and the narrow, one-lane road that leads to it from the village of Blackey follows the creek up the valley, passing by a few houses and an old wooden church before climbing up the steep mountainside to the schoolhouse. Although situated on the crest of a high ridge and surrounded by beautiful thick woods, the Carcassonne School is less than a quarter-mile from the devastation of an enormous mountaintop removal site. The wooden building, where the dance takes place, was originally built as a K-12 school in 1931, but it was renovated in the 1960s during the War on Poverty. The community raised the necessary funds by holding box suppers. No longer used as a school, it now serves as a community center for weddings, parties, reunions, a weekly quilting club, and other events.

In 1967 Clifton and Ruby Caudill and other local residents wanted to revive the Saturday night house dances that were once common in their community. The Caudills once told me of the dances of their youth, where, following a supper of chicken and dumplings, the furniture would be moved from the

Figure 14.3. Carcassonne Square Dance—"Circle Up Four and Do-si-do" (Carcassonne, Kentucky, 1990). Photo: Phil Jamison

largest room to make space for a four-couple square set. These house dances ended with World War II, when many mountain communities were split up as people moved away in search of work. When dances resumed after the war, they took place in bars and roadhouses, where alcohol (and sometimes guns) created a less family-friendly atmosphere. The monthly dance the Caudills started at Carcassonne close to 50 years ago is now the longest continuously running community square dance in Kentucky.

The dancing at Carcassonne takes place in the school's main assembly room, a long room still outfitted with the coal-burning stove that once heated the building. A small raised platform at one end of the room serves as a stage for the musicians. The dance floor can accommodate about thirty dancers, and an equal number of nondancers and spectators typically fill the folding chairs at the far end of the room. In an adjacent room, hot dogs, soft drinks, coffee, and candy are sold at a concession counter. The square dance scene in the movie *Coal Miner's Daughter* was filmed at Carcassonne, and Marion Summer and Lee Sexton, who appeared in that film, are among the many musicians who have played for dances there over the years. Until his death in 2009, Charlie Whitaker (1929–2009), who grew up in the Carcassone community, was the main caller.[11]

The dances at Carcassonne are big-ring square dances with visiting-couple figures for two couples: "Right-Hands Across," "Basket," "Bird in the Cage," "Duck for the Oyster," "Take a Peek," "Figure Eight," "Wave the Ocean," "Clover Leaf," and many others. The dancers start out in a large circle, moving to the left. Then one couple leads out and makes a circle of four with the couple to their right. These two couples then perform a visiting-couple figure, followed by a distinctive Kentucky-style "Do-si-do," in which the women pass in front of their partners and walk counterclockwise around them, without letting go of hands. This is similar to the Surry County "Do-si-do," but here the man ducks under his own arm as his partner passes to his left and around him. The dancers swing their opposites and their own partners, and then all couples promenade counterclockwise around the room before forming the big ring again. This sequence repeats with the active couple moving on to dance with the next couple to the right. If the circle is large, a second couple across the circle will spontaneously lead out and dance the figure as well. During the course of each dance, two or three different figures are called.[12] Although Whitaker called out the dance figures from the floor (as do callers in Surry County), over the years I have seen other callers at Carcassonne call from the stage, using a microphone. Several times during the course of the evening, dance tunes are played for freestyle flatfooting (or "hoedowning," as it is still known locally). There are also cakewalks and the Virginia Reel, but no waltzes, two-steps, or any other couple dances.

As in Surry County, the future of the square dances at Carcassonne is uncertain. Most of the older dancers who started it have now passed away. Those who remain can no longer dance, and, sadly, few of the next generation, now middle-aged, appear to have any interest in traditional square dancing. These dances used to be held year-round, but attendance has declined, and they no longer take place during the winter months. Although before his death, Charlie Whitaker trained a young teenaged apprentice to call dances, the viability of the Carcassonne dance will depend on whether or not the next generation of dancers is interested in going up the mountain each month to socialize and dance the old-time square dances at the old schoolhouse.[13]

Glenville, West Virginia

Every June, dancers from across West Virginia converge on the town of Glenville for several evenings of old-time square dancing at the West Virginia State Folk Festival. The atmosphere is similar to that of a county fair, with food vendors selling barbeque, lemonade, and funnel cakes. The local crowd, which includes families as well as groups of teenagers, gathers around the large plywood dance floor—twenty-four feet by sixty-four feet—built on one of the side streets in town. An old-time band is set up on the stage at one end, and when it's time for the dance to begin, dancers of all ages fill the floor with sets of four couples. There is no walk-through or teaching, and newcomers must learn on the fly, taking friendly cues and accepting helpful pushes and pulls from the more experienced dancers. Mack Samples of Clay County, Bill Ohse of Jackson County, Lou Maiuri of Nicholas County, and several other West Virginia callers take turns calling the dances each evening.

The dances at Glenville are for the most part traditional visiting-couple squares. These four-couple dances begin with a few introductory figures, such as "Circle to the Left," "Single File Back to the Right," "Grand Right and Left,"

Figure 14.4. Glenville Square Dance (Glenville, West Virginia, 2012). Photo: Becky Hill

and "Promenade Home." The main part of each dance consists of a variety of visiting-couple figures, called for each of the four couples in succession. "Take a Little Peek," "Duck for the Oyster," "Peek-a-Boo Over, Peek-a-Boo Back," and "Mow the Wheat and Sow the Clover" are a few of more than a dozen dance figures in the local repertoire. Some of the dance figures are the same as those encountered by Sharp and Karpeles in eastern Kentucky a century ago ("Chase the Rabbit," "Shoot the Owl," "Figure Eight," "Bird in the Cage," "Lady Round the Lady and the Gent Also"); others have come into the tradition more recently, no doubt through the folk and square dance movement of the mid-twentieth century ("Forward Up Six," "Dip 'n Dive," "Texas Star," "Swing Sally Gooden"). After the active couple has finished dancing with each of the couples in the square, they "run a reel" (a series of hand turns) with the last couple. This reel for two couples, which is similar to the Southern hand-turning "Do-si-do" and the "Georgia Rang-Tang," is likely derived from the old Scots-Irish four-handed reels, and it serves as a sub-chorus preceding the "Grand Right and Left."

The callers at Glenville call out the dance figures from the stage using a microphone. This allows for a more modern calling style and colorful rhyming patter calls—"All join hands and circle to the South, Put a little moonshine in your mouth!"—what Sharp referred to as "a mixture of prose and doggerel rhyme." While the callers share a common repertoire of dance figures, each of them calls with a personal style and calling patter. As a way to surprise and challenge the experienced dancers, they call out a variety of different figures during the course of each dance in no apparent order and without advance warning. Some of the dancers, who have been doing these dances for years, know all of the figures; others are stumbling through them for the first time, learning by watching the more experienced dancers. Regardless of one's level of experience or expertise, however, all are welcome to participate on the dance floor.

The square dances continue one after another for several hours with only a few breaks. There are no couple dances, but at one point some cakes are raffled off in a cakewalk (see fig. 11.1), and several times during the evening, when the band plays a fast breakdown, individual dancers take to the floor for some freestyle flatfooting and clogging. When this happens, it is not uncommon to see two or more men facing off to dance, a scene reminiscent of the "cut-out jigs" and "break-down" contests of earlier times. Sometimes a circle of dancers spontaneously forms on the dance floor, and as in the African tradition, the dancers, one or two at a time, take turns dancing in the center of the ring.[14]

* * *

The dances at Surry County, Carcassonne, and Glenville clearly illustrate all of the defining features of traditional Southern squares. Whether in big rings (Surry County and Carcassonne) or in four-couple square sets (Glenville), these dances share the characteristic circular visiting-couple structure of the Southern square dance, with figures for pairs of couples. Three of the distinctive Southern visiting-couple figures ("Figure Eight," "Bird in the Cage," and variants of the Southern hand-turning "Do-si-do"), known at all three locales, reflect the English, African, and Scots-Irish roots of these dances. These Southern dances are accompanied by fast-paced, old-time fiddle music, and a dance caller coordinates the variable choreography and freeform timing of the dance figures, either out on the floor or from the stage using a microphone. In a typical evening, in addition to the old-time squares, the dancing in these communities also includes a mix of freestyle flatfooting and clogging, two-steps, cakewalks, and an occasional Virginia Reel. These community dances are firmly rooted in the traditional culture of the Appalachia region, and as living folk traditions they will likely change and evolve over time, as they have over the past two hundred years, when new dance traditions are incorporated with the old.[15]

Community Dances and Dance Communities

Although the dances at Surry County, Carcassonne, and Glenville are public events that draw dancers from beyond the local community, at their core they are community dances, and like the dances of earlier times that followed workings, they are a function of the communities in which they take place. Dancers and nondancers alike attend these intergenerational social gatherings, and everyone is welcome to participate, regardless of age, experience, or dancing ability. The atmosphere is informal, and the dancers do not wear any particular dancing outfits or special shoes. These public dances are vestiges of the community dances that were once common throughout rural America, and as in earlier times, the dancing not only serves the social needs of the individual dancers, but it strengthens the social bonds within the community as a whole. During the course of a square dance, dancers swing and interact with numerous other dancers, regardless of age or acquaintance, creating connections between the participants, even if just for the evening.

As traditional communities made up of extended families and close neighbors have disappeared, "community dances" (dances of a community) have become rare. Taking their place, however, are new "dance communities" (communities of dancers) that are not necessarily a function of the local community but are based on shared interests. In addition to traditional square dances, dancers in Appalachia can now take part in modern Western square dancing, contra dancing, swing dancing, contemporary clogging, and more, and regardless of the type of dance, bonds develop between people. Like the community dances of earlier times, these new dance communities provide the short-term benefits of recreation and social and physical contact, but they also build social capital in support of the long-term needs of the participants.[16]

15 The American Square Dance

A few years ago I was asked to call a square dance for a group of counselors at a summer camp in western North Carolina. When I arrived, it was immediately apparent that these young people were familiar with the common stereotypes associated with these American folk dances. Half of them came to the dance dressed up as hillbillies, with bib overalls, funny hats, and blacked-out teeth, and the other half showed up wearing cowboy hats, red bandanas, and Western boots. When I called, "Do-si-do" (the back-to-back type), they instinctively crossed their arms across their chests as they had no doubt seen in depictions of square dancing—something not done by experienced dancers at a "real" square dance.[1] Like most Americans living today, few of these young people had ever attended a "real" square dance—by that I mean a community-based, traditional square dance with live music. They were, however, clearly aware of the common images associated with these dances as they are represented in the media.

The square dance is often portrayed as the quintessential American folk dance, but it represents different things to different people. To some, these dances epitomize the "otherness" of the Appalachian region, an idea first popularized by the local-color writers of the late-nineteenth century; to others, these are the dances of the American pioneers and cowboys who migrated west during the nineteenth century. To Cecil Sharp and his disciples, they were survivals of English dances and an affirmation of this country's Anglo-Saxon identity and heritage. And to dancers at Surry County, North Carolina, Carcassonne, Kentucky, Glenville, West Virginia, and elsewhere in rural America, they are simply social entertainment for a Saturday night. Regardless of how one views these American folk dances, they remain a part of our national consciousness and identity in the twenty-first century.

Folk Dance and National Identity

For many Americans, their first, and in most cases only, exposure to square dancing was in a physical education class in elementary or middle school. Dancing has long been part of the physical education curriculum. As early as the 1850s, dancing master Charles Durang advocated that dancing be taught in American schools, and an English writer recommended it as "the very best safeguard against the evils of over mental education, to which young ladies are so subject."[2] Consequently, by the early twentieth century, nonmixed (single-gender) folk dancing came to be included alongside calisthenics and gymnastics in physical education programs on both sides of the Atlantic.

Folk dances, regardless of their origin, have often been romantically thought to be the true expression of a nation's preindustrial folk culture, and this was especially true with the heightened sense of nationalism of the early twentieth century. When Cecil Sharp succeeded in having Morris dancing adopted into the physical education curriculum in England in 1909, he portrayed these dances, which had been danced in England since the mid-fifteenth century, as an "English institution" (even though they are thought to have originated with the Moors of Spain).[3]

It is harder to define national culture and identity in the United States, a country whose population has always been ethnically and racially diverse. This was true even in colonial times, when Anglo-Americans were by far the dominant group. By the time of the first national census in 1790, people of Anglo-Saxon descent (English, Scots, and Scots-Irish), while still a majority, accounted for only 60 percent of the population. Germans, Irish, Dutch, French, Swedes, and other European immigrants, as well as indigenous Native Americans, accounted for 20% of the population, and the remaining 20% were of African descent.[4]

Immigrants continued to arrive from the British Isles and northern Europe throughout the nineteenth century, and in the late 1800s, when millions more began to arrive from Southern and Eastern Europe, many native-born Americans became alarmed. They feared that the country's supposed Anglo-Saxon racial purity was in danger of being diluted by this flood of Italians, Slavs, and Jews, whom they viewed as culturally and racially inferior.[5] This anti-immigrant sentiment fostered an increased level of nativism (a defensive type of nationalism) that, in 1890, led to the founding of the Daughters of the American Revolution, a hereditary patriotic society that contributed to the image of American national identity as white, Anglo-Saxon, and Protestant. Around this same time (in 1892) the Pledge of Allegiance was adopted as a way to instill a sense of nationalism in the children of America, immigrant as well as native born.

While some shunned these new immigrants, Progressive Era social reformers sought to assimilate them to mainstream American culture through social and educational programs.[6] Elizabeth Burchenal was one of these reformers.

Figure 15.1. "Fifteen Acres of Dancing Girls" at Central Park (New York City, 1912) (Elizabeth Burchenal, *Dances of the People*, 1913).

A physical education instructor at Columbia University's Teachers College, Burchenal was recruited in 1905 to direct a folk dance program for girls in the New York City public schools. Folk dancing was seen to serve a twofold purpose. First, it was thought to be a healthy alternative to the popular couple dances of that time. The "licentious" dances, which took place in dimly lit dance halls where alcohol was available, were thought to encourage sexual promiscuity, thus corrupting young people, especially adolescent girls and young women.[7] Second, Burchenal's folk dance program was intended to instill a sense of common heritage and national identity in the children of America. This imposed heritage, however, was a white, northern European one, introduced through a selective curriculum of dances drawn mostly from the British Isles and Scandinavia. Before long, "acres" of schoolgirls were performing maypole dances at annual May Day celebrations in New York's Central Park.

Building on her success in the New York City schools, Burchenal founded the American Folk-Dance Society in 1916, and she led a nationwide folk dance movement, training teachers and promoting folk dancing in schools throughout the country. As the result of her work, children at the Pine Mountain and Hindman Settlement Schools in eastern Kentucky, like their counterparts across America, began celebrating May Day with maypole dances.[8]

In the 1920s Grace Ryan (1894–1986), a professor of physical education at Central Michigan Normal College (now Central Michigan University), began to question why the folk dance curriculum of America consisted of European rather than American folk dances. Ryan believed that "all Americans should know, and be able to do, the folk dancing which belongs to America."[9] Ryan had grown up in rural Michigan, so she was familiar with the northern quadrilles and contra dances, but she began to collect square dances from other parts of the country, including the Midwest, the Rocky Mountains, and Appalachia. She published descriptions of these American dances in *The Handbook for Dances of Our Pioneers* (1926). Making these dances available

Figure 15.2. Maypole Dance at the Hindman Settlement School (Hindman, Kentucky, c. 1920s). Berea College Southern Appalachian Archives, Hindman Settlement School Records, 1899–1979, SAA 41

to dance leaders, Ryan helped make square dancing a standard part of the physical education curriculum of America.[10]

Another promoter of square dancing in the 1920s was Henry Ford (1863–1947). Ford was appalled by the modern couple dances and jazz music of the early twentieth century, and he wanted to turn back the clock and revive the "old-fashioned dancing" he had known in his youth in Michigan. A vocal anti-Semite and racist, Ford claimed that these dances of "the northern peoples" (white Europeans) were the "style of dancing which best fits with the American temperament."[11] This certainly would not have included the tango and the Charleston, which had recently become popular in America. In 1926 he published a dance manual called *"Good Morning"* (actually written by Benjamin Lovett, a dancing master from Massachusetts), which included instructions for a number of New England quadrilles and contra dances as well as the Virginia Reel, the minuet, the waltz, and other "round" dances. Unlike Burchenal and Ryan, who actively promoted folk dances through physical education and recreation programs, Ford was reacting to what he saw as the social decline of America. By eradicating the modern couple dances and reestablishing the dances of the nineteenth century, he sought to reaffirm America's Anglo-Saxon Protestant identity.[12]

Burchenal, Ryan, and Ford all wanted to revive the traditional dances of America, but this raises the question: What makes something "American?" While Ryan promoted the Midwestern dances of the pioneers, Burchenal and

Ford looked to New England for the "most typically American" folk dances. Burchenal described this region as "one of the old, most truly American sections of our country, where many generations of the same stock have grown up undisturbed by foreign influences."[13] Consequently, the "American" dances that appear in Ford's dance book and Burchenal's *American Country Dances* (1918) are primarily quadrilles and contra dances from New England. These were the dances that fit their idealized vision of America and reflected this country's supposed northern European, Anglo-Saxon heritage and national identity. As country music historian Bill Malone has pointed out, the culture that was seen as the most "American" was that which was the most British.[14]

While Burchenal and Ford regarded New England as one of the "most truly American sections of our country," others looked to the southern mountains. Berea College President William Frost had described the "highland stock" of eastern Kentucky, in 1899, as racially pure, "native born" Anglo-Saxons. According to Frost, these "mountain Americans," like the old Anglo-American stock of New England, had remained isolated from the impurities of recent "foreign immigration" and had preserved true "American" culture. It was through this lens that the southern Appalachian square dances came to be perceived not just as "Appalachian" or "Southern" but as "American" folk dances.

These dances, which the local-color writers a generation earlier had ridiculed as the outdated and unfashionable recreation of the southern mountaineers ("interminable reels and antiquated Cotillons"[15]), were soon being celebrated and performed onstage as true American folk dances. By 1926 students from the Pine Mountain School were giving demonstrations of the "Kentucky Mountain Running Set," and in 1928 square dance teams began to perform at Bascom Lunsford's Mountain Dance and Folk Festival in Asheville, North Carolina. During the 1930s square dance teams were also featured on stage at Virginia's White Top Folk Festival as well as at the National Folk Festival,[16] and in 1938, once mixed-gender dancing was allowed at Berea College, the Berea College Country Dancers began performing reenactments of Sharp's description of "Set Running."

When King George VI and Queen Elizabeth of England visited America in 1939, Bascom Lunsford was asked to arrange a performance of American folk dances at the Roosevelt White House. Lunsford brought not one but two square dance groups from the southern mountains. One was Sam Queen's Soco Gap Square Dance Team from western North Carolina, which had been a perennial favorite at the Mountain Dance and Folk Festival. The other was a square dance group from Skyline Farms, a Works Progress Administration community in the Cumberland Mountains of northern Alabama. Skyline Farms was one of twenty-six new communities built by the WPA in the 1930s to resettle tenant farmers and their families during the Great Depression, and square dancing was promoted there as a way to build a sense of community.[17] Grace Ryan came down from Michigan to the University of North

Figure 15.3. Square Dance at Skyline Farms (northern Alabama, 1937). Photo: Ben Shahn. Library of Congress Prints and Photographs Division (LC-USF33-006289-M3)

Carolina to train recreation leaders for these new settlements; Lunsford had been recruited (in 1934) to teach the dances at Skyline Farms.[18]

Hillbillies and Cowboys

The recognition and celebration of the Appalachian square dances as American folk dances during the 1920s and 1930s coincided with the early years of commercial recording and radio, and these new industries are responsible for the two common stereotypes that came to be associated with these dances: the hillbilly and the cowboy. Although the term "Hill-Billie" did not appear in print until 1900, the image created by the local-color writers of the southern mountaineers being ignorant and backward was well established in the public's mind by that time.[19] Consequently, when record companies began to record rural Southern dance music in the 1920s, this image was used to promote and market the music. Many of the early recordings included humorous skits that played up the hillbilly stereotypes. Bands were given colorful-sounding names, such as the Possum Hunters, the Fruit Jar Drinkers, and the Hill Billies, and musicians, who had earlier appeared in publicity photos wearing suits and ties, began to dress in bib overalls and rustic hats.

Early country music radio shows, such as the "National Barn Dance," contributed to the popularization of the hillbilly image. This variety show, which was first broadcast by WLS in Chicago in 1924, could be heard each Saturday night coast to coast. The performers who appeared on the "National

Barn Dance" included Midwesterners as well as Southerners—Bill Monroe, in his pre-bluegrass years, performed onstage as a dancer at these live radio broadcasts in the late 1920s—and though it was not explicitly billed as "hillbilly" music, the music featured on this radio program was promoted as being from the southern mountains, and the common hillbilly stereotypes were clearly understood.

Starting in the 1930s, country musicians who sought to distance themselves from the negative connotations associated with the hillbilly image looked to the West for a new identity. America's fascination with the West was nothing new: "Buffalo Bill" Cody had toured America with his Wild West show in the 1880s, and romantic western themes had been popular in dime novels and silent films. The western cowboys personified the spirit of America, and like the southern mountaineers, they were perceived as Anglo-Saxon.[20] (Never mind the fact that the earliest cowboys were the vaqueros of northern Mexico, and there were also Native American and African American cowboys.)

Gene Autry, while not the first singing cowboy, is the one most responsible for popularizing the western image in country music.[21] The son of an Oklahoma rancher, Autry began his singing career imitating yodeler Jimmie Rodgers, and in 1931 he started performing on WLS as "Oklahoma's Yodeling Cowboy." Dressed in western regalia, Autry soon became one of the biggest stars of the "National Barn Dance," inspiring other country musicians to likewise adopt western personas and costumes. When Rubye Blevins, a young singer from Arkansas, teamed up with a square dance band from Kentucky to perform on WLS in 1933, the group donned western outfits and changed their names to Patsy Montana and the Prairie Ramblers.[22] The following year, Autry went on to Hollywood, where he immortalized the singing cowboy in more than ninety films on the silver screen. Among those who followed him west to Hollywood was Leonard Slye, a singer and square dance caller from southern Ohio who became known as Roy Rogers. These singing cowboys of Hollywood, like those heard on the "National Barn Dance," romanticized the West, prompting "hillbilly" musicians across the country to trade in their bib overalls for cowboy hats.[23] Not everyone, however, embraced the western image. Back in Asheville, at the Mountain Dance and Folk Festival, Bascom Lunsford wanted to present mountaineers, not cowboys, so when musicians showed up wearing cowboy hats, he insisted that they remove them before appearing onstage.[24]

During the 1930s, following the trend in country music, square dancing likewise became associated with the West. This was largely due to Lloyd Shaw (1890–1958), a Colorado educator who taught folk dancing at the Cheyenne Mountain School in Colorado Springs. Shaw had been teaching his students European folk dances as well as the New England quadrilles and contras in Henry Ford's dance book, which he (Shaw) claimed was "the best book for anyone who is interested in these fine old dances."[25] At some point, however, Shaw became interested in the square dances that the cowboys had "enjoyed on the ranches and in the cow towns of the West," and he began to seek out callers, who still knew this "old American folk tradition of purely Western dancing."[26]

Shaw acknowledged that these "cowboy dances," like the square dances of the Ozarks and the Midwest, had roots in the southern mountains. Western fiddlers likewise played the old "Virginia reels" that had come west with the settlers during the nineteenth century, and "Bird in the Cage," a visiting-couple figure once danced at antebellum slave frolics in the South, was known throughout the Midwest and as far west as Colorado.[27] The square dances of southwest Texas, New Mexico, Arizona, and southern Colorado, however, also included figures adopted from the quadrilles that were not found in the Appalachian dances. Shaw, who was clearly influenced by Ford and Burchenal, attributes these figures to New England,[28] but it is more likely that they came from closer sources. During the nineteenth century, French quadrilles were popular along the rivers of the Midwest that flowed into the Mississippi, and Mexican Quadrilles ("Las Cuadrillas") were known in the Southwest during the early years of the Mexican Republic.[29] California, Nevada, Utah, most of Arizona, and parts of New Mexico, Colorado, and Wyoming, after all, were Mexican territory until 1848, when this territory was ceded to the United States at the end of the Mexican-American War.

Shaw began to teach these square dances to his students in 1934, and by 1936 he had formed an exhibition team of sixteen high-schoolers called the Cheyenne Mountain Dancers.[30] Like the singing cowboys of Hollywood, Shaw's dancers donned elaborate western costumes. Initially performing at festivals in Colorado, the Cheyenne Mountain Dancers soon gained national recognition, and they were invited to perform across the country, including at the National Folk Festival in Washington, D.C., in 1939. The following year, Shaw, who was once described as "an educator with the instincts of a showman and the zeal of a missionary,"[31] began teaching these "cowboy dances" to dance leaders from around the country at annual summer workshops. The popularity of Shaw's dances following World War II led to the development of modern Western square dancing, a recreational form of square dance that became popular throughout America during the second half of the twentieth century.[32] By that time, the association between square dancing and the West was firmly fixed in the minds of many Americans, and dancers at square dance clubs across the country, from southern California to New England, began dressing in western outfits like those worn by Shaw's dancers and the singing cowboys of Hollywood.[33]

The American Square Dance Revival

When the "National Barn Dance" began broadcasting in 1924, Missourian Tom Owen could be heard calling out square dance figures each Saturday night. Initially, his calls, like those on the 78-rpm recordings of that time, were similar to what one would have heard at a local barn dance—simple prompts with a little rhyming patter thrown in. During the 1930s, however, as the country music industry professionalized, calling styles changed, and dance callers, like the musicians, became entertainers. With the advent of the microphone to amplify their voices above the music, colorful rhyming patter calls became the norm. Callers across the country soon adopted this new style of calling, even in New England, where Earl "Happy" Hale, a professional dance caller from Bernardston, Massachusetts, who claimed to be known "from Maine to California," "[kept] the dances going with a thousand little 'fill-in' calls."[34]

In addition to patter calling, Hale was known for his singing square dance calls, a style of calling that likewise was made possible by the advent of the PA system. As in the older tradition of play parties and singing games from which this style of calling likely developed, the dance prompts take the place of the lyrics of a popular song or are sung to the melody of a fiddle tune. Grace Ryan referred to it in 1926 as a "Caller's Song."[35] One of Hale's dances, sung to Stephen Foster's popular minstrel song from the 1850s, "Camptown Races," includes the Southern figure, "Bird in the Cage."[36] Hale's calling style and dance repertoire clearly reflect the influence of the Midwestern callers whose dance calling could be heard on 78s as well as the weekly broadcasts of the "National Barn Dance."[37] This was a radical departure from the New England tradition of sparsely prompted quadrilles and contra dances. Beth Tolman and Ralph Page noted in 1937 that although these "modern quadrilles" were "regarded with contempt" by older dancers, "the newer generation found them fun to do . . . and so they became established throughout southern New England."[38] That same year (1937), Hale won a calling competition at the Eastern States Exposition, an agricultural fair in West Springfield, Massachusetts, and after being declared a "world champion square dance caller," he, too, was invited to perform on the "National Barn Dance" in Chicago.[39]

"Happy" Hale and the other professional dance callers of his era were part of a revival of square dancing in America that was in full swing by the 1940s. Newly-formed recreational square dance clubs began to meet at community centers, and fueled by a proliferation of square dance books and records, as well as Shaw's summer workshops, this dance revival led to the blending of regional traditions and the subsequent standardization of square dancing in America. Southern visiting-couple figures, which became widely known throughout the country, were now seen as "American" square dance figures.

A key figure in this square dance movement was Margot Mayo (1910–1974), a native of Texas, whose family was from Kentucky. Mayo, an amateur folklorist, was active in the urban folk revival movement, and in the early 1930s she founded a recreational folk dance group, called the American Square Dance Group, in New York City. In her book *The American Square Dance* (1943) Mayo describes "square sets" from rural New York State that include Southern visiting-couple figures, and while she distinguishes these dances from the quadrilles of the Northeast, she does not identify them as being Southern but rather "American" square dances (which is what they had become by that time).[40]

By the 1940s square dancing was so mainstream in America that square dancers appeared in advertisements for cigarettes, soft drinks, and beer,[41] and record companies soon began to produce square dance records. Unlike the earlier "Barn Dance" 78-rpm recordings of the 1920s, which included dance calls merely as a colorful complement to the music, the recordings of the 1940s, which were intended for dancers in recreational dance groups, featured professional callers. These recordings eliminated the need for live musicians, but they also contributed to the dissemination of new dances and the standardization of the dance repertoire. As a result, dances, such as "Forward Up Six," "Dip 'n Dive," "Duck for the Oyster," "Take a Peek," "Texas Star," and "Swing Sally Gooden," which were not part of the traditional dance repertoire of Appalachia in the early twentieth century, are now known in West Virginia and throughout the country.

The square dance revival of the mid-twentieth century is long past, recreational modern western square dancing is on the decline, and community dances are now rare. In recent years, however, there has been a renewal of interest in traditional old-time square dancing. A new generation of young callers and dancers has discovered these dances, and new dance venues have become established in scattered locations across the country, from the Appalachians to the Pacific Northwest. Since 2004 more than a dozen "Dare To Be Square" square dance weekends have taken place (in North Carolina, Virginia, West Virginia, Tennessee, Oregon, Washington, and California), and these workshops have fostered a new generation of callers.[42] The old square dance books and records from the 1940s and 1950s can still be found in many libraries, and new online resources are also available. These include the *Square Dance History Project*, an online archive that documents the history of square dancing in America through videos, photographs, audio files, and text.[43] Traditional squares continue to be danced at weddings, summer camps, festivals, and other events, including community dances, so it appears likely that these American folk dances will be around for future generations to enjoy.

Black Invisibility

During the square dance revival of the twentieth century, the traditional music and dances of the southern mountains were commonly portrayed as white European American culture and heritage. That is certainly how Sharp, Burchenal, Lunsford, Shaw, and others in the folk and recreational dance movement perceived these traditions. This view, however, overlooks the presence of black Americans and their significant contributions to the shared mountain culture. Romantic accounts of the "stalwart pioneers" who

Figure 15.4. Dare to Be Square (Helvetia, West Virginia, 2014). Photo: Lee Bidgood

cleared the land and settled the Appalachian frontier, likewise, seldom recognize the importance of black labor. John C. Campbell claimed, "There were few Negroes in the Highlands in the early times" and they were never "a factor in rural mountain life."[44] In fact, though, as discussed earlier, the early population of the southern backcountry was a "mixed Multitude of all Classes and Complexions,"[45] and there have been blacks in the southern mountains since the time of the earliest settlers. For the most part, however, they have been an unacknowledged presence in the predominantly white population. African American scholar Edward Cabbell has referred to this as the "invisibility" of blacks in Appalachia.[46]

The organizers of early folk festivals of the 1930s, who promoted a white, Anglocentric Appalachia, contributed to this perception. Bascom Lunsford spoke of possible Native American influence on the traditional dances of western North Carolina, and his Mountain Dance and Folk Festival included participants from Cherokee,[47] but he ignored the contributions of African Americans. Sam Queen, one of Lunsford's personal favorites ("the dancingest man in the land") had learned from Bob Love, an African American dancer and square dance caller; and just to the north, in Madison County, African American fiddler George Buckner was still active playing music at the Spring Creek community in the 1930s. This, however, was not the image of mountain culture that Lunsford chose to present. The only African American known to have participated at the Mountain Dance and Folk Festival was Billy Smith, a "little negro tap dancer" who performed at the festival in 1942.[48] Virginia's White Top Folk Festival (1931–1939) likewise did not include black performers; embracing the ideas of William Frost, Ellen Semple, and Cecil Sharp, its organizers portrayed "authentic" Appalachian music and folk dance as Anglo-American, as exemplified by performances of the sword dance team from the Pine Mountain School.[49] While both of these festivals celebrated and encouraged traditional musicians and dancers in white communities, they likely contributed to the neglect and decline of these same traditions in black communities.

The commercialization of Appalachian music in the 1920s and 1930s likewise contributed to the whitewashing of the music and dance traditions. Recording companies segregated artists by race for marketing purposes, and even though there were still black fiddlers in the southern mountains, they were not recorded. Only white fiddlers appeared on the "Hillbilly" records that purported to represent the rural music of the southern mountains; black artists were marketed in a separate catalog of "Race" records.[50]

The "black invisibility" described by Cabbell, however, is not unique to Appalachia but applies to America in general. Although there have been African Americans in North America for more than four hundred years, their contributions to American heritage, history, and culture have too often been ignored, overlooked, and forgotten. African slaves accompanied the Spanish explorers of the mid-sixteenth century, and by 1619, the year before the Pilgrims landed at Plymouth Rock, there were African slaves in the English colony of Virginia. Over the next two centuries, hundreds of thousands more enslaved Africans were brought to North America, and by 1807, when the importation of slaves to the United States was abolished, there were more than one million blacks in the United States (19 percent of the population), including more than 180,000 free blacks.[51] With the end of the external slave trade and natural population growth, the proportion of native-born blacks increased during the nineteenth century. At the same time, with the arrival of successive waves of European immigrants, the proportion of native-born whites declined. As a result, by 1860 the proportion of native-born blacks was higher than the proportion of native-born whites.[52] The ancestors of today's black Americans, on average, arrived in America during the decade that preceded the American Revolution. By comparison, the ancestors of Americans of European descent arrived, on average, one hundred years later.[53] Although the nativists of the late nineteenth century considered Americans of English ancestry who arrived before the revolution to be the "native stock," black Americans clearly have an equal claim to that title (as of course do Native Americans).

In 1976 the nation's bicentennial year, Western square dance caller Betty Casey characterized square dancing as "uniquely American." She wrote, "The format, many of the folk dance movements, and the terminology incorporated into the square dance were brought by early emigrants from other countries to the United States. Borrowed bits of foreign dances such as French quadrilles, Irish jigs, English reels, and Spanish fandangos have blended with American folkways and customs into the square dance."[54] Casey's perception of the roots of the American square dance is broader than Sharp's Anglocentric interpretation, but it remains a white, Eurocentric view that ignores the significant contributions that generations of black Americans have made to "American folkways and customs" for nearly four hundred years.

While Betty Casey and others rightly celebrate square dancing as being "uniquely American," if we were to list other types of music and dance that would also be considered "uniquely American," what would we include? Musical forms would include jazz, blues, ragtime, soul, gospel, rhythm and blues, swing, old-time music, bluegrass, country music, Cajun, Creole, zydeco, rock-and-roll, rap, hip-hop, and even barbershop quartet singing. Dance forms would include tap dance, swing dance, jazz dance, the Charleston, hip-hop, clogging, and more. It is no coincidence that *all* of these "uniquely American" forms of music and dance, if not originating in African American culture, were at least influenced by it, so it should come as no surprise that the same is true of the American square dance. African American author and historian W. E. B. Du Bois, who pointed out the "gift" of African music to American culture, wrote, "Would America have been America without her Negro people?"[55]

The countless black fiddlers who provided music and called out the figures at dances in America for more than two centuries are now gone, and, sadly, they are, for the most part, also forgotten. While the African-derived banjo provides tangible evidence of the African American influence on the Appalachian musical tradition, unfortunately no such clear artifact exists for the dances. In *The History of Square Dancing* (1957), S. Foster Damon states that dance calling was "invented" by "some smart American," but he makes no reference to the role of black musicians and their contributions to the tradition.[56] Claiming that dance calling was "America's only unique contribution to the Square Dance," the keynote speaker at the 57th National Square Dance Convention in 2008 similarly attributed it to "typical Yankee ingenuity."[57] Dance calling is without a doubt the single most important factor in the creation of these American folk dances; they would not exist without it. There is no evidence, however, to suggest that it was a (presumably) white Yankee innovation. Instead, all of my research indicates that it has roots in the African tradition and was first popularized by African American dance musicians. Dance calling not only transformed the European set dances into uniquely American dances, but it also made them accessible to all classes of people and facilitated their proliferation as folk dances throughout rural America.

National Folk Dance

To some people, the American square dance is more than just an old folk dance from the days of the pioneers and the cowboys; it is a symbol of our nation's heritage. Since the mid-1960s dancers involved in the modern Western square dance movement have sought to have square dancing officially designated by Congress as the "National Folk Dance of the United States of America,"[58] adding it to the relatively short and selective list of national symbols that includes the national anthem, the flag, the Great Seal, the bald eagle, and the American rose. Identifying square dancing as "part of the folklore of this Nation," proponents of this designation also claim that it promotes "good manners and proper etiquette," "fosters family unity," and "embodies democratic principles by dissolving arbitrary social distinctions among its participants."[59] While these benefits may be worthwhile (and perhaps true), the "Promenade Act" (as it came to be known), despite numerous efforts, has lacked sufficient support in Congress to become law.[60] After several failed attempts at legislation in the 1980s, this bill most recently came before the 108th Congress in 2003, and once again, House Resolution 645 ("To designate the square dance as the national folk dance") did not pass. Having failed repeatedly at the national level, a group of modern Western square dancers, the United Square Dancers of America (USDA), has instead focused its efforts at the state level, and as of 2015, thirty-one states have passed legislation designating square dancing as their official state folk dance.[61]

Folk dances, regardless of their origin, are informal, vernacular social dances that are transmitted through the oral tradition and are typically associated with a live folk music tradition. While traditional, community-based square dancing would meet these criteria, modern Western square dancing, which is a standardized, club-based, recreational activity performed to recordings of contemporary popular or commercial country music, does not. Although the latter has roots in the earlier traditional folk dances, that association alone does not make it a folk dance.

In support of the "Promenade Act," the USDA praises square dancing as "a great part of our American heritage and history."[62] Important questions, however, arise: How is "American heritage" being defined? Is it narrowly defined, as Anglo-Saxon (white), as in the minds of William Frost, Cecil Sharp, Elizabeth Burchenal, Henry Ford, Bascom Lunsford, Lloyd Shaw, and their followers? Or, does "American heritage" also include the little known and often unacknowledged contributions of other Europeans, African Americans, and Native Americans?

In a nation such as ours, with a diverse population made up of so many racial and ethnic groups, each with its own folk traditions, is it appropriate, or even possible, to designate one type of dance as *the* National Folk Dance? Traditional, community-based square dancing is certainly a form of American folk dance, but it is not the only one; to select it above other types of dance would be to ignore the diversity of our nation. What about the contributions that Latinos, Asians, and others have made to the culture and heritage of America? At a congressional committee hearing to consider the "Promenade Act" (House Resolution 1706) in 1984, Ralph Rinzler, who at that time was the assistant secretary for public service at the Smithsonian Institution, summed it up this way: "I, as a folklorist, find it difficult to comprehend, especially in a multicultural society like ours, how one could have a 'national folk dance.'"[63]

If one dance form were selected above all others as *the* national folk dance, the criteria and implications of such a decision would need to be considered carefully. Would such a national dance have to remain static and standardized, or would it be allowed to change and evolve over time, as folk traditions naturally do? What would it mean to have a dance represent the whole country? Is that possible in a country with as diverse a population as the United States? Would it have to be popular with and/or familiar to a certain percentage of the population? Would it have to reflect the influence of a certain percentage of ethnic or racial constituencies? And finally, can a dance form be considered a true folk dance if it is regulated and governed by private or public organizations? These are questions that would need to be raised and answered if we were to select a national folk dance.[64]

* * *

More than a dozen years ago, when I first started to investigate the roots and branches of these Appalachian dances, I naïvely thought that it would be a straightforward story. As a musician, dancer, and dance caller, I knew these traditions well. They are a part of the culture of southern Appalachia where I live, and I have participated in them for many years. Little did I know how challenging it would be to account for these largely undocumented American folk dances, which have so many layers and strands of cultural influence. These social dance traditions have never been static but have changed and evolved over time, reflecting changes in demographics, popular culture, modes of transportation, social customs, politics, technology, and other factors.

The Appalachian dances are clearly not the pure survivals of dances imported from Europe; they developed in the Southern backcountry during the nineteenth century, incorporating elements borrowed from a number of traditions. Their roots extend far from the southern mountains, and my research has led me not only throughout nineteenth-century America—from New England to New Orleans–but further afield—to Scotland, Ireland, England, France, Africa, and the West Indies. Their branches likewise extend beyond the southern mountains. These Southern dances are the foundation of the Midwestern and Western square dances, and today, Southern dance figures are known across the country, from Southern California to New England.

Similarly, team clogging has now spread far from its birthplace in western North Carolina, and flatfoot dancers can be found at old-time music jams and festivals from Boston to Berkeley.

No doubt there is still more to learn about these southern Appalachian dance traditions. I hope, however, that by exploring their history, I have contributed to our understanding of these American folk traditions and have dispelled some of the longstanding myths and misconceptions regarding their origins. The hoedowns, reels, and frolics of rural Appalachia are not the provenance or "racial inheritance" of one particular ethnic group; instead, they are the result of cultural exchange and the creolization of traditions that occurred in the Southern backcountry during the nineteenth century. These folk traditions are an important part of the cultural history of this country, and they are a reflection of the racial and cultural diversity—not just of the southern mountains, but of America.

Appendix

"Barn Dances with Calls" (1924–1933)

Table 2. Discography of 78-rpm Recordings with Southern Dance Callers (1924–1933)

Region One: Southwest Virginia/North Carolina/East Tennessee (11 Callers, 23 Recordings)				
Year	Caller	County/State	Musicians	Recordings
1924	Unknown	Grayson/VA	Whitter's Virginia Breakdowners	Mississippi Sawyer, Sourwood Mountain
1926 1927	Al Hopkins (b. 1889)	Watauga/NC	The Hill Billies Al Hopkins and His Buckle Busters	Walking in the Parlor Boatin' Up Sandy, Bug in the Taters
1927	G. H. (Hub) Mahaffey	Sullivan/TN	Dykes' Magic City Trio	Callahan's Reel, Cotton-Eyed Joe, Huckleberry Blues [East Tennessee Blues], Red Steer, Shortnin' Bread, Tennessee Girls
1927	Ben Jarrell	Surry/NC	Da Costa Woltz's Southern Broadcasters	John Brown's Dream, Richmond Cotillion
1927	Eck Dunford (b. 1880)	Carroll/VA	Ernest Stoneman and Blue Ridge Corn Shuckers	Old Time Corn Shuckin'—Pt. 2 [Ship That Never Returned]
1927	Unknown	Sullivan/TN	Vance's Tennessee Breakdowners	Tennessee Breakdown [Sally Goodin]
1927	Leonard Porter (b. 1898)	Russell/VA	Fiddlin' Powers and Family	Old Virginia Reel—Pt. 2 [Cumberland Gap/Flop-Eared Mule]
1927	Unknown	Danville, VA	Four Virginians	Swing Your Partner, New Coon in Town, Promenade All [Bill Bailey]
1928	G. B. Grayson (b. 1887)	Ashe/NC	G. B. Grayson and Henry Whitter	Old Jimmie Sutton
1928	Ernest Stoneman (b. 1893)	Carroll/VA	Ernest Stoneman and The Blue Ridge Corn Shuckers Sweet Brothers	A Serenade in the Mountains—Pt. 2 [Molly Put the Kettle On/Love Somebody] I'm Gonna Marry That Pretty Little Girl
1929	Unknown	Roanoke, VA	Roanoke Jug Band	Johnny Lover

Table 2. (*continued*)

Region Two: West Virginia (5 Callers, 12 Recordings)				
Year	Caller	County/State	Musicians	Recordings
1927	Unknown	Logan/WV	Williamson Brothers and Curry	The Fun's All Over
1928	Andy Patterson (b. 1889)	Wood/WV	Warren Caplinger	Chicken Reel
1928	Ernest Legg (b. 1904)	Kanawha/WV	Kessinger Brothers	Turkey in the Straw, Hell among the Yearlings, Forked Deer Hornpipe, Girl I Left Behind Me, Chicken in the Barnyard, Devil's Dream, Patty on the Turnpike, Wild Horse
1928	Unknown	Cabell/WV	Calaway's West Virginia Mountaineers	The Cornshucker's Frolic
1928	Frank Hutchison (b. 1897)	Logan/WV	Sherman Lawson and Frank Hutchison	Wild Hogs in the Red Brush [Miss McLeod's Reel]

Region Three: Kentucky/Southern Ohio/Southern Indiana (6 Callers, 20 Recordings)				
Year	Caller	County/State	Musicians	Recordings
1924	Sam Jones	Hamilton/OH	Stovepipe No. 1 (Sam Jones)	Cripple Creek/Sourwood Mountain, Turkey in the Straw
1929	Asa Martin (b. 1900)	Clark/KY	Doc Roberts	Girl I Left Behind, Who's Been Here Since I've Been Gone, Martha Campbell, Waltz the Hall
1932			Charlie Wilson and His Hillbillies	Cuttin' at the Point, Shelven Rock
1933			Charlie Wilson and His Hillbillies	Ride the Goat over the Mountain
			Hatton Brothers	Hook and Line, Wish I Had My Time Again
1931	Albert Crockett (born c. 1884)	Bath/KY	Crockett's Kentucky Mountaineers	Sugar in My Coffee
1931	Lee Day (b. 1900)	Grayson/KY	Lonesome Luke and His Farm Hands	Dogs in the Ashcan [Flop-Eared Mule], Wild Hog in the Woods, Beaver Valley Breakdown, Halfway to Arkansas
1931	Jess Hillard (born c. 1895)	Wayne/IN	Jess Hillard and His New Richmond Aces	Arkansas Traveler, Cackling Hen
1931	Unknown	Anderson/KY	Jimmie Johnson's String Band	Step Lively, Washington Quadrille

Region Four: Middle Tennessee (4 Callers, 9 Recordings)				
Year	Caller	County/State	Musicians	Recordings
1927	Dave Macon (b. 1870)	Warren/TN	Uncle Dave Macon	Sleepy Lou, Tom and Jerry
1928	Humphrey Bate (b. 1875)	Sumner/TN	Dr. Humphrey Bate and His Possum Hunters	Goin' Up-Town
1928	W. J. (Bill) Barret (born c. 1872)			Billy in the Lowground, Take Your Foot Out of the Mud
1928	George R. Miles (born c. 1889)	Davidson or Jackson(?)/TN	Crook Brothers String Band	Job in Getting' There [Shortnin' Bread], My Wife Died Friday Night, Going across the Sea, Love Somebody [Too Young to Marry]

Region Five: North Georgia/Western North Carolina (15 Callers, 25 Recordings)

Year	Caller	County/State	Musicians	Recordings
1924	Samantha Bumgarner (b. 1880)	Jackson/NC	Samantha Bumgarner	Fly around My Pretty Little Miss, Shout Lou
1924	Unknown	Buncombe/NC	J. D. Harris	Buckin' Mule, Whip the Devil Round the Stump
1925	Webb Phillips	Gwinnett/GA	Dixie String Band	Chickens Don't Roost Too High for Me
1927	John Carson (b. 1868)	Fannin/GA	Fiddlin' John Carson	Cotton-Eyed Joe
1927	Ted (Ezra) Hawkins	Gwinnett/GA	Gid Tanner and His Skillet Lickers	Fiddlers' Convention in Georgia pt. 2 [Bile Em Cabbage Down]
1927	Unknown	Dekalb/GA	Scottdale String Band	Chinese Breakdown, In the Shade of the Parasol, Hiawatha Breakdown, Hop Light Ladies, Old Folks Better Go to Bed [Soldier's Joy]
1927	Bill Chitwood (b. 1891)	Gordon/GA	Bill Chitwood	Kitty Hill
1928	Unknown	Fulton/GA	Hershal Brown's Washboard Band	Liberty
1928	Unknown	Fulton/GA	Watkin's Band	Bob Murphy, Gideon
1928	Unknown	Dekalb/GA	Scottdale String Band	Share 'em, Green Mountain Poker [Flop-Eared Mule]
1928	Jim Baxter	Gordon/GA	Andrew and Jim Baxter	Georgia Stomp
1929	Unknown	Hall/GA	Chumbler, Coker, and Rice	Alabama Square Dance—Pt. 1 [Black Eyed Susie], Alabama Square Dance—Pt. 2
1930	John Dilleshaw (b. 1896)	Paulding/GA	Seven Foot Dilly	Square Dance Fight on Ball Top Mountain—Pt. 1 [Soldier's Joy], Square Dance Fight on Ball Top Mountain—Pt. 2 [Liberty]
1932	Unknown	Unknown/GA	Clayton McMichen and Riley Puckett	Hog-Trough Reel [McMichen's Reel]
1932	Clayton McMichen (b. 1900)	Bartow/GA	Clayton McMichen's Georgia Wildcats	Arkansas Traveler

Region Six: Mississippi (3 Callers, 6 Recordings)

Year	Caller	County/State	Musicians	Recordings
1927	Unknown	Leake/MS	Leake County Revelers	Leather Britches
1928	A. D. Coggin	Lee/MS	Floyd Ming and His Pep Steppers	Old Red, Tupelo Blues, White Mule
1930	Fonzo Cannon	Hinds/MS	Freeny's Barn Dance Band	Mississippi Square Dance—Pt 1 [Fire on the Mountain], Mississippi Square Dance—Pt 2 [Sally Ann]

Table 3. Dance Forms and Figures on 78-rpm Recordings (1924–1933)

REGION/STATE	VA	NC	TN	NC	VA	TN	VA	VA	NC	VA	VA	WV	WV	WV	WV	WV	OH	KY
CALLER MUSICIANS	Unknown (Whitter)	Al Hopkins	G. H. (Hub) Mahaffey	Ben Jarrell	Eck Dunford	Unknown (Vance)	Leonard Porter	Unknown (Virginians)	G. B. Grayson	Ernest Stoneman	Unknown (Roanoke)	Unknown (Williamson)	Andy Patterson	Ernest Legg	Unknown (Calaway)	Frank Hutchison	Sam Jones	Asa Martin
YEAR	1924	1926	1927	1927	1927	1927	1927	1927	1928	1928	1929	1927	1928	1928	1928	1928	1924	1929
DANCE FORM																		
Visiting couples	■	■	■	■	■	■	■	■	■	■	■	■	■	■	■	■		■
Four-couple square	■	■	■	■	■	■	■		■		■	■	■	■	■	■	■	■
Big ring								■		■								
FIGURES																		
Circle (eight or big ring)	■	■	■	■	■	■	■		■	■	■	■		■		■	■	■
Circle Four	■	■				■		■			■	■	■	■				■
Swing Opposite, Swing Partner		■	■				■	■			■			■				■
Balance					■	■		■		■	■	■	■	■	■	■		■
Right Hands Across, Left Back		■	■				■	■	■		■	■						■
Promenade	■	■	■	■	■	■	■	■	■	■		■	■	■		■	■	■
Grand Right and Left	■	■			■		■				■	■	■	■	■	■		■
Bird in the Cage	■		■										■	■	■	■		■
Ocean Wave																■		
Basket		■					■								■	■		■
Single File									■			■		■				■
Swing Ma and Pa (Adam and Eve)		■	■	■			■							■				■
Double Elbow Swing														■		■		■
Partner Right, Partner Left														■				
Lady Round Lady, Gent Also														■				■
Do-si-do (hand-turning)												■		■				■
Ladies Back to Back, Gents Around	■	■	■	■			■	■			■							■
Chase the Rabbit														■	■			
Jig Figure														■				
Do-si-do (circular)							■											
Shoo-Fly Swing																		
Allemande Left, Grand Right and Left													■	■				
Half Promenade													■	■				
Ladies Right Hands Across				■										■	■			
Divide the Ring														■				■
Right and Left Through													■					
Figure Eight			■						■									■
Ladies Chain													■					
Pokey-Four														■				
Swing Three				■		■												
Cowboy Loop																		
Outside Circle, Inside Swing																		
Sashay																		

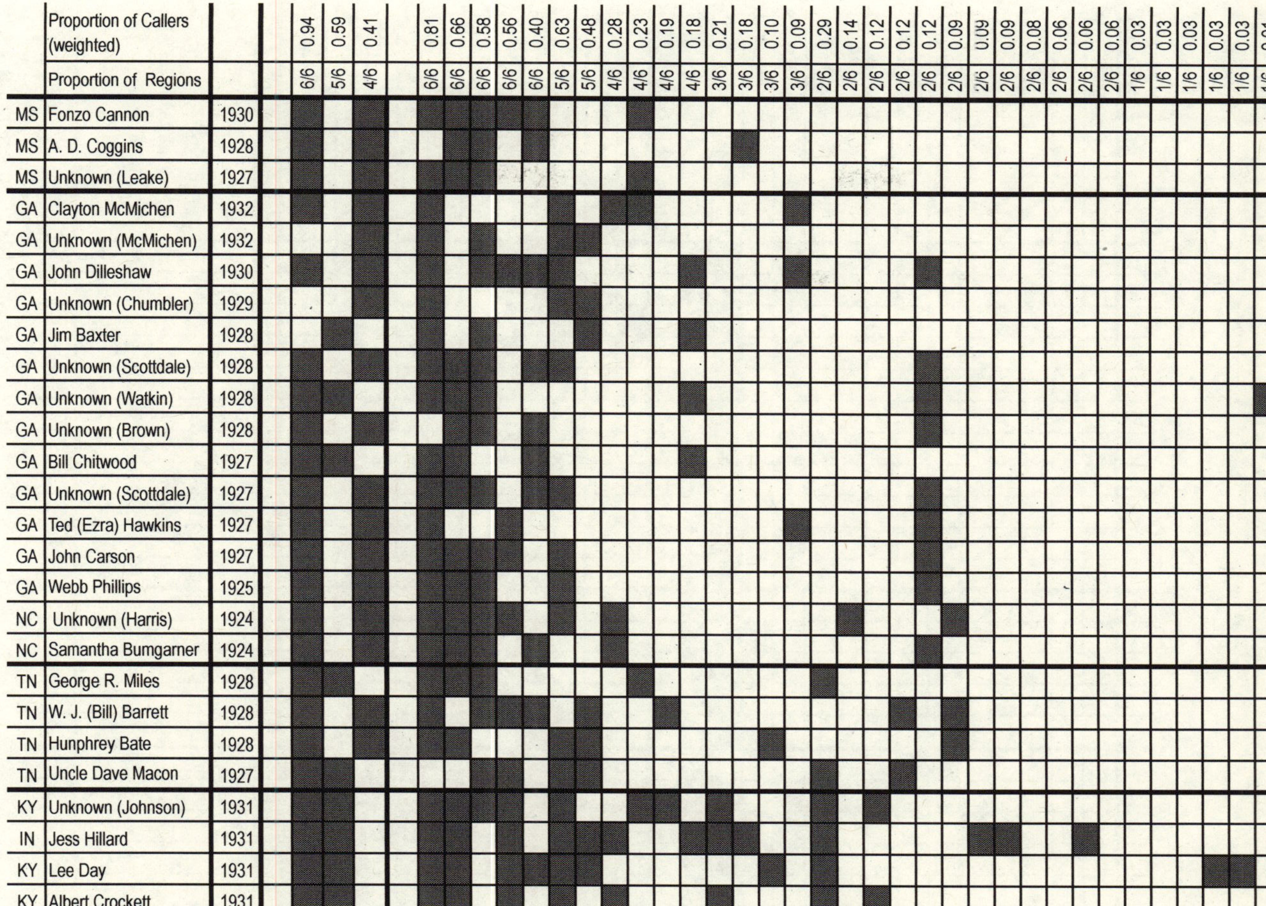

Proportion of Callers (weighted)
Proportion of Regions
0.94 0.59 0.41 0.81 0.66 0.58 0.56 0.40 0.63 0.48 0.28 0.23 0.19 0.18 0.21 0.18 0.10 0.09 0.29 0.14 0.12 0.12 0.12 0.09 0.09 0.09 0.08 0.06 0.06 0.06 0.03 0.03 0.03 0.03 0.03 0.01
6/6 5/6 4/6 6/6 6/6 6/6 6/6 6/6 5/6 5/6 4/6 4/6 4/6 4/6 3/6 3/6 3/6 3/6 2/6 2/6 2/6 2/6 2/6 2/6 2/6 2/6 2/6 2/6 2/6 2/6 1/6 1/6 1/6 1/6 1/6 1/6
MS Fonzo Cannon 1930
MS A. D. Coggins 1928
MS Unknown (Leake) 1927
GA Clayton McMichen 1932
GA Unknown (McMichen) 1932
GA John Dilleshaw 1930
GA Unknown (Chumbler) 1929
GA Jim Baxter 1928
GA Unknown (Scottdale) 1928
GA Unknown (Watkin) 1928
GA Unknown (Brown) 1928
GA Bill Chitwood 1927
GA Unknown (Scottdale) 1927
GA Ted (Ezra) Hawkins 1927
GA John Carson 1927
GA Webb Phillips 1925
NC Unknown (Harris) 1924
NC Samantha Bumgarner 1924
TN George R. Miles 1928
TN W. J. (Bill) Barrett 1928
TN Hunphrey Bate 1928
TN Uncle Dave Macon 1927
KY Unknown (Johnson) 1931
IN Jess Hillard 1931
KY Lee Day 1931
KY Albert Crockett 1931

Table 4. Calling Styles, Terminology, and Instrumentation on 78-rpm Recordings (1924–1933)

REGION/STATE	VA	NC	TN	NC	VA	TN	VA	VA	NC	VA	VA	WV	WV	WV	WV	WV	OH	KY	KY	KY	IN	KY
CALLER MUSICIAN	Unknown (Whitter)	Al Hopkins	G. H. (Hub) Mahaffey	Ben Jarrell	Eck Dunford	Unknown (Vance)	Leonard Porter	Unknown (Virginians)	G. B. Grayson	Ernest Stoneman	Unknown (Roanoke)	Unknown (Williamson)	Andy Patterson	Ernest Legg	Unknown (Calaway)	Frank Hutchison	Sam Jones	Asa Martin	Albert Crockett	Lee Day	Jess Hillard	Unknown (Johnson)
YEAR	1924	1926	1927	1927	1927	1927	1927	1927	1928	1928	1929	1927	1928	1928	1928	1928	1924	1929	1931	1931	1931	1931
CALLING STYLE																						
Shouted prompts	■	■	■	■	■		■	■	■	■	■	■			■	■		■	■	■	■	■
Chanted (pitched calls)						■							■	■			■	■	■			
Sung calls																	■	■	■			
Rhyming patter												■	■	■		■		■	■	■	■	■
TERMINOLOGY																						
"corner"				■			■				■		■	■	■		■				■	■
"home"	■	■	■					■					■	■		■		■	■	■	■	■
"to your places..."	■		■				■								■	■	■	■			■	
"first four," "quadrille"																		■				■
"set"			■															■				
INSTRUMENTATION																						
Guitar	■	■	■		■	■	■	■	■	■	■	■	■	■	■	■	■	■	■	■	■	■
Fiddle	■	■	■	■	■	■	■	■	■	■	■	■	■	■	■	■		■	■	■	■	■
Tenor Banjo													■							■		■
Banjo (five-string)	■	■		■	■		■			■	■							■	■			
Mandolin							■				■										■	
Ukulele		■					■					■										
Bass																						
Harmonica																	■					
Kazoo																	■					
Bones																			■			
Autoharp			■																			
Piano		■																				
Tiple								■														
Washboard																						
TEMPO (AVG BPM)	129	129	133	141	123	141	128	134	133	127	133	137	145	138	129	124	113	134	134	144	131	136

	Proportion of Callers (weighted)		0.85	0.29	0.15	0.27	0.58	0.57	0.25	0.14	0.04	0.96	0.89	0.32	0.31	0.16	0.15	0.09	0.07	0.03	0.03	0.02	0.02	0.02	0.01	
	Proportion of Regions		6/6	4/6	3/6	2/6	6/6	6/6	5/6	2/6	2/6	6/6	6/6	5/6	4/6	4/6	3/6	2/6	2/6	1/6	1/6	1/6	1/6	1/6	1/6	
MS	Fonzo Cannon	1930	■				■	■				■	■	■												121
MS	A. D. Coggins	1928	■									■	■			■										133
MS	Unknown (Leake)	1927	■				■	■				■	■	■												136
GA	Clayton McMichen	1932	■						■			■	■	■												134
GA	Unknown (McMichen)	1932	■				■					■	■	■												136
GA	John Dilleshaw	1930	■				■	■				■	■	■				■								118
GA	Unknown (Chumbler)	1929	■					■				■	■			■										132
GA	Jim Baxter	1928	■				■					■	■													103
GA	Unknown (Scottdale)	1928	■				■	■				■				■										127
GA	Unknown (Watkin)	1928	■				■					■		■		■										131
GA	Unknown (Brown)	1928	■				■					■	■												■	145
GA	Bill Chitwood	1927	■		■			■				■	■													127
GA	Unknown (Scottdale)	1927	■					■	■			■				■										124
GA	Ted (Ezra) Hawkins	1927	■									■	■	■												132
GA	John Carson	1927	■		■		■					■	■	■												129
GA	Webb Phillips	1925	■					■				■	■	■												120
NC	Unknown (Harris)	1924	■					■					■		■											126
NC	Samantha Bumgarner	1924	■												■											138
TN	George R. Miles	1928		■			■			■		■		■					■							124
TN	W. J. (Bill) Barrett	1928	■	■			■	■				■	■		■		■	■								134
TN	Hunphrey Bate	1928	■	■	■		■					■	■		■		■	■								140
TN	Uncle Dave Macon	1927	■				■	■	■	■		■	■		■											130

Glossary of Dance Terms, Figures, and Steps

Dance Terms

active couple (or dancer)	Couple (or dancer) who leads a dance figure.
Boulangère	French circle dance popular at the beginning of the nineteenth century.
breakdown	Traditional rural Southern step dancing; fast Southern dance tune.
buckdance	Traditional rural Southern step dancing.
calling	Verbal prompts given to dancers during the course of a dance.
change	Chorus figure of a cotillion; part of a quadrille; an individual square dance.
Charleston	Popular social dance of the 1920s.
clogging (clog dance)	Percussive Southern step dancing.
contra dance	American descendant of the longways English country dance (see introduction, n17).
corner	Adjacent dancer (other than one's partner) in a square dance.
cotillion	French square dance, popular in the late eighteenth century; the music that accompanied these dances.
country dance	English set dance, popular in Europe and North America during the eighteenth century. The predominant form was the longways set for any number of couples, with partners facing each other in two opposing lines. In these progressive dances, the couples move one place up or down the set during each iteration of the dance figures.
double quadrille	Quadrille for eight couples, with two couples on each side of the square.

figure	Short, choreographed sequence of dance movements.
flatfooting	Style of buckdance with the feet close to the floor.
frolic	Informal rural dance party.
German (German Cotillion)	Nineteenth-century parlor dance game, popular from the 1840s through the 1880s, involving couple dancing, the trading of dance partners, and party favors.
hoedown	Traditional rural Southern step dancing; informal rural dance event; fast Southern dance tune.
home	Initial position of a couple in a square dance.
hornpipe	British stage step dance from the late eighteenth century; the dance tunes (4/4 time, with dotted rhythm) that accompanied these dances.
inactive couple (or dancer)	Couple (or dancer) who does not lead a dance figure but may participate in the performance of one initiated by an active couple (or dancer).
jig	Lively solo step dance; the dance tunes that accompanied these dances. This term was once used for any type of fast step dance or tune, not necessarily one in 6/8 time (compound duple meter) as it is today.
line dance	Choreographed dance consisting of a repeated sequence of steps performed simultaneously by individual dancers standing in lines. These gender-free dances, which first became popular in the 1970s, are most often associated with country western music.
longways set	Dance formation with partners facing each other in two opposing lines.
march	Formal nineteenth-century ballroom promenade; the music that accompanied these dances.
Maypole dance	English folk dance in which dancers weave a pattern of intertwining ribbons around a pole. Traditionally performed on May Day to celebrate the coming of summer.
minuet	Formal eighteenth-century French couple dance; the music that accompanied these dances.
modern Western square dancing	Recreational, club-based form of American square dance that became popular in the mid-twentieth century (see introduction, n17).
morris dance	English folk dance with rhythmic stepping and dance figures involving the use of sticks, swords, handkerchiefs, and jingling bells. Thought to have originated with the Moors of Spain.
opposite	The other person's partner (one's corner) in a two-couple pairing; the couple (or dancer) across the set in a four-couple square.
pantomime dance	Dance that imitates the motion of animals or common activities.
patter	Rhythmic, rhyming dance prompts.

play party	Dance games accompanied by singing rather than instrumental music.
progressive dance	Dance in which a traveling (active) couple dances with successive couples in the set.
promiscuous figure	Nineteenth-century quadrille figure that involved trading partners.
quadrille	French square dance from the first quarter of the nineteenth century combining a number of earlier cotillion figures into a longer dance, most often with five distinct parts ("changes"); traditional square dance of New England and the Northeast.
reel	Scottish and Irish dances that involve setting steps alternating with a weaving traveling figure; fast dance tunes (in 4/4 time) that accompany these dances; rural Southern set dances.
ring shout	African American religious dance from the Sea Islands of Georgia and South Carolina, characterized by dancers moving with shuffling steps in a single-file, counterclockwise circle.
round dance	Circular folk dance; couple dance, such as the waltz or two-step, in which couples travel counterclockwise around the dance floor.
Running Set	Cecil Sharp's name for the traditional square dances of eastern Kentucky.
set	Group of dancers; group of dances; to perform setting steps.
set dance	Dance, such as a square dance, contra dance, or reel, for two or more couples, involving movement through a series of dance figures.
setting step	Footwork performed in place as part of a set dance.
Sicilian circle	Large, circular set with pairs of couples facing each other (as in a contra dance).
singing square	Square dance in which the dance prompts are sung as lyrics to a song.
square dance	Set dance involving four couples in a square formation or any number of couples in a circle; event involving these dances.
step dance	Dance (such as buckdancing, flatfooting, and clogging) involving rhythmic and often percussive footwork.
Virginia reel	American variant of the English longways dance "Sir Roger de Coverley"; six-handed reels that were popular in Virginia during the late eighteenth and early nineteenth centuries; generic term for rural Southern dances and dance tunes during the nineteenth century.
visiting-couple figure	Dance figure performed with successive couples in a set.
Western square dance (traditional)	Traditional square dances of southwest Texas, New Mexico, Arizona, and southern Colorado that developed during the second half of the nineteenth century.

Dance Figures

Allemande	One-handed turn. The name comes from the French word for a late-eighteenth-century German couple dance that involved couples turning with intertwined arms.
Basket	For two or more couples in a circular set: The men join hands behind the women's backs and the women join hands behind the men's backs; the formation then spins to the left (clockwise).
Bird in the Cage	Individual dancer within a ring of dancers.
Bouquet Waltz	(see Waltz-Swing)
Box the Gnat	Partners trade places with the right hands joined, the woman turning to her left under the raised arms.
Cast-off	In a longways set: The top couple separates, the dancers turning individually down the outside of their respective sides of the set.
Chase the Rabbit (Chase the Squirrel)	For two couples: Following the pattern of a figure eight, the active couple, with the woman in the lead, passes single file between the inactive couple and to the left around the inactive woman; the active woman then leads through the inactive couple a second time, her partner following, passing to the right around the inactive man; the figure is then repeated with the man in the lead.
Cheat (Coquette, Cheat 'em If You Can, Cheat 'em or Swing 'em)	Active woman (or man) may swing a designated dancer or "cheat" and swing another.
Circle Eight	Eight dancers join hands and circle to the left (clockwise).
Circle Four	Two couples (four dancers) join hands and circle to the left (clockwise).
Clover Leaf (Four-Leaf Clover)	For two couples in a circle: One couple passes under the raised hands of the other couple, bringing their joined hands over their heads to form a four-leaf clover.
Cowboy Loop (Mountaineer Loop, Rip and Snort)	For two (or more) couples in a circle: The active couple passes under the raised hands of the inactive couple, the actives dropping hands and separating, the active man leading to the left around the inactive woman, the active woman leading to the right around the inactive man. The inactive couple turns under their joined hands.
Cross Over	In a four-couple square: Two couples (or two dancers) exchange places across the set.
Divide the Ring (Cutting Off Three, Two, and One)	In a four-couple set: The active couple goes across the set and between the opposite couple, the woman going to the right and the man to the left, around the outside of the set to their home position; the same couple goes forward a second time, but splits apart before reaching the opposite couple, the woman to the

	right around the couple on the right, the man to the left around the couple on the left, to their home position; then the same couple goes forward a third time, the woman passing through the couple on the right and the man through the couple on the left to their home position.
Do-si-do (circular) (Dos-á-ballonette)	For two couples: Circle of four in which first the women and then the men face out (back to back).
Do-si-do (hand-turning)	For two couples: A series of alternating hand turns starting with a left-hand turn with one's partner, followed by a right-hand turn with the opposite partner, and then this is repeated.
Do-si-do (Kentucky-style)	For two couples: The woman walks in a counterclockwise direction in front of and around her partner without dropping hands. As she passes behind his back, he ducks under his right arm.
Do-si-do (Northern) (Dosado)	Two dancers move around each other, passing right shoulders, passing back-to-back (without turning), and then backing up to places.
Double-Elbow Swing (Double-L Swing, Lock Chain Swing)	Grand Right and Left, involving alternating right and left elbow swings.
Duck for the Oyster	For two couples: Without letting go of hands, the active couple moves forward and back under an arch made by the inactive couple. The inactive couple then moves forward and back under an arch made by the active couple. Finally, the active couple passes under the inactive couple's raised hands, separating behind the inactive man and woman to original places.
Figure Eight (Lady Round the Lady and the Gent Round the Gent)	For two couples: The active couple, with the woman in the lead, passes single file between the inactive couple. The active woman goes to the left around the inactive woman, and the active man goes to the right around the inactive man. The active couple turns with a right hand when they meet and then passes between the inactive couple a second time. This time, she goes to the right behind the inactive man, and he goes to the left behind the inactive woman.
Georgia Rang-Tang (Georgia Alabam, Running a Reel)	For two couples: Similar to the hand-turning Do-si-do, but starting with a right-hand turn with the opposite, followed by a left-hand turn with one's partner. This is repeated.
Going Down Town	In a four-couple set: The active couple moves across the set to the opposite couple; the two couples join hands and as a unit they move back across the set to the active couple's original place, then back again to the opposite couple's place.

Go to Cuba — Four men circle to the left around one woman. She chooses one of the men to swing, and her partner swings that man's partner.

Grand Right and Left (Grande Chaine, Rights and Lefts) — In a four-couple set or a big ring: Dancers pull past their partners with a right hand, the next person with a left hand, alternating with rights and lefts until they meet their partners.

Half Promenade — Two couples trade places using a Promenade figure, the men passing left shoulders.

Hey — Weaving figure in which dancers pass right and left shoulders alternately, following the path of a figure eight, without taking hands.

In and Out the Windows — Line of dancers is led back through itself, snaking in and out under the arms of the other dancers

Jig Figure — All of the women (or the men) swing the man (or woman) to their right, and then the next, continuing all the way around the set.

King's Highway — After promenading up the center of the floor toward the band, the couples separate, the women going to the right and the men to the left, single file to the bottom of the hall, where they meet and promenade up the center again. Queen's Highway is the same, except the women go to the left, and the men go to the right.

Ladies Back to Back — Women move to the center of the set and stand back to back, while the men go single file to the right (counterclockwise) around them.

Ladies Chain — Two women trade places, pulling by each other with right hands joined, meeting the opposite man with a left hand, and turning to place.

Lady Round the Lady and the Gent Also — For two couples: A variant of "Chase the Rabbit" (see above) in which the active man follows his partner through the inactive couple and to the left around the inactive woman. The active woman then continues in a figure-eight pattern, leading through the inactive couple a second time, and to the right around the inactive man. The active man, however, does not follow ("Lady round the gent, but the gent don't go").

London Bridge — During a Promenade, one couple reverses direction, making an arch over the other couples; the couples following do likewise.

Ocean Wave (Garden Gate, Wave the Ocean) — For two couples: both couples move forward and back, the active couple passing between the inactive couple; this is repeated with the inactive couple passing forward and back between the active couple.

Outside Circle, Inside Swing — A circle of dancers moves to the left (clockwise) while one couple swings in the center.

Pokey-Four	Two couples polka around each other.
Promenade	Dancers march counterclockwise around the set (or dance floor) as couples, the woman on the man's right side.
Right and Left Through	Two couples trade places by passing through each other, the women passing left shoulders.
Right-Hands Across	For two couples: The two men join right hands and the two women join right hands, and with arms crossed in the center, all circle to the left (clockwise).
Shoo-Fly Swing (Treat 'em All Right)	In a circle set: One couple steps into the center of the set and turns with a right hand; the woman then turns her corner (the next man) with a left hand and returns to her partner for another right-hand turn; she works her way around the set counterclockwise, alternately turning each of the other men with a left hand and her partner (who stays in the center of the set) with a right hand. The other couples follow up.
Shoot the Owl	For two couples: One man (or woman) circles with another couple; that couple raises their joined hands, making an arch, and "pops" the dancer through to his (or her) partner.
Single File	Dancers move counterclockwise in a single file circle.
Swing	Waltz Swing: Two dancers (in the couple dance position) spin around clockwise. Swing, Swing Three, Swing Four: two or more dancers, with hands joined, circle to the left.
Swing Ma and Pa (Adam and Eve, Girl from Arkansas)	For two couples: Active man swings the opposite woman (or man), then the opposite man (or woman), and then his partner.
Take a Peek	For two couples: The active couple moves forward and separates around the inactive couple, peeking at each other behind the inactive couple's backs.
Waltz Swing (Bouquet Waltz, Four-by-Four)	Two circles of dancers turn to the left (clockwise) while at the same time passing to the right of the other circle, moving counterclockwise around the floor. (See also Swing.)
Wild Goose Chase	The active man leads his partner by the hand through the inactive couple, to the left behind the inactive woman and back into the center of the set; still leading his partner by the hand, he turns to the right, following a clockwise path and then through the inactive couple a second time, this time leading to the right around the inactive man.
Wind Up the Ball of Yarn	Dancers are led, with hands joined, in a clockwise spiral into the center of the set, and then out again counterclockwise.

Dance Steps

Balance	Setting step in which two or more dancers, with joined hands, step forward and back.
Chug (Drag-Slide)	Forward-and-back sliding motion with the feet on the floor.
Double Shuffle	Shuffle step done twice.
Heel-and-Toe	Percussive step involving the heel and toe alternately striking the floor.
Pigeon Wing (Ailes de Pigeon)	French setting step from the late eighteenth century, involving a leap into the air and clicking of the heels.
Sashay (Chassé)	Sideways, gliding traveling step, with one foot "chasing" the other, as in a gallop.
Shuffle	Percussive step in which the toe ("double toe"), or the heel and then the toe, strikes the floor as the foot moves forward and back.
Windmill (Wagonwheel)	Clogging step in which one leg is rotated in a circle behind the dancer.

Notes

Preface

1. "The Barn Dance" (1929); "The Shindig" (1930); "Toby the Milkman" (1931); "The Farmer" (1931).

2. Buddy Ebsen, who played the role of Jed Clampett, was an accomplished tap dancer. See https://www.youtube.com/watch?v=22UKBv4b4zo (accessed December 30, 2014).

3. Susan Eike Spalding's recent publication, *Appalachian Dance: Creativity and Continuity in Six Communities* (2014), which examines the dance traditions of six communities in Appalachia, addresses this deficit. S. Foster Damon's *The History of Square Dancing* (1957) focuses primarily on the social dances of New England and the Northeast and devotes only a few sentences to the southern Appalachian dances. In *A Time to Dance* (1977) Richard Nevell includes a section on "Southern Appalachian Mountain Dancing." *Communities in Motion* (1995), edited by Susan Eike Spalding and Jane Harris Woodside, has some excellent articles and case studies of dance communities in Appalachia and elsewhere in North America.

4. Frank Smith, *Appalachian Square Dance*, 13–15.

5. An example of 6/8 time is the Mother Goose rhyme: "To market, to market, to buy a fat pig, Home again, home again, jiggety-jig." The syllables of the words are grouped in threes, and "jiggety-jig" means fast.

Introduction. Appalachia and Appalachian Dance

1. In the 1960s, the Appalachian Regional Commission (ARC), a federal-state agency, defined Appalachia using a more expansive boundary based on economic indicators as well as politics. The ARC boundary extends from northern Mississippi to southern New York and currently includes 420 rural counties in thirteen states: Alabama, Georgia, Kentucky, Maryland, Mississippi, New York, North Carolina, Ohio, Pennsylvania, South Carolina, Tennessee, Virginia, and West Virginia.

2. Lanman, *Letters from the Alleghany Mountain*, 135.

3. Simms, *Cub of the Panther*, 32.

4. Strother, "Mountains," 516.

5. Harney, "Strange Land and Peculiar People."

6. Bellamy, "Middle-Aged Romance," 578, 644. Bellamy wrote under the pseudonym Kamba Thorpe.

7. Murfree, *In the Tennessee Mountains*, 228, 233.

8. Burnett, "Lodusky," 673.

9. Dromgoole, *Sunny Side of the Cumberland*, 124. Will Allen Dromgoole, like Mary Noailles Murfree, was from Murfreesboro, Tennessee.

10. See Shapiro, *Appalachia on Our Mind*.

11. Campbell, *Southern Highlander*, xxi.

12. Malone, "Music," 115.

13. Sharp and Karpeles, *Country Dance Book, Part 5*.

14. See Whisnant, *All That Is Native and Fine*.

15. For a discussion of "social dance," "folk dance," and "tradition," see LaVita, "Theorizing Dance Practice," and Nielsen, *Folk Dancing*.

16. The Electric Slide is a choreographed line dance that became popular in the 1970s.

17. Modern Western square dancing is a club-based form of American square dancing that developed out of the recreational square dance movement of the mid-twentieth century. This contemporary style has roots in the "cowboy" dances performed by the Cheyenne Mountain Dancers, a high-school exhibition team founded in the 1930s by Colorado educator Lloyd Shaw (see chapter 15). These dances were more complicated than the traditional square dances of the western United States, and following World War II, dancers in Southern California formed clubs to learn this modern style. Lessons are required to participate in this style of dancing, and by the early 1950s, square dance clubs had formed across the country. Emulating Shaw's dancers and identifying with the West, club dancers adopted western-style shirts with scarf ties for the men and square dance dresses with petticoats for the women. During the 1960s and 1970s, as professional callers equipped with record players and microphones invented new choreography to challenge the dancers, modern Western square dancing evolved away from the traditional square dances. This recreational square dancing is now done exclusively to recorded music, primarily commercial country and pop, which serves as a rhythmic or melodic background for the caller's improvisational patter or singing calls. (See Mayo, *Step by Step through Modern Square Dance History*.)

Contra dances, which are danced in longways sets, have been part of the New England dance tradition since colonial times, and prior to the 1980s they were seldom seen outside New England except as part of dance programs affiliated with the Country Dance and Song Society, such as those at Berea College in Kentucky and the John C. Campbell Folk School in western North Carolina. The contra dances that have become popular across America in recent years are not, however, the traditional dances from New England but reflect a modern style (sometimes called "modern urban contra") that has developed since the 1970s. Although contra dancing can now be found within the Appalachian region and is sometimes mistakenly thought to represent Appalachian heritage, like modern Western square dancing, it is a transplanted form: the dances one sees in Asheville, North Carolina, Charleston, West Virginia, and Knoxville, Tennessee, are recent compositions and are no different from those found in Massachusetts, Florida, or California. For more on modern contra dancing, see Dart, *Contra Dance Choreography*.

Chapter 1. Diversity and Cultural Transmission in the Southern Mountains

1. William Goodell Frost, "Our Contemporary Ancestors." Others have suggested a cultural connection between Appalachia and the Scottish Highlands, despite the fact that Highland Scots were a relatively insignificant minority among the early settlers. Charles Jackson Ryder referred to the Appalachian people as "American Highlanders" in 1892 (Shapiro, *Appalachia On Our Mind*, 107), an image that was perpetuated by two early influential studies of the southern Appalachian region, Horace Kephart's *Our Southern Highlanders* (1913) and John C. Campbell's *The Southern Highlander and His Homeland* (1921). This perceived association between Appalachia and the Scottish Highlands endures today. The logo of the Highland Brewing Company, a local microbrewery in Asheville, includes a tartan-clad Scottish bagpiper, and every summer tens of thousands of Scotophiles flock to the mountains of western North Carolina to attend the Grandfather Mountain Highland Games. This annual festival, which has taken place since the 1950s, professes to be a celebration of the culture and heritage of the Scottish Highlands. In addition to traditional Scottish athletic events, attendees dressed in kilts participate in bagpipe and drum competitions and Scottish country dancing.

2. Semple, "Anglo-Saxons," 6.

3. Woodmason, *Carolina Backcountry*, 56.

4. It is estimated that during the 1700s, as many as two hundred thousand Scots-Irish came to America (Leyburn, *The Scotch-Irish*, 176). Most arrived in Philadelphia, and many traveled down the Great Wagon Road through the Shenandoah Valley of Virginia to the Carolina Piedmont and the southern mountains.

5. Woodmason, *Carolina Backcountry*, 246, 51, 60.

6. By 1790, there were more than nineteen thousand blacks in the core Appalachian region (Williams, *Appalachia*, 111).

7. "Population Schedules of the Second Census of the United States, 1800."

8. See Nobles, *American Frontiers*.

9. Ashe, *Travels in America*, 100.

10. Inscoe, "Slavery," 35.

11. Royall, *Sketches*.

12. Williams, *Appalachia*, 111. Estimates of the black population of Appalachia vary according to how the region is defined and which counties are included.

13. Stuckert, *Black Populations*.

14. Inscoe, "Race and Racism," 106; Perdue, "Red and Black," 27.

15. Hundley, *Social Relations*, 197.

16. Inscoe, "Race and Racism," 107.

17. Stuckert, *Black Populations*, 7, 8; Semple, "Anglo-Saxons," 7.

18. Semple, "Anglo-Saxons," 6.

19. Lanman, *Letters from the Alleghany Mountains*, 124.

20. Royall, *Sketches*, 28, 56.

21. Ritchie, *Singing Family*, 80–81.

22. Dunaway, *Slavery*, 89.

23. Keelboats had sails and could be pulled with ropes or poled upriver.

24. Eslinger, *Running Mad for Kentucky*, 57.

25. Baily, *Journal of a Tour*, 151.

26. Ellis, *Kentucky River*, 8; Clark, *Middle West*, 102.

27. Flint, *Recollections*, 14.

28. Collins, *Adventures*, 18.

29. Hall, *Letters from the West*, 183.

30. Thorpe, "Remembrances of the Mississippi," 37.

31. Toulmin, *Western Country*, 66.

32. Green, *Kentucky Gazette*, 6.

33. Staples, *History of Pioneer Lexington*, 225, 266.

34. Hunter, *Steamboats*, 12, 17, 40, 41.

35. *Western Monthly Review* (Cincinnati, 1827), quoted in Hunter, *Steamboats*, 29.

36. Ludlow, *Dramatic Life*, 136.

37. Merrick, *Old Times*, 157.

38. Clarke and Clarke, *Narratives*, 47, 76, 77, 83.

39. For more about the influence of African American musicians on the early minstrel performers, see Sacks and Sacks, *Way Up North in Dixie*, and Carlin, *Birth of the Banjo*.

40. During the 1880s more than one hundred flatboats traveled each year from Kentucky and West Virginia down the Big Sandy River to the Ohio River, and during the winter of 1885–86, three hundred boats floated down the Holston River to Knoxville (Hunter, *Steamboats*, 57–58).

41. Hunter, *Steamboats*, 58.

42. Frost, "Our Contemporary Ancestors," 3.

43. Waller, *Feud*, 120.

44. A "sawyer" is a submerged tree that rises and falls with a river's current.

45. This well-known Southern dance tune, which appears in Knauff's *Virginia Reels* (1839), may have derived its name from the Forked Deer River of West Tennessee.

Chapter 2. The Southern Square Dance

1. During the second half of the nineteenth century, a third square dance tradition developed in the West. These dances, which are a composite of the Southern and Northern dance traditions, are discussed in chapter 15.

2. This orientation supposedly originated when men wore sheaths for knives (or swords). Most men are right-handed, so the sheath was typically worn on the left-hand side, and a man's partner stood to his right. See Pieter Bruegel's oil on panel, "The Wedding Dance" (1566).

3. A musical phrase is a short section of music that terminates with a natural pause. For example, the song "Happy Birthday" consists of four short musical phrases.

4. Tucker, *Valley of Shenandoah*, 121.

5. Sharp, *Autograph Notebook*, 24.

6. This is clear not only in the published dance manuals of the urban dancing masters but also in an unpublished, handwritten, dance caller's notebook ("Prompter") of 1884 in which F. P. Morse of East Barnard, Vermont, recorded the fixed sequences of figures for twenty-three dances: nine contras, eleven quadrilles, one lancer, and two Sicilian circles (Morse, "Prompter").

7. This same phenomenon occurs in the Minianka culture of West Africa, where drummers create rhythms that follow and support the movements of dancers (Diallo and Hall, *Healing Drum*, 98).

Chapter 3. Square Roots

1. Crockett, *Narrative*, 59.

2. The word "reel," meaning to weave from side to side, dates back to the 1400s (*Oxford English Dictionary*, 328).

3. Flett and Flett, "History of the Scottish Reel, I," 113. This dance for three dancers, known as "alman haye" (German haye), is mentioned in *The Complaynt of Scotlande* (1549).

4. The term "hand" is used to indicate people (as in "farmhands" or "All hands on deck!"), not appendages with five digits.

5. Doddridge, *Notes*, 104, 123.

6. Durang, *Fashionable Dancer's Casket*, 186–87.

7. "Suas i Lár baill" ("Dance up Centre") is similar to "Ocean Wave"; "Uilinn i n-uilinn" ("Link Arms") is similar to "Elbow Swings"; "Cúl le cúl" ("Back to Back") resembles "Dos-á-ballonette"; "An dá lúib" ("Figure Eight") is similar to "Chase the Rabbit"; and "Uilinn i n-uilinn laistiar" ("Link at the Back") resembles "Swing at the Wall." (O'Keefe and O'Brien, *Handbook of Irish Dances*, 17, 20, 22, 26, 32). Hugh Thurston noted some of these similarities in "The Origin of the Appalachian Square Dance" (1969).

8. O'Keefe and O'Brien, *Handbook of Irish Dances*, 72; "Rang-Tang," slang for orangutan, may refer to the swinging movement of the arms in this dance figure. Bascom Lamar Lunsford first heard this dance figure called by that name in 1903 in Mills River, in western North Carolina. (Lunsford, *Spirit of the Dance*, 26). In Surry County, North Carolina, it is now known as "Georgia Alabam," likely a corruption of the word "Allemande."

9. Mead, *Travels*, 62, 29.

10. Harris, "Knob Dance," 48–49; Harris, "Bart Davis's Dance," 144–49.

11. Zeigler and Grosscup, *Heart of the Alleghanies*, 91–92.

12. Biss Honeycutt, interview (April 3, 1993).

13. Vallancey, *Collectanea*, 477; "4, 6, 8, 12, and 16 hand reels" can be found in O'Keefe's and O'Brien's *Handbook of Irish Dances* (5).

14. Boswell, *Tour to the Hebrides*, 242.

15. Tucker, *Valley of Shenandoah*, 121.

16. Ellen Mordecai, quoted in Montgomery, *Sketches of Old Warrenton*, 45.

17. Friedland, "Square Dancing," 686.

18. Hugh Thurston suggested in 1969 that the Appalachian square dance evolved from an old Irish round dance called the *rinncí fighte*. See Thurston, "Origin."

19. Bellamy, "Middle-Aged Romance," 644; Burnett, "Lodusky," 673.

20. Alan Jabbour, interview with Tommy Jarrell (1968), AFC; Neithammer, "Tommy Jarrell's Family Stories," 27; James Lawson, interview (September 11, 2009).

21. Margaret Dean-Smith, in Playford's *English Dancing Master*, 35.

22. The eighteen editions of Playford's *Dancing Master*, published between 1651 and 1728, include more than one thousand dances. While only thirty-eight of the 104 dances in Playford's first edition are longways sets "for as many as will," more than 95 percent of the dances in the final edition of 1728 use this formation.

23. Putnam, *History of Middle Tennessee*, 273.

24. Citing an advertisement for a London dancing master who "plays the Country Dances and Cotillions on the Harp, and directs the proper Figures," Kate Van Winkle Keller and Charles Cyril Hendrickson have suggested that country dance figures were prompted in England in the 1770s (Keller and Hendrickson, *George Washington*, 109). This, however, likely refers to the prompting of students at a dancing school, not a public ball.

25. There was a dancing master at William and Mary College in eastern Virginia as early as 1716, and by 1729 "country-dances" were being taught at dancing schools in Philadelphia. During the 1730s and 1740s dancing schools were established in New York, Newport, Rhode Island, Charleston, South Carolina, New Orleans, and elsewhere. Stanard, *Colonial Virginia*, 142; Bridenbaugh, *Cities in the Wilderness*, 438, 435, 117, 441; Sublette, *World That Made New Orleans*, 80.

26. Whitefield, *Journals*, 376.

27. Cohen, *South-Carolina Gazette*, 82; Keller, *Dance and Its Music*, 389.

28. Keller, *Dance and Its Music*, 84; Marks, *America Learns to Dance*, 41.

29. Ellen Mordecai, quoted in Montgomery, *Sketches of Old Warrenton*, 49.

30. In modern Western square dancing, dancers are referred to as "girls" and "boys." This terminology is likely the consequence of square dancing being taught in schools during the twentieth century (see chapter 15).

31. Stanard, *Colonial Virginia*, 144.

32. Bailey, *Life and Adventures*, 22.

33. Reeves, "Extracts," 471.

34. Jones, *America and French Culture*, 255.

35. Janson, *Stranger in America*, 400.

36. Audubon, *Ornithological Biography*, 2:578.

37. Audubon, *Audubon*, 58; Federal Reserve Bank of Minneapolis, http://www.minneapolisfed.org/community_education/teacher/calc/hist1800.cfm (accessed June 21, 2014).

38. This is not the simple hand turn known today, but one with intertwined arms, adopted from an eighteenth-century German couple dance by that name.

39. Keller, *If the Company*, 35; Cohen, *South-Carolina Gazette*, 39.

40. von Closen, *Revolutionary Journal*, 169.

41. Hunter, *Quebec to Carolina*, 207–8.

42. Howe, *Historical Collections of Ohio*, 274.

43. Cooke, *Leather and Silk*, 176.

44. Boggs, *Alexander Letters*, 121. Englishman Whitman Mead referred to similar informal step dances at a "dancing party" at Tarborough, North Carolina, in 1817: "North Carolina scamper downs, or what would be more descriptive, scamper dances, were the favourite figures of the party. . . . The best account I can give of them is, scamper, scamper, scamper" (Mead, *Travels*, 67).

45. Alan Jabbour, interview with Tommy Jarrell (1968), AFC.

46. Baylor, *Behind the Blue Ridge*, 274.

47. *Diary; or, Loudon's Register*, 3; *Gazette of the United States*, 4.

48. Some dancers today still refer to individual square dances as "changes."

49. Wright, *Views*, 27.

50. The dance repertoire of F. P. Morse of East Barnard, Vermont (1884) included more quadrilles (twelve) than contra dances (nine) (Morse, "Prompter").

51. Collins, *Adventures*, 138. Quadrilles could be danced with four, eight, twelve, or any multiple of four.

52. Haney, *Mountain People of Kentucky*, 52.

53. Sharp and Karpeles, *Country Dance Book, Part 5*.

54. Uncle Dave Macon, "Sleepy Lou"; Charlie Wilson and His Hillbillies, "Shelven Rock."

55. Buckingham, *Slave States of America*, 546–47; MacCorkle, *White Sulphur Springs*, 138; Paulding, *Letters from the South*, 1:232–33; Reniers, *Springs of Virginia*, 78, 105, 237.

56. Featherstonhaugh, *Excursion through the Slave States*, 17–18.

57. Lanman, *Letters from the Alleghany Mountains*, 125, 117.

58. A related figure appears in one of Playford's dances of 1651, "Mage on a Cree." Playford, *English Dancing Master*, 20.

59. Barrow, "Georgia Corn Shucking," 878.

60. Austen, *Pride and Prejudice*, 14; de Guardiola, "What Did Jane Austen Dance?"

61. The "interminable Boulanger" was known as far north as Quebec, where it was danced at a ball in 1835 (*North American Magazine* 5:279).

62. Simms, "Sketch of Craven County," 410.

63. *Collection of the Most Favorite Cottillions*, 30.

64. The hands are switched in some versions of La Boulangère. See Howe, *American Dancing Master*, 91.

65. Perdue, Barden, and Phillips, *Weevils in the Wheat*, 187.

66. Haney, *Mountain People of Kentucky*, 52; Dr. Humphrey Bate, "Goin' Up Town" and "Take Your Foot Out of the Mud and Put it in the Sand"; J. D. Harris, "Whip the Devil Round the Stump." This same figure was known, in Tidewater Virginia in the 1930s as the "Single Wardance." (Sinclair, "Square Dance Figures," 410).

67. Timberlake, *Memoirs*, 102.

68. Lawson, *New Voyage*, 44.

69. Cresswell, *Journal*, 109.

70. Norton, *Journal*, 55. These coiling ring dances were not unique to the South. In 1784 an observer in upstate New York wrote of Native American dancers moving in a "spiral line" around a fire. See "Journal of Griffith Evans, Clerk to the Presbyterian

Commissioners at Fort Stanwix and Fort McIntosh, 1784–1785," *PMHD* 45, no. 2 (April 1941): 213–14, quoted in Keller, *Dance and Its Music*, 473.

71. Keller, "*If the Company*," 32.

72. Byrd, *Secret Diary*, 425.

73. John Josselyn, *Two Voyages to New England* (Boston: William Veazie, 1865), 103, quoted in Pichierri, *Music in New Hampshire*, 18.

74. Cresswell, *Journal*, 111.

75. Norton, *Journal*, 41–42, 151. Craig Mishler documented a similar fusion of Native American and British dances in the Yukon of Canada and Alaska. French Canadians and Scots who worked for the Hudson Bay Company introduced fiddling as early as 1840, and by 1862 the Qwich'in Indians were dancing "Scotch reels of four and jigs." See Mishler, *Crooked Stovepipe*, 18–19, 103.

76. Speck and Broom, *Cherokee Dance and Drama*, 11, 24, 35.

77. Walker Calhoun, interview (November 14, 2005).

78. Lunsford, *Spirit of the Dance*, 62.

79. John Atkins, "*A Voyage to Guinea, Brasil, and the West-Indies, in His Majesty's Ships, the Swallow and Weymouth* . . . (London: Ward and Chandler, 1735), 53, quoted in Epstein, *Sinful Tunes and Spirituals*, 5.

80. James Grainger, "The Sugar Cane," in Gilmore, *Poetics of Empire*, 160.

81. Munsell, *Collections on the History of Albany* (1865), quoted by Stuckey, *Going through the Storm*, 67. Pinkster Day celebrations took place in New York from the 1750s until the mid-1800s. Originally a religious holiday observed by Dutch colonists and settlers at the time of the Pentecost (in late May or early June), by the early nineteenth century it had become primarily an African American holiday celebrated by slaves and free blacks with music and dancing.

82. John Pierpont, *Journal* (1805), 10–13, quoted in Epstein, *Sinful Tunes and Spirituals*, 84.

83. *Born in Slavery: Kentucky Narratives*, 7:113, BIS.

84. Latrobe, *Journal*, 181.

85. Hazzard-Gordon, "Dancing under the Lash," 104.

86. Heckscher, "Afro-Chesapeake Inventions."

87. Anderson, *From Slavery to Affluence*, 32.

88. *Born in Slavery: Texas Narratives*, 16.2:58, BIS.

89. Stuckey, *Slave Culture*, 11. Traces of these burial dances appear in the African American folklore of the South. In "Bur Rabbit in the Red Hill Churchyard," a folktale collected by Edward C. L. Adams in central South Carolina in the 1920s, Brer Rabbit plays his fiddle on top of a grave. He is joined by Brer Mockin' Bird, who whistles the "chune," and they are encircled by the "little birds an' beasts" of the forest, who "form dey self into a circle 'round de grave. (Adams, *Tales of the Congaree*, 235).

90. Hearn, "Levee Life," 60. The musical legacy of these riverboat workers can be heard on several 78-rpm recordings made in 1924 by African American musician and dance caller Sam Jones ("Stovepipe No. 1") of Cincinnati, who called out dance figures while playing the harmonica and guitar. See chapter 7.

91. Hearn borrows this term from the "Double Quadrilles" that were danced in formal ballrooms at that time with eight couples, two on each side of a square set (Howe, *Complete Ball-Room Hand Book*, 20).

92. Hearn, "Levee Life," 68.

93. Barrow, "Georgia Corn Shucking," 878.

94. *Born in Slavery: Alabama Narratives*, 1:280, BIS; *Born in Slavery: Georgia Narratives*, 4.3:124, BIS. A reference to these eight-couple African American ring dances appears in the words of a "Negro Folk Rhyme" collected in 1922: "Han's up sixteen! Circle to de right!" See Talley, *Negro Folk Rhymes*, 1.

95. Kent, "Frolics," 9.

96. Harris, "Sporting Epistle," 30.

97. De Garmo, *Prompter*, 7; *Beadle's*, 15. These were not the first dances to be called "squares." Playford's *English Dancing Master* (1651) includes "square dances for eight," Joseph Doddridge referred to four-handed reels in "square sets" (Doddridge, *Notes*, 104), and James Boswell danced "country squares" in rural Scotland in the late eighteenth century (Boswell, *Tour to the Hebrides*, 242).

98. Harben, *Westerfelt*, 54.

Chapter 4. Transforming Tradition

1. Sharp and Karpeles, *Country Dance Book*, 5:19.

2. Latrobe, *Journal*, 172.

3. Prior to the twentieth century, hair cutting was mostly an African American profession. Black barbers could be found throughout North America—from New England to New Orleans and as far west as Minnesota and British Columbia. Music and cutting hair were compatible occupations, and many barbers were also fiddlers and dance callers. This may account for the title of the Kentucky fiddle tune "Yellow Barber" and perhaps also the traditional tune ending, "Shave and a haircut, two bits."

4. Djedje, *Fiddling in West Africa*, 22; Minton, "West African Fiddles," 299.

5. Ottley and Weatherby, *Negro in New York*, 9; Virginia Writers' Program, *Negro in Virginia*, 35.

6. Keller, *Dance and Its Music*, 2007. These fiddlers were from the following states: Connecticut (50), Delaware (12), Georgia (5), Maryland (43), Massachusetts (34), New Jersey (33), New York (40), North Carolina (7), Pennsylvania (48), Rhode Island (15), South Carolina (18), and Virginia (84). Additional accounts of black musicians playing for white dancers come from across the country in the given years: Virginia 1773 (Feyock, 1995), 1840 (Buckingham, 1968), c. 1860 (Reniers, 1941), 1873 (King, 1972); North Carolina 1775 (Battle, 1907), 1800 (Bernard, 1969), c. 1840 (Battle, 1907), c. 1850 (Avirett, 1901); South Carolina c. 1800 (Gilman, 1998), 1825 (Bernhard, 1828); Kentucky 1838 (Lucas, 1992); Philadelphia 1801 (Bernard, 1969); New Jersey 1807 (Irving, 1983); Mississippi 1817 (Ludlow, 1880); New Orleans 1819 (Latrobe, 1905), 1826 (Bernhard, 1828); New York State 1832 (Coke, 1833), 1868 (Bronner, 1987); Massachusetts 1832 (Arfwedson, 1969); Chicago 1834 (Hoffman, 1912); Tennessee c. 1850 (Branch, 1912); Alabama 1853 (Epstein, 1977); Ohio 1853 (Collins, 1986); Missouri 1857 (Collins, 1986); Minnesota 1850s (Heine, 2012); Louisiana 1859 (Ripley, 1912).

7. Nathaniel Bouton, *History of Concord* (Concord, N. H.: Sanborn, 1856), 252, quoted in Pichierri, *Music in New Hampshire*, 55.

8. Stanton, "'Those Who Labor,'" 166; Lucas, *History*, 35.

9. de Crèvecoeur, *Sketches*, 96.

10. Mott, *Biographical Sketches*, 48; Irving, "Salmagundi," 99.

11. Montgomery, *Sketches*, 44.

12. Gilman, *Recollections*, 76.

13. Northup, *Twelve Years a Slave*, 52, 137, 149. The Academy Award–winning film, *12 Years a Slave* (2013), was adapted from Northup's memoir.

14. C. A. Bryce, "Dusky 'Fiddlers' of Olden Days Tenderly Recalled," *Richmond Times-Dispatch*, May 22, 1921, quoted in "The Banjo in Virginia," Blue Ridge Institute and Museum, Ferrum College, Ferrum, Virginia.

15. "A Mississippi Planter," "Management," 625.

16. Buckingham, *Slave States of America*, 336.

17. Arthur, *Western North Carolina*, 502.

18. Lucas, *History*, 106.

19. *Virginia Gazette and Winchester Advertiser*, October 8 and 15, 1788, quoted in Keller, *Dance and Its Music*, 237.

20. Southern, *Music of Black Americans*, 54.

21. Cresswell, *Journal*, 30.

22. Schoepf, *Travels*, 311.

23. Sharp and Karpeles, *Country Dance Book*, 5:18.

24. Jabbour, "Fiddle Tunes of the Old Frontier," available at http://www.alanjabbour.com/fiddle_tunes_old_frontier.html (accessed October 16, 2011).

25. In 1839, George Knauff published a collection of "Virginia Reels." These include American versions of Scottish, English, French, and Irish dance tunes, as well as an equal number of tunes, such as "Ohio River" ("Boatman's Dance"), that are native to America (Knauff, *Virginia Reels*).

26. Titon, *Fiddle Tunes*, 21.

27. Stanton, "'Those Who Labor,'" 166; Irving, "Salmagundi," 330.

28. Dock Boggs quoted in "'I Always Loved the Lonesome Songs.'"

29. Hobart Smith, quoted in Conway, *African Banjo Echoes*, 141.

30. In 1773 dancing master William Fearson posted a notice for the return of his runaway slave, "Fiddler Billy" (Feyock, "Dance," 219).

31. Cohen, "Negro Folk Game," 183–84.

32. When dancing English country dances, the top couple had the privilege of "calling" the dance, which simply meant choosing the next dance and announcing the figures before it started. English dancing master Thomas Wilson wrote in 1815 that "calling of the dance" may also involve the lead couple "setting the company an example, and directing [fellow dancers] (when required) in the performance of the Dance" (*Complete System*, 172). Neither of these examples implies the continuous calling or prompting of the figures throughout the dance, either from the dance floor or the stage.

33. Szwed and Marks, "Afro-American Transformation," 32.

34. Ireland, *Life*, 28.

35. Others likewise have referred to calling as "chanting." See D. L., "Ball in the Far West," and Moore, *Ole Mistis*.

36. Bernhard, *Travels*, 212.

37. Trollope, *Domestic Manners*, 155.
38. Arfwedson, *United States and Canada*, 220–21.
39. Coke, *Subaltern's Furlough*, 204.
40. Longstreet, *Georgia Scenes*, 124, 127.
41. Kemble, *Journal*, 312.
42. Johnson, who was described as an "inventor-general of cotillions," was the first African American composer to have his work published as sheet music and the first to give public concerts. See AfriClassical.com—African Heritage in Classical Music, available at http://chevalierdesaintgeorges.homestead.com/JohnsonF.html (accessed October 25, 2014).
43. Avirett, *Old Plantation*, 168.
44. African American dance callers could also be found in the Midwest. One was Kentucky-born fiddler and barber William Taylor, who called dances in St. Paul, Minnesota, in the 1850s (Heine, "William Taylor").
45. Quadrilles, descended from the nineteenth-century French dances, are still danced in Jamaica and elsewhere in the West Indies today. These dances are directed by a "commandeur," who calls out the figures with rhythmic patter (Sublette, *World*, 274). See also Manuel, *Creolizing Contradance*.
46. Sublette, *World*, 57; King-Dorset, *Black Dance*, 24.
47. Irving, "Salmagundi," 122–23.
48. Curtin, *Atlantic Slave Trade*, 143.
49. Gilman, *Recollections*, 76.
50. D. L., "Ball in the Far West," 22.
51. Wentworth, "Address at the Reception," 151.
52. Durang, *Fashionable Dancer's Casket*, 28.
53. Brooks, *Ball-Room Monitor*, 50.
54. Collins, *Biography*, 106.
55. John Francis Campbell, *Short American Tramp*, 352–53.
56. Moore, *Ole Mistis*, 213.
57. The Kessinger Brothers, "Devil's Dream," 1928. Not everyone found such excessive verbiage attractive. According to Bascom Lamar Lunsford, "An occasional rhyme is certainly not objectionable . . . but the continuous repetition of childish rigmarole begins to 'taste of the can.' . . . The directional calls are all you need" (Lunsford, *Spirit of the Dance*, 5).
58. Dance calling appears in Harris, "At Teague Poteet's" (1884); Miles, *Spirit of the Mountains* (1905); Haney, *Mountain People of Kentucky* (1906); Samuel Johnson, *Life in the Kentucky Mountains* (1908); and Fox, *Heart of the Hills* (1912).
59. Harben, *Westerfelt*, 53.
60. Megginson, *African American Life*, 326.
61. *Born in Slavery: Mississippi Narratives*, 9:145–146, BIS.
62. Bronner, *Old-Time Music Makers*, 16; Laufman, "Tradition," 33. Edward Peterson (b. 1843), an African American fiddler and Civil War veteran from Geneseo, New York, played and called at local dances in western New York State into the 1930s (Kimball, "Old-Time Dance Music").

63. Hancock, *Emigrants' Five Years*, 249.

64. Clendenen, *Fashionable Quadrille Book*, 3.

65. Cleveland, *Dancing*, 29.

66. Barrow, "Georgia Corn Shucking," 878.

Chapter 5. Cecil Sharp and the Kentucky Running Set

1. Deschamps, letter to Peter Rogers, August 3, 1975, quoted in Spalding, *Appalachian Dance*, 138.

2. Evelyn Kendrick Wells, quoted in Yates, Bradtke, and Taylor, *Dear Companion*, 17.

3. Sharp and Karpeles, *Country Dance Book*, 5:14–15.

4. Cecil Sharp correspondence to Mrs. Helen O. Storrow, September 11, 1917, quoted in Yates, Bradtke, and Taylor, *Dear Companion*, 17.

5. "Cecil Sharp's Appalachian Diaries" (September 18, 1917), VWML.

6. Ibid. (October 2, 1917).

7. Ibid. (October 3, 1917).

8. Karpeles, *Cecil Sharp*, 164. Throughout their travels, Sharp was constantly plagued by headaches, fevers, coughing, asthma, toothaches, dysentery, and exhaustion.

9. "Cecil Sharp's Appalachian Diaries" (October 12, 1917), VWML.

10. Ibid., (October 8, 1917).

11. Sharp, *Country Dance Book*, 1:9.

12. Karpeles, *Cecil Sharp*, 86.

13. "Cecil Sharp's Appalachian Diaries," VWML.

14. Ibid., (June 19, 1915).

15. Cecil Sharp, quoted in Campbell, *Southern Highlander*, 70.

16. Cecil Sharp, correspondence to Mrs. Oppé, August 14, 1916, quoted by Yates, Bradtke, and Taylor, *Dear Companion*, 8.

17. Sharp, *Country Dance Book*, 5:9.

18. Ibid., 10, 12, 23.

19. Ibid., 23–24.

20. English country dances with progressive visiting-couple figures include "Chirping of the Nightingale," "Mill-Field," "Peppers Black," "Rose is White and Rose is Red," and "Up Tails All" (Playford, *English Dancing Master*, 53, 30, 35, 33, 82). Visiting-couple figures can also be found in some of the French cotillions and quadrilles. See Werner's *Book 18 for the Year 1785*, *Violin, without a Master* (1850), and Schell's *Prompting* (1890).

21. Sharp and Karpeles, *Country Dance Book*, 5:9.

22. Baylor, *Behind the Blue Ridge*, 274.

23. The majority (70 percent) of the Southern callers, who recorded dance calls on 78s, used the Promenade as a chorus figure. (See appendix, table 3.)

24. Although Sharp acknowledges that "promenade" is a French term, he generally avoids French dance terminology, preferring to use English country dance terms. He likewise describes "Rights and Lefts" as a "Circular-hey, handing" (Sharp and Karpeles, *Country Dance Book*, 5:31).

25. Ibid., 13.

26. They describe twenty-one figures, but more appear in their transcriptions of dance calls.

27. Coulon, *Hand-book of Dancing*, 81. Although they do not mention "Pop Goes the Weasel" by name, Sharp and Karpeles use the word "pop" to describe the motion in the Kentucky figure "Shoot the Owl."

28. Robert M. Keller, "The Dancing Master." "Ladies in the centre back-to-back" is a figure in "The Fine Companion" and "Jenny Pluck Pears" (1651); a figure resembling "Rights and Lefts" appears in "Buckingham House or Chelsea Reach" (1657); and a figure similar to "Lock Chain Swing" appears in "Oranges and Lemons" (1686).

29. Sharp and Karpeles, *Country Dance Book*, 5:9, 11, 12.

30. See Gomme, *Traditional Games*. Alice Gomme was a founding member of the English Folk-Song Society in 1898. In 1909, she and Sharp co-authored a series of instructional manuals of Children's Singing Games for use in British schools, and in 1911, she helped Sharp found the English Folk Dance Society. Her analysis of children's games was based on the idea of cultural evolution and survivals, a popular idea of her time, in which all cultures evolve from savagery and barbarism to civilization. Gomme believed that children's games, imitating adult activities, preserved ancient religious and social practices of an earlier stage of civilization. As a mentor and close colleague, Gomme, with her books and ideas, obviously influenced Sharp's thinking.

31. Sharp and Karpeles, *Country Dance Book*, 5:11. In his discussion of the origin of "Wind up the Ball [of] Yarn," Sharp cites Gomme, who relates it to "winding games" in which dancers spiral into a coil and then reverse direction to unwind. Later, however, he (mistakenly?) uses this same name for a figure more commonly known as the "Grapevine Twist." Sharp and Karpeles, *Country Dance Book*, 5:34; Gomme, *Traditional Games*, 1:119 and 2:384, 386, 510.

32. Sharp and Karpeles, *Country Dance Book*, 5:11.

33. *Ball-Room Instructer*, 32; Flett and Flett, *Traditional Dancing in Scotland*, 243. The "Basket" figure also appears in the Ukrainian folk dance, "Kolomeyka." See Burchenal, *Folk Dances from Old Homelands*, 32.

34. Sharp and Karpeles, *Country Dance Book*, 5:12; Flett and Flett, *Traditional Dancing in Scotland*, 1.

35. Sharp likens "Tucker" to "The Jolly Miller," but in fact it more closely resembles a singing game called "Pig in the Parlor." Sharp and Karpeles, *Country Dance Book*, 5:35.

36. *Ball-room Manual*, 26; Brooks, *Ball-Room Monitor*, 60.

37. Poore, *Reminiscences*, 74.

38. *Ball-room Instructer*, 33.

39. Sharp and Karpeles, *Country Dance Book*, 5:41. Sharp attributes this dance figure to Playford's "Rose Is White and Rose Is Red," which also has circles of three, but without the revolving motion. See Jamison, "The Bouquet Waltz."

40. Sharp (mistakenly?) describes all of the turns being done with the left hand. This figure usually alternates with right and left hand turns.

41. Sharp and Karpeles, *Country Dance Book*, 5:29.

42. Durang, *Fashionable Dancer's Casket*, 191. This figure, which was one of the change figures of the French cotillions, likely has roots in a German couple dance called the "Allemande."

43. Sharp and Karpeles, *Country Dance Book*, 5:13–14.

44. Similar hand-turning figures appear in Irish four-handed reels ("Uilinn i n-uilinn") as well as circular reels ("Deas Láma Anonn") (O'Keefe and O'Brien, *Handbook of Irish Dances*, 58, 30).

45. Wilder, *Little House*, 105–6.

46. Bill Monroe, "Uncle Pen," ©1951, Hill and Range.

47. In some of the late-eighteenth-century cotillions, the "Right and Left Through" serves a similar role as a subchorus following a visiting-couple figure. See Griffiths, *Collection*, "The Coquet"; Ives, *Twenty-Four Figures*, "Lá Monoco." In 1953 leaders in the modern Western square dance movement renamed this Southern hand-turning figure (sometimes spelled "Docey-Doe") "Do Paso" as a way to differentiate it from the Northern back-to-back "Do-si-do." For more on the "Do-si-do," see Jamison, "Old Folks."

48. Sharp and Karpeles, *Country Dance Book*, 5:10.

49. Sharp, *Country Dance Book*, 2:9, 12.

50. Sharp and Karpeles, *Country Dance Book*, 5:20.

51. See preface (herewith), n5.

52. Sharp and Karpeles, *Country Dance Book*, 5:18.

53. "Give the Fiddler a Dram" and "Hog-Eyed Man."

54. Sharp and Karpeles, *Country Dance Book*, 5:18.

55. Maud Karpeles in Sharp, *English Folk Songs*, xviii; Sharp, *Autograph*, 24. It is unfortunate that Sharp and Karpeles paid so little attention to the music. The previous year, Sharp had criticized earlier ballad collectors, who collected only the words of ballads and not the music. He wrote, "The two elements should never be dissociated . . . to sever one from the other is to remove the gem from its setting" (Campbell and Sharp, *English Folk Songs*, xii).

56. Sharp and Karpeles, *Country Dance Book*, 5:17. Although the Appalachian "jigs" heard by Sharp would have been in 4/4 time, he provides instructions for patting in 6/8 time. Perhaps he envisioned English dancers patting along with country dance jigs while performing the Running Set.

57. Hearn, "Levee Life," 68.

58. Sharp and Karpeles, *Country Dance Book*, 5:17.

59. Jacqie Malone, *Steppin' on the Blues*, 15.

60. Barrow, "Georgia Corn Shucking," 878.

61. Sharp and Karpeles, *Country Dance Book*, 5:19.

62. Ibid., 23. The dance calls transcribed by Sharp and Karpeles include the words "yaller girls," a term for women of mixed race.

63. Ibid., 7.

64. Cecil J. Sharp, introduction to Campbell and Sharp, *English Folk Songs*, iv.

65. Sharp and Karpeles, *Country Dance Book*, 5:14.

66. Campbell and Sharp, *English Folk Songs*, vi.

67. Sharp correspondence to Mrs. Storrow, July 30, 1917, quoted in Yates, "Cecil Sharp in America."

68. Karpeles, *Cecil Sharp*, 166.

69. Ibid., 146.

70. Maude Karpeles diary, July 31, 1917, quoted in Yates, "Cecil Sharp in America."

71. "Cecil Sharp's Appalachian Diaries" (July 31, 1917), VWML.

72. Sharp and Karpeles did eventually collect some British ballads from two African American singers.

73. Karpeles diary, August 1, 1917, quoted in Yates, "Cecil Sharp in America."

74. "Cecil Sharp's Appalachian Diaries" (August 30–September 1, 1918), VWML.

75. Sharp and Oppé, *Dance*, 31–32.

76. Semple, "Anglo-Saxons," 150, 156.

77. Cecil Sharp quoted in *Asheville Citizen*, "Pen and Plate Club Hears Cecil Sharp" (June 14, 1917).

78. Karpeles, "Some Additional Figures," 39.

79. John L. Turner interview, 1975, SAA; Marguerite Bidstrup interview, 1972, SAA.

80. Flett and Flett, *Traditional Dancing in Scotland*, 187.

81. Neithammer, "Tommy Jarrell's Family Stories," 26.

82. Karpeles, "Some Additional Figures," 39.

83. In a description of a "ho-down" in eastern Kentucky in 1906 the "sets" include figures and dance terminology ("first four") from the quadrilles (Haney, *Mountain People of Kentucky*, 52–53); on a 1927 recording of the East Tennessee band, Dyke's Magic City Trio, Hub Mahaffey calls out, "Get your partners for the next set" (Dyke's Magic City Trio, "Shortenin' Bread"). On a 1932 recording of Charlie Wilson and His Hillbillies, Kentucky caller Asa Martin announces that he will call a "set," "one more little quadrille" (Charlie Wilson and His Hillbillies, "Shelven Rock"). Today, musicians perform "sets" of music, and I suspect that this term comes from the five or six separate dance tunes once played for a set of quadrilles.

84. Lunsford, *Spirit of the Dance*, 11.

85. Spalding, *Appalachian Dance*, 136.

86. "Evelyn Wells Letters," 024, PMSS.

87. Ibid., 018.

88. Sharp and Karpeles, *Country Dance Book*, 5:16.

Chapter 6. Sharp's Legacy

1. "A Record of Pine Mountain Settlement School, Pine Mountain, Harlan County, Kentucky (Wells and Hench Compilation, 1913–1928)," 54, PMSS.

2. Ibid., 55.

3. Ibid., 162.

4. Ibid., 53.

5. Ibid., 55.

6. *New York Times*, January 3, 1929; *New York Times*, November 15, 1936; *New York Times*, October 30, 1938.

7. John L. Turner, interview (July 1, 1975), SAA.

8. Alan Lomax, Pine Mountain School, Kentucky, August 1937, AFC.

9. Grazia Combs, interview (July 15, 1975), SAA.

10. Sharp published folk dances collected from the living tradition as well as his interpretations of Playford's dances in four previous volumes.

11. Sharp and Karpeles, *Country Dance Book*, 5:15.

12. Kennedy, *English Folk Dancing*, 92.

13. Sharp and Karpeles, *Country Dance Book*, 5:23.

14. Six years earlier, Sharp acknowledged that this step used in his re-creations of English country dances "may or may not be historically accurate" (Sharp, *Country Dance Book*, 2:23).

15. Karpeles, "Some Additional Figures," 39–42.

16. For an extensive review of the literature on southern Appalachian square dancing, see Jamison, "Southern Appalachian Square Dance."

17. Email from Susan Spalding, Berea College (March 30, 2012).

18. Boyd, *Descriptions*, 34, 39.

19. Shaw, *Cowboy Dances*, 29, 30.

20. Mayo, *American Square Dance*, 54.

21. Smith, *Appalachian Square Dance*, 13, 15, 17.

22. Hutchins, letter to Frank Smith (February 4, 1937), SAA.

23. Email from Harry Rice, Berea College (January 31, 2007).

24. Spalding, *Appalachian Dance*, 159.

25. A 1974 performance of "Set Running" by the Berea College Country Dancers can be seen on YouTube at http://www.youtube.com/watch?v=TA3l9reVQZo&feature=related (accessed October 25, 2014).

26. Frank Smith founded this annual, weeklong workshop in 1938 after attending the American branch of the English Folk Dance Society's summer dance week at the Pinewoods Camp in Plymouth, Massachusetts (Spalding, *Appalachian Dance*, 152). The Berea College Christmas Country Dance School continues to offer classes in "a variety of English, American, Irish, and Scandinavian" dance, including the "Kentucky Running Set" (which, until 2009, was called "Kentucky Set Running"). See http://www.berea.edu/ccds (accessed November 20, 2014).

27. Dorothy Shaw, "The Appalachian Mountain Dance," in "History and Heritage of Modern American Square Dancing," European Association of American Square Dancing Clubs, http://eaasdc.eu/eu/fileadmin/eaasdc2/archive/history/shehisto.pdf (accessed November 27, 2014).

28. Sharp and Karpeles, *Country Dance Book*, 5:8.

29. Sharp, *Autograph Notebook*, 45.

30. Ibid.

31. Buchanan, "Dance Figures," Annabel Morris Buchanan Papers #4020, folder 324, SHC; Sinclair, *Tidewater Virginia*, 410.

32. Levin, *Kentucky Square Dances*, 29.

33. Ryan, *Dances of Our Pioneers*, 33.

34. O'Keefe and O'Brien, *Handbook of Irish Dances*, 22.

35. Keller and Hendrickson, *George Washington*, 109.

36. Sharp, *Autograph Notebook*, 46, 47.

37. Sinclair, *Tidewater Virginia*, 408.

Chapter 7. "Barn Dances with Calls" (1924–1933)

1. Texas fiddler Eck Robertson, who recorded several old-time fiddle tunes for Victor Records in New York in 1922, was the first of many to be recorded.

2. A few years later (in 1926), Tom Owen recorded dance calls, accompanied by "His Barn Dance Trio of WLS."

3. Reneau and Austin reunited five months later for a second recording session in New York. Billing themselves as the Blue Ridge Duo, they re-recorded "Turkey in the Straw" as well as "Arkansas Traveler," with Austin reciting dance calls and remarks almost verbatim to those on the earlier recording.

4. Bill Chitwood and His Georgia Mountaineers, "Kitty Hill."

5. There is one instance where a caller clearly copies an earlier recording. In November 1928, only a few months after the release of the Kessinger Brothers' recordings of "Turkey in the Straw" and "Hell among the Yearlings," two musicians, billed as the Hobbs Brothers recorded (different) tunes, though marketed under those same titles, with an unidentified caller reciting Ernest Legg's recorded calls almost word for word. The following year, in 1929, these same musicians again copied Legg's dance calls from two more recently released Kessinger Brothers recordings, "Devil's Dream" and "Patty on the Turnpike." For this reason, and the fact that I have been unable to determine the identity of the Hobbs Brothers, their recordings are not included in this study.

6. Two other African American musicians who included dance calls on their recordings are Arthur "Blind" Blake ("West Coast Blues," 1926) and Henry Thomas ("Old Country Stomp," 1928).

7. Sharp and Karpeles, *Country Dance Book*, 5:19.

8. Kessinger Brothers, "Turkey in the Straw."

9. The term "allemande," indicating a hand turn with another dancer, appears on only one recording by a caller in northern West Virginia. All of the rest of these Southern callers use the term "turn" for this common figure.

Chapter 8. The Virginia Reel

1. "Right Word at the Right Time," 39.

2. A variety of six-handed reels were also known in the British Isles. In Scotland, the Sixsome Reel took the form of two three-handed reels performed side by side in parallel lines, a woman between two men in one line and a man between two women in the other (Emmerson, *Social History of Scottish Dance*, 179). In Ireland the Six-Hand Reel was danced with a man between two women in each line (Brennan, *Story of Irish Dance*, 97). For additional descriptions of the six-handed reel, see Keller, *Dance and Its Music*, 184–85, and Howe, *American Dancing Master*, 88.

3. An illustration of a six-handed reel by Canadian historical illustrator Charles William Jefferys appears in *The Picture Gallery of Canadian History, vols. 2 and 3* (Toronto: Ryerson, 1945–50).

4. Robert Hunter, *Quebec to Carolina*, 207–8.

5. Enys, *American Journals*, 234, 347, n12.

6. Janson, *Stranger in America*, 400.

7. Paulding, *Letters from the South*, 189. Referring to the music, Paulding writes, "One of the favourite Virginia reels is, 'Fire in the mountains, run boys, run'" (116).

8. Mitchell, *Spirit of the Old Dominion*, 173. A puncheon floor consists of logs split down the middle and turned flat side up.

9. Stueckrath, "Upper Country of South Carolina," 693.

10. Perdue, Barden, and Phillips, *Weevils*, 226.

11. Longstreet, *Georgia Scenes*, 15; Taliaferro, *Fisher's River*, 115.

12. Guild, *Old Times in Tennessee*, 42–43.

13. Other tunes mentioned by Guild include "Molly Put the Kettle On," "Leather Britches," and "Billy in the Wild Woods" (ibid., 43).

14. Simms, "Craven County," 409.

15. Wilson, *Analysis of Country Dancing*, 112. This dance derives its name from Sir Roger de Coverley, a fictitious character featured in essays written in 1711 and 1712 by English author and politician Joseph Addison.

16. Wilson, *Complete System*, 100–101. Perhaps referring to an earlier dance by the same name that appears in Playford's collections from 1695 to 1728, Wilson claims that this dance was composed "about 100 years ago." That dance, however, is a progressive country dance and bears no resemblance to Wilson's "Sir Roger de Coverley."

17. Wilson, *Analysis*, 112–14.

18. Poore, *Reminiscences*, 74, 29.

19. Hillgrove, *Scholars' Companion*, 72.

20. *Collection of the Most Favorite Cottillions*, 30; "The amusements of the night were invariably wound up by the *Boulanger*, or Sir Roger de Coverley" (*New Monthly Magazine, and Literary Journal, Volume 1* [London: Colburn, 1821], 292).

21. Kemble, *Journal*, 290.

22. "McKernan's Dance History," http://mckernansdancehistory.shutterfly.com (accessed March 20, 2014).

23. Durang, *Durang's Terpsichore*, 156.

24. *Beadle's*, 24.

25. Simms, "Craven County," 410.

26. Lanman, *Haw-Ho-Noo*, 144; Jane M. G. Turnbull and Marion Turnbull, *American Photographs, 2nd ed.* (London: Newby, 1860), 2:70, quoted in Emery, *Black Dance*, 140.

27. *Born in Slavery: Texas Narratives*, 16.3:91; *Born in Slavery, Texas Narratives*, 16.2:234–35, LOC-BIS.

28. De Garmo, *Prompter*, 30.

29. Strother, "Mountains," 803.

30. Murfree, "Dancin' Party," 233.

31. McDowell, *Dialect Tales*, 157.

32. Buchanan, "White Top Folk Trails—Dances and Games," Annabel Morris Buchanan Papers, no. 4020, folder 355C, SHC. Lloyd Shaw of Colorado likewise wrote in 1939, "I have never seen it with the country folk" (*Cowboy Dances*, 124).

33. *Daughters of the American Revolution Magazine*, 12:293.

34. Ibid., 16:1236.

35. *Masquerades, Tableaux and Drills*, 92.

36. "The Old Virginia Reel: A Christmas Reverie in Verse," *Richmond Planet*, December 26, 1908.

37. Burchenal, *American Country Dances*, vi.

38. "Encyclopedic Discography of Victor Recordings."

39. "The Victor in the Schools."

40. *American School Board Journal* (February 1919), 55.

41. Ibid. (May 1919), 65.

42. "Old Time Dancing Party."

43. Ryan, *Handbook*, 161. That same year the Virginia Reel also appeared in Henry Ford's dance book *Good Morning* (114).

44. Walker Calhoun, interview (November 14, 2005); James Lawson, interview (September 11, 2009); Spalding, *Appalachian Dance*, 205.

45. Tolman and Page, *Country Dance Book*, 114.

46. Shaw, *Cowboy Dances*, 125–26.

Chapter 9. Religion and Dancing

1. Loyal Jones, interview (March 16, 2006).

2. Wagner, *Adversaries of Dance*, 27.

3. Ibid., 4, 8.

4. Mather, "Arrow," 106.

5. Owenby, *Subduing Satan*, 119.

6. Whitefield, *Journals*, 379.

7. Woodmason, *Carolina Backcountry*, 244.

8. Mott, *Biographical Sketches*, 48–49.

9. Cartwright, *Autobiography*, 34, 206.

10. Johnson, *Ante-Bellum North Carolina*, 93.

11. Pike, *Catching The Tune*, 16.

12. Brown, *Frank C. Brown Collection*, 7:151–52.

13. Nixon, *Cross Woodis*, 9.

14. Lyell, *Second Visit*, 269–70.

15. Gannett, "Freedmen at Port Royal," 10.

16. *The Nation* (1867), quoted in King, *Great South*, 618.

17. Parrish, *Slave Songs*, 85.

18. Abrahams, *African American Folktales*, 56–57.

19. *African-American Experience in Ohio 1850–1920*, available at http://dbs.ohiohistory.org/africanam (accessed October 25, 2014).

20. See Parrish, *Slave Songs*; Jones and Hawes, *Step It Down*.

21. Botkin, *American Play-Party Song*.

22. Howe, *Historical Collections of Ohio*, 367.

23. Crockett, *Narrative*, 60.

24. *Sketches and Eccentricities*, 45–50. Variants of this singing game, "Oats, Peas, Beans and Barley Grow," were known throughout rural America in the nineteenth century.

25. *Ball-room Manual*, 26. Dance calls to "Old Dan Tucker" can be heard on a recording made in 1925 by Judge Sturday's Orchestra from Missouri. "Old Dan Tucker" also appears as a circle dance for "any number of couples" in Henry Ford's *Good Morning* (1926).

26. Haney, *Mountain People of Kentucky*. Its inclusion in a 1911 U.S. Government publication, *Social Plays, Games, Marches, Old Folk Dances, and Rhythmic Movements for Use in Indian Schools*, may have popularized this play party.

27. Dromgoole, *Sunny Side*, 127.

28. Owenby, *Subduing Satan*, 120; Annabel Morris Buchanan Papers, SHC.

29. Ritchie, *Singing Family*, 191.

30. Jean Ritchie, interview (July 2001).

31. For more on play parties, see Botkin, *American Play-Party Song*: Jamison, "Fly to the East, Fly to the West."

32. Marguerite Bidstrup interview, 1972, SAA.

33. Hamby, *Memories of Grassy Creek*, 74.

34. Jensen, *History*, 27.

35. Marguerite Bidstrup interview, 1973, SAA.

Chapter 10. Couple Dances

1. Felton was an outspoken writer and progressive who later became the first woman to serve in the United States Senate (though only for one day).

2. Felton, *Country Life in Georgia*, 51.

3. *Philadelphia Gazette* (March 2, 1797), 4.

4. Arfwedson, *United States and Canada*, 220.

5. Aldrich, *From the Ballroom to Hell*, 19.

6. Durang, *Fashionable Dancer's Casket*, 55.

7. Strother, "Winter in the South," 735.

8. Strother, "Mountains," 516.

9. Gardner, *Modern Dancing*, 7–8, 30–31.

10. "Round and Square Dances," *New York Times* (June 19, 1881).

11. Elias Howe, *Complete Ball-Room Hand Book*.

12. "Pokey Four" called by Ernest Legg appears on the Kessinger Brothers' "Patty on the Turnpike."

13. *The German*, 128.

14. Cellarius, *Drawing-Room Dances*, ii.

15. *The German*, 11.

16. See Dodworth, *Dancing and Its Relations*.

17. *Cartier and Baron's*, 37.

18. Ibid., 37.

19. MacCorkle, *White Sulphur Springs*, 138.

20. Reniers, *Springs of Virginia*, 219.

21. Farlow, Lane, and Oliver, *Haywood Homes*; Jenkins, "Social Dance," 20, 22; Zeigler and Grosscup, *Heart of the Alleghanies*, 343.

22. Warner, *On Horseback*, 121.

23. It is not clear how or why this name became attached to this mixer. See "What's with This Paul Jones Thing Anyway?" at http://www.kickery.com/2014/08/paul-jones-survey.html (accessed December 20, 2014).

24. Coll and Rosiere, *Dancing Made Easy*, 111.

25. Bill Ohse, interview (August 6, 2010).

26. Spalding, "Aesthetic Standards," 231; Worth, "Denton Dance," 13.

27. Burchenal, *Dances of the People*, 79.

28. Wilson, *Complete System*, 320; Bernhard, *Travels*, 111.

29. During the nineteenth century freed African Americans brought the Grand March to Liberia, where it is still common at weddings and other festive occasions. See http://pancocojams.blogspot.com/2012/02/grand-march-liberia-west-africa.html (accessed December 28, 2012).

30. *Ballroom Instructer*, 29–30.

31. Hillgrove, *Complete Practical Guide*, 86–87.

32. Cellarius, *Drawing-Room Dances*, 129.

33. De Garmo, *Prompter*, 73.

34. Harvey, *Wehman's*, 34. In 1898 Alice Gomme described a similar figure from Cornwall, called "Snail's Creep" (see Gomme, *Traditional Games*, 2:386).

35. Sharp and Karpeles, *Country Dance Book*, 5:11.

36. The Grand March was performed as part of graduation exercises at Boothbay (Maine) Region High School in 2013. See http://www.youtube.com/watch?v=R2n5GTOJi5Q (accessed November 16, 2013).

Chapter 11. The Cakewalk

1. Rohrbough, *Handy Play Party Book*, 53.

2. Milnes, *Play of a Fiddle*, 115.

3. Sir Henry Piers, *A Chorographical History of the County West-Meath*, quoted in Danaher, *Year in Ireland*, 80.

4. Ibid., 81.

5. Cohen, "Negro Folk Game," 183–84.

6. Stearns and Stearns, *Jazz Dance*, 22.

7. *Born in Slavery: Georgia Narratives*, 4.2:348, BIS.

8. Toll, *Blacking Up*, 78.

9. For more on the stereotypes associated with the cakewalk, see Baldwin, "Cakewalk."

10. Stearns and Stearns, *Jazz Dance*, 117.

11. "The Cake Walk: A Richmond Christmas Festival," *Frank Leslie's Illustrated Newspaper*, December 31, 1870, 261–62.

12. *New York Times*, January 11, 1883.

13. *St. Louis Republic*, quoted in *Hartford [Kentucky] Herald*, March 23, 1892.

14. Johnson, *Autobiography of an Ex-Colored Man*, 62–63.

15. *Kansas City Gazette*, February 27, 1899.

16. Toll, *Blacking Up*, 195.

17. Peterson, *Century of Musicals*, 92–93.

18. Abbott and Seroff, *Out of Sight*, 206.

19. The expression, "It was a Cakewalk" was used as early as 1863. *Online Etymology Dictionary*, http://www.etymonline.com (accessed November 28, 2014).

20. "Walking for a Cake: Eleven Couples Competed, and Mr. Marshall and Miss Hammett Won First Prize," *New York Times*, February 7, 1897.

21. Stearns and Stearns, *Jazz Dance*, 122.

22. Others include the "Black Bottom," "Ballin' the Jack," the Charleston, and numerous animal dances.

23. Fletcher, *100 Years of the Negro*, 123.

24. Wirth, *Complete Quadrille Call Book*, 44. The Cakewalk craze went international in 1900, when John Phillip Sousa's band performed Cakewalk music at the Paris Exhibition. Ragtime pieces, called "Cakewalks," soon became popular, including Claude Debussy's 1909 composition "Golliwog's Cakewalk."

25. Warner, *On Horseback*, 149.

26. *Harper's New Monthly Magazine* 59 (October 1879): 799.

27. *The* [Earlington, Kentucky] *Bee*, July 26, 1894.

Chapter 12. Appalachian Step Dance

1. Sharp and Karpeles, *Country Dance Book*, 5:8, 16.

2. The Carter Fold was founded in 1979 by Janette Carter, the daughter of Sara and A. P. Carter.

3. The great variability of personal dance styles in Appalachia can be seen in Mike Seeger's film *Talking Feet: Solo Southern Dance: Buck, Flatfoot and Tap* (1987). This excellent documentary, which features twenty-four traditional dancers from West Virginia, Kentucky, Virginia, and North Carolina, is now available online at http://www.folkstreams.net/film,121.

4. Lucas, *History*, 35.

5. Ottley and Weatherby, *Negro in New York*, 9–10. Regarding Pinkster Day, see chapter 3, note 81.

6. Stearns and Stearns, *Jazz Dance*, 15.

7. Pinckard, *Notes on the West Indies*, 231; James Grainger, "The Sugar Cane" in Gilmore, *Poetics of Empire*, 160–61.

8. Nathan, *Dan Emmett*.

9. Wood, "'Gimme de Kneebone Bent,'" 8.

10. John Atkins, "*A Voyage to Guinea, Brasil, and the West-Indies, in His Majesty's Ships, the Swallow and Weymouth* . . . (London: Ward and Chandler, 1735), 53, quoted in Epstein, *Sinful Tunes*, 5.

11. These dance competitions would take place on a "shingle," a wide board "about five to six feet long, of large width." De Voe, *Market Book*, 344.

12. *Jig, Clog, and Breakdown*, 5.

13. Contemporary examples include African American dancers John Dee Holeman (b. 1929) and Fris Holloway (1919–2008) of North Carolina, and white dancer Thomas Maupin (b. 1938) of Tennessee.

14. Spelman, "Relation of Virginia," cxiv.

15. Lawson, *New Voyage to Carolina*, 45.

16. "Complaynt of Scotlande" (1549); "Christ's Kirk on the Green"; "The Complaynt of the Papyngo" (1530) in Lyndsay, *Poetical Works*; Dauney, *Ancient Scottish Melodies*.

17. Dean-Smith, "Jig."

18. Emmerson, *Social History*, 262.

19. The legacy of these percussive step dances can perhaps be seen in the traditional Irish sean-nós (old-style) step dancing still found in the Connemara Gaeltacht (Irish-speaking) region of western Ireland today.

20. Adams, *Diary and Autobiography*, 1:172.

21. Burnaby, *Travels*, 26.

22. Benjamin Latrobe encountered this kind of dance, likely the Bamboula, in New Orleans in 1819 (Latrobe, *Journal*, 180).

23. Stewart, *Island of Jamaica*, 269–70.

24. Cresswell, *Journal*, 53.

25. Doddridge, *Notes*, 104.

26. Letter to Abigail Goddard quoted in Keller and Hendrickson, *George Washington*, 81.

27. Connor, Lefler, and Wilson, *Documentary History*, 82.

28. Bernard, *Retrospections of America*, 207–8.

29. *Born in Slavery: Texas Narratives*, 16.4:34, BIS.

30. Baylor, *Behind the Blue Ridge*, 273; Wilder, *Little House*, 107.

31. *Born in Slavery: Texas Narratives*, 16.4:34, BIS.

32. Hearn, "Levee Life," 68.

33. Keller, *Dance and Its Music*, 259.

34. Durang, *Memoir*, 11.

35. Emery, *Black Dance*, 180.

36. Durang, *Memoir*, 22.

37. Elias Howe, *Complete Ball-Room Hand Book*, 23.

38. Several decades after John Durang's death, his son Charles published a list of the steps his father used in the "Pas de Matelot" or "Sailor Hornpipe—Old Style" (Charles Durang, *Ball-Room Bijou*, 158).

39. Taliaferro, *Fisher's River*, 185.

40. Nathan, *Dan Emmett*, 84.

41. Peacock, *Sketches*, 92.

42. Wyeth, *With Sabre and Scalpel*, 62.

43. Dromgoole, *Sunny Side of the Cumberland*, 127.

44. Christian, "Joe Hood."

45. Milnes, *Play of a Fiddle*, 116.

46. Instructions for the "Double Shuffle" and the "Heel-and-Toe" appear in *Jig, Clog, and Breakdown Dancing* (1873).

47. Edward Henry Durell [Henry Didimus, pseud.], quoted in Blesh and Janis, *They All Played Ragtime*, 83.

48. Jane M. G. Turnbull and Marion Turnbull, *American Photographs*, 2nd ed. (London: Newby, 1860), 2:70, quoted in Emery, *Black Dance*, 140.

49. Dickens, "Poor Mercantile Jack," 46. The step "Cover the Buckle," also called "Cut-the-Buckle," was a popular setting step for Scottish reels at the end of the eighteenth century. This step involved crossing one foot over the buckle of the shoe on the other foot. John Durang used "Cut the Buckle" in his hornpipe dancing. By the early nineteenth century "Cover-the-Buckle" was also used in Irish step dancing (Emmerson, *Social History*, 171).

50. Howe, *Complete Ball-Room Hand Book*, 4, 23.

51. Olmsted, *Cotton Kingdom*, 350; Baylor, *Behind the Blue Ridge*, 275.

52. Biss Honeycutt, interview (April 3, 1993).

53. "Dandy Jim ob Caroline" (1844), Nathan, *Dan Emmett*, 86.

54. Nathan, *Dan Emmett*, 86; Compan's *Dictionaire de Danse* (1787) describes the Entrechat as striking the legs together three times while in the air.

55. Durang, *Memoir*, 11–12.

56. An account from 1818–1835 mentions dancers doing "pigeon wings" and "double shuffles" in Perry County, Alabama (Cauthen, *With Fiddle*, 206).

57. Guild, *Old Times in Tennessee*, 42–43.

58. Longstreet, *Georgia Scenes*, 29.

59. Harris, "Sporting Epistle," 30.

60. *Born in Slavery: Texas Narratives*, 16.2:243, BIS.

61. *Born in Slavery: Texas Narratives*, 16.1:10, BIS. A unique and frequently quoted description of the "Pigeon Wing," lacking any mention of the crossing of the legs or clicking of the heels, comes from former Virginia slave Fannie Berry, who described "cuttin' de pigeons wings" as "flippin' yo' arms an' legs roun' an' holdin' yo' neck stiff like a bird do" (Virginia Writers' Program, *Negro in Virginia*, 92). This may be another case of dance terminology being indiscriminately applied to an unrelated step.

62. Stearns and Stearns, *Jazz Dance*, 191.

63. Wilder, *Little House*, 107; *Asheville Citizen*, December 21, 1947.

64. Gallini, *Critical Observations*, 176.

65. *Dictionary of American Regional English*, 1:370.

66. In 1851 author Lewis W. Paine referred to these dances as a "regular teardown" (Paine, *Six Years in a Georgia Prison*, 183).

67. Claiborne, *Life and Correspondence*, 42.

68. Twain, *Life on the Mississippi*, 49.

69. Baylor, *Behind the Blue Ridge*, 275.

70. Bartlett, *Dictionary of Americanisms*, 48–49.

71. *Born in Slavery: Georgia Narratives*, 4.2:284, BIS.

72. *Jig, Clog, and Breakdown Dancing*, 11–12.

73. Bartlett, *Dictionary of Americanisms*, 197.

74. *Gentleman's Vade Mecum* 1, no. 12 (March 21, 1835), Philadelphia, quoted in Mathews, *Dictionary of Americanisms*; Strother, "Adventures," 8.

75. Gunderson, *Log-Cabin Campaign*, 128; Zeigler and Grosscup, *Heart of the Alleghanies*, 91.

76. Jamison, "'Square Dance' at Carcassonne, Kentucky."

77. T. B. Thorpe, "Remembrances of the Mississippi," 37.

78. Jerry Duke suggested in 1984 that the term "buck" was related to the word "buccaneer (Duke, *Clog Dance*, 27). He cites Carl Bridenbaugh, who wrote in 1952 that during the eighteenth century, slaves near Charleston, South Carolina, referred to poor whites using "the West Indian Negro label of 'bockorau' (buccaneer), which with time became 'po' buckra'" (Bridenbaugh, *Myths and Realities*, 65). The term "buck," however, is older than that. It comes from Old English and has been used to refer to male deer, goats, and other animals since before the twelfth century. This

is more likely its source in reference to male slaves. The term commonly used for female slaves, "wenches," meaning female servant, likewise comes from Old English.

79. *Born in Slavery: Texas Narratives*, 16.1:38, BIS.

80. Smith, "Lancashire," 156.

81. Cauthen, *With Fiddle*, 193.

82. Contemporary cloggers refer to this as a "drag-slide."

83. Breathnach, *Folk Music*, 42.

84. Irving, "Salmagundi," 123.

85. *Sketches and Eccentricities of Col. David Crockett*, 37.

86. Fulcher, "Traditional Dance," 14.

87. Speck and Broom, *Cherokee Dance and Drama*, 71–79.

88. Seeger, *Talking Feet*.

89. Conway, *African Banjo Echoes*, 68; Fulcher, "Traditional Dance"; Seeger, *Talking Feet*.

90. Stuckey, *Slave Culture*, 11; *Born in Slavery: Georgia Narratives*, 4.1:99, BIS; *Born in Slavery: Texas Narratives*, 16.2:137, BIS.

91. *Wichita Daily Eagle*, April 28, 1894.

92. John Reeves, interview (April 21, 1993).

93. Emery, *Black Dance*, 228.

94. Seeger, *Talking Feet*; Fulcher, "Traditional Dance."

95. Jamison, "Willard Watson."

96. The Lancashire Clog is from Lancashire, England, where cotton-mill workers wore wooden-soled clogs. British and Irish sailors may have introduced these dances to America in the 1830s (Krause, "Step Dancing"). The earliest documented performance of this dance was in Boston in 1845 (Smith, "Lancashire," 71).

97. Tucker, *Clog Dancing*, 5.

98. Collins, *Biography*, 246.

99. In *The Gold Rush* (1925), Chaplin demonstrates his knowledge of stage step dancing in a comical scene involving dinner rolls on forks.

100. Helen Frost, *Clog Dance Book*, 18, 34.

101. Murfree, *In the Tennessee Mountains*, 227.

102. *Twin City Sentinel*, May 1, 1924; Jamison, "Jubilant Spirit."

103. This term appears in the *Asheville Times*, August 4, 1933.

104. Matthews, *Cutting a Dido*, 66.

105. Betty Garland, interview (February 17, 1993). In 1993 I received a grant from the Folklife Section of the North Carolina Arts Council to document traditional step dancers in western North Carolina. I filmed more than forty dancers, ages fifty-five to eighty-five. See Jamison, "'A Jubilant Spirit within Me.'" Videos of these dancers, as well as audio interviews, which are housed at the Southern Folklife Collection at Chapel Hill, will be available for viewing online at www.philjamison.com.

106. Pauline Zimmerman, interview (February 11, 1993).

Chapter 13. Clogging: Appalachian Step Dance on Stage

1. Painter, *German Invasion*, 17.

2. Albert Burnette, interview (August 18, 2001).

3. *Asheville Citizen*, June 5, 1928.

4. *Asheville Times*, June 5, 1928.

5. *Asheville Citizen*, June 6, 1928, quoted in Jones, *Minstrel of the Appalachians*, 43.

6. *Asheville Times*, June 6, 1928.

7. *Asheville Times*, August 4, 1933.

8. *Asheville Citizen*, August 10, 1952.

9. In 1965 the festival's Folk Heritage Committee considered banning taps (MDFF Committee Meeting Notes, September 2, 1965, SCRL), and in 1972 the committee announced: "Metal taps for the shoes of clog dancers will not be permitted" (*Asheville Citizen*, July 20, 1972). This rule, however, was ignored by the dancers and discarded the following year.

10. One of western North Carolina's premier freestyle clogging teams of the 1970s, the Southern Appalachian Cloggers of Haywood County are featured in the documentary film *Full of Life A-Dancin'*.

11. *Asheville Citizen*, July 31, 1959.

12. *Asheville Citizen*, August 10, 1952.

13. *Asheville Times*, August 12, 1977.

14. *Asheville Citizen*, August 9, 1959. This group was founded by Mr. and Mrs. E. B. Smathers, formerly of western North Carolina.

15. For more on the Mountain Dance and Folk Festival, see Whisnant, "Finding the Way."

16. *Asheville Times*, August 9, 1942.

17. James Kesterson, interview (February 26, 2012).

18. Footage from this 1964 documentary by David Hoffman appears in *Ballad of a Mountain Man: The Story of Bascom Lamar Lunsford* (PBS Video, 1989). Hoffman has rereleased this same film as *The Complete Bascom Lamar Lunsford Story* (Varied Directions, 2012).

19. *Asheville Citizen*, July 20, 1972.

20. Available variously at http://www.youtube.com. See, for example, http://www.youtube.com/watch?v=QmJj6LZogms (accessed October 25, 2014).

21. For more on the Blue Ridge Mountain Dancers, see Jamison, "James Kesterson's Blue Ridge Mountain Dancers."

22. MDFF Committee Meeting Notes, May 9, 1974, SCRL.

23. *Asheville Citizen*, August 4, 1974.

24. These include the Philadelphia Folk Festival (1974–1978), the National Folk Festival (1975–1976), the Great Hudson River Revival (1977–1978), and the Chicago, Winnipeg, and Vancouver folk festivals in 1979.

25. As early as 1986, Maryland-based dancers Joan Kaminkow (Cope) and Lynn Hamberger taught Green Grass steps and style in England. That same year, the Fiddle Puppet Dancers made the first of eleven annual tours of the United Kingdom. In 1988 the Minnesota-based Wild Goose Chase Cloggers performed and taught workshops at the Sidmouth Folk Festival, and during the past twenty-five years, American dancer Ira Bernstein has taught Green Grass steps and style on frequent tours of the British Isles. Dancers from the British Isles have also attended dance workshops in the United States.

26. "The Clogging List—UK Appalachian Dancer Teams." See http://www.bluefields.org.uk/clogginglist.html (accessed July 12, 2011).

27. For more on the Green Grass Cloggers, see Jamison, "Green Grass Cloggers."

28. Bill Nichols, telephone interview (November 17, 2008).

29. Other contemporary clogging organizations include On Stage America (Utah, 1981) and Clogging Champions of America (1998).

30. Frank Hall has noted a similar development in Irish step dancing, where competitions sanctioned by governing organizations have likewise led to the standardization and codification of a traditional dance form. See Hall, *Competitive Irish Dance*.

31. "2010–2011 NCHC Rules & Guidelines," http://www.clog.org/NCHC/National_Championships/2012-2013%20Rules.pdf (accessed January 18, 2014).

32. Ibid.

33. See "American Racket Cloggers: Kentucky Running Set (2010)," YouTube, http://www.youtube.com/watch?v=uKcioKEmmNw&feature=related (accessed October 25, 2014).

34. Orthner, "What is Clogging?" available at http://www.kerriclogs.com/about.html (accessed October 25, 2014).

Chapter 14. Community Dance in Appalachia

1. Taliaferro, *Fisher's River*, 114.

2. Norman, *Portion of My Life*, 22.

3. It is possible that this designation of "odd" and "even" couples is the consequence of square dances being performed on stage at the Mountain Dance and Folk Festival starting in 1928, as there is no evidence of the terms "odd" and "even" being used prior to that time, and they do not appear on any of the 78-rpm recordings of Southern dance callers recorded between 1924 and 1933.

A similar choreographic change occurred in contra dances. When danced in private homes, the sets tended to be short, and only the top couple would initiate the dance figure; the other couples would follow up once they had reached the top of the set. In larger public ballrooms, however, the sets grew in size, and the dances became exceedingly long. Consequently, as a way to speed up the pace of the dances, these longways sets were subdivided into "minor sets." One dancing master, who recommended this "triple-minor set" formation in 1858, wrote, "It is usual for those at the foot of the set to wait until the first couple has passed down, and they have arrived at the head of the set; but there is no good reason why they should so wait, as every fourth couple should commence with the first couple" (Elias Howe, *Complete Ball-Room Hand Book*, 23). This "triple-minor" form was prevalent until the twentieth century, when "duple-minor sets," with every other couple being active, became the common form of contra dances.

4. For more on the Farmer's Ball, see Jamison, "Old Farmer's Ball."

5. Arnold Ferguson, interview (August 24, 2001).

6. For more on the community dances of western North Carolina, see Jamison, "'Square Dancing' in Haywood County."

7. Taliaferro, *Fisher's River*, 114.

8. Norman, *Portion of My Life*, 21.

9. Wayne Jarrell, interview (February 18, 2005).

10. "Breaking up Christmas" dances, now sponsored by the Surry County Arts Council, still take place in Mt. Airy.

11. Although Whitaker grew up in rural eastern Kentucky, he was clearly a product of the folk dance movement of the twentieth century (see chapter 15). He first learned English country dances in the mid-1940s while attending a nearby settlement school, and he later participated in international folk dancing as a student at Peabody College. Whitaker went on to teach folk dancing at the Pine Mountain Settlement School (1956–1965) and Alice Lloyd College; after retiring and moving back to Carcassonne, he continued to teach folk dance classes in nearby counties in eastern Kentucky (Spalding, *Appalachian Dance*, 205).

12. Videos of the Carcassonne dance made in 1991 can be seen at the Square Dance History Project, http://squaredancehistory.org.

13. For more on the Carcassonne dance, see Jamison, "'Square Dance' at Carcassonne, Kentucky"; Spalding, *Appalachian Dance*.

14. For more on old-time community square dancing in West Virginia, see Dalsemer, *West Virginia Square Dances* and *Reel 'em, Boys, Reel 'em*.

15. For profiles of additional community dances in the Appalachian region, see Spalding, *Appalachian Dance*.

16. For more on community dances and dance communities, see Hast, "Performance, Transformation, and Community"; Dart, *Contra Dance Choreography*; and Bealle, *Old-Time Music and Dance*.

Chapter 15. The American Square Dance

1. I suspect that this crossing of the arms in the Do-si-do comes from Elizabeth Burchenal's folk dance curriculum, which included a Russian folk dance with "arms folded, elbows shoulder-high," as well as a Finnish folk dance in which the dancers pass back-to-back with folded arms. Burchenal, *Folk Dances and Singing Games* (1909), 46; (1933), 66.

2. Marks, *America Learns to Dance*, 80; Webster, *Dancing*, 1.

3. Sharp, *Morris Book*.

4. Parrillo, *Diversity in America*, 69.

5. Higham, *Strangers in the Land*, 142.

6. See Tomko, *Dancing Class*.

7. In an antidance tract published in 1893, Baptist preacher William W. Gardner warned that these "licentious" modern social dances led to "the violation of the Seventh Commandment." Citing official reports, Gardner claimed that "three-fourths (3/4) of the abandoned girls . . . [in New York City] . . . were ruined by dancing," and "three-fifths (3/5) of the fallen women . . . [in St. Louis] . . . attribute their fall to promiscuous dancing" (Gardner, *Modern Dancing*, 31).

8. For more on the folk dance movement of the early twentieth century and its influence on the Pine Mountain Settlement School, Berea College, and the dance traditions of Appalachia, see Spalding, *Appalachian Dance*.

9. Ryan, *Handbook*, v.

10. Another folk dance publication from this era is Ida Levin's *Kentucky Square Dances*, published by the Recreation Council of Louisville, Kentucky, in 1928. Levin

describes "old square dances" from "the Kentucky Mountains" that involve visiting-couple figures for "any number of couples" in a circle set (Levin, *Kentucky Square Dances*).

11. Ford, *Good Morning*, 8.

12. The illustrations in Ford's book show dancers dressed for a formal ball: the men in white ties and tails and the women in full-length dresses.

13. Burchenal, *American Country Dances*. Burchenal wanted to "revive" the old New England dances, which were being displaced by "modern dancing." This collection of dances, published in 1918, consists primarily of New England contra dances, but it also includes the Virginia Reel, which Burchenal describes as "nothing more or less than the well-known popular English countrydance known as 'Sir Roger de Coverly,'" and Dan Tucker, "an old favorite in the Middle West."

14. Malone and Stricklin, *Southern Music/American Music*, 34.

15. Bellamy, "Middle-Aged Romance," 578.

16. In its first five years, the National Folk Festival was held at St. Louis, Missouri (1934), Chattanooga, Tennessee (1935), Dallas, Texas (1936), Chicago, Illinois (1937), and Washington, D.C. (1938).

17. Campbell and Coombs, "Skyline Farms."

18. Casey, *International Folk Dancing*, 32; Lunsford, *Spirit of the Dance*, 2.

19. Harkins, *Hillbilly*, 49.

20. Malone, *Singing Cowboys*, 73.

21. Jimmie Rodgers had earlier romanticized the West with "T for Texas" (1927) and "Yodeling Cowboy" (1929).

22. In 1937 the Prairie Ramblers recorded three 78s with Southern square dance figures called out by bass player Jack Taylor. Taylor's calls include two visiting-couple figures, "Bird in the Cage" and "Lady Round Lady, and Gent Round Gent," and the "Texas Star." ("Raise the Roof in Georgia" [ARC 7-08-60], "Bacon Rind" [ARC 7-08-60], "Kansas City Rag" [ARC 7-11-61].)

23. For more about the transformation of country music's image, see Malone, *Singing Cowboys*.

24. *Ballad of a Mountain Man.*

25. Shaw, *Cowboy Dances*, 28.

26. Ibid., 9.

27. "Bird in the Cage" is mentioned as a "favorite figure" in a fictional account of a dance at a Colorado ranch in 1893 (Fuller, "At the Keith Ranch," 764), and it also appears among the calls at a "ho-down" in eastern Kentucky in 1906 (Haney, *Mountain People of Kentucky*, 52). A similar unnamed figure was danced as part of a quadrille in Michigan in 1889 (Strassburg, *Call Book*, 22). See also appendix, table 3.

28. Shaw, *Cowboy Dances*.

29. Owens, *American Square Dances*, 18. For more on *las cuadrillas* of colonial Mexico, see Aurora Lucero-White, Eunice Hauskins, and Helene Mareau, *Folk Dances of the Spanish-Colonials of New Mexico* (1940); Jack Loeffler, Katherine Loeffler, and Enrique R. Lamadrid, *La música de los Viejitos: Hispano Folk Music of the Rio Grande Del Norte* (1999).

30. Email from Bill Litchman (November 20, 2013).

31. Parkhill, "Swing That Pretty Gal!"

32. See introduction, n17.

33. The association between square dancing and the West was reinforced by Shaw's seminal square dance book, *Cowboy Dances* (1939), which includes illustrations of dancers in cowboy hats and western attire.

34. Tolman and Page, *Country Dance Book*, 183–84.

35. Ryan's book includes the singing square dance, "Girl I Left Behind Me." Ryan, *Dances of Our Pioneers*, 19.

36. Tolman and Page, *Country Dance Book*, 181.

37. Ibid., 183–84. Hale's repertoire included visiting-couple squares that had been recorded on 78-rpm recordings ten years earlier by midwestern callers Tom Owen (1926) and Ed Goodreau (1927).

38. Ibid., 78.

39. *Oakland Tribune*, October 16, 1937.

40. The only dances Mayo specifically identifies as Southern are big-set square dances for many couples, which, borrowing Sharp's terminology, she refers to as "The Running Set." Mayo's American Square Dance Group can be seen performing "The Running Set," accompanied by Pete Seeger (who was involved in the group) in Seeger's 1947 short film "To Hear Your Banjo Play." SDHP, available at http://squaredancehistory.org/items/show/655 (accessed December 20, 2014). For more on old-time square dancing in rural New York State, see Kimball, "Country Dancing."

41. "Square Dance in Advertisements," SDHP, available at http://squaredancehistory.org/items/show/929 (accessed March 17, 2013). Perhaps the most bizarre of these ads is a 1948 television commercial for Lucky Strike cigarettes, featuring eight cigarettes square dancing in a barn to "Turkey in the Straw." See http://archive.org/details/LuckyStr1948_2 (accessed March 17, 2013).

42. These independently organized weekend workshops are intended to promote old-time square dancing, which has declined in many places around the country since the 1980s, due in part to the widespread popularity and dominance of modern contra dancing. See Jamison, "Community Dances in the Eighties"; Jamison, "Community Dances in the 21st Century," available at http://www.philjamison.com; see also www.daretobesquare.org.

43. "The Square Dance History Project" is jointly sponsored by the Country Dance and Song Society; CALLERLAB—The International Association of Square Dance Callers, the Lloyd Shaw Foundation; ARTS-dance: Alliance of Round, Traditional, and Square-Dance, the Square Dance Foundation of New England; and the University of New Hampshire, Special Collections. See http://squaredancehistory.org.

44. Campbell, *Southern Highlander*, 94.

45. Woodmason, *Carolina Backcountry*, 56.

46. Cabbell, "Black Invisibility," 3.

47. The Smoky Mountain Dance Team from Cherokee won first place at the Mountain Dance and Folk Festival in 1932, and in 1935 the winning band was the Carolina Hotshots, from Soco Gap, "composed for the most part of Cherokee Indians or persons of Cherokee family relationship." *Asheville Times*, August 7, 1932; *Asheville Times*, July 4, 1935.

48. *Asheville Times*, August 9, 1942.

49. For a discussion of the Whitetop Festival, see Whisnant, *All That is Native and Fine*.

50. For more on the decline of square dancing and old-time music in African American communities in Appalachia during the first half of the twentieth century, see Spalding, *Appalachian Dance*.

51. U.S. Census, http://www.census.gov (accessed December 19, 2011).

52. Dunaway, *Slavery*, 257.

53. Wood, "Gimme de Kneebone Bent," 7.

54. Casey, *Complete Book*, 4.

55. Du Bois, *Souls of Black Folk*, 193.

56. Damon, *History of Square Dancing*, 25.

57. Maczko, "Keynote Address."

58. Square Dance Legislation Collection.

59. "Promenade Act."

60. Under the "Promenade Act," square dancing is broadly defined to include a number of different types of dance that some square dance club members participate in—round dances, contra dances, line dances, heritage dances, and clogging. While the "Promenade Act" may have originally been conceived as a way to honor American heritage during the nation's bicentennial in 1976, today it appears to be more about promoting modern Western square dancing. Participation in square dance clubs has been declining since the 1980s, and supporters of the bill state that this legislation would "have a positive effect on recruiting new dancers" by giving square dancing "more visibility." See United Square Dancers of America, http://www.usda.org (accessed January 13, 2013). In 1976 nearly forty thousand dancers attended the annual National Square Dance Convention; in 2011 attendance had dropped to just over thirty-seven hundred (National Square Dance Convention).

61. United Square Dancers of America.

62. Ibid.

63. Mangin, "State Folk Dance Conspiracy."

64. Ibid. These and other questions were raised and discussed at congressional hearings in 1984 and 1988. See Square Dance Legislation Collection.

Bibliography

Abbreviations, Archives, and Collections

ABC	"An American Ballroom Companion: Dance Instruction Manuals ca. 1490–1920," Library of Congress, Music Division, available at http://memory.loc.gov/ammem/dihtml/dihome.html.
AFC	American Folklife Center, Library of Congress, Washington, D.C.
BIS	"Born in Slavery: Slave Narratives from the Federal Writers' Project, 1936–1938." Library of Congress, Manuscript Division, available at http://memory.loc.gov/ammem/snhtml/snhome.html.
BLLC	Bascom Lamar Lunsford Collection, Mars Hill University, Mars Hill, North Carolina.
CA	"Chronicling America: Historic American Newspapers," Library of Congress.
DAS	"Documenting the American South," University Library, University of North Carolina at Chapel Hill, http://docsouth.unc.edu.
EAC	W. L. Eury Appalachian Collection, Belk Library, Appalachian State University, Boone, North Carolina.
IA	Internet Archive, https://archive.org.
LOC	Library of Congress, Washington, D.C.
MOA	"Making of America," available at http://quod.lib.umich.edu/m/moagrp.
PMSS	Pine Mountain Settlement School Collections, Pine Mountain Settlement School Library, Bledsoe, Kentucky.
SAA	Southern Appalachian Archives, Hutchins Library, Berea College, Berea, Kentucky.
SCRL	Special Collections, D. H. Ramsey Library, University of North Carolina at Asheville.
SDHP	"Square Dance History Project," available at http://squaredancehistory.org.
SHC	Southern Historical Collection, Wilson Library, University of North Carolina, Chapel Hill, North Carolina.
VWML	Vaughn Williams Memorial Library, Cecil Sharp House, London.

Interviews

Ira Bernstein, Asheville, North Carolina, August 19, 2011.

Albert Burnette, Canton, North Carolina, August 18, 2001.

Walker Calhoun, Swannanoa, North Carolina, November 14, 2005.

Arnold Ferguson, Swannanoa, North Carolina, August 24, 2001.

Betty Garland, Sylva, North Carolina, February 17, 1993.

Biss Honeycutt, Yancey County, North Carolina, April 3, 1993.

Wayne Jarrell, Mt. Airy, North Carolina, February 18, 2005.

Loyal Jones, Berea, Kentucky, March 16, 2006.

James Kesterson, Hendersonville, North Carolina, 1989, and February 26, 2012.

James Lawson, Mt. Airy, North Carolina, September 11, 2009.

Bill Nichols, Telephone interview, Easley, South Carolina, November 17, 2008.

Bill Ohse, Clifftop, West Virginia, August 6, 2010.

John Reeves, Lake Junaluska, North Carolina, April 21, 1993.

Jean Ritchie, Swannanoa, North Carolina, July 2001.

Pauline Zimmerman, Madison County, North Carolina, February 11, 1993.

Internet Sources

2010–2011 NCHC Rules and Guidelines, available at http://www.clog.org/NCHC/National_Championships/2012-2013%20Rules.pdf (accessed January 18, 2014).

"African-American Experience in Ohio 1850–1920, Works Progress Administration Ex-Slave Narratives," Ohio Historical Center Archives Library, American Memory, LOC, available at http://dbs.ohiohistory.org/africanam (accessed December 26, 2007).

AfriClassical.com—African Heritage in Classical Music, available at http://chevalierdesaintgeorges.homestead.com/JohnsonF.html (accessed October 23, 2010).

Berea College Christmas Country Dance School, available at http://www.berea.edu/ccds (accessed December 2, 2014).

"Cecil Sharp's Appalachian Diaries 1915–1918." Vaughn Williams Memorial Library, available at http://library.efdss.org/cgi-bin/introsharpdiaries.cgi (accessed December 2, 2014).

The Clogging List—UK Appalachian Dancer Teams, available at http://www.bluefields.org.uk/clogginglist.html (accessed July 12, 2011).

de Guardiola, Susan. "What Did Jane Austen Dance?" (November 1, 2009), Capering and Kickery, available at http://www.kickery.com/2009/11/what-did-jane-austen-dance.html (accessed November 26, 2010).

"Encyclopedic Discography of Victor Recordings," Special Collections, University of California, Santa Barbara Library, available at http://victor.library.ucsb.edu (accessed December 2, 2014).

Federal Reserve Bank of Minneapolis, available at http://www.minneapolisfed.org/community_education/teacher/calc/hist1800.cfm (accessed June 21, 2014).

Jabbour, Alan. "Fiddle Tunes of the Old Frontier." Essay delivered at Indiana State University, Terre Haute, Indiana (December 6, 2001), available at http://www.alanjabbour.com/fiddle_tunes_old_frontier.html (accessed October 16, 2011).

Keller, Robert M. "The Dancing Master, 1651–1728: An Illustrated Compendium." Country Dance and Song Society, 2000, available at http://www.izaak.unh.edu/nhltmd/indexes/dancingmaster.

Maczko, Jim. "Keynote Address," 57th National Square Dance Convention, Wichita, Kansas, June 2008, available at http://www.57nsdc.com/Flyers/KeynoteSpeaker/index.htm (accessed August 21, 2008).

McKernan, Michael. "McKernan's Dance History," available at http://mckernans dancehistory.shutterfly.com (accessed March 20, 2014).

National Square Dance Convention, available at http://www.nsdcnec.com/past.htm (accessed January 7, 2012).

"Online Etymology Dictionary," available at http://www.etymonline.com (accessed November 28, 2014).

Orthner, Kerri. "What is Clogging?" available at http://www.kerriclogs.com/about.html (accessed July 13, 2011).

"Population Schedules of the Second Census of the United States, 1800," reel 29, North Carolina, vol. 1, 158: IA (accessed January 7, 2014).

"Promenade Act," H. R. 645, 108th Congress, 2003, available at http://thomas.loc.gov/cgi-bin/query/z?c108:H.R.645.IH (accessed January 17, 2012).

Shaw, Dorothy. "The Appalachian Mountain Dance." European Association of American Square Dancing Clubs. Available at http://eaasdc.eu/eu/fileadmin/eaasdc2/archive/history/shehisto.pdf (accessed November 27, 2014).

The Square Dance Legislation Collection, AFC 1984/024. American Folklife Center, LOC, Washington, DC, 1994, available at http://www.loc.gov/folklife/guides/squaredance.html (accessed August 25, 2008).

United Square Dancers of America, available at http://www.usda.org (accessed December 19, 2011).

United States Census, available at http://www.census.gov (accessed December 19, 2011).

Yates, Mike. "Cecil Sharp in America: Collecting in the Appalachians," *Musical Traditions Internet Magazine* (January 15, 1999), available at http://www.mustrad.org.uk/articles/sharp.htm (accessed October 27, 2008).

Recordings

Dr. Humphrey Bate and His Possum Hunters, "Billy in the Lowground" (Brunswick 239), 1928.

———, "Goin' Up-Town" (Brunswick 232), 1928.

———, "Take Your Foot Out of the Mud" (Brunswick 243), 1928.

Andrew and Jim Baxter "Georgia Stomp" (Victor 38002), 1928.

The Blue Ridge Duo (George Reneau and Gene Austin), "Arkansas Traveler" (Edison 51422), 1924.

———, "Turkey in the Straw" (Edison 51502), 1924.

Hershal Brown's Washboard Band, "Liberty" (Victor 40070), 1928.

Samantha Bumgarner, "Fly around My Pretty Little Miss" (Columbia 146), 1924.

———, "Shout Lou" (Columbia 146), 1924.

Calaway's West Virginia Mountaineers, "The Cornshucker's Frolic" (Gennett 6545), 1928.
Warren Caplinger, "Chicken Reel" (Vocalion 5222), 1928.
Fiddlin' John Carson, "Cotton-Eyed Joe" (OKeh 45122), 1927.
Bill Chitwood, "Kitty Hill" (OKeh 45162), 1927.
Chumbler, Coker, and Rice, "Alabama Square Dance—Pt. 1" (Broadway 8234), 1929.
———, "Alabama Square Dance—Pt. 2" (Broadway 8234), 1929.
Crockett's Kentucky Mountaineers, "Sugar in My Coffee" (Crown 3075), 1931.
Crook Brothers String Band, "Going across the Sea" (Victor 40099), 1928.
———, "Job in Getting' There" (Victor 40020), 1928.
———, "Love Somebody" (Victor 40099), 1928.
———, "My Wife Died Friday Night" (Victor 40020), 1928.
Seven Foot Dilly (John Dilleshaw), "Square Dance Fight on Ball Top Mountain—Pt. 1" (Vocalion 5419), 1930.
———, "Square Dance Fight on Ball Top Mountain—Pt. 2" (Vocalion 5419), 1930.
Dixie String Band, "Chickens Don't Roost Too High for Me" (Paramount 33160), 1925.
Dykes' Magic City Trio, "Callahan's Reel" (Vocalion 5181), 1927.
———, "Cotton-Eyed Joe" (Brunswick 120), 1927.
———, "Huckleberry Blues" (Brunswick 129), 1927.
———, "Red Steer" (Vocalion 5181), 1927.
———, "Shortnin' Bread" (Brunswick 125), 1927.
———, "Tennessee Girls" (Brunswick 120), 1927.
Four Virginians, "New Coon in Town" (OKeh 45181), 1927.
———, "Promenade All" (OKeh 45201), 1927.
———, "Swing Your Partner" (OKeh 45181), 1927.
Freeny's Barn Dance Band, "Mississippi Square Dance—Pt. 1" (OKeh 45533), 1930.
———, "Mississippi Square Dance—Pt. 2" (OKeh 45533), 1930.
G. B. Grayson and Henry Whitter, "Old Jimmie Sutton" (Gennett 6436), 1928.
J. D. (Dedrick) Harris, "Buckin' Mule" (Broadway 1963), 1924.
———, "Whip the Devil Round the Stump" (Broadway 1964), 1924.
Hatton Brothers, "Hook and Line" (Champion 16628), 1933.
———, "Wish I Had My Time Again" (Champion 16628), 1933.
Jess Hillard and His New Richmond Aces, "Arkansas Traveler" (Champion 16333), 1931.
———, "Cackling Hen" (Champion 16333), 1931.
The Hillbillies, "Walking in the Parlor" (Vocalion 5024), 1926.
Al Hopkins and His Buckle Busters, "Boatin' Up Sandy" (Brunswick 182), 1927.
———, "Bug in the Taters" (Brunswick 182), 1927.
Jimmie Johnson's String Band, "Step Lively" (Champion 16389), 1931.
———, "Washington Quadrille" (Champion 16389), 1931.
Kessinger Brothers, "Chicken in the Barnyard" (Brunswick 256), 1928.
———, "Devil's Dream" (Brunswick 256), 1928.
———, "Forked Deer Hornpipe" (Brunswick 247), 1928.
———, "Girl I Left Behind Me" (Brunswick 267), 1928.

———, "Hell among the Yearlings" (Brunswick 235), 1928.
———, "Patty on the Turnpike" (Vocalion 5248), 1928.
———, "Turkey in the Straw" (Brunswick 235), 1928.
———, "Wild Horse" (Vocalion 5248), 1928.
Sherman Lawson and Frank Hutchison, "Wild Hogs in the Red Brush" (OKeh 45274), 1928.
Leake County Revelers, "Leather Britches" (Columbia 15149), 1927.
Lonesome Luke and His Farm Hands, "Beaver Valley Breakdown" (Champion 16269), 1931.
———, "Dogs in the Ashcan" (Champion 16229), 1931.
———, "Halfway to Arkansas" (Champion 16269), 1931.
———, "Wild Hog in the Woods" (Champion 16229), 1931.
Uncle Dave Macon, "Sleepy Lou" (Vocalion 5156), 1927.
———, "Tom and Jerry" (Vocalion 5165), 1927.
Clayton McMichen's Georgia Wildcats, "Arkansas Traveler" (Gennett 7011), 1932.
Clayton McMichen and Riley Puckett, "Hog-Trough Reel" (Gennett 7011), 1932.
Floyd Ming and His Pep Steppers, "Old Red" (Victor 21294), 1928.
———, "Tupelo Blues" (Victor 21534), 1928.
———, "White Mule" (Victor 21534), 1928.
Fiddlin' Powers and Family, "Old Virginia Reel—Pt. 2" (OKeh 45268), 1927.
George Reneau, "Turkey in the Straw" (Vocalion 14812), 1924.
Roanoke Jug Band, "Johnny Lover" (OKeh 45423), 1929.
Doc Roberts, "Girl I Left Behind" (Gennett 6826), 1929.
———, "Martha Campbell" (Supertone 9397), 1929.
———, "Waltz the Hall" (Supertone 9670), 1929.
———, "Who's Been Here Since I've Been Gone" (Gennett 6826), 1929.
Scottdale String Band, "Chinese Breakdown" (OKeh 45103), 1927.
———, "Green Mountain Poker" (OKeh 45279), 1928.
———, "Hiawatha Breakdown" (OKeh 45158), 1927.
———, "Hop Light Ladies" (OKeh 45158), 1927.
———, "In the Shade of the Parasol" (OKeh 45103), 1927.
———, "Old Folks Better Go to Bed" (OKeh 45173), 1927.
———, "Share 'em" (OKeh 45256), 1928.
Ernest Stoneman and the Blue Ridge Corn Shuckers, "Old Time Corn Shuckin'—Pt. 2" (Victor 20835), 1927.
———, "A Serenade in the Mountains, pt. 2" (Victor 21518), 1928.
Stovepipe No. 1 (Sam Jones), "Cripple Creek/Sourwood Mountain" (Columbia 201), 1924.
———, "Turkey in the Straw" (Columbia 201), 1924.
Judge Sturdy's Orchestra, "Old Dan Tucker [Old Country Dance]" (Victor 20102), 1925.
Sweet Brothers, "I'm Gonna Marry That Pretty Little Girl" (unissued), 1928.
Gid Tanner and His Skillet Lickers, "Fiddlers' Convention in Georgia—Pt.2" (Columbia 15140), 1927.

Vance's Tennessee Breakdowners, "Tennessee Breakdown" (OKeh 45151), 1927.
Watkin's Band, "Bob Murphy" (Victor 21405), 1928.
———, "Gideon" (Victor 21405), 1928.
Whitter's Virginia Breakdowners, "Mississippi Sawyer" (OKeh 7005), 1924.
———, "Sourwood Mountain" (OKeh 7005), 1924.
Williamson Brothers and Curry, "The Fun's All Over" (OKeh 45108), 1927.
Charlie Wilson and His Hillbillies, "Cuttin' at the Point" (Champion 16528), 1932.
———, "Ride the Goat over the Mountain" (Champion 16601), 1933.
———, "Shelven Rock" (Champion 16528), 1932.
Da Costa Woltz's Southern Broadcasters, "John Brown's Dream" (Gennett 6220), 1927.
———, "Richmond Cotillion" (Gennett 6220), 1927.

Films

The Complete Bascom Lamar Lunsford Story. 1989. DVD. David Hoffman. Varied Directions, 2012.
Full of Life A-Dancin'. DVD. Robert Fiore and Richard Nevell, 1978.
Reel 'em, Boys, Reel 'em. DVD. Gerald Milnes and Becky Hill. Elkins, West Virginia: Augusta Heritage, 2014.
Step Back Cindy: Old Time Dancing in Southwest Virginia. DVD. Anne Lewis Johnson and Susan Spalding. Whitesburg, Ky.: Appalshop, 1990.
Talking Feet: Solo Southern Dance, Buck, Flatfoot and Tap. DVD. Mike Seeger and Ruth Pershing (1987), Washington, D.C.: Smithsonian Folkways, 2007.

Newspapers and Periodicals

American School Board Journal 58, nos. 2 and 5 (February and May 1919).
Asheville Citizen (June 5, 1928; December 21, 1947; August 10, 1952; July 31, 1959; August 9, 1959; July 20, 1972; August 4, 1974).
Asheville Times (June 5, 1928; June 6, 1928, August 7, 1932; August 4, 1933; July 4, 1935; August 9, 1942; August 12, 1977).
[Earlington, Kentucky] Bee, (July 26, 1894), "Chronicling America: Historic American Newspapers," LOC.
"The Cake Walk: A Richmond Christmas Festival." *Frank Leslie's Illustrated Newspaper*, December 31, 1870, 261–62.
The Diary; or, Loudon's Register 197 (October 1, 1792), New York.
Gazette of the United States 11, no. 1377 (February 6, 1797), Philadelphia.
Harper's New Monthly Magazine 59 (October 1879).
Hartford [Kentucky] Herald, (March 23, 1892), CA.
Kansas City Gazette (February 27, 1899).
New Monthly Magazine and Literary Journal, vol. 1 (London: Colburn, 1821).
New York Times (January 11, 1883; January 3, 1929; November 15, 1936; October 30, 1938).
North American Magazine, vol. 5 (Sherman, 1835).
Oakland {California] Tribune (October 16, 1937).
"The Old Virginia Reel: A Christmas Reverie in Verse," *Richmond Planet*, December 26, 1908, CA.

"Pen and Plate Club Hears Cecil Sharp." *Asheville Citizen*, June 14, 1917.

Philadelphia Gazette and Universal Daily Advertiser 16, no. 2604 (March 2, 1797): 4.

"Round and Square Dances." *New York Times*, June 19, 1881.

Twin City Sentinel (Winston-Salem, N.C.) (May 1, 1924).

"Walking for a Cake: Eleven Couples Competed, and Mr. Marshall and Miss Hammett Won First Prize." *New York Times*, February 7, 1897.

Wichita Daily Eagle (April 28, 1894).

Print Sources

Abbott, Lynn, and Doug Seroff. *Out of Sight: The Rise of African American Popular Music, 1889–1895*. Jackson: University Press of Mississippi, 2002.

Abrahams, Roger D. *African American Folktales: Stories from Black Traditions in the New World*. New York: Pantheon, 1985.

———. *Singing the Master: The Emergence of African American Culture in the Plantation South*. New York: Pantheon, 1992.

Adams, Edward C. L. *Tales of the Congaree* (1928). Robert G. O'Meally, ed. Chapel Hill: University of North Carolina Press, 1987.

Adams, John. *The Adams Papers / Diary and Autobiography of John Adams, Vol. I: Diary 1755–1770*. L. H. Butterfield, ed. Cambridge: Harvard University Press, 1961.

Aimwell, Absalom. "A Pinkster Ode For the Year 1803." *New York Folklore Quarterly* 8 (Spring 1952): 31–45.

Aldrich, Elizabeth. *From the Ballroom to Hell: Grace and Folly in Nineteenth Century Dance*. Evanston, Ill.: Northwestern University Press, 1991.

Anderson, Robert. *From Slavery to Affluence: Memoirs of Robert Anderson, Ex-Slave*. 1927. Steamboat Springs, Colo.: Steamboat Pilot, 1967.

Arfwedson, Carl D. *The United States and Canada in 1832, 1833 and 1834*. 2 vols. 1834. New York: Johnson Reprint, 1969.

Arthur, John Preston. *Western North Carolina: A History (from 1730 to 1913)*. Raleigh, N.C.: Edwards and Broughton, 1914.

Ashe, Thomas. *Travels in America, Performed in 1806, for the Purpose of Exploring the Rivers Alleghany, Monongahela, Ohio, and Mississippi, and Ascertaining the Produce and Condition of Their Banks and Vicinity*. London: Sawyer, 1808.

Audubon, John James. *Ornithological Biography*. Vol. 2. Edinburgh: Black, 1834.

Audubon, Maria R. *Audubon and His Journals*. New York: Scribner's, 1897.

Austen, Jane. *Pride and Prejudice*. 1813. Carol Howard, introduction and notes. New York: Barnes and Noble, 2003.

Avirett, James Battle. *The Old Plantation; How We Lived in Great House and Cabin before the War*. New York: Neely, 1901.

Bailey, Robert. *The Life and Adventures of Robert Bailey, An Autobiography*. 1822. Marceline, Mo. / Berkeley Springs, W.V.: Warm Springs Echoes, 1978.

Baily, Francis. *Journal of a Tour in Unsettled Parts of North America in 1796 and 1797*. London: Baily, 1856.

Baldwin, Brook. "The Cakewalk: A Study in Stereotype and Reality." *Journal of Social History* 15, no. 2 (1981): 205–18.

The Ball-Room Instructer. New York: Huestis and Craft, 1841, ABC.

The Ball-room Manual of Contra Dances and Social Cotillons, With Remarks on Quadrilles and Spanish Dance. Belfast, Maine: Washburn, 1863, ABC.

"The Banjo in Virginia." Blue Ridge Institute and Museum, Ferrum College, Ferrum, Virginia.

Barrow, David C., Jr. "A Georgia Corn Shucking." *Century Illustrated Monthly Magazine* 24 (1882): 873–78.

Bartlett, John Russell. *Dictionary of Americanisms*. New York: Little, Brown, 1859.

Battle, Kemp P. *History of the University of North Carolina, 1789–1868*. Vol. 1. Raleigh, N.C.: Edwards and Broughton, 1907.

Baylor, Frances Courtenay. *Behind the Blue Ridge: A Homely Narrative*. Philadelphia: Lippincott, 1887.

Beadle's Dime Ball-Room Companion and Guide to Dancing. New York: Beadle, c. 1868, ABC.

Bealle, John. *Old-Time Music and Dance: Community and Folk Revival*. Bloomington: Indiana University Press, 2005.

Bellamy, Elizabeth Whitfield [Kamba Thorpe, pseud.] "A Middle-Aged Romance." *Appletons' Journal: A Magazine of General Literature* 11, nos. 268–70 (May 9–23, 1874), MOA.

Bernard, John. *Retrospections of America, 1797–1811*. 1887. New York: Blom, 1969.

Bernhard, Duke of Saxe-Weimar Eisenach. *Travels through North America, during the Years 1825 and 1826*. 2 vols. Philadelphia: Carey, Lea, and Carey, 1828.

Blesh, Rudi, and Harriet Janis. *They All Played Ragtime: The True Story of an American Music*. New York: Knopf, 1950.

Boggs, Marion Alexander, ed. *The Alexander Letters, 1787–1900*. Athens: University of Georgia Press, 1980.

Boswell, James. *A Tour to the Hebrides*. Frederick A. Pottle and Charles H. Bennett, eds. New York: Viking, 1936.

Botkin, B. A. *The American Play-Party Song*. 1937. New York: Ungar, 1963.

Boyd, Neva Leona. *Descriptions of English and American Country Dances*. Chicago: self-published, 193?.

Boyd, Neva L., and Tressie M. Dunlavy. *Old Square Dances of America*. Chicago: Recreational Training School, 1925.

Branch, Mary Polk. *Memoirs of a Southern Woman: "Within the Lines" and a Genealogical Record*. Chicago: Branch, 1912. Electronic edition, Academic Affairs Library, University of North Carolina at Chapel Hill, 1998.

Breathnach, Breandán. *Folk Music and Dances of Ireland*. Rev. ed. Dublin: Mercier, 1977.

Brennan, Helen. *The Story of Irish Dance*. Kerry, Ireland: Brandon, 1999.

Bridenbaugh, Carl. *Cities in the Wilderness: The First Century of Urban Life in America, 1625–1742*. 1938. New York: Capricorn, 1964.

———. *Myths and Realities: Societies of the Colonial South*. Baton Rouge: Louisiana State University Press, 1952.

Bronner, Simon J. *Old-Time Music Makers of New York State*. Syracuse, N.Y.: Syracuse University Press, 1987.

Brooks, C. *The Ball-Room Monitor*. Philadelphia: Johnson, 1866, ABC.

Brown, Frank C. *Frank C. Brown Collection of North Carolina Folklore*. Vol. 7. Durham, N.C.: Duke University Press, 1964.

Buckingham, J. S. *The Slave States of America*. Vol. 1. 1842. New York: Negro Universities Press, 1968.

Burchenal, Elizabeth. *American Country Dances*. Vol. 1. New York: Schirmer, 1918.

———. *Dances of the People: A Second Volume of Folk-Dances and Singing Games*. New York: Schirmer, 1913.

———. *Folk Dances and Singing Games*. New York: Schirmer, 1909.

———. *Folk Dances and Singing Games*. Rev. ed. New York: Schirmer, 1933.

———. *Folk Dances from Old Homelands*. New York: Schirmer, 1922.

Burnaby, Rev. Andrew. *Travels through the Middle Settlements in North-America*. 2nd ed. 1775. Ithaca, N.Y.: Cornell University Press, 1968.

Burnett, Frances Hodgson. "Lodusky." *Scribner's Monthly* 16 (September 1877): 673.

Byrd, William. *The Secret Diary of William Byrd of Westover 1709–1712*. Louis B. Wright and Marion Tinling, eds. Richmond, Va.: Dietz, 1941.

Cabbell, Edward J. "Black Invisibility and Racism in Appalachia: An Informal Survey." In *Blacks in Appalachia*, ed. William H. Turner and Edward J. Cabbell (Lexington: University Press of Kentucky, 1985).

Campbell, David, and David Coombs. "Skyline Farms: A Case Study of Community Development and Rural Rehabilitation." *Appalachian Journal* 10 (Spring 1983): 244–54.

Campbell, John C. *The Southern Highlander and His Homeland*. New York: Sage, 1921.

Campbell, John Francis. *A Short American Tramp on the Fall of 1864*. Edinburgh: Edmonston and Douglas, 1865. American Notes: Travels in America, 1750–1920. LOC.

Campbell, Olive Dame, and Cecil J. Sharp. *English Folk Songs from the Southern Appalachians*. New York: Putnam, 1917.

Carlin, Bob. *The Birth of the Banjo: Joel Walker Sweeney and Early Minstrelsy*. Jefferson, N.C.: McFarland, 2007.

Cartier and Baron's Practical Illustrated Waltz Instructor, Ball Room Guide, and Call Book. New York: De Witt, 1879, ABC.

Cartwright, Peter. *Autobiography of Peter Cartwright, the Backwoods Preacher*. Cincinnati: Swormstedt and Poe, 1859, IA.

Casey, Betty. *The Complete Book of Square Dancing and Round Dancing*. New York: Doubleday, 1976.

———. *International Folk Dancing U.S.A.* New York: Doubleday, 1981.

Cauthen, Joyce H. *With Fiddle and Well-Rosined Bow*. Tuscaloosa: University of Alabama Press, 1989.

Cellarius, Henri. *The Drawing-Room Dances*. London: Churton, 1847, ABC.

Christian, Jacky. "Joe Hood—Old-Time Buck Dancer." *Old Time Herald* 4, no. 8 (May 1995): 12–14, 60.

"Christ's Kirk on the Green." *Two Ancient Scottish Poems: The Gaberlunzie-Man and Christ's Kirk on the Green*. Notes by John Callander. Edinburgh: Robertson, 1782, IA.

Claiborne, John Francis Hamtramck. *Life and Correspondence of John A. Quitman*. New York: Harper, 1860, MOA.

Clark, Dan Elbert. *The Middle West in American History*. New York: Crowell, 1937.

Clarke, Lewis Garrard, and Milton Clarke. *Narratives of the Sufferings of Lewis and Milton Clarke,* 1846, DAS.

Clendenen, F. Leslie. *Prof. Clendenen's Fashionable Quadrille Book and Guide to Etiquette.* Davenport, Iowa: Clendenen, 1895, ABC.

Cleveland, C. H., Jr. *Dancing at Home and Abroad*. Boston: Ditson, 1878, ABC.

Cohen, Hennig. "Negro Folk Game in Colonial South Carolina." *Southern Folklore Quarterly* 16 (September 1952): 183–84.

———. *The South-Carolina Gazette: 1732–1775*. Columbia: University of South Carolina Press, 1953.

Coke, E. T. (Edward Thomas). *A Subaltern's Furlough: Descriptive Scenes of the United States, Upper and Lower Canada, New-Brunswick, and Nova Scotia, during the Summer and Autumn of 1832*. Vol. 1. New York: Harper, 1833.

Coll, Charles J., and Gabrielle Rosiere. *Dancing Made Easy*. New York: Clode, 1922, ABC.

A Collection of the Most Favorite Cottillions. Philadelphia: Blake, c. 1810.

Collins, Thomas. *The Adventures of T. C. Collins-Boatman: Twenty-Four Years on the Western Waters, 1849–1873*. Herbert L. Roush Sr., ed. Baltimore, Md.: Gateway, 1985.

———. *The Biography of T. C. Collins, Written by Himself, Part One, 1832–1873*. Herbert L. Roush Sr., ed. Baltimore: Gateway, 1986.

Compan, Charles. *Dictionnaire de Danse*. 1787. New York: Broude, 1974.

The Complaynt of Scotlande. 1549. Introduction by James Murray. London: Early English Text Society, 1872, IA.

Connor, R. D. W., Hugh T. Lefler, and Louis R. Wilson, eds. *A Documentary History of the University of North Carolina, 1776–1799.* Chapel Hill: University of North Carolina Press, 1953.

Conway, Cecelia. *African Banjo Echoes in Appalachia: A Study of Folk Traditions.* Knoxville: University of Tennessee Press, 1995.

Cooke, John Esten. *Leather and Silk* [reprint of *Leather Stocking and Silk*]. New York: Dillingham, 1854.

Coulon. *Coulon's Hand-book of Dancing*. London: Hammond, 1873, ABC.

Cresswell, Nicholas. *The Journal of Nicholas Cresswell, 1774–1777*. New York: Dial, 1924.

Crockett, David. *A Narrative of the Life of David Crockett of the State of Tennessee.* 1834. Facsimile edition with annotations and introduction by James A. Shackford and Stanley J. Folmsbee. Knoxville: University of Tennessee Press, 1973.

Curtin, Philip D. *The Atlantic Slave Trade*. Madison: University of Wisconsin Press, 1969.

D. L. "A Ball in the Far West." *The Ladies' Companion* 7 (May 1837): 21–23.

Dalsemer, Robert G. *West Virginia Square Dances*. New York: Country Dance and Song Society of America, 1982.

Damon, S. Foster. *The History of Square Dancing*. Barre, Mass.: Barre Gazette, 1957.

Danaher, Kevin. *The Year in Ireland.* Cork: Mercier, 1972.

Dart, Mary McNab. *Contra Dance Choreography: A Reflection of Social Change*. New York: Garland Publishing, 1995.

Daughters of the American Revolution Magazine 12. National Society of the Daughters of the American Revolution, 1898 (Google eBook).

Daughters of the American Revolution Magazine 16. National Society of the Daughters of the American Revolution, 1900 (Google eBook).

Dauney, William. *Ancient Scotish Melodies, from a Manuscript of the Reign of King James VI*. Edinburgh, 1838.

Dean-Smith, Margaret. "Jig." *The New Grove Dictionary of Music Online*, edited by L. Macy (accessed January 16, 2003).

de Crèvecoeur, St. John. *Sketches of Eighteenth Century America: More "Letters from an American Farmer."* 1792. New Haven, Conn.: Yale University Press, 1925.

De Garmo, William B. *The Prompter*. New York: Raymond and Caulon, 1865, ABC.

De Voe, Thomas F. *The Market Book: A History of the Public Markets of New York*. 1862. New York: Kelley, 1970.

Diallo, Yaya, and Mitchell Hall. *The Healing Drum: African Wisdom Teachings*. Rochester, Vt.: Destiny, 1989.

Dickens, Charles. "Poor Mercantile Jack" In *The Uncommercial Traveller* (1860). Oxford: Oxford University Press, 1997.

Dictionary of American Regional English. Vol. 1. Frederic G. Cassidy, ed. Cambridge, Mass: Belknap, 1985.

Djedje, Jacqueline Cogdell. *Fiddling in West Africa: Touching the Spirit in Fulbe, Hausa, and Dagbamba Cultures*. Bloomington: Indiana University Press, 2008.

Doddridge, Joseph. *Notes on the Settlement and Indian Wars, of the Western Parts of Virginia and Pennsylvania from 1763 to 1783, Inclusive, Together with a Review of the State of Society and Manners of the First Settlers of the Western Country*. 1824. Repr., Pittsburgh: Ritenour and Lindsay, 1912.

Dodworth, Allen. *Dancing and Its Relations to Education and Social Life, with a New Method of Instruction*. New York: Harper, 1900, ABC.

Dromgoole, Will Allen. *The Sunny Side of the Cumberland: A Story of the Mountains*. Murfreesboro, Tenn.: n.p., 1886.

Du Bois, W. E. B. *The Souls of Black Folk*. 1903. David W. Blight and Robert Gooding-Williams, eds. Boston: Bedford, 1997.

Duke, Jerry. *Clog Dance in the Appalachians*. San Francisco: Duke, 1984.

Dunaway, Wilma A. *Slavery in the American Mountain South*. Cambridge: Cambridge University Press, 2003.

Durang, Charles. *The Ball-Room Bijou and Art of Dancing: Containing the Figures of the Polkas, Mazurkas, and other Popular New Dances, with Rules for Polite Behavior*. Philadelphia: Fisher, 1850, IA.

———. *Durang's Terpsichore; or, Ball Room Guide*. Philadelphia: Turner and Fisher, 1848.

———. *The Fashionable Dancer's Casket; or The Ballroom Instructor*. 1856. Bedford, Mass.: Applewood, 1996.

Durang, John. *The Memoir of John Durang*. Alan S. Downer, ed. York, Penn.: University of Pittsburgh Press, 1966.

Ellis, William E. *The Kentucky River*. Lexington: University of Kentucky, 2000.

Emery, Lynne Fauley. *Black Dance, From 1619 to Today*. Hightstown, N. J.: Princeton, 1988.

Emmerson, George S. *Rantin' Pipe and Tremblin' String: A History of Scottish Dance Music*. Montreal: McGill-Queen's University Press, 1971.

———. *A Social History of Scottish Dance*. Montreal: McGill-Queens University Press, 1972.

Enys, John. *The American Journals of Lt. John Enys*. Elizabeth Cometti, ed. Syracuse, N.Y.: Syracuse University Press, 1976.

Epstein, Dena J. *Sinful Tunes and Spirituals: Black Folk Music to the Civil War*. Urbana: University of Illinois Press, 1977.

Eslinger, Ellen, ed. *Running Mad for Kentucky: Frontier Travel Accounts*. Lexington: University Press of Kentucky, 2004.

Farlow, Betsy, Dan Lane, and Duane Oliver. *Haywood Homes and History*. Hazelwood, N.C.: Farlow, 1993.

Featherstonhaugh, George William. *Excursion through the Slave States from Washington on the Potomac to the Frontier of Mexico, 1834–1835*. 1844. New York: Negro Universities Press, 1968.

Felton, Rebecca Latimer. *Country Life in Georgia in the Days of My Youth*. Atlanta: Index, 1919, DAS.

Feyock, Merry. "Dance, Our Dearest Diversion: Historical Dance Reconstruction in Colonial Williamsburg." In Eike and Woodside, *Communities in Motion*.

Flett, J. F., and T. M. Flett. "The History of the Scottish Reel as a Dance-Form, I." *Scottish Studies 16*. School of Scottish Studies, University of Edinburgh, 1972.

———. "The History of the Scottish Reel as a Dance-Form, II." *Scottish Studies 17*. School of Scottish Studies, University of Edinburgh, 1973.

———. *Traditional Dancing in Scotland*. London: Routledge and Kegan Paul, 1964.

Fletcher, Tom. *100 Years of the Negro in Show Business*. 1954. New York: Da Capo, 1984.

Flint, Timothy. *Recollections of the Last Ten Years in the Valley of the Mississippi*. 1826. George R. Brooks, ed. Carbondale: Southern Illinois University Press, 1968.

Ford, Mr. and Mrs. Henry. *Good Morning*. Dearborn, Mich.: Dearborn Pub., 1926.

Fox, John, Jr. *Heart of the Hills*. New York: Burt, 1912.

Friedland, LeeEllen. "Folk Dance History." In *International Encyclopedia of Dance*, edited by Selma Jeanne Cohen (New York: Oxford University Press, 1998), 3:29–38.

———. "Square Dancing." In *International Encyclopedia of Dance*, edited by Selma Jeanne Cohen (New York: Oxford University Press, 1998), 5:685–90.

———. "Traditional Folkdance in Kentucky." *Country Dance and Song* 10 (1979): 5–19.

Frost, Helen. *The Clog Dance Book*. New York: Barnes, 1921.

Frost, William Goodell. "Our Contemporary Ancestors in the Southern Mountains." *Atlantic Monthly* (1899), SCRL.

Fulcher, Bobby. "Traditional Dance on the Cumberland Plateau, Part 1." *Old Time Herald* 3, no. 4 (May 1992): 11–16, 56.

Fuller, Anna. "At the Keith Ranch." *Century Illustrated Monthly Magazine* 45. Scribner, 1893.

Furnivall, Frederick J. *Captain Cox, His Ballads and Books*. London: 1871, IA.

Gallini, Giovanni-Andrea. *Critical Observations on the Art of Dancing*. London: R. Dodsley, 1770 (Google eBook).

Gannett, Edward Channing. "The Freedmen at Port Royal." *North American Review* 101 (1865): 10.

Gardner, William W. *Modern Dancing: In the Light of Scripture and Facts*. Louisville, Ky.: Baptist Book Concern, 1893.

The German. How to Give It. How to Lead It. How to Dance It. Chicago: Jansen, McClurg, 1879.

Gilman, Caroline Howard. *Recollections of a Southern Matron*. New York: Harper, 1838.

Gilmore, John. *The Poetics of Empire: A Study of James Grainger's The Sugar Cane*. London: Athlone, 2000.

Goertzen, Chris, and Alan Jabbour. "George P. Knauff's Virginia Reels and Fiddling in the Antebellum South." *American Music* 5, no. 2 (Summer, 1987): 121–44.

Gomme, Alice Bertha. *The Traditional Games of England, Scotland, and Ireland, Vol. 1 (1894) and Vol. 2 (1898)*. London: Thames and Hudson, 1984.

Green, Karen Mauer. *Kentucky Gazette, 1787–1800*. Baltimore: Gateway, 1983.

Griffiths, John. *A Collection of the Newest Cotillions, and Country Dances*. Northampton, Mass.: Butler, 1788.

Guild, Josephus Conn. *Old Times in Tennessee, with Historical, Personal, and Political Scraps and Sketches*. 1878. Knoxville, Tenn.: Tenase, 1971.

Hall, Frank. *Competitive Irish Dance: Art, Sport, Duty*. Madison, Wisc.: Macater Press, 2008.

Hall, James. *Letters from the West; Containing Sketches of Scenery, Manners, and Customs; And Anecdotes Connected with the First Settlement of the Western Sections of the United States*. London: Colburn, 1828.

Hamby, Zetta Barker. *Memories of Grassy Creek: Growing up in the Mountains on the Virginia–North Carolina Line*. Jefferson, N.C.: McFarland, 1998.

Hancock, William. *An Emigrants' Five Years in the Free States of America*. London: Newby, 1860.

Haney, William H. *The Mountain People of Kentucky*. Cincinnati, Ohio: Clarke, 1906.

Harben, Will N. *Westerfelt*. New York: Harper, 1901.

Harkins, Anthony. *Hillbilly: A Cultural History of an American Icon*. New York: Oxford University Press, 2004.

Harney, Will Wallace. "Strange Land and Peculiar People." *Lippincott's Magazine* 12 (October 1873): 429–38. Repr. in *Appalachian Images in Folk and Popular Culture*, edited by W. K. McNeil, 45–58. Ann Arbor, Michigan: UMI Research, 1989.

Harris, George Washington. "Bart Davis's Dance." In *Sut Lovingood's Yarns*, edited by M. Thomas Inge (New Haven, Conn: College and University Press, 1966).

———. "The Knob Dance—A Tennessee Frolic." In Inge, *High Times and Hard Times*.

———. "Sporting Epistle from East Tennessee." 1843. In Inge, *High Times and Hard Times*.

Harris, Joel Chandler. "At Teague Poteet's: A Sketch of the Hog Mountain Range." In *Mingo and Other Sketches in Black and White* (New York: McKinlay, Stone, and MacKenzie, 1884).

Harvey, J. H. *Wehman's Complete Dancing Master and Call Book*. New York: Wehman, 1889, ABC.

Hast, Dorthea. "Performance, Transformation, and Community: Contra Dance in New England." *Dance Research Journal* 25.1 (1993): 21.

Hazzard-Gordon, Katrina. "Dancing under the Lash: Sociocultural Disruption, Continuity, and Synthesis." In *African Dance: An Artistic, Historical, and Philosophical Inquiry*, edited by Kariamu Welsh-Asante (Trenton, N.J.: Africa World, 1996).

Hearn, Lafcadio. "Levee Life: Haunts and Pastimes of the Roustabouts, Their Original Songs and Peculiar Dances." 1876. *The Folklore Historian: Journal of the Folklore and History Section of the American Folklore Society* 21 (2004): 59–72.

Heckscher, Jurretta Jordan. "The Afro-Chesapeake Inventions of American Dance." In *Ballroom, Boogie, Shimmy Sham, Shake: A Social and Popular Dance Reader*, edited by Julie Malnig (Urbana: University of Illinois Press, 2009).

Heine, John R. "William Taylor: First Fiddler of Minnesota." Unpublished manuscript, 2012.

Higham, John. *Strangers in the Land: Patterns of American Nativism, 1860–1925*. New Brunswick, N.J.: Rutgers University Press, 2002.

Hillgrove, Thomas. *A Complete Practical Guide to the Art of Dancing*. New York: Dick and Fitzgerald, 1863, ABC.

———. *The Scholars' Companion and Ball-room Vade Mecum*. New York: Turnbull, 1857, ABC.

Hoffman, Charles Fenno. "A Winter in the West." 1835. In *Reminiscences of Early Chicago*, with an introduction by Mabel McIlvaine, 1–26 (Chicago: Donnelley, 1912).

Howe, Elias. *American Dancing Master, and Ball-Room Prompter*. Boston: Howe, 1862.

———. *Complete Ball-Room Hand Book*. Boston: Ditson, 1858, ABC.

Howe, Henry. *Historical Collections of Ohio*. Cincinnati: Derby, Bradley, 1847.

Hudson, Charles. *The Southeastern Indians*. Knoxville: The University of Tennessee Press, 1976.

Hundley, Daniel R. *Social Relations in Our Southern States*. 1860. Baton Rouge: Louisiana State University Press, 1979.

Hunter, Louis C. *Steamboats on the Western Rivers: An Economic and Technical History*. 1949. New York: Octagon, 1969.

Hunter, Robert. *Quebec to Carolina in 1785–1786*. Edited by Louis B. Wright and Marion Tinling. San Marino, Calif.: Huntington Library, 1943.

"'I Always Loved the Lonesome Songs.'" *Sing Out!* 14, no. 3 (July 1964): 32–39.

Inge, M. Thomas, ed. *High Times and Hard Times: Sketches and Tales by George Washington Harris*. Nashville, Tenn.: Vanderbilt University Press, 1967.

Inscoe, John C. "Race and Racism in Nineteenth-Century Southern Appalachia: Myths, Realities, and Ambiguities." In *Appalachia in the Making: The Mountain South in the Nineteenth Century*, edited by Mary Beth Pudup, Dwight B. Billings, and Altina L. Waller (Chapel Hill: University of North Carolina Press, 1995).

———. "Slavery and African Americans in the Nineteenth Century." In *High Mountains Rising*, edited by Richard A. Straw and H. Tyler Blethen (Urbana: University of Illinois Press, 2004).

Ireland, James. *The Life of the Rev. James Ireland*. 1819. Repr., West Liberty, Ky.: Johnson, 1981.

Irving, Washington. "Salmagundi." *History, Tales and Sketches*. 1807. New York: Library of America, 1983.

Ives, John H. *Twenty-Four Figures of the Most Fashionable Country Dances: Together with Eight Cotillions, for the Year Eighteen Hundred*. New Haven, Conn.: Read and Morse, 1799.

Jamison, Phil. "The Bouquet Waltz." *Old-Time Herald*, 11, no. 3 (February 2008): 8–10.

———. "The Cakewalk." *Old-Time Herald* 3, no. 6 (November 1992): 13–16.

———. "Community Dances in the Eighties: Dare to Be Square!" *Old-Time Herald* 1, no. 6 (November 1988): 21–24, 35.

———. "Community Dances in the 21st Century: Dare to Be Square!" *Old-Time Herald* 9. no. 3 (February 2004): 8–12.

———. "Fly to the East, Fly to the West: Play-Parties, Square Dancing, and Old-Time Music." *Old-Time Herald* 9, no. 2 (November 2003): 8–11.

———. "The Green Grass Cloggers: The Appalachian Spirit Goes International." In Eike and Woodside, *Communities in Motion*.

———. "James Kesterson's Blue Ridge Mountain Dancers: Stepping between Tradition and Precision." *Old-Time Herald* 2, no. 1 (August 1989): 24–27.

———. "'A Jubilant Spirit within Me. . . .' Buckdance, Flatfoot, or Clogging?" *Old-Time Herald* 4, no. 2 (November 1993): 14–17, 51.

———. "The Old Farmer's Ball." *Old-Time Herald* 5, no. 5 (August 1996): 9–11.

———. "The Old Folks Danced the Do-si-do." *Old-Time Herald* 8, no. 4 (May 2002): 15–21, 52.

———. "'Square Dance' at Carcassonne, Kentucky." *Old-Time Herald* 2, no. 7 (November 2001): 12–16.

———. "'Square Dancing' in Haywood County." *Old-Time Herald* 8, no. 2 (November 2001): 12–16.

———. "Willard Watson: Old-Time Flatfoot Dancer." *Old-Time Herald* 1, no. 3 (February 1988): 18–19.

Jamison, Philip A. "The Southern Appalachian Square Dance: African-American Influence on European-American Dance in Appalachia." Master's thesis, Appalachian Studies, Appalachian State University, Boone, North Carolina, August 2007.

Janson, Charles William. *The Stranger in America, 1793–1806*. 1807. New York: Press of the Pioneers, 1935.

Jenkins, Jane R. "Social Dance in North Carolina before the Twentieth Century." PhD diss., University of North Carolina—Greensboro, 1978.

Jensen, Henry G. *A History of Warren Wilson College*. Warren Wilson College, 1974.

Jig, Clog, and Breakdown Dancing Made Easy. New York: James, 1873.

Johnson, Guion Griffis. *Ante-Bellum North Carolina: A Social History.* Chapel Hill: University of North Carolina Press, 1937.

Johnson, James Weldon. *The Autobiography of an Ex-Colored Man*. 1912. New York: Penguin, 1990.

Johnson, Samuel. "Life in the Kentucky Mountains. By a Mountaineer." *Independent* 65 (July 9, 1908): 72–82. Repr. in *Appalachian Images in Folk and Popular Culture*, edited by. W. K. McNeil (Ann Arbor, Michigan: UMI Research, 1989).

Jones, Bessie, and Bess Lomax Hawes. *Step It Down: Games, Plays, Songs, and Stories from the Afro-American Heritage*. New York: Harper and Row, 1972.

Jones, Howard Mumford. *America and French Culture 1750–1848*. Chapel Hill: University of North Carolina Press, 1927.

Jones, Loyal. *Minstrel of the Appalachians*. 1984. Lexington: University of Kentucky Press, 2002.

Karpeles, Maud. *Cecil Sharp: His Life and Work*. Chicago: University of Chicago Press, 1967.

———. "Some Additional Figures for Set-Running." *Journal of the English Folk Dance Society* 2, no. 3 (1930): 39–50.

Keller, Kate Van Winkle. *Dance and Its Music in America, 1528–1789*. Hillsdale, N.Y.: Pendragons, 2007.

———. *"If the Company Can Do It!"* Sandy Hook, Conn.: Hendrickson, 1991.

Keller, Kate Van Winkle, and Charles Cyril Hendrickson. *George Washington: A Biography in Social Dance*. Sandy Hook, Conn.: Hendrickson, 1998.

Kemble, Frances Anne. *Journal of Frances Anne Kemble*. Vol 1. 1835. New York: Blom, 1970.

Kennedy, Douglas. *English Folk Dancing: Today and Tomorrow*. London: Bell, 1964.

Kent, Dot. "Frolics: African American House Dance Traditions of the North Carolina Piedmont." *Old Time Herald* 5, no.7 (February 1997): 9–11, 32.

Kephart, Horace. *Our Southern Highlanders*. New York: Macmillan, 1913.

Kimball, James. "Country Dancing in Central and Western New York State." *New York Folklore* 14, nos. 3–4, 1988.

———. "Old-Time Dance Music in Western New York." *Voices: The Journal of New York Folklore* 29 (Spring–Summer 2003). http://www.nyfolklore.org/pubs/voic29-1-2/oldtime.html.

King, Edward. *The Great South*. 1879. Edited by Magruder Drake and Robert R. Jones. Baton Rouge: Louisiana State University Press, 1972.

King-Dorset, Rodreguez. *Black Dance in London, 1730–1850*. Jefferson, N.C.: McFarland, 2008.

Kirschner, Don S. "The Perils of Pleasure: Commercial Recreation, Social Disorder and Moral Reform in the Progressive Era." *American Studies* 21, no. 2 (1980): 27–42.

Knauff, G. P. *Virginia Reels, No. 3*. Baltimore, Md.: Willig, 1839. Music for the Nation: American Sheet Music, LOC.

Krause, Rhett. "Step Dancing on the Boston Stage: 1841–1869." *Country Song and Dance* 22 (June 1992).

Lanman, Charles. *Haw-Ho-Noo; or, Records of a Tourist*. Philadelphia: Lippincott, Gramibo, 1850.

———. *Letters from the Alleghany Mountains*. New York: Putnam, 1849.

Latrobe, Benjamin Henry. *The Journal of Latrobe*. New York: Appleton, 1905.

Laufman, Dudley. "The Tradition of Fiddling and Calling in New England." *Fiddler Magazine* (Summer 1999): 31–37.

LaVita, James A. "Theorizing Dance Practice: Toward an Ethnography of Movement." PhD diss., University of Texas at Austin, 1998.

Lawson, John. *A New Voyage to Carolina*. 1709. Edited by Hugh Talmage Lefler. Chapel Hill: University of North Carolina Press, 1967.

Levin, Ida. *Kentucky Square Dances*. Louisville, Ky.: Recreation Council, 1928.

Leyburn, James G. *The Scotch-Irish: A Social History*. Chapel Hill: University of North Carolina Press, 1962.

Loeffler, Jack, Katherine Loeffler, and Enrique R. Lamadrid. *La música de los Viejitos: Hispano Folk Music of the Rio Grande Del Norte.* Albuquerque: University of New Mexico Press, 1999.

Longstreet, Augustus. *Georgia Scenes*. New York: Harper, 1840. Repr. Upper Saddle River, N.J.: Literature House / Gregg, 1969.

Lucas, Marion B. *A History of Blacks in Kentucky*, Vol. 1: *From Slavery to Segregation, 1760–1891*. Kentucky Historical Society, 1992.

Lucero-White, Aurora, Eunice Hauskins, and Helene Mareau. *Folk Dances of the Spanish-Colonials of New Mexico*. Rev. 2nd ed. Santa Fe, New Mexico: Examiner, 1940.

Ludlow, Noah Miller. *Dramatic Life as I Found It*. St. Louis: Jones, 1880.

Lunsford, Bascom Lamar. "The Spirit of the Dance." Unpublished manuscript, 1942, BLLC.

Lyell, Charles. *A Second Visit to the United States of North America*. New York: Harper, 1850.

Lyndsay, David. *The Poetical Works of Sir David Lyndsay*. Edited by David Laing. Edinburgh: Patterson, 1879, IA.

MacCorkle, William Alexander. *The White Sulphur Springs*. New York: Neale, 1916.

Malone, Bill C. "Music." In *High Mountains Rising: Appalachia in Time and Place*, edited by Richard A. Straw and H. Tyler Blethen (Urbana: University of Illinois Press, 2004).

———. *Singing Cowboys and Musical Mountaineers: Southern Culture and the Roots of Country Music*. Athens: University of Georgia Press, 1993.

Malone, Bill C., and David Stricklin. *Southern Music/American Music*. Rev. ed. Lexington: University Press of Kentucky, 2003.

Malone, Jacqui. *Steppin' on the Blues: The Visible Rhythms of African American Dance*. Urbana: University of Illinois Press, 1996.

Mangin, Julie. "The State Folk Dance Conspiracy: Fabricating a National Folk Dance." *Old-Time Herald* 4, no. 7 (Spring 1995): 9–12.

Manuel, Peter, ed. *Creolizing Contradance in the Caribbean*. Philadelphia: Temple University Press, 2009.

Marks, Joseph E., III. *America Learns to Dance: A Historical Study of Dance Education in America Before 1900*. Brooklyn, N.Y.: Dance Horizons, 1957.

Masquerades, Tableaux and Drills. New York: Butterick, 1906, ABC.

Mather, Increase. "An Arrow against Profane and Promiscuous Dancing Drawn out of the Quiver of the Scriptures." 1685. *I See America Dancing, Selected Readings 1685–2000*. Urbana: University of Illinois Press, 2002.

Mathews, Mitford M., ed. *A Dictionary of Americanisms on Historical Principles*. Chicago: University of Chicago Press, 1951.

Matthews, Gail V. S. "Cutting a Dido: A Dancer's-Eye View of Mountain Dance in Haywood County, N.C." Master's thesis, Indiana University, 1983.

Mayo, Jim. *Step by Step through Modern Square Dance History*. Self-published, 2003.

Mayo, Margot. *The American Square Dance*. New York: Sentinel, 1943.

McDowell, Katherine [Sherwood Bonner, pseud.]. *Dialect Tales*. New York: Harper, 1883.

Mead, Whitman. *Mead's Travels in North America.* 1820. Facsimile. Bedford, Mass.: Applewood, 2007.

Meade, Guthrie T., Jr., with Dick Spottswood and Douglas S. Meade. *Country Music Sources: A Biblio-Discography of Commercially Recorded Traditional Music*. Chapel Hill: Southern Folklife Collection, University of North Carolina, 2002.

Megginson, W. J. *African American Life in South Carolina's Upper Piedmont, 1780–1900*. Columbia: University of South Carolina Press, 2006.

Merrick, George Byron. *Old Times on the Upper Mississippi: The Recollections of a Steamboat Pilot from 1854 to 1863*. Cleveland: Clark, 1909.

Miles, Emma B. *The Spirit of the Mountains*. 1905. Foreword by Roger D. Abrahams. Introduction by David E. Whisnant. Knoxville: University of Tennessee Press, 1975.

Milnes, Gerald. *Play of a Fiddle*. Lexington: University of Kentucky Press, 1999.

Minton, John. "West African Fiddles in Deep East Texas." In *Juneteenth Texas: Essays in African-American Folklore*, edited by Francis Edward Abernethy, Alan B. Govenar, and Patrick B. Mullen (Denton, Texas: University of North Texas Press, 1996).

Mishler, Craig. *The Crooked Stovepipe: Athapaskan Fiddle Music and Square Dancing in Northeast Alaska and Northwest Canada*. Urbana: University of Illinois Press, 1993.

"A Mississippi Planter." "Management of Negroes Upon Southern Estates." *Debow's Review, Agricultural, Commercial, Industrial Progress and Resources* 10, no. 6 (June 1851): 621–27, MOA.

Mitchell, Stephen T. *The Spirit of the Old Dominion*. Richmond: Shepherd and Pollard, 1827.

Montgomery, Lizzie Wilson. *Sketches of Old Warrenton, North Carolina*. Raleigh, N.C.: Edwards and Broughton, 1924.

Moore, John Trotwood. *Ole Mistis and Other Songs and Stories from Tennessee*. Nashville: Cokesbury, 1897.

Morse, F. P. "Prompter." Unpublished, handwritten, dance-caller's notes. East Barnard, Vermont, 1884.

Mott, Abigail. *Biographical Sketches and Interesting Anecdotes of Persons of Color*. 2nd ed. New York: Mahlon Day, 1837 (Google eBook).

Murfree, Mary Noailles [Charles Egbert Craddock, pseud.]. *In the Tennessee Mountains*. 23rd ed. Boston: Houghton Mifflin, 1893.

Napier, Patrick E. *Kentucky Mountain Square Dancing*. Berea, Ky.: Self-published, 1960.

Nathan, Hans. *Dan Emmett and the Rise of Early Negro Minstrelsy*. Norman: University of Oklahoma Press, 1962.

Neithammer, Nancy Dols. "Tommy Jarrell's Family Stories 1830–1925, Part 1." *Old-Time Herald* 3, no. 1 (Fall 1991).

Nevell, Richard. *A Time to Dance*. New York: St. Martin's, 1977.

Newell, William Wells. *Games and Songs of American Children*. 1883. New York: Dover, 1963.

Nielsen, Erica. *Folk Dancing.* Westport, Conn.: Greenwood, 2010. Nixon, Alfred. *Cross Woodis: Character Sketch*. N.p.: Journal Press, 1905.

Nobles, Gregory H. *American Frontiers: Cultural Encounters and Continental Conquest*. New York: Hill and Wang, 1997.

Norman, William M. *A Portion of My Life: Being of Short and Imperfect History Written While a Prisoner of War on Johnson's Island, 1864*. Winston-Salem, N.C.: Blair, 1959.

Northup, Solomon. *Twelve Years a Slave*. 1853. Edited by Sue Eakin and Joseph Logsdon. Baton Rouge: Louisiana State University Press, 1968.

Norton, John. *The Journal of Major John Norton 1809–1816*. Edited by Carl F. Klinck and James J. Talman. Toronto: Champlain Society, 1970.

O'Keefe, J. G., and Art O'Brien. *A Handbook of Irish Dances*. 1912. Dublin: Gill, 1944.

"Old Time Dancing Party." *Farm and Fireside*, 1926.

Olmsted, Frederick Law. *The Cotton Kingdom: A Traveller's Observations on Cotton and Slavery in the American Slave States*. 1861. New York: Knopf, 1953.

Ottley, Roi, and William J. Weatherby, eds. *The Negro in New York: An Informal Social History*. New York: Praeger, 1967.

Owenby, Ted. *Subduing Satan: Religion, Recreation, and Manhood in the Rural South: 1865–1920*. Chapel Hill: University of North Carolina, 1990.

Owens, Lee. *American Square Dances of the West and Southwest*. Palo Alto, Calif.: Pacific, 1949.

The Oxford English Dictionary. 2nd ed. Oxford: Claredon, 1989.

Paine, Lewis W. *Six Years in a Georgia Prison*. New York: n.p., 1851.

Painter, Jacqueline Burgin. *The German Invasion of Western North Carolina*. Asheville, N.C.: Biltmore, 1992.

Parkhill, Forbes. "Swing That Pretty Gal!" *Saturday Evening Post*, August 2, 1941, 18–19, 58–60.

Parrillo, Vincent N. *Diversity in America*. Thousand Oaks, Calif.: Pine Forge, 2009.

Parrish, Lydia. *Slave Songs of the Georgia Sea Islands*. 1942. Hatboro, Penn.: Folklore, 1965.

Paulding, James Kirke. *Letters from the South*. Vol. 1. New York: Harper, 1835.

Peacock, Francis. *Sketches Relative to the History and Theory, but More Especially to the Practice of Dancing*. Aberdeen: Chalmers, 1805, ABC.

Perdue, Charles L., Jr., Thomas E. Barden, and Robert K. Phillips, eds. *Weevils in the Wheat: Interviews with Virginia Ex-Slaves*. Charlottesville: University Press of Virginia, 1976.

Perdue, Theda. "Red and Black in the Southern Appalachians." In *Blacks in Appalachia*, ed. William H. Turner and Edward J. Cabbell (Lexington: University Press of Kentucky, 1985.

Peterson, Bernard L. *A Century of Musicals in Black and White: An Encyclopedia of Musical Stage Works by, about, or involving African Americans*. Westport, Conn.: Greenwood, 1993.

Pichierri, Louis. *Music in New Hampshire, 1623–1800*. New York: Columbia University Press, 1960).

Pike, Martha V. *Catching the Tune*. Edited by Janice Gray Armstrong. Stony Point, N.Y.: Museum at Stony Point, 1984.

Pinckard, George. *Notes on the West Indies*. Vol. I. London: Longman, Hurst, Rees and Orm, 1806.

Playford, John. *The English Dancing Master*. 1651. Facsimile reprint with introduction, bibliography, and notes by Margaret Dean-Smith. London: Schott, 1957.

Poore, Benjamin Perley. *Perley's Reminiscences of Sixty Years in the National Metropolis*. Philadelphia: Hubbard, 1886, available at http://openlibrary.org/books.

Putnam, A. W. *History of Middle Tennessee; or, Life and Times of Gen. James Robertson*. 1859. Repr. New York: Arno, 1971.

Reeves, Enos. "Extracts from the Letter-books of Lieutenant Enos Reeves, of the Pennsylvania Line." *Pennsylvania Magazine of History and Biography* 21 (1897), IA.

Reniers, Perceval. *The Springs of Virginia: Life, Love, and Death at the Waters, 1775–1900*. Chapel Hill: University of North Carolina Press, 1941.

"The Right Word at the Right Time." *Appletons' Journal* 3, no. 41 (January 8, 1870): 37–40, MOA.

Ripley, Eliza Moore Chinn McHatten. *Social Life in Old New Orleans: Being Recollections of My Girlhood*. New York: Appleton, 1912. DAS, University Library, University of North Carolina at Chapel Hill, available at http://docsouth.unc.edu.

Ritchie, Jean. *Singing Family of the Cumberlands*. Oxford: Oxford University Press, 1955.

Rohrbough, Lynn. *Handy Play Party Book*. Delaware, Ohio: Cooperative Recreation, 1940.

Royall, Anne [A Traveler, pseud.]. *Sketches of History, Life, and Manners in the United States*. New Haven, Conn., 1826.

Russell, Tony. *Country Music Records: a Discography, 1921–1942*. New York: Oxford University Press, 2004.

Ryan, Grace L. *The Handbook for Dances of Our Pioneers*. New York: Barnes, 1926.

Sachs, Curt. *World History of the Dance*. Translated by Bessie Schönberg. 1937. New York: Norton, 1963.

Sacks, Howard L., and Judith Rose Sacks. *Way Up North in Dixie*. Washington: Smithsonian Institution Press, 1993.

Sanders, J. Olcutt. "Finding List of Southeastern Square Dance Figures." *Southern Folklore Quarterly* 6, no. 4 (December 1942): 263–75.

Schell, John M. *Prompting: How to Do It*. 1890. Boston: Fischer, 1948.

Schoepf, Johann David. *Travels in the Confederation, 1783–1784, Part 1*. 1788. Translated and edited by Alfred J. Morrison. New York: Bergman, 1968.

Seeger, Mike. *Talking Feet: Buck, Flatfoot, and Tap; Solo Southern Dance of the Appalachian, Piedmont, and Blue Ridge Mountain Regions*. Berkeley, Calif.: North Atlantic, 1992.

Semple, Ellen Churchill. "The Anglo-Saxons of the Kentucky Mountains: A Study of Anthropogeography." *Geographical Journal* 17 (June 1901), IA.

Shapiro, Henry. *Appalachia on Our Mind: The Southern Mountains and Mountaineers in the American Consciousness, 1870–1920*. Chapel Hill: University of North Carolina, 1978.

Sharp, Cecil J. *The Cecil Sharp Autograph Notebook Collection*. "Folk Dance Notes," vol. 4, 1918, EAC.

———. *The Country Dance Book, Part 1*. 1909. Rev. 2nd ed. Revised and edited by Maud Karpeles (1934). Wakefield, Yorkshire: EP, 1975.

———. *The Country Dance Book, Part II*. 1911. 3rd ed., 1927. Wakefield, Yorkshire: EP, 1975.

———. *English Folk Songs from the Southern Appalachians, Vols. 1 and 2*. Edited by Maud Karpeles. London: Oxford University Press, 1932.

———. *The Morris Book.* London: Novello, 1907.

Sharp, Cecil J., and Maud Karpeles. *The Country Dance Book, Part 5*. London: Novello, 1918. Reprint, Yorkshire, England: EP, 1976.

Sharp, Cecil, and A. P. Oppé. *The Dance: An Historical Survey of Dancing in Europe*. 1924. Totowa, N.J.: Rowman and Littlefield, 1972.

Shaw, Lloyd. *Cowboy Dances*. Caldwell, Id.: Caxton, 1950.

———. *The Round Dance Book: A Century of Waltzing*. Caldwell, Id.: Caxton, 1949.

Sheppard, Cherie. "The Fiddle Puppets/Footworks Dance Ensemble: History in Motion with Innovation to Boot." *Old-Time Herald* 9, no. 6 (November 2004): 11–15.

Simms, William Gilmore. *The Cub of the Panther*. 1869. Edited by Miriam Jones Shillingsburg. Fayetteville: University of Arkansas Press, 1997.

——— [F. A. P., pseud.]. "Historical and Social Sketch of Craven County." *Southern Quarterly Review* 9, no. 18 (April 1854): 377–428. MOA.

Sinclair, Caroline B. "Square Dance Figures of Tidewater Virginia." *Journal of Health and Physical Education* 8, no. 7 (September 1937): 407–10, 445–47.

Sketches and Eccentricities of Col. David Crockett of West Tennessee. 1833. Anonymous. New York: Arno, 1974.

Smith, Frank H. *The Appalachian Square Dance*. Berea, Ky.: Berea College, 1955.

Smith, Kathryn Kari Anne. "The Lancashire Clog Hornpipe Dance on the American Stage, 1840–1940, Vols. 1 & 2." Ph.D. diss., Boston University, 2002.

Social Plays, Games, Marches, Old Folk Dances and Rhythmic Movements: For Use in Indian Schools. Washington, D.C.: GPO, 1911.

Southern, Eileen. *The Music of Black Americans: A History*. 2nd ed. New York: Norton, 1983.

Spalding, Susan Eike. "Aesthetic Standards in Old Time Dancing in Southwest Virginia: African-American and European-American Threads." PhD diss., Temple University, 1993.

———. *Appalachian Dance: Creativity and Continuity in Six Communities.* Urbana: University of Illinois Press, 2014.

———. "Frolics, Hoedowns, and Four-Handed Reels: Variations in Old-Time Dancing in Three Southwest Virginia Communities." In Spalding and Woodside, *Communities in Motion*.

Spalding, Susan Eike, and Jane Harris Woodside, eds. *Communities in Motion*. Westport, Conn: Greenwood, 1995.

Speck, Frank G., and Leonard Broom. *Cherokee Dance and Drama*. 1951. Repr. Norman: University of Oklahoma Press, 1983.

Spelman, Henry. "Relation of Virginia" (c. 1609). In *Travels and Works of Captain John Smith*, vol. 1, edited by Edward Arber (Edinburgh: Grant, 1910).

Stanard, Mary Newton. *Colonial Virginia: Its People and Customs*. Philadelphia: Lippincott, 1917.

Stanton, Lucia. "'Those Who Labor for My Happiness': Thomas Jefferson and His Slaves." In *Jeffersonian Legacies*, edited by Peter S. Onuf, 147–80 (Charlottesville: University of Virginia Press, 1993).

Staples, Charles R. *The History of Pioneer Lexington (Kentucky) 1779–1806*. 1939. Lexington, Ky.: Lexington-Fayette County Historical Commission, 1973.

Stearns, Marshall, and Jean Stearns. *Jazz Dance: The Story of American Vernacular Dance*. 1968. New York: Da Capo, 1994.

Stewart, John. *A View of the Past and Present State of the Island of Jamaica: With Remarks on the Moral and Physical Condition of the Slaves, and on the Abolition of Slavery in the Colonies*. Edinburgh: Oliver and Boyd, 1823 (Google eBook).

Strassburg, Herman A. *Call Book of Modern Quadrilles*. Detroit, Mich.: American Music, 1889, ABC.

Strother, David Hunter [Porte Crayon, pseud.]. "The Adventures of Porte Crayon and His Cousins." *Harper's New Monthly Magazine* 10, no. 55 (December 1854).

———. "The Mountains." *Harper's New Monthly Magazine* 45, no. 268 (September 1872), and 45, no. 270, (November 1872).

———. "A Winter in the South, Sixth Paper." *Harper's New Monthly Magazine* 16, no. 96 (May 1858), and 17, no. 99 (August 1858).

Stuckert, Robert P. *Black Populations of Southern Appalachian Counties*. Berea, Ky.: Berea College, 1987.

Stuckey, Sterling. *Going through the Storm: The Influence of African-American Art in History*. New York: Oxford University Press, 1994.

———. *Slave Culture: Nationalist Theory and the Foundations of Black America*. Oxford: Oxford University Press, 1987.

Stueckrath, George H. "The Upper Country of South Carolina," *Debow's Review, Agricultural, Commercial, Industrial Progress and Resources* 27, no. 6 (December 1859), MOA.

Sublette, Ned. *The World That Made New Orleans: From Spanish Silver to Congo Square*. Chicago: Hill, 2008.

Szwed, John F., and Morton Marks. "The Afro-American Transformation of European Set Dances and Dance Suites." *Dance Research Journal* 20 (1988): 29–36.

Taliaferro, Harden E. [Skitt, pseud.]. *Fisher's River (North Carolina) Scenes and Characters*. 1859. New York: Arno, 1977.

Talley, Thomas W. *Negro Folk Rhymes*. New York: Macmillan, 1922.

Thorpe, Thomas Bangs. "Remembrances of the Mississippi." *Harper's New Monthly Magazine* 12, no. 67 (December 1855): 25–39.

Thurston, Hugh. "The Origin of the Appalachian Square Dance." *Northern Junket* 9, no. 11 (1969): 2–7, and 9, no. 12 (1969): 8–13, SDHP.

Timberlake, Henry. *Lieut. Henry Timberlake's Memoirs, 1756–1765, with Annotation, Introduction and Index by Samuel Cole Williams*. Marietta, Ga.: Continental, 1948.

Titon, Jeff Todd. *Old-Time Kentucky Fiddle Tunes*. Lexington: University Press of Kentucky, 2001.

Toll, Robert C. *Blacking Up: The Minstrel Show in Nineteenth Century America*. New York: Oxford University Press, 1974.

Tolman, Beth, and Ralph Page. *The Country Dance Book*. 1937. Brattleboro, Vt.: Greene, 1976.

Tomko, Linda F. *Dancing Class: Gender, Ethnicity, and Social Divides in American Dance, 1890–1920*. Bloomington: Indiana University Press, 1999.

Toulmin, Harry. *The Western Country in 1793: Reports on Kentucky and Virginia*. San Marino, Calif.: Huntington Library, 1948.

Trollope, Frances. *Domestic Manners of the Americans*. 1832. Edited with an introduction by Donald Smalley. New York: Knopf, 1949.

Tucker George. *The Valley of Shenandoah, Vol. 2*. 1824. Chapel Hill: University of North Carolina Press, 1970.

Tucker, Henry. *Clog Dancing Made Easy*. New York: De Witt, 1874.

Tyler, Paul L. "The Rise of Rural Rhythm." In *The Hayloft Gang: The Story of the National Barn Dance*, edited by Chad Berry, 19–71 (Urbana: University of Illinois Press, 2008).

Twain, Mark. *Life on the Mississippi*. Boston: Osgood, 1883.

Vallancey, Charles. *Collectanea de Rebus Hibernicis, Vol. 4*. Dublin: White, 1786, IA.

The Victor in the Schools. Camden, N.J.: Victor Talking Machine Co., 1915.

Violin, without a Master. Boston: Ditson, 1850.

Virginia Writers' Program. *The Negro in Virginia*. New York: Hastings, 1940.

von Closen, Ludwig. *The Revolutionary Journal of Baron Ludwig von Closen, 1780–1783*. Evelyn M. Acomb, ed. Chapel Hill: University of North Carolina Press, 1958.

Wagner, Ann. *Adversaries of Dance: From the Puritans to the Present*. Urbana: University of Illinois Press, 1997.

Waller, Altina L. *Feud: Hatfields, McCoys, and Social Change in Appalachia, 1860–1900*. Chapel Hill: University of North Carolina Press, 1988.

Warner, Charles Dudley. *On Horseback: A Tour in Virginia, North Carolina, and Tennessee*. Boston: Houghton Mifflin, 1889.

Webster, Alfred, Mrs. *Dancing, as a Means of Physical Education: With Remarks on Deformities, and Their Prevention and Cure*. London: Bogue, 1851, ABC.

Wentworth, John. "Address at the Reception to the Settlers of Chicago Prior to 1840," May 27, 1879. In *Reminiscences of Early Chicago*, 125–52 (Chicago: Donnelley, 1912).

Werner, Francis. *Book 18 for the Year 1785, 8 Cotillions, 6 Favorite Country Dances and Two Minuets*, 1785.

Whisnant, David E. *All That Is Native and Fine*. Chapel Hill: University of North Carolina Press, 1983.

———. "Finding the Way between the Old and the New: The Mountain Dance and Folk Festival and Bascom Lamar Lunsford's Work as a Citizen." *Appalachian Journal* 7, nos. 1–2 (Autumn/Winter 1979–1980): 135–54.

Whitefield, George. *Journals (1737–1741), to Which Is Prefixed His "Short Account" (1746) and "Further Account" (1747)*. Edited by William V. Davis. Gainesville, Fla.: Scholar's Facsimiles and Reprints, 1969.

Wilder, Laura Ingalls. *Little House in the Big Woods*. New York: Harper, 1932.

Williams, John Alexander. *Appalachia: A History*. Chapel Hill: University of North Carolina Press, 2002.

Wilson, Thomas. *An Analysis of Country Dancing*. London: Calvert, 1808, ABC.

———. *The Complete System of English Country Dancing*. London: Sherwood, Neeley and Jones, 1815, ABC.

Wirth, A. C. *Complete Quadrille Call Book and Dancing Master*. Chicago: Drake, 1902.

Wood, Peter H. "'Gimme de Kneebone Bent': African Body Language and the Evolution of American Dance Forms." In *The Black Tradition in American Dance*, edited by Gerald E. Myers, 7–8 (Durham, N.C.: 1988).

Woodmason, Charles. *The Carolina Backcountry on the Eve of the Revolution: The Journal and Other Writings of Charles Woodmason, Anglican Itinerant*. Edited by Richard J. Hooker. Chapel Hill: University of North Carolina Press, 1953.

Worth, Lynn. "The Denton Dance Story." *Old-Time Herald* 6, no. 4 (Summer 1998).

Wright, Frances. *Views of Society and Manners in America*. New York: Bliss White, 1821.

Wyeth, John Allen. *With Sabre and Scalpel: The Autobiography of a Soldier and Surgeon*. New York: Harper, 1914, DAS.

Yates, Michael, Elaine Bradtke, and Malcolm Taylor, eds. *Dear Companion: Appalachian Traditional Songs and Singers from the Cecil Sharp Collection*. London: English Folk Dance and Song Society, 2004.

Zeigler, Wilbur G., and Ben S. Grosscup. *The Heart of the Alleghanies*. Raleigh, N.C.: Williams, 1883.

Index

PHIL JAMISON is nationally known as a dance caller, old-time musician, and flatfoot dancer. He has called dances, performed, and taught at music festivals and dance events throughout the United States and overseas since the early 1970s, including over thirty years as a member of the Green Grass Cloggers. His flatfoot dancing was featured in the film *Songcatcher*, for which he also served as Traditional Dance consultant. From 1982 through 2004, he toured and played guitar with Ralph Blizard and the New Southern Ramblers, and he also plays fiddle and banjo. In 2004, he cofounded Dare To Be Square!, a weekend workshop for square dance callers. Jamison teaches mathematics and Appalachian music at Warren Wilson College, where he coordinates the Old-Time Music and Dance Week at the Swannanoa Gathering, and he writes at www.philjamison.com.

Music in American Life

Only a Miner: Studies in Recorded Coal-Mining Songs *Archie Green*
Great Day Coming: Folk Music and the American Left *R. Serge Denisoff*
John Philip Sousa: A Descriptive Catalog of His Works *Paul E. Bierley*
The Hell-Bound Train: A Cowboy Songbook *Glenn Ohrlin*
Oh, Didn't He Ramble: The Life Story of Lee Collins, as Told to Mary Collins *Edited by Frank J. Gillis and John W. Miner*
American Labor Songs of the Nineteenth Century *Philip S. Foner*
Stars of Country Music: Uncle Dave Macon to Johnny Rodriguez *Edited by Bill C. Malone and Judith McCulloh*
Git Along, Little Dogies: Songs and Songmakers of the American West *John I. White*
A Texas-Mexican *Cancionero*: Folksongs of the Lower Border *Américo Paredes*
San Antonio Rose: The Life and Music of Bob Wills *Charles R. Townsend*
Early Downhome Blues: A Musical and Cultural Analysis *Jeff Todd Titon*
An Ives Celebration: Papers and Panels of the Charles Ives Centennial Festival-Conference *Edited by H. Wiley Hitchcock and Vivian Perlis*
Sinful Tunes and Spirituals: Black Folk Music to the Civil War *Dena J. Epstein*
Joe Scott, the Woodsman-Songmaker *Edward D. Ives*
Jimmie Rodgers: The Life and Times of America's Blue Yodeler *Nolan Porterfield*
Early American Music Engraving and Printing: A History of Music Publishing in America from 1787 to 1825, with Commentary on Earlier and Later Practices *Richard J. Wolfe*
Sing a Sad Song: The Life of Hank Williams *Roger M. Williams*
Long Steel Rail: The Railroad in American Folksong *Norm Cohen*
Resources of American Music History: A Directory of Source Materials from Colonial Times to World War II *D. W. Krummel, Jean Geil, Doris J. Dyen, and Deane L. Root*
Tenement Songs: The Popular Music of the Jewish Immigrants *Mark Slobin*
Ozark Folksongs *Vance Randolph; edited and abridged by Norm Cohen*
Oscar Sonneck and American Music *Edited by William Lichtenwanger*
Bluegrass Breakdown: The Making of the Old Southern Sound *Robert Cantwell*
Bluegrass: A History *Neil V. Rosenberg*
Music at the White House: A History of the American Spirit *Elise K. Kirk*
Red River Blues: The Blues Tradition in the Southeast *Bruce Bastin*
Good Friends and Bad Enemies: Robert Winslow Gordon and the Study of American Folksong *Debora Kodish*
Fiddlin' Georgia Crazy: Fiddlin' John Carson, His Real World, and the World of His Songs *Gene Wiggins*
America's Music: From the Pilgrims to the Present (rev. 3d ed.) *Gilbert Chase*
Secular Music in Colonial Annapolis: The Tuesday Club, 1745–56 *John Barry Talley*
Bibliographical Handbook of American Music *D. W. Krummel*

Goin' to Kansas City *Nathan W. Pearson, Jr.*

"Susanna," "Jeanie," and "The Old Folks at Home": The Songs of Stephen C. Foster from His Time to Ours (2d ed.) *William W. Austin*

Songprints: The Musical Experience of Five Shoshone Women *Judith Vander*

"Happy in the Service of the Lord": Afro-American Gospel Quartets in Memphis *Kip Lornell*

Paul Hindemith in the United States *Luther Noss*

"My Song Is My Weapon": People's Songs, American Communism, and the Politics of Culture, 1930–50 *Robbie Lieberman*

Chosen Voices: The Story of the American Cantorate *Mark Slobin*

Theodore Thomas: America's Conductor and Builder of Orchestras, 1835–1905 *Ezra Schabas*

"The Whorehouse Bells Were Ringing" and Other Songs Cowboys Sing *Collected and Edited by Guy Logsdon*

Crazeology: The Autobiography of a Chicago Jazzman *Bud Freeman, as Told to Robert Wolf*

Discoursing Sweet Music: Brass Bands and Community Life in Turn-of-the-Century Pennsylvania *Kenneth Kreitner*

Mormonism and Music: A History *Michael Hicks*

Voices of the Jazz Age: Profiles of Eight Vintage Jazzmen *Chip Deffaa*

Pickin' on Peachtree: A History of Country Music in Atlanta, Georgia *Wayne W. Daniel*

Bitter Music: Collected Journals, Essays, Introductions, and Librettos *Harry Partch; edited by Thomas McGeary*

Ethnic Music on Records: A Discography of Ethnic Recordings Produced in the United States, 1893 to 1942 *Richard K. Spottswood*

Downhome Blues Lyrics: An Anthology from the Post–World War II Era *Jeff Todd Titon*

Ellington: The Early Years *Mark Tucker*

Chicago Soul *Robert Pruter*

That Half-Barbaric Twang: The Banjo in American Popular Culture *Karen Linn*

Hot Man: The Life of Art Hodes *Art Hodes and Chadwick Hansen*

The Erotic Muse: American Bawdy Songs (2d ed.) *Ed Cray*

Barrio Rhythm: Mexican American Music in Los Angeles *Steven Loza*

The Creation of Jazz: Music, Race, and Culture in Urban America *Burton W. Peretti*

Charles Martin Loeffler: A Life Apart in Music *Ellen Knight*

Club Date Musicians: Playing the New York Party Circuit *Bruce A. MacLeod*

Opera on the Road: Traveling Opera Troupes in the United States, 1825–60 *Katherine K. Preston*

The Stonemans: An Appalachian Family and the Music That Shaped Their Lives *Ivan M. Tribe*

Transforming Tradition: Folk Music Revivals Examined *Edited by Neil V. Rosenberg*

The Crooked Stovepipe: Athapaskan Fiddle Music and Square Dancing in Northeast Alaska and Northwest Canada *Craig Mishler*

Traveling the High Way Home: Ralph Stanley and the World of Traditional Bluegrass Music *John Wright*

Carl Ruggles: Composer, Painter, and Storyteller *Marilyn Ziffrin*

Never without a Song: The Years and Songs of Jennie Devlin, 1865–1952 *Katharine D. Newman*

The Hank Snow Story *Hank Snow, with Jack Ownbey and Bob Burris*

Milton Brown and the Founding of Western Swing *Cary Ginell, with special assistance from Roy Lee Brown*

Santiago de Murcia's "Códice Saldívar No. 4": A Treasury of Secular Guitar Music from Baroque Mexico *Craig H. Russell*

The Sound of the Dove: Singing in Appalachian Primitive Baptist Churches *Beverly Bush Patterson*

Heartland Excursions: Ethnomusicological Reflections on Schools of Music *Bruno Nettl*

Doowop: The Chicago Scene *Robert Pruter*

Blue Rhythms: Six Lives in Rhythm and Blues *Chip Deffaa*

Shoshone Ghost Dance Religion: Poetry Songs and Great Basin Context *Judith Vander*

Go Cat Go! Rockabilly Music and Its Makers *Craig Morrison*

'Twas Only an Irishman's Dream: The Image of Ireland and the Irish in American Popular Song Lyrics, 1800–1920 *William H. A. Williams*

Democracy at the Opera: Music, Theater, and Culture in New York City, 1815–60 *Karen Ahlquist*

Fred Waring and the Pennsylvanians *Virginia Waring*

Woody, Cisco, and Me: Seamen Three in the Merchant Marine *Jim Longhi*

Behind the Burnt Cork Mask: Early Blackface Minstrelsy and Antebellum American Popular Culture *William J. Mahar*

Going to Cincinnati: A History of the Blues in the Queen City *Steven C. Tracy*

Pistol Packin' Mama: Aunt Molly Jackson and the Politics of Folksong *Shelly Romalis*

Sixties Rock: Garage, Psychedelic, and Other Satisfactions *Michael Hicks*

The Late Great Johnny Ace and the Transition from R&B to Rock 'n' Roll *James M. Salem*

Tito Puente and the Making of Latin Music *Steven Loza*

Juilliard: A History *Andrea Olmstead*

Understanding Charles Seeger, Pioneer in American Musicology *Edited by Bell Yung and Helen Rees*

Mountains of Music: West Virginia Traditional Music from *Goldenseal* *Edited by John Lilly*

Alice Tully: An Intimate Portrait *Albert Fuller*

A Blues Life *Henry Townsend, as told to Bill Greensmith*

Long Steel Rail: The Railroad in American Folksong (2d ed.) *Norm Cohen*

Goin' to Kansas City *Nathan W. Pearson, Jr.*
"Susanna," "Jeanie," and "The Old Folks at Home": The Songs of Stephen C. Foster from His Time to Ours (2d ed.) *William W. Austin*
Songprints: The Musical Experience of Five Shoshone Women *Judith Vander*
"Happy in the Service of the Lord": Afro-American Gospel Quartets in Memphis *Kip Lornell*
Paul Hindemith in the United States *Luther Noss*
"My Song Is My Weapon": People's Songs, American Communism, and the Politics of Culture, 1930–50 *Robbie Lieberman*
Chosen Voices: The Story of the American Cantorate *Mark Slobin*
Theodore Thomas: America's Conductor and Builder of Orchestras, 1835–1905 *Ezra Schabas*
"The Whorehouse Bells Were Ringing" and Other Songs Cowboys Sing *Collected and Edited by Guy Logsdon*
Crazeology: The Autobiography of a Chicago Jazzman *Bud Freeman, as Told to Robert Wolf*
Discoursing Sweet Music: Brass Bands and Community Life in Turn-of-the-Century Pennsylvania *Kenneth Kreitner*
Mormonism and Music: A History *Michael Hicks*
Voices of the Jazz Age: Profiles of Eight Vintage Jazzmen *Chip Deffaa*
Pickin' on Peachtree: A History of Country Music in Atlanta, Georgia *Wayne W. Daniel*
Bitter Music: Collected Journals, Essays, Introductions, and Librettos *Harry Partch; edited by Thomas McGeary*
Ethnic Music on Records: A Discography of Ethnic Recordings Produced in the United States, 1893 to 1942 *Richard K. Spottswood*
Downhome Blues Lyrics: An Anthology from the Post–World War II Era *Jeff Todd Titon*
Ellington: The Early Years *Mark Tucker*
Chicago Soul *Robert Pruter*
That Half-Barbaric Twang: The Banjo in American Popular Culture *Karen Linn*
Hot Man: The Life of Art Hodes *Art Hodes and Chadwick Hansen*
The Erotic Muse: American Bawdy Songs (2d ed.) *Ed Cray*
Barrio Rhythm: Mexican American Music in Los Angeles *Steven Loza*
The Creation of Jazz: Music, Race, and Culture in Urban America *Burton W. Peretti*
Charles Martin Loeffler: A Life Apart in Music *Ellen Knight*
Club Date Musicians: Playing the New York Party Circuit *Bruce A. MacLeod*
Opera on the Road: Traveling Opera Troupes in the United States, 1825–60 *Katherine K. Preston*
The Stonemans: An Appalachian Family and the Music That Shaped Their Lives *Ivan M. Tribe*
Transforming Tradition: Folk Music Revivals Examined *Edited by Neil V. Rosenberg*

The Crooked Stovepipe: Athapaskan Fiddle Music and Square Dancing in Northeast Alaska and Northwest Canada *Craig Mishler*

Traveling the High Way Home: Ralph Stanley and the World of Traditional Bluegrass Music *John Wright*

Carl Ruggles: Composer, Painter, and Storyteller *Marilyn Ziffrin*

Never without a Song: The Years and Songs of Jennie Devlin, 1865–1952 *Katharine D. Newman*

The Hank Snow Story *Hank Snow, with Jack Ownbey and Bob Burris*

Milton Brown and the Founding of Western Swing *Cary Ginell, with special assistance from Roy Lee Brown*

Santiago de Murcia's "Códice Saldívar No. 4": A Treasury of Secular Guitar Music from Baroque Mexico *Craig H. Russell*

The Sound of the Dove: Singing in Appalachian Primitive Baptist Churches *Beverly Bush Patterson*

Heartland Excursions: Ethnomusicological Reflections on Schools of Music *Bruno Nettl*

Doowop: The Chicago Scene *Robert Pruter*

Blue Rhythms: Six Lives in Rhythm and Blues *Chip Deffaa*

Shoshone Ghost Dance Religion: Poetry Songs and Great Basin Context *Judith Vander*

Go Cat Go! Rockabilly Music and Its Makers *Craig Morrison*

'Twas Only an Irishman's Dream: The Image of Ireland and the Irish in American Popular Song Lyrics, 1800–1920 *William H. A. Williams*

Democracy at the Opera: Music, Theater, and Culture in New York City, 1815–60 *Karen Ahlquist*

Fred Waring and the Pennsylvanians *Virginia Waring*

Woody, Cisco, and Me: Seamen Three in the Merchant Marine *Jim Longhi*

Behind the Burnt Cork Mask: Early Blackface Minstrelsy and Antebellum American Popular Culture *William J. Mahar*

Going to Cincinnati: A History of the Blues in the Queen City *Steven C. Tracy*

Pistol Packin' Mama: Aunt Molly Jackson and the Politics of Folksong *Shelly Romalis*

Sixties Rock: Garage, Psychedelic, and Other Satisfactions *Michael Hicks*

The Late Great Johnny Ace and the Transition from R&B to Rock 'n' Roll *James M. Salem*

Tito Puente and the Making of Latin Music *Steven Loza*

Juilliard: A History *Andrea Olmstead*

Understanding Charles Seeger, Pioneer in American Musicology *Edited by Bell Yung and Helen Rees*

Mountains of Music: West Virginia Traditional Music from *Goldenseal* *Edited by John Lilly*

Alice Tully: An Intimate Portrait *Albert Fuller*

A Blues Life *Henry Townsend, as told to Bill Greensmith*

Long Steel Rail: The Railroad in American Folksong (2d ed.) *Norm Cohen*

The Golden Age of Gospel *Text by Horace Clarence Boyer; photography by Lloyd Yearwood*
Aaron Copland: The Life and Work of an Uncommon Man *Howard Pollack*
Louis Moreau Gottschalk *S. Frederick Starr*
Race, Rock, and Elvis *Michael T. Bertrand*
Theremin: Ether Music and Espionage *Albert Glinsky*
Poetry and Violence: The Ballad Tradition of Mexico's Costa Chica *John H. McDowell*
The Bill Monroe Reader *Edited by Tom Ewing*
Music in Lubavitcher Life *Ellen Koskoff*
Zarzuela: Spanish Operetta, American Stage *Janet L. Sturman*
Bluegrass Odyssey: A Documentary in Pictures and Words, 1966–86 *Carl Fleischhauer and Neil V. Rosenberg*
That Old-Time Rock & Roll: A Chronicle of an Era, 1954–63 *Richard Aquila*
Labor's Troubadour *Joe Glazer*
American Opera *Elise K. Kirk*
Don't Get above Your Raisin': Country Music and the Southern Working Class *Bill C. Malone*
John Alden Carpenter: A Chicago Composer *Howard Pollack*
Heartbeat of the People: Music and Dance of the Northern Pow-wow *Tara Browner*
My Lord, What a Morning: An Autobiography *Marian Anderson*
Marian Anderson: A Singer's Journey *Allan Keiler*
Charles Ives Remembered: An Oral History *Vivian Perlis*
Henry Cowell, Bohemian *Michael Hicks*
Rap Music and Street Consciousness *Cheryl L. Keyes*
Louis Prima *Garry Boulard*
Marian McPartland's Jazz World: All in Good Time *Marian McPartland*
Robert Johnson: Lost and Found *Barry Lee Pearson and Bill McCulloch*
Bound for America: Three British Composers *Nicholas Temperley*
Lost Sounds: Blacks and the Birth of the Recording Industry, 1890–1919 *Tim Brooks*
Burn, Baby! BURN! The Autobiography of Magnificent Montague *Magnificent Montague with Bob Baker*
Way Up North in Dixie: A Black Family's Claim to the Confederate Anthem *Howard L. Sacks and Judith Rose Sacks*
The Bluegrass Reader *Edited by Thomas Goldsmith*
Colin McPhee: Composer in Two Worlds *Carol J. Oja*
Robert Johnson, Mythmaking, and Contemporary American Culture *Patricia R. Schroeder*
Composing a World: Lou Harrison, Musical Wayfarer *Leta E. Miller and Fredric Lieberman*
Fritz Reiner, Maestro and Martinet *Kenneth Morgan*

That Toddlin' Town: Chicago's White Dance Bands and Orchestras, 1900–1950 *Charles A. Sengstock Jr.*

Dewey and Elvis: The Life and Times of a Rock 'n' Roll Deejay *Louis Cantor*

Come Hither to Go Yonder: Playing Bluegrass with Bill Monroe *Bob Black*

Chicago Blues: Portraits and Stories *David Whiteis*

The Incredible Band of John Philip Sousa *Paul E. Bierley*

"Maximum Clarity" and Other Writings on Music *Ben Johnston, edited by Bob Gilmore*

Staging Tradition: John Lair and Sarah Gertrude Knott *Michael Ann Williams*

Homegrown Music: Discovering Bluegrass *Stephanie P. Ledgin*

Tales of a Theatrical Guru *Danny Newman*

The Music of Bill Monroe *Neil V. Rosenberg and Charles K. Wolfe*

Pressing On: The Roni Stoneman Story *Roni Stoneman, as told to Ellen Wright*

Together Let Us Sweetly Live *Jonathan C. David, with photographs by Richard Holloway*

Live Fast, Love Hard: The Faron Young Story *Diane Diekman*

Air Castle of the South: WSM Radio and the Making of Music City *Craig P. Havighurst*

Traveling Home: Sacred Harp Singing and American Pluralism *Kiri Miller*

Where Did Our Love Go? The Rise and Fall of the Motown Sound *Nelson George*

Lonesome Cowgirls and Honky-Tonk Angels: The Women of Barn Dance Radio *Kristine M. McCusker*

California Polyphony: Ethnic Voices, Musical Crossroads *Mina Yang*

The Never-Ending Revival: Rounder Records and the Folk Alliance *Michael F. Scully*

Sing It Pretty: A Memoir *Bess Lomax Hawes*

Working Girl Blues: The Life and Music of Hazel Dickens *Hazel Dickens and Bill C. Malone*

Charles Ives Reconsidered *Gayle Sherwood Magee*

The Hayloft Gang: The Story of the National Barn Dance *Edited by Chad Berry*

Country Music Humorists and Comedians *Loyal Jones*

Record Makers and Breakers: Voices of the Independent Rock 'n' Roll Pioneers *John Broven*

Music of the First Nations: Tradition and Innovation in Native North America *Edited by Tara Browner*

Cafe Society: The Wrong Place for the Right People *Barney Josephson, with Terry Trilling-Josephson*

George Gershwin: An Intimate Portrait *Walter Rimler*

Life Flows On in Endless Song: Folk Songs and American History *Robert V. Wells*

I Feel a Song Coming On: The Life of Jimmy McHugh *Alyn Shipton*

King of the Queen City: The Story of King Records *Jon Hartley Fox*

Long Lost Blues: Popular Blues in America, 1850–1920 *Peter C. Muir*

Hard Luck Blues: Roots Music Photographs from the Great Depression *Rich Remsberg*
Restless Giant: The Life and Times of Jean Aberbach and Hill and Range Songs *Bar Biszick-Lockwood*
Champagne Charlie and Pretty Jemima: Variety Theater in the Nineteenth Century *Gillian M. Rodger*
Sacred Steel: Inside an African American Steel Guitar Tradition *Robert L. Stone*
Gone to the Country: The New Lost City Ramblers and the Folk Music Revival *Ray Allen*
The Makers of the Sacred Harp *David Warren Steel with Richard H. Hulan*
Woody Guthrie, American Radical *Will Kaufman*
George Szell: A Life of Music *Michael Charry*
Bean Blossom: The Brown County Jamboree and Bill Monroe's Bluegrass Festivals *Thomas A. Adler*
Crowe on the Banjo: The Music Life of J. D. Crowe *Marty Godbey*
Twentieth Century Drifter: The Life of Marty Robbins *Diane Diekman*
Henry Mancini: Reinventing Film Music *John Caps*
The Beautiful Music All Around Us: Field Recordings and the American Experience *Stephen Wade*
Then Sings My Soul: The Culture of Southern Gospel Music *Douglas Harrison*
The Accordion in the Americas: Klezmer, Polka, Tango, Zydeco, and More! *Edited by Helena Simonett*
Bluegrass Bluesman: A Memoir *Josh Graves, edited by Fred Bartenstein*
One Woman in a Hundred: Edna Phillips and the Philadelphia Orchestra *Mary Sue Welsh*
The Great Orchestrator: Arthur Judson and American Arts Management *James M. Doering*
Charles Ives in the Mirror: American Histories of an Iconic Composer *David C. Paul*
Southern Soul-Blues *David Whiteis*
Sweet Air: Modernism, Regionalism, and American Popular Song *Edward P. Comentale*
Pretty Good for a Girl: Women in Bluegrass *Murphy Hicks Henry*
Sweet Dreams: The World of Patsy Cline *Warren R. Hofstra*
William Sidney Mount and the Creolization of American Culture *Christopher J. Smith*
Bird: The Life and Music of Charlie Parker *Chuck Haddix*
Making the March King: John Philip Sousa's Washington Years, 1854–1893 *Patrick Warfield*
In It for the Long Run *Jim Rooney*
Pioneers of the Blues Revival *Steve Cushing*
Roots of the Revival: American and British Folk Music in the 1950s *Ronald D. Cohen and Rachel Clare Donaldson*
Blues All Day Long: The Jimmy Rogers Story *Wayne Everett Goins*

Yankee Twang: Country and Western Music in New England *Clifford R. Murphy*
The Music of the Stanley Brothers *Gary B. Reid*
Hawaiian Music in Motion: Mariners, Missionaries, and Minstrels *James Revell Carr*
Sounds of the New Deal: The Federal Music Project in the West *Peter Gough*
The Mormon Tabernacle Choir: A Biography *Michael Hicks*
The Man That Got Away: The Life and Songs of Harold Arlen *Walter Rimler*
A City Called Heaven: Chicago and the Birth of Gospel Music *Robert M. Marovich*
Blues Unlimited: Essential Interviews from the Original Blues Magazine *Edited by Bill Greensmith, Mark Camarigg, and Mike Rowe*
Hoedowns, Reels, and Frolics: Roots and Branches of Southern Appalachian Dance *Phil Jamison*

The University of Illinois Press
is a founding member of the
Association of American University Presses.

University of Illinois Press
1325 South Oak Street
Champaign, IL 61820-6903
www.press.uillinois.edu